# Sir John Denham (1614/15–1669) Reassessed

T0386208

*Sir John Denham (1614/15–1669) Reassessed* shines new light on a singular, colourful yet elusive figure of seventeenth-century English letters. Despite his influence as a poet, wit, courtier, exile, politician and surveyor of the king's works, Denham remains a neglected figure. The original essays in this interdisciplinary collection provide the sustained modern critical attention his life and work merit.

The book both examines for the first time and reassesses important features of Denham's life and reputations: his friendship circles, his role as a political satirist, his religious inclinations, his playwriting years, the personal, political and literary repercussions of his long exile; and offers fresh interpretations of his poetic magnum opus, *Coopers Hill*. Building on the recent resurgence of scholarly interest in royalists and royalism, this lively account of Denham's influence questions assumptions about neatly demarcated seventeenth-century chronological, geographic and literary boundaries. What emerges is a complex man who subverts as well as reinforces conventional characterisations of court wit, gambler and dilettante.

**Dr Philip Major** is an Associate Lecturer in English literature at Birkbeck, University of London. He is the author of *Writings of Exile in the English Revolution and Restoration.* He has edited a collection of essays on *Literatures of Exile in the English Revolution and its Aftermath, 1640–1685*, and on *Thomas Killigrew and the Seventeenth-century English Stage*, and co-edited *England's Fortress: New Perspectives on Thomas, 3rd Lord Fairfax.* He has written articles on seventeenth-century literature for a variety of peer-review journals, including *The Times Literary Supplement, Review of English Studies, Renaissance and Reformation / Renaissance et Reforme, and Seventeenth Century*, and also has chapters in a number of edited collections.

*Cover and frontispiece illustration*: Detail from 'Portrait of an Old and a Younger Man (John Taylor and John Denham)', 1643, by William Dobson (1610–1646), oil on canvas. The Samuel Courtauld Trust, The Courtauld Gallery, London.

# Sir John Denham (1614/15–1669) Reassessed

The State's Poet

**Edited by Philip Major**

Routledge
Taylor & Francis Group

LONDON AND NEW YORK

First published 2016 by Routledge

2 Park Square, Milton Park, Abingdon, Oxfordshire OX14 4RN
52 Vanderbilt Avenue, New York, NY 10017

*Routledge is an imprint of the Taylor & Francis Group, an informa business*

First issued in paperback 2019

*British Library Cataloguing in Publication Data*
A catalogue record for this book is available from the British Library

*Library of Congress Cataloging-in-Publication Data*
Names: Major, Philip, editor.
Title: Sir John Denham (1614/15–1669) reassessed : the state's poet / edited by Philip Major.
Description: Burlington, VT : Ashgate, 2016. | Includes bibliographical references and index.
Identifiers: LCCN 2015038652 | ISBN 9781472458414 (hardcover) | ISBN 9781472479570 (ebook) | ISBN 9781472479587 (epub)
Subjects: LCSH: Denham, John, Sir, 1615–1669—Criticism and interpretation.
Classification: LCC PR3409.D2 Z88 2016 | DDC 821/.4—dc23
LC record available at http://lccn.loc.gov/2015038652

ISBN: 978-1-4724-5841-4 (hbk)
ISBN: 978-0-367-88104-7 (pbk)

Typeset in Times New Roman
by Apex CoVantage, LLC

# Contents

# Figures

# Contributors

**Victoria Anker** holds a doctorate in English Literature from the University of Edinburgh. Her doctoral thesis, 'The Uses of Ceremony: Performing Power in the First Civil War', examined performances of military, monarchical, and religious rituals as the methodical enforcement of competing political authorities during the First Civil War (1642–1646). Her ongoing research explores ambassadorial interactions with the royal court and parliament during the 1640s in order to consider how international observers made sense of the civil wars. More broadly, she is interested in political culture (and representations thereof) and the role of ceremony and protocol within the Caroline court.

**Naomi Howell** is Associate Research Fellow in Medieval Studies at the University of Exeter and contributes to the European Research Council-funded project 'The Past in its Place'. Her areas of interest include tombs and funerary sculpture in medieval literature and society, particularly in the Anglo-Norman milieu. More broadly, she is interested in the wider cultural and material contexts which inform the relationship of the living with the past. She is completing a book on monuments and the memory of violence in twelfth-century romance.

**Philip Major** is an Associate Lecturer in English at Birkbeck, University of London. He is the author of *Writings of Exile in the English Revolution and Restoration* (Ashgate, 2013). He has edited the collections of essays *Literatures of Exile in the English Revolution and Its Aftermath* (Ashgate, 2010), *Thomas Killigrew and the Seventeenth-Century English Stage* (Ashgate, 2013), and (with Andrew Hopper) *England's Fortress: New Perspectives on Thomas, 3rd Lord Fairfax* (Ashgate, 2014). He has also written a number of articles and chapters on seventeenth-century literature.

**Amin Momeni** gained his Master of Letters in English Literature at the Department of English, University of Birmingham. His thesis, 'Representations of Persia and Persians on the English Stage, 1580–1685', reveals the ways in which dramatic depictions of Safavid Persia and Persians actively participated in foreign and domestic policy debates in Tudor-Stuart England. He holds an MA in English Renaissance Literature from Eastern Mediterranean University,

Cyprus (2011), and a BA in English Literature and Language from the University of Isfahan, Iran (2009).

**Marcus Nevitt** is a Senior Lecturer in Renaissance Literature at the University of Sheffield. He is the author of *Women and the Pamphlet Culture of Revolutionary England, 1640–1660* (Ashgate, 2006) as well as numerous articles on seventeenth-century royalism.

**Timothy Raylor** is Professor of English at Carleton College, Minnesota. His publications include *The Essex House Masque of 1621: Viscount Doncaster and the Jacobean Masque* (2000), *Cavaliers, Clubs, and Literary Culture: Sir John Mennes, James Smith, and the Order of the Fancy* (1994), the edited collection *The Cavendish Circle* (a special issue of the *Seventeenth Century* 1994), and articles on various aspects of the literary and intellectual history of seventeenth-century England in *English Manuscript Studies*, *English Literary Renaissance*, *Historical Journal*, *Huntington Library Quarterly*, *Renaissance Quarterly*, and *Renaissance Studies*, *Review of English Studies*, and the *Seventeenth Century*. He is currently working, with Stephen Clucas, on an edition of *De corpore*, for the Clarendon edition of the works of Thomas Hobbes.

**Philip Schwyzer** is Professor of Renaissance Literature at the University of Exeter. Much of his research focuses on cultural memory and the uses of the past in early modern England and Wales. He is the author of studies including *Shakespeare and the Remains of Richard III* (Oxford, 2013), *Archaeologies of English Renaissance Literature* (Oxford, 2007), and *Literature, Nationalism, and Memory in Early Modern England and Wales* (Cambridge, 2004). He is the Principal Investigator for the European Research Council-funded project 'The Past in its Place', exploring how locales such as Cooper's Hill and Runnymede have served as sites of national memory from the Middle Ages to the present.

**Geoffrey Smith** was Head of History at Melbourne Grammar School for a number of years. He is now an Honorary Fellow in the School of History at the University of Melbourne. He is the author of *The Cavaliers in Exile, 1640–1660* (Palgrave Macmillan, 2003), *Royalist Agents, Conspirators and Spies: Their Role in the British Civil Wars, 1640–1600* (Ashgate, 2011), and of several articles.

**John Stubbs** wrote his PhD at Cambridge (2005) on Shakespeare and 'farfetched' rhetoric. He is the author of two books, *Donne: The Reformed Soul* (Viking and Norton, 2006) and *Reprobates: The Cavaliers of the English Civil War* (Viking and Norton, 2010).

**Rory Tanner** holds a doctorate in English Literature from the University of Ottawa. His ongoing research describes the literary roots of the 'Age of Party', considering parliamentary rhetoric alongside the writing and reading of political poetry through the middle decades of the seventeenth century. His academic interests also include early-modern devotional writing and manu-script miscellanies.

**J.P. Vander Motten** is emeritus Professor of English Literature at Ghent University. His publications include a book on the playwright Sir William Killigrew and several articles on aspects of Restoration drama and on such authors as Thomas Killigrew, Sir Richard Flecknoe, Margaret Cavendish, and Aphra Behn. He has recently edited a special issue of *English Studies* on cultural relations between the Low Countries and England in the seventeenth century.

# Acknowledgements

Steering this volume through to publication has been made possible only due to the assistance of a number of people, to whom I offer sincere thanks. I have greatly appreciated and benefited from the generous advice of Graham Parry, whose knowledge of and enthusiasm for the topic helped convince me that this project was worth pursuing. It has been a pleasure to work with all of the contributors, who have made my task a simple one. The anonymous reviewer of the manuscript made a number of helpful suggestions which were gratefully implemented. Finally, and as usual, the staff at Ashgate and at Taylor & Francis (with special thanks to Erika Gaffney and Autumn Spalding, respectively) have been unfailingly supportive and efficient.

# Abbreviations

| | |
|---|---|
| Add. MS | Additional Manuscript |
| Banks, *PW* | Theodore Howard Banks, Jr (ed.), *The Poetical Works of Sir John Denham* (New Haven: Yale University Press, 1928, repr. 1969) |
| BL | British Library |
| Bodl. | Bodleian Library |
| Denham, *PT* | John Denham, *Poems and Translations with The Sophy. Written by the Honourable Sir John Denham Knight of the Bath* (London: Henry Herringman, 1668) |
| *CClSP* | *Calendar of the Clarendon State Papers*, ed. O. Ogle, W.H. Bliss, W.D. Macray, and F.J. Routledge, 5 vols (Oxford, 1869–1970) |
| *CSPD* | *Calendar of State Papers, Domestic Series* |
| *DNB* | *Dictionary of National Biography* |
| HMC | Historical Manuscripts Commission |
| *ODNB* | *Oxford Dictionary of National Biography: From the Earliest Times to the Year 2000*, ed. H.C.G. Matthew and B. Harrison, 60 vols (Oxford: Oxford University Press, 2004) |
| *OED* | *Oxford English Dictionary* |
| O Hehir, *EH* | Brendan O Hehir, *Expans'd Hieroglyphicks: A Critical Edition of Sir John Denham's Coopers Hill* (Berkley and Los Angeles: University of California Press, 1969) |
| O Hehir, *HD* | Brendan O Hehir, *Harmony from Discords: A Life of Sir John Denham* (Berkeley and Los Angeles: University of California Press, 1968) |
| SP | State Papers, National Archives, London |

# Introduction

*Philip Major*

## I

Towards the end of his 'Brief Life' of Sir John Denham, John Aubrey related the following anecdote:

> He was generally temperate as to drinking: but one time when he was a student at Lincolne's-Inne, having been merry at the tavern with his camerades, late at night, a frolick came into his head, to get a playsterer's brush and a pott of inke, and blott out all the signes between Temple-Bar and Charing-crosse, which made a strange confusion the next day.[1]

Aubrey's intention was to share a humorous vignette of his subject's youthful years. Yet he also provides a useful analogy for today's early modern student and scholar, who could be forgiven for perceiving that the signs illuminating Denham's life and literary legacy have been similarly obscured. The feeling persists that we have failed adequately to take the measure of 'the state's poet': despite his influence as a poet, playwright, translator, wit, courtier, exile, diplomat, politician, and Surveyor of the King's Works, Denham remains a comparatively understudied figure. This is evidenced by, and derives from, a conspicuous shortage of modern publications: the most recent book-length studies are Brendan O Hehir's biography of 1968, and the same author's critique of *Coopers Hill* a year later; while the newest edition of the poems, edited by Theodore Banks, was first published in 1928.[2]

The metaphorical brush and inkpot concealing Denham from contemporary view is, in part, the historiographical imbalance in seventeenth-century British

---

1 John Aubrey, '*Brief Lives*', *Chiefly of Contemporaries, Set Down by John Aubrey, between the Years 1669 & 1696*, ed. Andrew Clark, 2 vols (Oxford: Clarendon Press, 1898), i, p. 220.

2 O Hehir, *HD*; idem, *EH*; Banks, *PW*. Academic articles on Denham have continued to be published, albeit sporadically, such as Tanya Caldwell, 'John Dryden and John Denham', *Texas Studies in Literature and Language*, 46.1 (Spring 2004), 49–72, and Jerome de Groot, 'John Denham and Lucy Hutchinson's Commonplace Book', *Studies in English Literature*, 48.1 (2008), 147–63.

studies, obtaining since at least the 1940s, which has seen parliamentarians and radicals, for a variety of reasons, subjected to consistently closer scrutiny than their (as broadly conceived) monarchy-supporting peers. A corollary of this understandable though ultimately distorted focus has been implicitly to downplay the significance and variety of the conservative opposition to the seismic, revolutionary events of the mid-seventeenth century. Politically, philosophically, and culturally, Denham was an intrinsic part of that opposition, though as we shall see there were moments during the 1650s when his loyalty to the Crown was questioned.

There has been a welcome if belated shift of emphasis in recent years, with Crown followers below the highest levels of the attenuated court now receiving a more equitable level of attention. The growing number of studies on royalism, particularly over the last fifteen or so years, has extended our knowledge and deepened our understanding of the royalist credo and, particularly, the multifarious and multivalent literary responses to defeat and displacement.[3] An appreciably more complex and nuanced picture of royalism is emerging which has made redundant some of the critical framework of previous generations of historians and literary scholars. Thanks to recent scholarship we also have a much better insight into the royalist exile and its cultural manifestations, a topic of direct relevance to Denham,[4] and the same can be said for studies on royalist networks of friendship and patronage, royalist print culture of the Interregnum, and the oppositional nature of Church of England adherence. All told, it is a far more auspicious critical environment for a major study of Denham than has existed for some considerable time.

But if his royalist credentials no longer debar him from scholarly enquiry, why does Denham, in particular, warrant reassessment? There are, after all, features of his life and character which are undeniably unappealing, ostensibly giving credence to the familiar label of shallow and disreputable cavalier. Neither Banks nor O Hehir resorted to hagiography; both revealed the congenital gambling and consequent habitual debt (notwithstanding an early essay against gambling, *The*

---

3  See, for example, Robert Wilcher, *The Writing of Royalism, 1628–1660* (Cambridge: Cambridge University Press, 2001), and idem, *The Discontented Cavalier: The Work of Sir John Suckling in Its Social, Religious, Political, and Literary Contexts* (Newark: University of Delaware Press, 2007); Andrew Lacey, *The Cult of King Charles the Martyr* (Woodbridge: Boydell, 2003); Hero Chalmers, *Royalist Women Writers, 1650–1689* (Oxford: Clarendon Press, 2004); Jason McElligott and David L. Smith (eds), *Royalists and Royalism during the English Civil Wars* (Cambridge: Cambridge University Press, 2007), and idem, *Royalists and Royalism during the Interregnum* (Manchester: Manchester University Press, 2010); John Stubbs, *Reprobates: The Cavaliers of the English Civil War* (Cambridge: Cambridge University Press, 2012); Philip Major (ed.), *Thomas Killigrew and the Seventeenth-Century English Stage* (Farnham: Ashgate, 2013).

4  See Geoffrey Smith, *The Cavaliers in Exile, 1640–1660* (Basingstoke: Palgrave, 2003); Christopher D'Addario, *Exile and Journey in Seventeenth-Century Literature* (Cambridge: Cambridge University Press, 2007); Philip Major (ed.), *Literatures of Exile in the English Revolution and Its Aftermath, 1640–1690* (Farnham: Ashgate, 2010), and idem, *Writings of Exile in the English Revolution and Restoration* (Farnham: Ashgate, 2013).

*Anatomy of Play*), the alleged syphilis, the blatant preferment enjoyed at the Restoration, and, perhaps more pathetically, the temporary madness (announcing to Charles II that he was the Holy Ghost), and the humiliation of his role as public cuckold, when his young second wife, Margaret Brooke, became the mistress of the Duke of York. Putting to one side his literary accomplishments, Denham has been described as an 'ineffective warrior, temporizing conspirator, uninspired surveyor general, and dutiful Member of Parliament', his character 'grouped under three general heads: impetuous generosity or loyalty; irresolution and weakness of will; and self-regard in its various forms of self-preservation, self-indulgence, and self-aggrandizement'.[5] For Herbert Berry, he was a 'systematic if a rather well-meaning and repentant wastrel'.[6]

A relative paucity of portraiture has not helped Denham's cause, a situation possibly created, and probably perpetuated, by the intermittent physical effects of syphilis: Pepys recalls that, 'among others, Sir J. Denham he told me he had cured it after it was come to an ulcer all over his face'.[7] Aubrey's assessment of his physical appearance is ambivalent at best:

> He was of the tallest, but a little incurvetting at his shoulders, not very robust. His haire was but thin and flaxen, with a moist curle. His gate was slow, and was rather a stalking (he had long legges) [...] his eie was a kind of light goose-gray, not big; but it had a strange piercingness, not as to shining and glory, but (like a Momus) when he conversed with you he look't into your very thoughts.[8]

On the other hand, few would dispute that Denham also displayed the redeeming features acknowledged in this book: survivability, an infectious love of life, and humour. To his single elegist, Christopher Wase (who had enjoyed with him the patronage of the Earl of Pembroke), he was the consummate court wit; hence the absence of further poetic commemoration was incomprehensible:

> What means this silence, that may seeme to doome
> Denham to an undistinguished tombe?
> Is it astonishment? or deep respect
> To matchlesse witt? It cannot be neglect.
> What e'er th' excuse, it must not be allow'd
> In loathed oblivion so much worth to shrowd.[9]

---

5  O Hehir, *HD*, pp. 1, 195.

6  Herbert Berry, 'Sir John Denham at Law', *Modern Philology*, 71.3 (February 1974), 266–76 (p. 266).

7  Samuel Pepys, *The Diary of Samuel Pepys*, ed. Robert Latham and William Matthews, 11 vols (Berkeley: University of California Press, 1971–83), v, p. 242.

8  Aubrey, *'Brief Lives'*, i, p. 222.

9  SP 29/270, fols 329–30.

It is Denham's protean nature, his ability to reinvent himself, which most commands our attention. Within royalist circles, at least, he may not have possessed the charisma of Killigrew, or commanded the loyalty shown to Carew, but Denham's life was unusually full, even for the times in which he lived. Studying at Lincolns Inn may have been a conventional route to have followed for the son of a judge,[10] but thereafter few figures—much less poets—can lay claim to have been a political satirist, captured and lost a castle in the civil war, been High Sheriff of Surrey, acted as a personal confidant, envoy, and courier of Henrietta Maria, Charles I, and Prince Charles, undertaken a diplomatic mission to Poland, been sent on royalist spying assignments (resulting in banishment from London), gone temporarily insane, and, as Surveyor General, organised the coronation of Charles II, and recommended the appointment of the nation's most celebrated architect, Christopher Wren. Moreover, though an MP at the Restoration for a notorious rotten borough, he sat on numerous commissions, including the Council of Plantations, which was influential in furthering the interests of British foreign trade.

The common thread is his loyalty to the Crown: Aubrey asserts, probably correctly, that Denham was 'much beloved by King Charles the First, who valued him for his ingenuity'.[11] But just how significant a figure he was within royalist circles is a moot point. Ó Hehir claims that he was 'not a very prominent cavalier', while Hilton Kelliher states that he 'occupied in political terms a moderately distinguished place'.[12] Even mid-ranking courtiers, however, are worthy of scholarly attention, and there are aspects of Denham's loyalism which are noteworthy in their own right. As a royalist political propagandist he was in and out of prison in the mid-1640s and -1650s, and considered important enough to be named as one of those persons 'to be removed from His Majesty's Counsels, and to be restrained from coming within the Verge of the Court' in the peace negotiations of November 1644.[13] In 1648 he was sent on a mission to treat with the Committee of States on the king's behalf, and, though William Crofts receives most of the credit for it in the surviving sources,[14] his mission to Poland in 1650—with Crofts—to raise money for the exiled Prince Charles was a huge financial success, cryptically celebrated in his poem, 'On My Lord Croft's and my Journey into Poland, from whence we Brought 10000 L. for his Majesty by the Decimation of his Scottish Subjects There'. As a royalist agent in England, it has been claimed that he formed a clandestine group as a successor to the Sealed Knot,[15] and, after services

10  For the judge Sir John Denham (1559–1639), see *ODNB*.

11  Aubrey, '*Brief Lives*', i, p. 218.

12  Ó Hehir, *HD*, p. 119, f.n.; Hilton Kelliher, 'John Denham: New Letters and Documents', *British Library Journal*, 12 (1986), 1–20 (p. 1).

13  *Journals of the House of Lords*, vii, p. 55.

14  For the most comprehensive account of the mission in English, see Andrew B. Pernal and Rosanne P. Gasse, 'The 1651 Polish Subsidy to the Exile Charles II', *Oxford Slavonic Papers*, n.s., 32 (1999), 1–50.

15  David Underdown, *Royalist Conspiracy in England* (New Haven: Yale University Press, 1960), pp. 303–04. The claim gives added piquancy to the lines from *Coopers Hill*, 'Some study plots, and some those plots t'undo, / Others to make 'em, and undo 'em too'.

rendered as Surveyor General at Charles II's coronation, which impressed Pepys,[16] the king created him knight of the Honourable Order of the Bath.

This is not to say—chiming with recent studies emphasising the contingency of monarchical allegiance—that Denham's support for the monarchy was always consistent or unqualified. Denham's father supported Judge George Croke (1559–1641) in his deprecation of the Crown in the hugely contentious Ship-Money disputes of the 1630s, and the poet saw fit to write an admiring 'Elegy on the death of Judge Croke'.[17] The self-preservation identified by O Hehir is adduced not least by Denham's friendly relations with members of the Council of State during the Interregnum: he was the 'sort of man who would always fraternize with the enemy'.[18] And the epithet of 'the state's poet', this volume's subtitle, has an ambivalent provenance: coined by a Cromwellian spy in Paris in a letter to Thurloe, it may suggest a rueful, if misplaced, perception on the part of the royalists with whom the spy was mingling that Denham had returned to England to become the de facto poet laureate of the Commonwealth.[19] Even the ardour of the royalism in *Coopers Hill* has been contested, with at least one critic claiming it betrays a poet who was far from being a divine right ideologue.[20]

Ultimately, it is Denham the writer to whom we return.[21] His literary reputation has always rested chiefly on his celebrated topographical poem, *Coopers Hill*, written on the eve of the civil war, though subsequently republished in various iterations. It is a work which, attested by this book, continues to intrigue and captivate literary scholars,[22] and to generate divergent critical responses. In *Carmen Votivum* (1665), the Jesuit and author Maurice Newport termed it Denham's most beautiful poem ('pulcherrimo poëmate'), its author the richest talent ('detissimus ingeni').[23] Dryden thought it 'the exact Standard of good Writing',[24] and high praise was also forthcoming from Herrick, Pope, and Addison. Of lines 189–92, Johnson wrote,

> so much meaning is comprized in so few words; the particulars of resemblance are so perspicaciously collected, and every mode of excellence separated from its adjacent fault by so nice a line of limitation; the different parts

---

16  *Pepys Diary*, 23 April 1661.
17  Banks, *PW*, pp. 156–58.
18  O Hehir, *HD*, p. 195.
19  Ibid., p. 100.
20  See Wilcher, *The Writing of Royalism*, p. 76.
21  Another tale from Aubrey gives an initial, mostly misleading impression of literary dilettantism. According to Aubrey, when the poet George Wither was imprisoned during the civil war, 'Sir John Denham went to the king, and desired his majestie not to hang him, for that whilst G.W. lived he should not be the worst poet in England'. Aubrey, *'Brief Lives'*, i, p. 221.
22  James Loxley, for example, has described it as a 'masterly piece of map-making'; *Royalism and Poetry in the English Civil Wars: The Drawn Sword* (Basingstoke: Palgave, 1997), p. 85.
23  M.N. Anglo [Maurice Newport], … *Carmen Votivum* (London, 1665), pp. 2, 108, note c.
24  Anthony Wood, *Athenae Oxonienses*, ed. Philip Bliss, 4 vols (London, 1813–20; repr. New York: Johnson Reprint Society, 1967), iii, p. 825.

of the sentence are so accurately adjusted; and the flow of the last couplet is so smooth and sweet; that the passage, however celebrated, has not been praised above its merit. It has beauty peculiar to itself, and must be numbered among those felicities which cannot be produced at will by wit and labour, but must rise unexpectedly in some hour propitious to poetry.[25]

Of his later compositions, Denham's Preface to his *Poems and Translations* (1668) downplays, in formulaic fashion, his literary responses to the 'arguments' given to him by Prince Charles in Holland and France 'to divert and put off the evil hours of our banishment, which now and then fell not short of your Majesties expectation'. Yet, as this study will affirm, there was more to Denham's literary output than one poem. Coterminous with *Coopers Hill* is *The Sophy* (1642), a politically allusive verse tragedy centred on the reign of Shah Abbas I of Persia, a play whose contemporary popularity is reflected in Edmund Waller's remark that, upon its publication, Denham 'broke-out like the Irish Rebellion—threescore thousand strong before anybody was aware'.[26] Translations of Book 2 of the *Aeneid*, published as *The Destruction of Troy*, and of Corneille's *Horace*, followed, as well as multiple verses, many satirical, such as his eight contributions to *Certain verses written by severall of the authors friends*, a collection of hostile responses to Sir William Davenant's *Gondibert* (1651). Denham's Preface goes on to privilege his non-literary services to the king:

> when men are young, and have little else to do, they might well vent the overflowings of their Fancy that way, but when they were thought fit for more serious Employments, if they still persisted in that course, it would look, as if they minded not the way to any better.

However, along with his *A Version of the Psalms of David* (1714), these 'overflowings of […] Fancy' make up a body of work which, written during a momentous period of British history, is eminently worthy of re-examination through modern critical lenses.

## II

Established and emerging academics have helped this volume give shape to 'a curiously indistinct figure'.[27] To varying degrees, each has employed critical frameworks developed in recent scholarship, allowing for fresh thinking about and approaches towards influential Crown supporters of the mid-seventeenth century. For example, the malleability and instability of language under the pressure

25  Samuel Johnson, *The Lives of the Most Eminent English Poets: With Critical Observations on Their Works*, 2 vols (London: P.C. and J. Rivington, 1821), i, p. 57.
26  Aubrey, '*Brief Lives*', i, p. 217.
27  Banks, *PW*, p. 1.

of defeat and exile, and the contingency of royalist notions of loyalty, find full expression throughout the volume. It is to be hoped that these ten chapters, individually and collectively, not only open new windows onto Denham himself, repainting the 'signes between Temple-Bar and Charing-crosse', but also pave the way for further studies which consider the nuances of civil war and Restoration royalism, and its impact on seventeenth-century letters.

In the opening chapter, John Stubbs considers Denham as a 'cavalier'. If Denham has been and probably always shall be classified as a 'cavalier poet', what does this term actually mean? In thinking of cavaliers, most will picture the heroes of the royalist campaigns—the Marquess of Newcastle, Sir Ralph Hopton, and above all Prince Rupert. Yet when London gangs first taunted members of the king's unofficial bodyguard as 'cavaliers' in 1641, they had in mind a figure of another stamp. The term was associated often with the poet Sir John Suckling, who became notorious during the 1630s for his gambling and frequent lapses of gallantry, and who in a public letter on the parliamentary crisis declared that the 'people are naturally not gallant, nor much cavalier'. This, it was felt, was high talk from a 'roaring boy', a boaster famous for declining to fight a duel and arranging for assassins to dispatch his challenger. As Stubbs argues, the word 'cavalier', connoting courtesy, chivalry, and refinement, thus became tied up with its anti-type, and assigned as an ironic honour to the king's private militia. Thus, paradoxically, Hopton, Rupert, and company were never true cavaliers in its original partisan sense. On the other hand, Denham was—to a certain extent. His military career was manifestly more Sucklingtonian than Rupertian. Yet, as with many of his fellow literary royalists (including Suckling), the cavalier profile provides a useful key to understanding Denham in the ways he did and did not match it. This chapter discusses the matches as a means of drawing more sharply his idiosyncrasies, poetic and personal.

Next, Geoffrey Smith examines the wide range of experiences Denham underwent between the end of the civil war and the Restoration that shaped both his career and his writing. He endured periods both in prison and in exile, where he travelled extensively and where at different times he was attached to three different Stuart households, those of Queen Henrietta Maria, of the Prince of Wales, later Charles II, and of James, Duke of York. He was employed as a courier in the king's cause, as an envoy with William Crofts on a money-raising mission to Poland, and became involved in royalist conspiracies in England. These experiences considerably widened the range of Denham's friends and acquaintances while at the same time involving him in the factional rivalries that constantly tore at the unity of the king's party.

As Smith reveals, at different times during this period Denham was drawn into the company of significant noblemen like the Duke of Buckingham, the Marquess of Ormond, and the Earl of Oxford; of courtiers in the queen's favour like Lord Jermyn, John Ashburnham, and Sir John Berkeley; of fellow poets like Edmund Waller, Sir Richard Fanshawe, and Abraham Cowley; of convivial hard drinking and gambling 'good fellows' like Sir John Mennes, Sir John Poley, Thomas Killigrew, Crofts, William Murray; and of 'professional' conspirators like Daniel O'Neill, Humphrey Boswell, and members of the Sealed Knot and Lord Mordaunt's Great Trust. Smith's analysis of Denham's relationships during this period shines a torch on some of the significant elements in his career, how these helped to shape his reputation, and the insights they give us into his character.

In the following chapter, Marcus Nevitt re-reads one of the most famous documents in Restoration theatre history in order to cast new light on some of the conflicts and collaborations which helped shape the theatre of the early 1660s. The Lord Chamberlain's order of December 1660, granting Sir William Davenant and the Duke's Company exclusive performance rights to eleven old plays, has, until now, only ever been read for what it says about the status of Shakespeare and other Jacobean dramatists in the re-modelled theatrical culture of 1660. No commentator has hitherto considered the place of Denham's sole unperformed play, *The Sophy*, in Davenant's astonishingly modest list of plays. This essay puts Denham's play back into that document and explores the ways in which the Restoration theatrical settlement was influenced by royalist literary culture during the Interregnum, in particular the relationship of Denham and Davenant, whose rivalry during the 1650s was notorious. Through an analysis of a variety of manuscript and printed texts by these authors, Nevitt argues that the competition amongst theatre companies amid the well-documented scramble for plays in 1660 was intense but hardly fresh; it had its origins in long-standing cavalier conflicts. In the process, the chapter raises an important methodological issue, suggesting that an interdisciplinary approach to the drama of the period, a willingness to think across chronological boundaries and turn to different kinds of historical and literary record, is the surest way to render the stubborn silences of Restoration theatre history more meaningful.

The next chapter examines *The Sophy* from a more conspicuously Persian perspective. Here, Amin Momeni argues that though an explicit and direct parallel between Denham's Shah Abbas I and Charles I is elusive, there are nonetheless references in the play which remind us of Charles's strategic misjudgements as king. He suggests that Denham seeks to allude to Charles through the dramatisation of two different royal Islamic Persian figures: Shah Abbas and his son Mirza. These two characters function in combination as the embodiment of mistakes made by Charles during his reign. Denham was not the only playwright in the period to draw such parallels: Robert Baron's tragedy *Mirza*, entered in the Stationers' Register in 1655, also invites its reader to draw comparisons between the tragic Persian prince, Mirza, and the deposed and executed Charles I. In essence, then, Momeni's reading of *The Sophy*, through its focus on Denham's representations of Islamic Persia and Persians in the play, aims to cast into bolder relief the play's commentary on contemporary affairs, and, at the same time, situate Denham's play in the broader context of the politically allusive theatre of the civil wars and Interregnum.

In Chapter 5, Victoria Anker offers a fresh analysis of Denham's political satires written during the First Civil War (1642–46). Whilst recent scholarship has sought to emphasise the complexities and legacy of Denham beyond *Coopers*

*Hill*, few have returned to the early years of Denham's career in the king's employ. In addressing this imbalance, Anker situates Denham's satirical works within the contemporary social and political maelstrom; as entering into a dialogue both with fellow royalists and the parliamentarian opposition. Two texts come under close scrutiny: the ballads 'A Western Wonder' (1643) and 'A Second Western Wonder' (1643). Whilst evidence suggests these ballads did not appear in print until *Rump Songs* (1662), the author argues that the setting of both works to common tunes facilitated their broad dissemination. Despite the apparently artless lyrics and witty rhymes, Denham's texts reveal an acute awareness of events during the civil war, from military engagements to religious changes. Anker concludes that in these ballads we can see the beginnings of the bald humour that dominated Denham's later works whilst in exile. More importantly, the satires preached the royalist tenets of loyalty, community, and order which many still thought attainable.

Denham's political writing comes under further examination in the following chapter, by Rory Tanner. The parliament of 1640 signalled the end of Charles I's personal rule, and at the same time provoked a crucial debate among MPs as to their responsibilities within a deliberative political assembly. Their attention in the Short and Long Parliaments to matters of debate, rhetoric, and decision-making soon precipitated in popular writing a broader discussion among those who sought to gauge the efficacy of discourse (whether in parliament or in public) within the English polity. As Tanner shows, Denham's writing looms large in this body of work, which enjoyed a two-way relationship with Westminster. The author identifies Denham, both in his shorter, scribally published poems, and in *Coopers Hill*, as a sceptical royalist voice responding to the nascent parliamentary literary culture of the early 1640s, challenging the aims and motivation of those who—ostensibly for the sake of the country—immersed themselves in the new oppositional discourse.

In Chapter 7, I examine the text and context of a long-neglected Denham work, *A Version of the Psalms of David*. The enduring image of Denham's religion is his claim to Charles II, during his short-lived episode of insanity, to be the Holy Ghost. This was considered all the more eccentric because he 'despised religion'. But did he? Clearly, poems such as 'The Progress of Learning' rail against religious enthusiasm. On the other hand, Samuel Johnson wrote that '[Denham] appears, whenever any serious question comes before him, to have been a man of piety, he consecrated his poetical powers to religion, and made a metrical version of the Psalms of David'.[28] This considerable literary undertaking has attracted little modern critical attention, yet it shows a radically different side to the cavalier poet. It also provides additional insight into Denham's little-known charitable works for poor widows, whom he housed in alms houses near his Egham estate; about which, I speculate, he may have written his first poem. As for literary merit, Johnson thought Denham had failed; but Denham's version was deemed

---

28  Johnson, *The Lives*, i, p. 54.

aesthetically pleasing enough by Samuel Woodford to warrant, in 1668, his composing a poem 'To the Honourable Sir John Denham upon his New Version of the Psalms'.

Denham's pre-eminent work, *Coopers Hill*, is the topic of the three remaining studies. In Chapter 8, Timothy Raylor considers the significance of an important allegory in the poem, promoted by 'J.B.', the publisher, in his note to the reader of the 1655 edition, as 'that excellent Allegory of the Royall Stag (which among others was lop't off by the Transcriber) skilfully maintain'd without dragging or haling in Words and Metaphors, as the fashion now is with some that cannot write, and cannot but write'. O Hehir has exposed as disingenuous J.B.'s implication that this extension of the famous stag hunt scene arose from the re-emergence of missing material, rather than from Denham's own revision. And further doubts are cast on J.B.'s credibility by the recent discovery of a single copy of an edition dated '1653' which, minus the prefatory note, is almost identical to the 1655 edition. However, the second part of J.B.'s message—the distinction drawn between Denham's deft control of the stag allegory and that lacking in similar works by poetic rivals—has hitherto resisted explanation.

Here, Raylor argues, J.B. is on firmer ground: the expanded passage is indeed a repudiation of contemporary writers who indulge in voguish 'dragging or haling in [of] Words and Metaphors', and who have thereby fallen short of matching Denham's linguistic effects. In identifying the authors J.B. alludes to, and establishing the reasons for the author's revision, this chapter not only solves a Denham mystery but also casts the intense debate over poetic reform among sections of the royalist exile community in the late 1640s and '50s into bolder relief.

The penultimate chapter, by J.P. Vander Motten, assesses an intriguing element in the eighteenth-century reception of *Coopers Hill*. Denham's late seventeenth- and eighteenth-century reputation is amply illustrated by the biographical accounts and the various editions of his collected works, and, as far as *Coopers Hill* is concerned, its inclusion in numerous collections of British poets, anthologies, and critical essays, in which the poem was almost universally hailed, not least by Johnson, as having set the standard for later Augustan poetry. Imitations followed. Once such, which has hitherto escaped critical attention, was *Cooper's Well* (1767), published anonymously as a 'fragment' by Denham 'found amongst the Papers of a late Noble Lord' (title page). A parody of Denham's poem in its length, verse form, constituent parts, and descriptive nature (though not in its political/philosophical dimension), *Cooper's Well* is actually an erotic poem in the mode of Lord Rochester, the 'noble lord' to whom it is dedicated, substituting the inexhaustible riches of the female body for Denham's reflections on the natural scenery around Cooper's Hill. Documenting an episode in the critical fortunes of one of the most anthologised of English seventeenth-century poems, Vander Motten provides a detailed discussion of *Cooper's Well* and its debt to *Coopers Hill*. In the process, he explores the eighteenth-century poem's contexts, including John Armstrong's *The Economy of Love* (1739) and some minor works by Edward Thompson (1738?–1786), to whom the Denham imitation is sometimes attributed.

He also examines the literary 'uses' in the satirical or parodic vein to which *Coopers Hill* was put, a century after its inclusion in *Poems and Translations*.

In the volume's concluding essay, Naomi Howell and Philip Schwyzer's premise is that *Coopers Hill* has rarely seemed more timely or relevant than it does today. The year 2015 marked not only the four hundredth anniversary of Denham's birth but the eight hundredth anniversary of Magna Carta, an event with which the Runnymede landscape was indelibly associated. Reading Runnymede as a very English *lieu de mémoire*, this chapter situates Denham's poem at the hinge of this landscape's cultural history. The first section examines the generally glancing yet intriguing references to Runnymede and its environs in medieval and early modern literature, in texts including the thirteenth-century *Histoire de Guillaume le Marechal*. The second examines the historical vision of *Coopers Hill*, with a focus on that parcel of the Thames floodplain where 'was that Charter seal'd, wherein the Crown / All marks of arbitrary power lays down'.

The final section examines the cultural and material reception of Denham's poem in the memorial landscape of Runnymede and Cooper's Hill in the twentieth and twenty-first centuries. The clustering of memorials in this landscape—including the John F. Kennedy Memorial, the Commonwealth Air Forces Memorial, and the American Bar Association's Magna Carta Memorial—suggests an ongoing contest over the meaning and ownership of the past in this place, a contest much enlivened by the presence, since 2012, of an ecovillage on Cooper's Hill inhabited by a group of modern-day 'Diggers'. These are conflicts that Denham's poem, with its pessimistic vision of national history, might be said to predict. Yet perhaps no lines of the poem seem more prescient than those concluding verses that imagine the river breaking its banks and 'mak[ing] its power its shores'. In this era of human-made climate change and catastrophic flooding, Howell and Schwyzer argue, nature is less and less the teacher of moderation Denham hoped it would be, and Runnymede seems fated to spend a good part of the years to come underwater.

# 1 Denham as Cavalier

*John Stubbs*

## I

Describing Sir John Denham as a cavalier ought to be a matter of simple historical shorthand. As a cavalry officer in the king's English army and subsequently, on leaving active service through injury, serving as occasional councillor to the king himself; as an exile and activist during the years of the English republic, and then a court official, rewarded with an unlikely place during the post-Restoration years of the 'Cavalier' Parliament, Denham's credentials as cavalier surely require little elaboration. The following chapter, though, sets out to consider what people meant when they first described certain men as 'hotspur Cavaliers', and then to see how well this idea fits Denham.

In calling 'cavaliers' to mind, one inevitably thinks of Prince Rupert, capturing Essex's guns and coach at Edgehill, or Sir Ralph Hopton, expelling the parliamentarians from Cornwall; or, if the frame is widened, the Marquess of Newcastle, combining the virtues of poet, horseman, diplomat, patron of the arts, and commander in the field. From the royalist perspective, the historical aura of the cavalier is coloured by a spectrum of doomed heroism, refinement, and panache, with a tinge of the tragic that might be taken, unkindly, as bathetic. The ideal is captured in Hopton's affecting letter to his opposite number and old friend Sir William Waller, as the royalists pressed the parliamentarians back towards Bath in June 1643.[1] Hopton's lament on 'this war without an enemy', one of the most resonant phrases to emerge from the vast and multitudinous clash of forces pressed under the headings of 'king' and 'parliament', was a rhetorical palliative for the brute force and savage sectarianism released across the three kingdoms by the civil wars. Indeed, it recalled the class of baroque and metaphysical paradoxes such men had had greater leisure to explore and savour in peacetime.[2] Such

---

1 S.R. Gardiner, *History of the Great Civil War, 1642–1649*, 4 vols (London: Longmans, 1901), i, pp. 167–68.
2 An intimate, introspective, and opaque manner which of course differed in kind from the clear, public, and impersonal poetic which Earl Miner characterised as 'cavalier' in his influential study, *The Cavalier Mode from Jonson to Cotton* (Princeton: Princeton University Press, 1971). The relationship between the 'Jonsonian' and 'metaphysical' styles has formed a duality almost as vexed as

niceties were afforded less and less easily as time wore on: for Hopton was writing at the high point of the royalist campaign. His famous letter does though point up a reality which confronts any student of the civil-war chronicles: in England, the armies of the civil war consisted of men who, despite the images we have of cavalier lovelocks and roundhead short backs and sides, dressed similarly, shared interests and customs to a much greater degree than the political points which divided them, and were equally varied in their shades and strengths of religious devoutness. Meanwhile, the two symbolic figureheads of each army, Charles and Cromwell, were equally 'puritanic' and *un*-cavalier in their approach to worship.

Cavaliers, then, were hard to pick out in the melange of battle, amid the wounded laid out on village streets or stacked in corridors and outhouses, or among the survivors making the most of an evening's pass. Civil-war historians of the past half-century in any case began to use the word 'cavalier' with extreme care in discussions of the period. It must be applied only to the post-1641 years, since there is still general agreement that the word became synonymous with a 'royalist' faction in something like the way described by the Earl of Clarendon. As clashes in the street became frequent between demobbed officers, who had appointed themselves members of the king's bodyguard, and crowds of protesters supporting Charles's enemies, 'they who were looked upon as servants to the King [were] then called "Cavaliers", and the other of the rabble contemned and despised under the name of "Roundheads"'.[3]

The historical consensus against speaking of 'cavaliers' before the period of absolute crisis in the latter half of 1641 is founded on the fact that no 'royalist' (or 'pro-Charles') faction existed until then.[4] Thus it is meaningless, the argument

that of roundhead and cavalier. Miner traced the lineage of the latter in his earlier book, *The Metaphysical Mode from Donne to Cowley* (Princeton: Princeton University Press, 1969). For a sense of the variety of literary languages active at the time, however, and the overlap and friction between them, see Thomas N. Corns, *Uncloistered Virtue: English Political Literature, 1640–60* (Oxford: Clarendon Press, 1992), David Norbrook, *Writing the English Republic: Poetry, Rhetoric and Politics, 1627–1660* (Cambridge: Cambridge University Press, 1999)—in which the deployment of a concept of 'illocutionary' speech acts (p.10, and passim) is as relevant for royalist as for republican writings—and, more radically and expansively still, John Kerrigan, *Archipelagic English: Literature, History and Politics, 1603–1707* (Oxford: Oxford University Press, 2008).

3   Edward Hyde, Earl of Clarendon, *The History of the Rebellion and Civil Wars in England*, ed. by W. Dunn Macray, 6 vols (Oxford: Clarendon Press, 1958), i, p. 456.

4   The following works are suggested merely as starting points (and signposts) in a vast and expanding bibliography on the mid-seventeenth-century factions. On the culture and literature of the early Caroline court, see Kevin Sharpe, *Criticism and Compliment: The Politics of Literature in the England of Charles I* (Cambridge: Cambridge University Press, 1990). For an overview of the wider political context, see G.E. Aylmer, 'Collective Mentalities in Mid-Seventeenth-Century England, I: The Puritan Outlook', *Transactions of the Royal Historical Society*, fifth series, 36 (1986), 1–25; idem, 'Collective Mentalities in Mid-Seventeenth-Century England, 2: Royalist Attitudes', *Transactions of the Royal Historical Society*, 37 (1987), 1–30; David L. Smith, *Constitutional Royalism and the Search for Settlement c. 1640–1649* (Cambridge: Cambridge University Press, 1994) and Jason McElligott and David L. Smith (eds), *Royalists and Royalism during the English Civil Wars* (Cambridge: Cambridge University Press, 2007) contain challenging responses to the work of the

runs, to speak of cavaliers in the 1630s since that would suggest the existence of a royalist faction at court before the schism that led to the civil wars came about. Such a line of thinking would fall in with the now repudiated and purport-edly 'deterministic' view of the whole mid-century period as one of revolution.[5] The revisionist argument indeed might be taken further, both conceptually and chronologically. For it is obvious that many in the parliamentarian ranks, had they considered it as an abstract question, would have declared themselves avowedly 'royalist'. They weren't fighting the king but, as successive parliamentary ordi-nances insisted, his 'evil councillors'. Or, granted that they were fighting a bad king, many were not fighting against monarchy per se—although many certainly were, profoundly and proudly. Equally, many who by the summer of 1642 had found themselves in the ranks of the cavalier armies had no distinct idea that they were fighting for royalty as a distinct political concept. Many among Charles's critics and sceptics—including Sir Ralph Hopton—enlisted in the royal forces purely to suppress what had become a rebellion. Hopton had spoken up in the Commons against the fallen royal favourite, the Earl of Strafford, who went to the block in April 1641; yet he supported Charles on the splintering issue of the king's right to levy Ship Money independently of Parliament. In November 1641 he opposed the 'Grand Remonstrance' against Charles, which detailed the king's wrongs against his people and demanded justice. 'Cavaliers', in such notable instances, were figures who were clearly unsure about themselves *as* cavaliers, if the term is equated strictly with 'royalist'—a concept which, in the early months and years of the war, arguably has little meaning either. There were royalists una-ware that that is what they were; and future regicides who still took monarchy for granted.[6] Despite the strength of the image—long hair in ringlets, lace collar, and trimmings; floppy hat, embroidered suit, and bucket-topped boots—the idea of

1980s: in the latter, more specifically see Malcolm Smuts, 'The Court and the Emergence of a Royalist Party' (pp. 43–65) and David Scott, 'Counsel and Cabal in the King's Party, 1642–1646' (pp. 112–35). To varying extents these studies respond to and engage with the narratives of, among others, Paul Hardacre, *The Royalists during the Puritan Revolution* (The Hague: Nijhoff, 1956), Brian Wormald, *Clarendon: Politics, History and Religion* (Cambridge: Cambridge University Press, 1951) and, on the continuity (and sometimes lack thereof) between the royalist and Tory identities in English political life, Sir Keith Feiling, *A History of the Tory Party, 1660–1714*, rev. edn (Oxford: Clarendon Press, 1965).

5 The papers collected in John Morrill, *The Nature of the English Revolution* (Oxford: Routledge, 1993) and Blair Worden, *God's Instruments: Political Conduct in the England of Oliver Cromwell* (Oxford: Oxford University Press, 2012) provide a cumulative idea of how the vast historiography on 'revolutionary' (or, indeed unrevolutionary) England has developed and variegated over the decades.

6 On the diverse positions which came to recognise themselves as 'royalist' over the years and dec-ades, and the expressions they took on, see Jerome de Groot, *Royalist Identities* (Basingstoke: Macmillan, 2004), James Loxley, *Royalism and Poetry in the English Civil Wars: The Drawn Sword* (Basingstoke: Macmillan, 1997), Lois Potter, *Secret Rites and Secret Writing: Royalist Literature, 1641–1660* (Cambridge: Cambridge University Press, 1971), Robert Wilcher, *The Writing of Roy-alism, 1628–1660* (Cambridge: Cambridge University Press, 2001) and Hero Chalmers, *Royalist Women Writers, 1650–1689* (Oxford: Oxford University Press, 2004).

the cavalier is ambiguous, disputed, notional. Of what use, then, is it to apply such an epithet to a personality as shadowy and evasive as Sir John Denham, sometime cavalry commander in the royal army, councillor, exile, and latterly the king's Surveyor of Works? By the time Hopton wrote of 'this war without an enemy' in April 1643, Denham was a decided partisan: he had just published, in March, a pungently anti-Parliament verse satire, *Mr. Hampdens speech occasioned upon the Londoners petition for peace*. Ballads in a similar, traditionally 'cavalier' vein followed. He soon joined the royal garrison at Oxford, and by the end of 1644, as tentative moves towards peace gained pace, was effectively branded an enemy of the people by parliamentary articles which listed him among those to be prohibited from advising the king. Here was an out-and-out cavalier: yet it is impossible to forget that Denham was among those who, like Hopton and a great many cavaliers, had their doubts or held differing views on different topics. The rhetorical mood permeating Hopton's letter is not merely one of fellowship but genuine aporia. Similarly, the great meditation on kingship and history in *Coopers Hill*, in the original published version, had offered an almost uniquely levelled critique of the elements to blame for the grave pre-war situation, pointing up individual monarchic stubbornness and short-sightedness, as well as the cynical motives of those with interests in the City of London supporting a populist cause. Denham printed a revised edition of the poem in 1644, but the expansiveness of his initial inspiration, with its call for all to think within the traditional parameters of political consensus, is still unmistakeable. Was this a cavalier?[7]

The notion as such actually becomes historically useful again when we break down, even if only for the span of a discussion, the narrow equivalence between 'cavalier' and 'royalist'. It becomes easier when we accept, again if only provisionally, that royalism itself was not an especially coherent or homogenous concept in the early 1640s. The taxonomic cleansing carried out by the leading revisionist historians of the period has brought many benefits, but imposed simplifying strictures of its own. The helpfulness of the word as a source of historical texture and colour can be recovered by laying aside the political sense of its meaning and concentrating on its social and even literary connotations. Rather than a term, we are dealing with a cloud of associations, in which a traditionally 'cavalier' writer such as Denham may emerge, paradoxically, in greater clarity.

Two points should be made at the outset from Clarendon's elegantly high-handed sketch of how rival factions in the early struggle came to christen one another. First, the cavaliers are 'servants of the king' and the roundheads belong to the 'rabble'. The paramount distinction between cavaliers and non-cavaliers is thus one of class. A cavalier, as the word has always signified in the romance languages, is *un chevalier*, a gentleman, or more precisely, a horseman granted

---

7 *Coopers Hill* is regarded as a landmark, and sensitively treated, by (among others) Thomas N. Corns, *A History of Seventeenth-Century Literature*, rev. edn (Oxford: Blackwell, 2014), pp. 253–56, Loxley, *Royalism and Poetry*, pp. 84–86, and (especially) Wilcher, *The Writing of Royalism*, pp. 75–86, 130–33, and (commenting helpfully on scholarship on the revision of the poem), 339–42.

certain feudal privileges as a knight. Servants of the king, whether one finds them helping to secure the precincts of Whitehall or—as in Clarendon's case—holding out for justice in the Commons, are not to be found among the lower classes. Secondly, even though it is not clear whether these royal servants are first branded cavaliers by the rabble—or whether they assume the title for themselves—it is obvious that the word has not emerged from a vacuum: it means something, and must have meant something in 1631 as well as 1641. By exploring some of its earlier associations, we might learn something about those it came to describe; and then be able to determine how well this term described Denham.[8]

## II

Early in 1639 a Scottish Protestant mercenary, Sir James Lumsden, applied for permission to leave his Swedish regiment so that he could return and fight with the Covenanters who were defying King Charles: when he said that the call of God and his country was one 'I cannot disobey as a cavalier who loves his honour', he used the word in its flat sense of 'knight and gentleman'. He was writing in French, but to an English ear that hardly mattered. 'Cavalier' would always be a foreign word, a linguistic luxury import, and would betoken either refinement or pretentiousness depending on one's point of view.[9] Later, 'cavalier' could be intended as the highest praise, as when John Aubrey dubbed Sir Philip Sidney 'the most accomplished cavalier of his time'.[10] This entry in *Brief Lives* is no doubt tainted with post-war associations of 'cavalier', and there may be a surreptitious or even quite unconscious attempt to conscript the distinguished Elizabethan to the restored royalist cause. But, as an example of usage, Aubrey's paean to Sidney is typical: the cavalier embodied the accomplishments and virtues of the courtier, a blend of chivalry and finesse. These were the connotations monarchists emphasised, after the Restoration, insofar as they accepted or even cultivated the label. Yet there was also a rakish flavour to conceptions of the cavalier which was tolerated with varying ease. Kevin Sharpe, in his classic study of *The Personal Rule of Charles I*, suggested that the word referred most frequently to 'a gallant or a gay blade'.[11] However, the cut of the cavalier's jib in the literature in English of the earlier seventeenth century is consistently more disreputable and comic. The word's foreignness, its closeness to old enemies,

---

8  For a more detailed discussion of the term and its connotations, see Graham Roebuck, 'Cavalier', in Claude J. Summers and Ted-Larry Pebworth (eds), *The English Civil Wars in the Literary Imagination* (Columbia: University of Missouri Press, 1999), pp. 9–26.

9  David Stevenson, *The Scottish Revolution, 1637–44*, 2nd edn (Edinburgh: John Donald, 2003), p. 130; quoting T.A. Fischer, *The Scots in Sweden* (Edinburgh: Otto Schulz, 1907), pp. 114–15. Future Covenanter officers regularly described themselves as chevaliers in the correspondence Fischer translates.

10  John Aubrey, *'Brief Lives', Chiefly of Contemporaries, Set Down by John Aubrey, between the Years 1669 & 1696*, ed. Andrew Clark, 2 vols (Oxford: Clarendon Press, 1898), ii, p. 247.

11  Kevin Sharpe, *The Personal Rule of Charles I* (New Haven: Yale University Press, 1992), p. 233.

made it immediately suspect: as applied in 1641, it carried a distinct whiff of Charles's brief quixotic career as a *caballero*, when he had journeyed as a young man to Madrid to court the infanta Maria. To the Protestant mob, he hardly righted matters by marrying another papist, Henrietta Maria of France. These prejudices were backed up in works that were becoming canonical. In Jonson, the cavalier is invariably a demobbed comrade of the drunkard and cut-throat, ready for the hangman. In Shakespeare, the 'cavalleria' are frequenters of broth-els.[12] The second, ironic sense of cavalier is thus an outright subversion of the first, and together they give an idea of the exchange of insults in and about West-minster in late autumn 1641. If the 'rabble' branded the king's servants cavaliers, they intended it in the second, subversive sense of the word; which their oppo-nents, shunning the charge of debauchery and dishonour, converted back to the former, panegyric sense.[13]

To close in on the word as it sounded in the late 1630s and early 1640s, it makes sense to consider the example of one man with whom both senses became strongly associated. The courtier, dramatist, and poet Sir John Suckling was dead by the time the rabble clashed with the king's unapproved bodyguard, but he had long been a figurehead of the cavalleria. He was one of the period's most notori-ous gamesters, who had frittered away his patrimony in covering up his losses. It was said that on suffering a particularly bad night at the card table, after hiding away for a short interval he would make himself the talk of the town by appearing in a new sumptuous suit (such as the one in which he was painted by Van Dyck), making light of his debts and expenses. London shopkeepers were wary of trust-ing him for sixpence. Among his great indulgences were productions of his plays, funded from his own pocket. Suckling followed the contemporary rage amid the titled classes for masques on the model of the great spectacles put on at Whitehall and the Inns of Court, and spent lavishly for costumes and scenery for his plays at Blackfriars Theatre. He wrote three finished dramas, all of which displayed a talent for dialogue and speechwriting, and a good sense of story. Suckling freely admitted his works were not perfect: describing himself in an influential poem recounting 'A Sessions of the Poets', he acknowledged that

> He loved not the Muses so well as his sport;
> And prized black eyes, or a lucky hit
> At bowls, above all the Trophies of Wit.[14]

---

12 Ben Jonson, *Every Man in His Humour* (1.4.135), ed. Robert S. Miola (Manchester: Manches-ter University Press, 2000), p. 118; William Shakespeare, *Pericles* (Sc. 19), ed. Roger Warren (Oxford: Oxford University Press, 2003), p. 193.

13 On the near-synonymy of 'cavalier' and 'malignant' in Parliamentarian literature, see Roebuck, 'Cavalier', pp. 17–23.

14 Sir John Suckling, 'A sessions of the Poets' (ll. 73–8), in Thomas Clayton (ed.), *The Works of Sir John Suckling*, vol. 2: *The Non-dramatic Works* (Oxford: Clarendon Press, 1971), p. 74. The scholarship of Clayton in his introduction to this volume (pp. xxiv–lxiv), that of Herbert Berry, 'Sir John Suckling's poems and letters from manuscript', in *Studies in the Humanities Departments of*

Suckling, who was thirty in 1639, lived the life of a rake on returning in 1632 from a spell of cavalry training and diplomatic service in central Europe. His letters from the continent reveal a satirical turn of mind, light-hearted on the whole but far from immune to the madness of the unfolding Thirty Years' War, largely accepting self-interest and the love of power as constants in the universe of politics. His response to these forces was a lifelong commitment to insouciance. When his sister's much older husband, a quadruple widower, hanged himself, he advised her to enjoy her freedom:

> I would not have you so much as enquire whether it were with his garters or his Cloak-bag strings [...] Curiosity would be here as vain, as if a Cuckold should enquire whether it upon the Couch or a Bed, and whether the Cavalier pull'd off his Spurrs first or not.[15]

The cavalier was for Suckling a guiding symbol in both life and writing. Elegance, pluck, and *sprezzatura* were the virtues to be cultivated. As the national crisis mounted in 1640, in a letter purportedly to his friend Henry Jermyn, he proposed that the king should simply act with a certain magnificence, the boldness of a gallant, to subdue his enemies and appease the public: 'For the People are naturally not valiant, and not much Cavalier'.[16] Boldness, he argued, would carry the day. The letter was published—whether with or without Suckling's authority is unclear—and caused outrage, since it only strengthened fears that the king was willing not only to quash parliamentary privilege but also to unhinge the constitution. Jermyn, the close confidant of the queen, one of the most louche presences in the royal court and in truth a far more influential person than Suckling, was manifestly a kindred spirit—a vilified gambler, fortune-hunter, and philanderer.

For since the early to mid-1630s Suckling's name had been drenched in scandal and a fair amount of ridicule. The most damaging affair was his pursuit of the heiress Ann Willoughby, daughter of Sir Henry, bt. He was challenged by a rival, the redoubtable Sir John Digby, on the road towards the Willoughby estate at Risley. Digby, a towering man and a formidable soldier, demanded that Suckling renounce his claim on Ann or provide satisfaction. Suckling, who was 'slight timberd' in stature,[17] refused, sensibly but most dishonourably, to draw his sword, and so his adversary set about him with a cudgel. Digby was risking serious displeasure in the highest places, since the king was said to have approved the match between Ann and Sir John if the lady's consent was genuine. Reports

the *University of Western Ontario*, no.1 (1960), and Kees Van Strien, 'Sir John Suckling in Holland', *English Studies*, 78 (1995), 443–54, has in recent years been supplemented on a grand scale by Robert Wilcher, *Discontented Cavalier: The Work of Sir John Suckling in Its Social, Religious, Political and Literary Contexts* (Newark, Delaware: University of Delaware Press, 2007).

15  Suckling 'to Martha Lady Southcot, October 1639', in Clayton, *Non-dramatic Works*, pp. 149–50.
16  Suckling, 'To Mr Henry German, in the Beginning of Parliament, 1640', in Clayton, *Non-dramatic Works*, p. 165.
17  Aubrey, *'Brief Lives'*, ii, p. 241.

of the *rodomontado* nonetheless put all the virtue on the side of Digby, and Suckling emerged as weak, boastful, and cowardly. He did himself little further good a few weeks later in the autumn of 1634 when he tried ambushing Digby with a group of toughs outside the private theatre at Blackfriars. Digby, reminding some of Sir Edward Herbert a generation earlier, saw off all his would-be assassins. Suckling spent a week fretting in prison until his friends at court managed to have him released.[18] As with most losses or setbacks, he responded ebulliently. All of his hugely costly productions, staged at court or Blackfriars, were put on in the years following the feud with Digby. His career reached its climax in a military excursion that was arguably his largest theatrical effort, and greatest flop. In 1637 Scotland rose up against Charles and Archbishop Laud's attempt to impose a prayer book on the Kirk. A large yet unevenly equipped English force was raised to suppress the forces of the rebel Covenant, in the first campaign of the Bishops' Wars. Suckling raised a cavalry unit at his own expense, paying characteristic attention to his men's uniforms and accoutrements. The hundred men in his troop were all fitted out in white doublets, scarlet coats, breeches, and cockaded hats.[19] In the aftermath of the crisis at Kelso in June 1638, when English forces retreated and scattered at the mere sight of the enemy, Suckling and his troopers were among the principals facing derision and outright scorn, unjustly as it happened, for the perceived debacle. It would be anachronistic to speak of Suckling's troop as civil-war cavaliers; yet in the rout of dandified gallants by doughty defenders of liberty one has all the makings of pro-Parliament caricature. Suckling, his finances now nearing desperation-point, had no shortage of enemies to offer jibes.

> When he came to the Camp, he was in a damp [a cold sweat]
> To see the Scots in sight a,
> And all his brave Troops like so many droops,
> To fight they had no heart a.
> And when the Allarme called all to arme,
> Sir *John* he went to shite a.[20]

The record in fact shows that charges of cowardice against Sir John were in this instance quite unfounded, yet as an established bragger and gamester he was a conveniently risible figure in the shaken royal court. To more reflective critics of the campaign, the imagined sight of Suckling and his red-coated beaux might have suggested a passage in Machiavelli's *Discourses on Livy*, much-studied by

18  William Knowler (ed.), *The Earl of Strafford's Letters and Dispatches*, 2 vols (London: William Bowyer, 1739–40), i, pp. 336–37. On this period in Suckling's life more generally, see Wilcher, 'The Stories of the Town: Gallant and Gamester', in *Discontented Cavalier*, pp. 85–120.

19  Aubrey, *'Brief Lives'*, ii, p. 242.

20  Sir John Mennes, 'Upon Sir John Suckling's Northern Discoverie' (ll. 25–30), Clayton, *Non-dramatic Works*, pp. 207–08.

those considering the virtues of a republic. The situation recalled a Roman army's standoff with Samnite forces.

> Assembling thereafter to the number of forty thousand, one-half of whom, to render their appearance of unusual splendour, were clad in white, with plumes and crests over their helmets, they took up their ground in the neighbourhood of Aquilonia. But Papirius, being sent against them, bade his soldiers be of good cheer, telling them that "feathers made no wounds, and that a Roman spear would pierce a painted shield".[21]

Over the few years that remained to him, and which included a second still more wretched showing against the Scots, Suckling became virtually synonymous with foolhardy endeavours. None was more so than the so-called second army plot to rescue the king's condemned viceroy of Ireland, the Earl of Strafford, and regain control of London for the Crown in 1641. Early in May, Suckling was involved in an abortive attempt to seize the Tower; made an ill-judged show of strength, in the company of sixty armed men at a tavern in Bread Street (near the birthplace of his much-admired Donne); and fled the country upon being charged with treason. With him, to Dieppe, went Jermyn and his friend William Davenant. He made his way to Paris, and died, of obscure causes, later that year.[22] Suckling and his public images had by this point long been living separate lives. The disparity between the clashing versions of his life became all the greater the more distant he became in living memory. Despite his flaws Suckling was evidently a thoughtful, creative, spirited and politically insightful individual. His mottled virtues, though, were predictably as irrelevant to enemies of the king as his undoubted faults were to posthumous defenders. He was singled out for attack in at least sixteen pro-Parliament tracts. Some of these dealt with him alone.[23] A broadside of 1641, *The Sucklington Faction*, gloated over his disgrace and departure. Though apparently ignorant of his death, his critic was in no doubt that Suckling had met with justice. He wished nothing less for other 'Sucklington' characters and 'roaring boys'.

> Here fits the prodigall children [...] acting *your* parts of hotspur Cavaliers and disguised ding-thrifts, habiting themselves after the fashions of the world, as one that is to travaile into a farre Countrey.

---

21  Niccolò Machiavelli, *Discourses on Livy* (Chapter 15), trans. by Ninian Hill Thomson (Mineola, NY: Dover, 2007), p. 48. Without pushing an analogy too far, it might be noted that the Samnites summon the strength for one last stand against the Romans by recourse to 'ancient sacrificial rite', which for certain readers might have seemed applicable to the 'papistical' liturgy in Charles's rejected prayer book. Ironically, the Samnites swear dreadful oaths never to turn their backs in battle.

22  On Suckling's last years, see Wilcher, *Discontented Cavalier*, pp. 272–330. On his role in the army plots (and for a fine prose-portrait in miniature), see also John Adamson, *The Noble Revolt: The Overthrow of Charles I* (London: Orion, 2007), pp. 279–85, 445–46.

23  'There were undoubtedly others', concludes his modern editor; Clayton, 'Introduction', *Non-dramatic Works*, p. lxvi.

Suckling had actually gone further, into the final undiscovered country; but his personal existence was irrelevant to the broader symbolic type which he and his brethren embodied. The godly author was perfectly satisfied that such 'hotspur Cavaliers' belonged among the reprobate—fallen 'not onely from piety to impuritie, but also from Christian verities, to Antichristian vanities, fopperies and trumperies'.[24]

To the above author, 'Cavalier' doesn't mean 'Royalist'; it means 'Sucklington'. It seems reasonable to extend such thinking to the protesters who were so angry with King Charles's surly cohorts later in 1641. A cavalier was a man who typified all that was seen to be wrong with the royal court. Such bodyguards were called 'cavaliers', ironically and scornfully, because they seemed specimens of the class of person to which Sir John Suckling had also belonged. By the mid-1640s 'cavalier' obviously had come to denote a soldier or supporter of the king's army. Fighting for Parliament, however, did not mean that you yourself were not a royalist. You might have believed strongly in monarchy, however much you lamented what 'evil counselors' had done to Charles. Fighting the cavaliers indicated that you were not a roaring boy, a rich lout ignoring the old constitution of England.

On the other side, being a cavalier meant being loyal to the king. It was a virtuous, heroic thing to be. There were even those who felt it was not so bad to be someone like Suckling. There had always been a large group at court who admired him, not all of them proven Sucklingtons. This allowed even Suckling to be rehabilitated. The 1640s saw commendatory editions of his works which took a modest place in the royalist canon of literary relics, and included a biography that is almost pure encomium.[25] After the Restoration, his literary reputation seemed secure. Late in the century, Congreve has a character mention him as 'natural, easy Suckling'.[26] Steele, in *The Tatler*, associates him with a coxcomb who feels obliged to give hourly proof of his courage, but apparently with no aspersion against Suckling himself. A quotation from a Suckling poem, somewhat

24  *The Sucklington Faction, or (Svcklings) Roaring Boys* (London, 1641), BL 669, fol. 4 (17.), Wing S6133, printed in facsimile as a foldout in William Carew Hazlitt (ed.), *The Poetical Works of Sir John Suckling*, 2nd edn (London: Reeves and Turner, 1892). On the derogatory and hagiographical images contemporaries furnished of Suckling in his last years and posthumously, see Wilcher, 'This Gentle and Princely Poet: The Making of the Cavalier', in *Discontented Cavalier*, pp. 331–46. Wilcher also reprints key polemical sources such as *The Sucklingtonian Faction* in the appendices to this book, pp. 347–55. 'Roaring boy' had been applied to rowdy antisocial types since Elizabethan times, often in connection with the theatre; see Judith Cook, *Roaring Boys: Playwrights and Players in Jacobean England* (London: Sutton, 2004).

25  Suckling's works were published as *Fragmenta Aurea*, 'golden pieces', and their importance in the process of royalist lamentation from the late 1640s on is assessed by Thomas N. Corns, 'Thomas Carew, Sir John Suckling and Richard Lovelace', in Thomas N. Corns (ed.), *The Cambridge Companion to English Poetry: Donne to Marvell* (Cambridge: Cambridge University Press, 1993), pp. 200–20 (pp. 200–02).

26  Herbert Davis (ed.), *The Way of The World* (IV.I.106), in *The Complete Plays of William Congreve* (Chicago: University of Chicago Press, 1967), p. 447.

surprisingly, is used to define the standard this new 'roaring boy' fails to reach.[27] In such approving notes, rightly or wrongly, the word 'cavalier' itself implicitly regains its old and primary meaning of knight and gentleman.

Yet the epithet would always have some tincture of the Sucklington. The fallen cockade, the broken sword, and the dampened swagger were the attributes the Parliamentary press would always try bringing out in their targeted cavaliers. For the Sucklington experience amounted to bafflement, the worst nightmare of every knight at arms. This was the fate allotted to the king's defeated general, 'the brave Marquess of *Newcastle*' when he fled in a fishing boat after Marston Moor. The outstanding courtier and builder, the refiner of dressage, governor to the Prince of Wales and patron of Jonson, was put on the Sucklington path of the cavalier:

> the brave Marquess of *Newcastle*, which made the fine plays, he danced so quaintly, played his part a while in the North, was soundly beaten, shew'd a pair of heels, and exit *Newcastle*.[28]

The cavalier seeking to preserve his self-image as hero and sweet gentleman would always be fighting the reptilian accuser who defined him by his lowest moment, and attributed the lowest motive to any questionable act. The disreputable connotation lasted into the eighteenth century. Another issue of *The Tatler*, just a few weeks after the one in which Suckling was quoted, mentioned a 'house, or rather a college, sacred to hospitality, and the industrious arts'. At the entrance is hieroglyphically drawn, a cavalier contending with a monster, with jaws expanded, ready to devour him.[29] The house, in a part of town famous for the freshest oysters and the plainest English, has been founded to combat ostentation and pretence. The meaning of the hieroglyphic is obscure, but apparently cautionary. The monster stands for the vanity of the cavalier himself, a vice which members of the house's 'Industry' rigorously oppose. To their enemies, cavaliers are devoured by their own inner failings. The true Sucklington, meanwhile, the cavalier of '41, only stops when he loses everything. Until then he is disregardful, obnoxiously so. He refuses to be eaten by disgrace. He puts a new splendid suit on his account, sells off more of his patrimony, and raises another troop of horse.

## III

How much of a Sucklington was Denham? Assuredly there are resemblances. He was a comeback specialist, an undaunted gentleman. He had powerful friends, even during the Interregnum, who helped him avoid paying the full cost of his actions. Late in life, he tasted the court's hemlock of shame, and, on recovering

---

27  Richard Steele, *The Tatler* (no. 57, 20 August 1709), 4 vols (London: J. Parsons, 1794), ii, p. 39.
28  Quoted in Geoffrey Trease, *Portrait of a Cavalier: William Cavendish, First Duke of Newcastle* (London: Macmillan, 1979), p. 143.
29  Steele, *The Tatler* (no. 73, 27 September 1709), ii, p. 130.

from the madness which overwhelmed him during his wife's fatal affair with the Duke of York, returned to the social scene with renewed and defiant vigour. Denham's last extrovert whirl, in Aubrey's telling, reads like one of Suckling's strutting shows of carelessness writ large.

There is of course ample literary evidence of Denham's royalism. By 1642, commissioned as Charles's High Sheriff in Surrey, he was writing as a cavalier in the standard historical sense. In arms and letters, he was a committed follower of the king. There is his elegy for Strafford, not published Until 1668 but clearly drafted shortly after the earl's execution in May 1641;[30] the 'Humble Petition of the Poets' to the five members, his burlesque on Hampden and the 'Western Wonder' poems. It has sometimes been pointed out how these, and the others in his clutch of wartime and republic-era lyrics, shift from the greater circumspection Denham revealed towards Charles's policies in *The Sophy* and the first version of *Coopers Hill*. Such a shift probably indicates the reality of a writer who held a developed view of the issues being forced into choosing a side in a war. It reflects the grief he felt about the situation and a burst of hostile feeling to the enemy with whom, he felt, the burden of guilt rested. Storm clouds are present in the view from Cooper's Hill, and the developing national emergency offered ever less space for even-handedness, and brought an equally increasing need for comic relief. Denham's journey from reflective commentator to partisan wit indicates the great expansion in the ranks of the cavaliers between the latter half of 1641 and the raising of the royal standard in 1642. The cavaliers had grown from a band of lawless desperados hanging around Whitehall to an army comprised of a probable majority of former moderates. An important moment in this transformation is likely to have been Charles's unlucky descent on Westminster to arrest the Five Members with his armed escort, only to find that the birds had flown. Denham commemorated the five right honourable gentlemen with something of the gaiety that Suckling might have treated it.

> According unto the blessed form you have taught us,
> We thank you first for the *Ills* you have brought us,
> For the *Good* we receive we thank him that gave it,
> And you for the Confidence only to crave it.[31]

There can be little doubt of Denham's subsequent allegiance to the royal cause, notwithstanding the insurance policy provided by his friendship with the Earl of Pembroke, a member of Cromwell's Council of State. Of more interest here is

---

30  Denham, 'On the Earl of Strafford's Trial and Death', Banks, *PW*, pp. 153–54. See Banks's transcript of the earlier version from a British Museum manuscript, Egerton 2421, in his note on p. 153. On the place of the elegy in the manuscript culture of the time, see de Groot, *Royalist Identities*, pp. 67–69.

31  Denham, 'To the Five Members of the Honourable House of Commons. The Humble Petition of the Poets' (ll. 9–12), Banks, *PW*, p. 128.

whether we might aptly place him among the earlier constitution of the cavaliers, the class of wealthy, arrogant no-goods of which John Suckling proved perhaps the crowning example. There is no evidence Denham was closely associated with Suckling himself or his circle before the war. In later decades, the picture presented by his connection with Sir William Davenant, poet laureate, a close friend of Suckling and in summer 1641 his fellow runaway, is ambiguous. Denham collaborated with Davenant in the 1660s and like him had been up to his neck in the espionage and conspiracy of the previous decade. He wrote biting criticisms, though, of Davenant's artistic pretensions in his epic poem, *Gondibert*, and commented harshly on the laureate's colonial misadventures and also on his wife. At first anonymous, Denham put his name to these and further jibes after Davenant's death. The bearing these insults have on their relationship will probably remain unclear. It was a time in which wits expected little mercy from each other, when relations might resume or continue after a clash of verses, fists, or blades to clear the air. The poems on the whole suggest a running joke rather than real and long-nursed dislike; Denham's final joshing elegy on Davenant reads affectionately.[32] His attitude to the Sucklingtons themselves is not to be determined by his mixed messages about Davenant any more, say, than the jocose way he treats Suckling's enemy Sir John Mennes in a mocking ballad about a mission to eat a pig in Bologna.[33]

The point at issue here, though, is not whether Denham knew or liked Suckling. Many liked Suckling who were not at all like him—notably his older and deeply inscrutable friend and comrade, Thomas Carew. The question is, might Denham have belonged among the cavaliers whose conduct Suckling and the Sucklingtons embodied in the early summer of 1641? Was he a roaring boy? It is important to bear in mind that such labels are broader than Suckling himself, and older than the crisis of the Short Parliament.

Suggesting an answer is only possible by looking back to the 1630s. There, a tantalising cavalier trait is evident in Denham's lifelong habit as a 'gamester'. Comparatively few rakes and gallants can have had access to the funds Suckling and Denham frittered away. Of the two, Denham's legacy was by far the more modest, yet he was little less compulsive when it came to cards and bowls. When he inherited his father's property and capital, 'the money was played away first, and next the plate was sold'.[34] The land soon followed. Denham's financial troubles are an important personal subtext of *Coopers Hill*, and the sense of self-inflicted disinheritance which so troubles the poem. The lines are uttered from a vantage point near Denham's house at Egham, 'The Place', a modest yet attractive and pleasantly situated former parsonage. As some of Denham's first readers

---

32  The lyrics, evidently copied by Denham himself into a copy of his 1668 *Poems*, are printed by Banks as Appendix A in Banks, *PW*, pp. 311–25.

33  Denham, 'To Sir John Mennis being invited from Calice to Bologne to eat a pig', Banks, *PW*, pp. 100–03.

34  Aubrey, *'Brief Lives'*, ii, p. 218.

knew well, the poet surveying the surrounding territory is a man left with no choice but to sell up his own stake in what he sees (and stands on).[35] Such mounting losses suggest a compulsion, something like a libidinal 'rejouissance', to borrow a word Denham applies mockingly to resolute promiscuity.[36] To respectable citizens, the practice was equally abhorrent. The broadside quoted earlier, *The Sucklington Faction*, belongs to a long tradition of proclamations and diatribes against the evils of gaming.

For Suckling, being the 'greatest gamester' was an integral part of his public persona, the ongoing court performance that his short adult life constituted. Denham adopted a third attitude to the sin. He is accredited by Aubrey with writing 'a little essay in 8vo, printed ... [Aubrey's memory failed him], *Against gameing and to shew the vanities and inconveniences of it*, which he presented to his father to let him know his detestation of it'.[37] Denham supposedly wrote the piece to calm his father's doubts about his reliability as an heir and it has been identified with a short tract entitled *The Anatomy of Play*, published anonymously in 1651.[38] Although much of what the essay has to say is somewhat 'commonplace',[39] it still quite thoughtfully breaks down the almost sadomasochistic relationship between punishers and practitioners in the debate on gambling. This debate paradoxically opened up precisely at a time when measures to eliminate English gambling had never been so severe: the *Anatomy*'s date of publication, during Denham's exile abroad, as moves against 'sports and games' of all kinds gathered pace in the English Commonwealth, is significant in this respect. There is an especially interesting passage where Denham faintly suggests that gambling was in some ways condoned and even expected in quarters where one might expect it to be condemned. He tells the story of a friend he accompanied to the house of 'a Great lady', where those gathered very frequently 'fell to play' and remained at the card table all night. The gentleman became renowned for the large tips he gave out in the household when luck was with him. The servants, instead of groaning at the lengthened working hours, would support the players avidly. Denham's friend's glass was never empty; his way downstairs was always lit. Butlers and footmen were 'ready to do all offices expecting their reward'. On the nights he was unlucky, however, such favours were withdrawn; 'he might stumble and break his neck down the staires, for any help he should have of them'.[40]

Denham has no intention of passing on the blame for the vice, but such paragraphs indicate the groups who stood to profit from the sin of prodigals. Besides the

---

35  'He sold it to John Thynne, Esq.', recorded Aubrey; *'Brief Lives'*, i, p. 219.
36  Denham, 'A Dialogue between Sir John Pooley and Mr Thomas Killigrew' (l.8), Banks, *PW*, p.103.
37  Aubrey, *'Brief Lives'*, i, p. 217.
38  *The Anatomy of Play: Written by a worthy and Learned Gent.: Dedicated to his Father, to shew his detestation of it* (London: G.P. for Nicholas Bourne, 1651).
39  O Hehir, *HD*, p. 9.
40  Denham, *The Anatomy of Play*, pp. 18–19; discussed by O Hehir, *HD*, p. 11.

servants in great houses where play occurred, we should also infer the numerous tradesmen, lenders and tavern-keepers who were all but dependant on gamesters and their victims. 'A mans winnings are as it were in jest', concludes Denham's anecdote, 'but his losses always prove in earnest'. Such was undoubtedly the case for a gamester who drained his entire stock, as Suckling did. Suggestively, Denham put one line in *The Sophy* which sounded a note of understanding for those in such a predicament. War itself, to such desperate men, sometimes remained the last available bet: 'now the wars are done, we have no pretences / To put off Creditors: I am haunted Sir … [by] Material and Substantial Devils'.[41] Before that point was reached, however, the relationship between the gamesters and their most vocal protesters could very often be symbiotic. Gaming benefited a 'grey' economic area; and at a symbolic level it provided moral failures easy to condemn.

It also illustrated the need of a guiding hand. The noted gallants frequently had a troubled relationship with their fathers. Sir John Suckling Senior had been a dynasty-builder and secretary of state. The elder Denham was a senior judge, a Baron of the Exchequer and former Lord Justice of Ireland, who famously ruled in favour of the Crown's adversaries in the matter of Ship Money. His personality was 'reverend and religious'.[42] Despite the assurances Denham the younger sought to give in *The Anatomy of Play*, and despite following him into the legal profession—he was called to the bar the year the elder Denham died—he clearly found it impossible to meet his father's expectations. Denham belonged, admittedly, to a generation which collectively failed or betrayed its paternal and ancestral legacies, from King Charles downwards. The English story of the civil wars is one of children clashing over what their forebears had intended their country to be. At his own level in the 1630s, Denham left in living memory a catalogue of almost helplessly rebellious indiscretions. In Aubrey's account, we see him laughing when the president of his Oxford college suggested he repay a debt, and running riot with a paint pot between Temple-Bar and Charing Cross, blotting out all the signs. 'Thy father [...] haz hanged many an honester man' was the verdict of Ralph Kettel, the president of Trinity College, Oxford, on Denham for his early conduct: a classically gruff expostulation on a rogue cavalier.[43] There was an ample stock of good humour behind this remark, and it should be noted that Kettell was adept at containing his undergraduates by resorting to the lesser evil: he always kept excellent beer in his college to prevent potential drunkards going into town 'to comfort their stomachs'.[44] Yet in the language of *The Anatomy of Play*, the confirmed gamester symbolised the collapse of the threefold trust on which Denham's patriarchal society depended, that 'from a Soveraigne, to a subject, a

---

41  Denham, *The Sophy* (1.2.276–81), Banks, *PW*, p. 245.
42  According to the puritan divine Richard Bernard, quoted in Wilfred Prest, 'Sir John Denham (1559–1639)', *ODNB*.
43  Aubrey, *'Brief Lives'*, ii, p. 18. There was an ample stock of good humour and reasonableness behind the remark, nevertheless.
44  Ibid., p. 20.

Father, to a son, or a Master, to a servant, of all which a Gamester makes himself incapable'.[45] Such a man was a walking vortex, a bringer of anarchy.

## IV

To critics of Sucklingtons as impure souls, the causes of such squandering tendencies were less interesting than the character of an errant son was rhetorically convenient. Intriguingly, to his most reliable contemporary biographer Denham resembled precisely the spirit of censure who pedalled such reprehension in myth. His singular piercing stare put John Aubrey in mind of 'a momus', the bearer of blame and ridicule. This spiteful and cynical if loquacious daemon was familiar to the early Stuart imagination from, among other treatments, Thomas Carew and Inigo Jones's celebrated court masque, *Coelum Britannicum*. (The shadow of a Momus prompts the passing thought that to certain ears 'cavalier' might have carried an echo of Latin *cavillator*, originally 'mocker' or 'scoffer'.) Aubrey's impression is borne out by other accounts and much of Denham's output: one thinks again of his sustained (and justified) teasing of Davenant. Yet Denham still stands as one of the most notorious victims of the Momus who served as the Restoration court's presiding spirit of scandal.

Quite a number of Denham's poems project the image of a cavalier libertine. One, *'Natura Naturata'*, rather drily and conventionally questions sexual taboos; another argues for 'Friendship and Single Life against Love and Marriage'. The latter, written in taut triplets, may well be a bleak commentary on Denham's traumatic second marriage. Yet amid all the stories collected about him, many of them with a pungent hint of fantasy about them, there are none to suggest Denham was much of a rake. Aubrey for one would undoubtedly have preserved anecdotal evidence of Denham philandering had he heard it. Instead, Denham was a man who married—unhappily on both occasions, if for very different reasons. His first marriage and family life was wrecked by the onset of civil war. His second was ill-augured as a result of misjudgement. It is striking that Denham proposed to Margaret Brooke, rather than pursuing an extramarital affair with her or another 'beautifull young lady'. His status and relative wealth made the course as possible for him as other ageing, ailing courtiers. In 1665 when they married, 'Sir John was ancient and limping', and he made the older man's perennial mistake of believing the young bride returned his love with equal ardour.[46] On his part, this may have been Denham just trying his luck and damning the consequences—and, naturally, placing a bet for the sake of Margaret's dowry. The court Momus saw to it, however, that Lady Denham was soon demanding that the king's brother publicly acknowledge her as his mistress. James was to visit her quite openly at the house her husband had built at Scotland Yard. Perhaps this was her attempt, cornered not by one but a pair of older predators, to call the royal lover's bluff; if so, it failed.

---

45  Denham, *The Anatomy of Play*, p. 11.
46  Aubrey, *'Brief Lives'*, ii, p. 218.

Her husband was attacked on all sides when 'fair Denham' died[47] and was implicated in her murder. Samuel Butler castigated him in verse; the mob was prepared to tear him apart. From beginning to end, his courtship of Margaret Brooke decked Denham in colours of folly. Yet, more importantly when it comes to understanding who he was, it also revealed him as naive. Perhaps the most striking incident in his biography, his well-known reaction to hearing of his wife's affair, when he turned back without viewing the quarry he had travelled to visit, indicates that he genuinely had no sense that Lady Denham might betray him— and how truly besotted he was. The dowry was no doubt gratefully accepted, to sponsor building projects and offset losses at Piccadilly, but really seems not to have been Denham's prime motive. In the field of one of the most notoriously liberated royal courts in English history, this hardly marks him out as a smooth operator. Rather, it brings to mind the description a contemporary gave Aubrey of Denham in early adulthood as 'the dreamingest young fellow', one from whom 'such things [...] as he haz left the world' might never be expected.[48] Marrying a much younger woman, later in life, and losing his mind at her adultery—such a course might, however, be predicted of such a detached and introverted character. How well it tallies with Aubrey's own impressions of Denham is open to dispute. Remembering the lean and stalking Surveyor of the King's Works, Aubrey had the sense of a figure who resembled 'Horace's mad poet striding with head held high into a well or ditch'.[49] When this portrait is established, Denham's gambling takes on a rather less Sucklington quality. One recalls how Aubrey says Denham was mostly 'rooked' by more competent players and card sharps.[50] Sucklingtons, naturally, might come in all shapes and sizes, with all manner of personalities. Suckling himself was diminutive and mercurial; his friend Jermyn was a somewhat ponderous man, with (said Marvell) a drayman's build and the backbone of an elephant.[51] Loping Denham, with his small-pox scars and his thinning sandy hair, might still have ridden with such cavaliers. He is, however, more lonely, more serious, the solitary watcher on the hilltop—and yet also giddier, more a victim of impulse. In some ways this figure with a hint of Momus in his bearing is less attractive than easy, natural Suckling and many of his cronies. But the greater complexity, depth, and learning in his writing is also an indication that he saw further. The cavalier stereotype does even Suckling an injustice; but there is much more still of Denham that evades and exceeds this misunderstood and much-simplified label. His modern editor betrays the fatigue of long and excellent service to his text with an underwhelming assessment of Denham as poet.[52] Yet

47  Andrew Marvell, 'The Last Instructions to a Painter' (1.342), in *The Poems and Letters of Andrew Marvell*, ed. H.M. Margoliouth, 2 vols (Oxford: Clarendon Press, 3rd edn, 1971), i, p. 156.
48  Aubrey, *'Brief Lives'*, i, p. 217.
49  O Hehir's fine paraphrase of Aubrey's quotation from *De Arte Poetica* (457–59), in *HD*, p. 17.
50  Aubrey, *'Brief Lives'*, i, p. 217.
51  Marvell, 'Last Instructions to a Painter' (1.34), *Poems and Letters*, ii, p. 148.
52  Banks, in his introduction to *Poetical Works*, admits: 'I cannot say that the judgement of time is not in the main just' (p. 26).

on every page of Denham's works a reader surrendering lofty expectations—the expectations nurtured, of course, by *Coopers Hill*—will find compelling aptness and moments of arresting strangeness:

> They who *Minerva* from *Joves* head derive,
> Might make Old *Homers* Skull the Muses Hive.[53]

Such oddities must have slipped every now and then from the dreamy man and startled his friends when he visited the Apsleys in Richmond during his early twenties. Their home lay conveniently on the road to town from Egham. His friend Allen Apsley was later a fellow royalist officer. Apsley's father, the late Sir Allen, had been lieutenant of the Tower, popular with celebrated inmates such as Sir John Eliot and Sir Walter Raleigh, and known as something of a gambler himself in his younger days. The younger Apsley's sister, Lucy, was the future essayist, poet, and biographer whose qualities as a writer have only very recently gained the attention and merit they deserve. She would marry Colonel John Hutchinson, the parliamentary soldier, whose puritan morals she passionately shared and for whose *Life* she is still best known. At some point she acquired and evidently liked a translation of the *Aeneid* books II-VI which Denham had worked on in the peaceful mid-1630s. Many years later, she copied Denham's translation into her commonplace book. This must have been a few years after Denham returned to the work himself, and published a revised version of a part of it, in 1651, as *The Destruction of Troy*.

Lucy Hutchinson's notebook is remarkable for the discipline with which she compiled it, and the eclectic range of works she included. Her selection was extremely non-partisan, though her approval of what she read was a complex matter. Hutchinson translated *De rerum natura* in its entirety, but then at some point wrote a long poem of her own repudiating, more or less completely, Lucretius's ideas.[54] When she transcribed lyrics by John Cleveland, or translations of the Psalms by Carew (a courtier of extremely low standing on the parliamentarian side), she was drawn to the merits and faults of the texts themselves: and the same principle must have guided her when she copied Denham's Virgil.[55] Hutchinson is such a singular thinker that her distant family friendship and personal acquaintance with Denham can explain only in part the route by which this partial English

---

53  Denham, 'The Progress of Learning' (ll. 65–66), Banks, *PW*, p. 116.

54  Reid Barbour and David Norbrook (eds), *The Works of Lucy Hutchinson*, 4 vols (Oxford: Clarendon Press, 2011–), i: *The Translation of Lucretius*; Lucy Hutchinson, *Order and Disorder*, ed. David Norbrook (Oxford: Blackwell, 2001).

55  Hutchinson's commonplace book is in the Nottinghamshire Archives, MS DD/Hul. Denham's Virgil takes up pp. 5–135. Cleveland's 'The Hue and Cry after Sir John Presbyter' is on pp. 247–49; 'Four Songs' by Carew (in addition to his Psalms on p. 144) are on pp. 231–35. See the archive catalogue entry by Jill Millman http://web.warwick.ac.uk/, and Jerome de Groot, 'John Denham and Lucy Hutchinson's Commonplace Book', *Studies in English Literature*, 48.1 (Winter 2008), 147–64.

*Aeneid* reached Hutchinson's pen; but the part such connections played should not be ignored. In her handwritten pages, something of the actual fluidity of Stuart society may be caught. Hutchinson's inclusion of Denham not only suggests her fierce independence of mind but also the freedom of intellectual movement that was still possible within her social world. Lines of dialogue and exchange existed that civil war had not entirely cut off. In the Apsley context, Denham was still the absent-minded, somewhat vice-prone associate of old, reduced neither to his roaring-boy markings nor his royalist baggage.

## V

The vestiges of the cavalier which hung about Denham only become important when you come to reflect on the outward identity of the translator who redid some of his work for the crisper, yet looser and more idiomatic version published in 1651. *The Destruction of Troy*, with its Ur-text in Hutchinson's notebook, has oddly greater poignancy even than the evolving *Coopers Hill*. For Denham's rendering of Aeneas narrating the desecration of his home, the focus and attention he brought to that particular section of his earlier effort, highlights surely a sense of his homeland's own lost legacy, a common inheritance lost to all.[56] It is more than the work of a cavalier writer, as Denham himself was more than a cavalier, in either the standard sense or the 'Sucklington' profile explored here. Yet the cavalier traces he carried—as a demonised gamester, a prodigal son, and a baffled knight, as well as a bold gentleman and respectable royalist—will always help us see more clearly the figure he cut in his own time.

---

56 On *The Destruction of Troy* and for a fine gauging of the attitudes to translation the poem incorporates see Potter, *Secret Rites and Secret Writing*, pp. 52–53. More broadly, for a survey of the attitudes (and survival tactics) of the displaced of the period, see Philip Major, *Writings of exile in the English Revolution and Restoration* (Farnham: Ashgate, 2013), especially the chapter on 'Ceremony and Grief in the Royalist Exile' (pp. 67–100). Jason McElligott explores the issues effecting the publication and circulation contexts of royalist writing during the 'Interregnum' in *Royalism, Print and Censorship in Revolutionary England* (Woodbridge: Boydell Press, 2007). The themes of many of the more recent discussions of the Royalist perspective during the Protectorate years are best understood by referring back, for example, to Hardacre, *The Royalists during the Puritan Revolution*, pp. 17–105.

# 2 'The good Fellow is no where a stranger'

## Friendship and Faction in the Travels of Sir John Denham, 1646–60

*Geoffrey Smith*

## I

> Mirth makes them not mad,
> Nor Sobriety sad;
> But of that they are seldom in danger:
> At *Paris,* at *Rome,*
> At the *Hague* they're at home;
> The good Fellow is no where a stranger.[1]

Fellowship, the delights of good company, of wine, women, and song, are promi-nent traditional characteristics of the cavalier. And during the long years of exile and defeat, of frequently crushed hopes and endless grinding poverty, Sir John Denham consistently showed himself as a 'good Fellow', welcome in a surpris-ingly wide range of the different groups and factions that comprised the 'king's party'. Whether we consider those who were attracted to the different Stuart households and courts in exile, of King Charles II, Queen Henrietta Maria, or James Duke of York, or the clients and followers of great nobles like the Duke of Buckingham and the Marquess of Ormond, or the companions of prominent cour-tiers like Sir John Berkeley and John Ashburnham, we will find Denham among them. He shared his exile with poets and scholars like Sir Richard Fanshawe, Abraham Cowley, and Edmund Waller, but seems to have been more at home with the hard drinkers and gamblers who frequented the Stuart courts, like Tom Killigrew, Sir John Mennes, and William Crofts. Denham's employment by the Stuarts as a courier and the periods he spent in England during the late 1640s and 1650s also led to his involvement in royalist conspiracy, drawing him into the murky and dangerous world of the Sealed Knot and the Great Trust, and into the company of plotters and spies like Daniel O'Neill and Alan Brodrick. Den-ham was 'at home' among all these varied, scattered, frequently quarrelsome,

---

1 'On Mr. *Tho. Killigrew's* Return From His Embassie From Venice, And Mr. *William Murray's* From Scotland', Banks, *PW*, pp. 111–12.

and mutually hostile groups and factions. He was certainly 'no where a stranger' among them, but how significant was his presence in them?

The range of Denham's travels between his first journey into exile in 1646 and the Restoration in 1660 to a great extent shaped his relationship with other groups of royalists. His first experience of exile began probably in June 1646 when, having been captured at the surrender of Dartmouth in January, he was brought to London to appear before the House of Lords, who after examination in May ordered his release, only to discover that Denham had then been re-arrested at the instigation of his creditors. Denham's release had once more to be ordered by the Lords, freeing him to escape his creditors by a flight to France.[2] A letter of intelligence on 28 June to Sir Edward Hyde, recently arrived on Jersey in the following of the Prince of Wales, reported Denham's presence in Caen, along with other prominent royalists, including Sir John Berkeley and John Ashburnham.[3]

In Caen, Denham was confronted with two options, to join either Prince Charles and his small following on Jersey or the party of royalists sent from Queen Henrietta Maria to persuade Charles to come to his mother in Paris. Denham decided to go to Paris. There he was drawn into a group of the queen's favoured advisors, among whom Lord Jermyn, Ashburnham, Berkeley, and the experienced Scottish intriguer Will Murray were prominent.[4] Representing the interests of the queen, they had been attempting to establish lines of communication with Charles I and to influence the shape of the settlement which the king was negotiating with the representatives of the army, who in August 1647 had installed him in Hampton Court.

A month earlier Denham had returned to England. According to his dedication in 1668 to Charles II of his *Poems and Translations*, 'After the delivery of your Royal Father's Person into the hands of the Army, I undertaking to the Queen that I would find some means to get access to him she was pleased to send me'.[5] In fact, access to Charles I was not all that difficult, even for notorious Malignants. Sir Richard Fanshawe, whose verses Denham praised when he saw the king, and his wife Ann visited Charles at Hampton Court several times in September and October.[6] Another visitor at Hampton Court was Ann Fanshawe's friend and companion in Oxford during the civil war, the beautiful Lady Isabella Thynne, a committed royalist with a taste for intrigue. Isabella, a daughter of the Earl of Holland, was married to the wealthy Wiltshire landowner Sir James Thynne,

2  *Journals of the House of Lords*, viii, pp. 313–14.
3  *CCISP*, i, p. 324; O Hehir, *HD*, pp. 68–72.
4  For employment of Ashburnham and Murray as negotiators and couriers between Charles I and the Queen, see John Bruce (ed.), *Charles I in 1646: Letters of King Charles the First to Queen Henrietta Maria* (London: Printed for the Camden Society, 1856), no. 63, pp. 6, 12–13, 25, 39, 51, 60, 63–67, 75.
5  'To the King', Banks, *PW*, p. 59.
6  John Loftis (ed.), *The Memoirs of Anne, Lady Halkett and Ann, Lady Fanshawe* (Oxford: Clarendon Press, 1979), pp. 96, 120. For Denham's admiration of Fanshawe, see 'To Sir Richard Fanshaw Upon His Translation of Pastor Fido', Banks, *PW*, p. 143.

gentleman of the privy chamber to Charles I and a member of the royalist parliament that sat in Oxford during the civil war.[7] It may have been during these war years in Oxford that Denham established his friendship with Isabella, a friendship renewed at Hampton Court and then later in exile. For the Thynnes were not exactly a devoted couple, and while Sir James retired to his Wiltshire estates after the surrender of Oxford, Lady Isabella contrived both a brief affair with Ormond and some dabbling in royalist plots, until in May 1649 it was reported that 'my Lady Isabella Thynne and Mrs Howard are escaped [...] from the rebels' and had fled to France where she joined the queen in Paris.[8]

Along with loyal visitors to the king like the Fanshawes and Isabella Thynne, there were a number of agents sent by the queen, of whom Denham was merely one. On 8 August a letter of intelligence to Hyde informed him that 'Jack Berkeley and Jack Denham' were in town, 'persons of good understanding employed betwixt the king and the army', while 'Jack Ashburnham was not far off'.[9] Denham was also accompanied by Colonel Sir Edward Ford, while Ashburnham on his journey from Paris encountered in Calais a fellow groom of the bedchamber, another experienced cavalier soldier and friend of Prince Rupert, Colonel William Legge, who joined him.[10]

Denham was thus one of a group of prominent royalists who in Berkeley's words were attempting 'to promote an Agreement between his Majestie and them [the army grandees], although precedence among these negotiators and advisors was accorded by the queen and Prince Charles to Berkeley and Ashburnham, as they 'might be supposed to have greater trust, both with the Queen in France, and with the King in England than either Sir Edward Ford or Mr. Denham had'.[11] Berkeley refers to a meeting at Woburn in late July, shortly before Charles reached Hampton Court, where the king sent for a group of about a dozen men 'of great Abilities and Integrity' to advise him.[12] With the exceptions of Ashburnham, Ford, and Berkeley, this was an assemblage of lawyers and divines, among whom Denham, with his legal background, would not have felt out of place.

7  Ibid., p. 115; Hilton Kelliher, 'John Denham: New Letters and Documents', *British Library Journal* (Spring 1986), 1–20 (p. 14); Thomas Carte, *The Life of James Duke of Ormond*, 6 vols (Oxford, 1851), iv, pp. 701–02; B.D. Henning (ed.), *The History of Parliament: House of Commons 1660–1690* (London, 1983), online edition; Antonia Fraser, *The Weaker Vessel: Woman's Lot in Seventeenth-Century England* (London: Phoenix Press, 1984), pp. 292–93.
8  *A Collection of Original Letters and Papers, Concerning the Affairs of England ... 1641–1660, Found among the Duke of Ormond's Papers*, ed. Thomas Carte, 2 vols (London, 1739), i, p. 286.
9  *CCISP*, i, p. 387.
10  John Berkeley, *Memoirs of Sir John Berkley, containing an Account of his Negotiations with Lieutenant General Cromwell, Commissary General Ireton and Other Officers of the Army* (London, 1699), pp. 4–6, 14; *CCISP*, i, p. 387; O Hehir, *HD*, pp. 73–74. For Ford and Legge, see P.R. Newman, *Royalist Officers in England and Wales, 1642–1660* (New York: Garland Publishing, 1981), pp. 140, 227–28.
11  Berkeley, *Memoirs*, pp. 4–5.
12  Ibid., p. 37.

The flight of Charles I from Hampton Court in November placed Denham in a difficult position. The details of the mismanaged decision to escape from Hampton Court, to head for the south coast and to escape by ship across the Channel to France, were largely confined to Ashburnham, Berkeley, and Legge. Did Denham have any knowledge of it? A letter to the Commons on 11 November 1647 claimed that 'some gentlemen passed this night over Kingston bridge, supposed to be his Majesty, with Sir Edward Ford, Sir John Bartlett [Berkeley?], Mr. Ashburnham and Mr. Denham'. This letter indicates that Denham was involved in the escape plan but the account is contradicted by Berkeley's, which names only himself, the king, Asburnham, Legge, and a servant in the group who fled from Hampton Court at night.[13] Berkeley in his *Memoirs* also asserted that Denham and Isabella Thynne had guaranteed the reliability and essential trustworthiness of Colonel Hammond, Parliament's governor of the Isle of Wight, while Denham, in his dedication of his poems 'To the King', claimed that at Charles's 'departure from Hampton Court, he was pleased to command me to stay privately at London, to send to him and receive from him all his Letters from and to all his correspondents at home and abroad, and I was furnished with nine several Cyphers in order to it'.[14] All this suggests that Denham was certainly aware that the king's flight from Hampton Court was imminent.

'This was a very sad time for all of us of the king's party', recalled Ann Fanshawe, 'for by their folly (to give it no worse name) Sir John B[erke]ley, since Lord B[erke]ley, and Mr. John Ashburnham of the King's bedchamber, who were drawn in by the cursed standing crew of the then standing army for the Parliament, perswade[d] the King to leave Hampton Court'.[15] The disastrous consequences of the mismanaged flight to the coast to a non-existent ship to take the king to France brought criticisms of incompetence or worse on those who had managed it and Denham did not escape censure for his perceived role in the affair. 'I dare not trust Denham, being Mr. Ashburnham's creature', wrote an anonymous London intelligencer on 8 February to the Earl of Lanark, the Duke of Hamilton's younger brother, who was being kept informed of the various schemes to enable the king to escape from Carisbrooke Castle.[16]

For approximately another nine months Denham remained in England, for the most part in London, where the complicated process of his attempts to compound for his diminished and scattered estates was slowly progressing.[17] His contribution to the royalist cause was now essentially that of courier and intelligencer, and he seems to have had little involvement in the various schemes to rescue the king from his increasingly rigorous confinement, although in January 1648 he briefly joined the king's principal servants who had been expelled to the mainland by

13  Ibid., pp. 46–50; Letter cited in Banks, *PW*, p. 13.

14  Berkeley, *Memoirs*, p. 56; 'To the King', Banks, *PW*, pp. 59–60.

15  *Halkett and Fanshawe Memoirs*, p. 120.

16  S.R. Gardiner (ed.), *The Hamilton Papers*, second series, 27 (London: Printed for the Camden Society, 1880), pp. 147–49, cited in O Hehir, *HD*, p. 78.

17  Ibid., pp. 76–82.

Colonel Hammond. Berkeley recounted a meeting with Ashburnham, Legge, and 'Mr. Denham (who was then come to us from London)', which decided to send Berkeley to the queen to explain and presumably justify their failure to rescue her husband.[18] It was as an intelligencer in London that Denham was now most seriously involved in the royalist underground. This involvement is demonstrated by his connection with the resourceful and daring Major Humphrey Boswell, an experienced agent considered by the authorities to be 'a very dangerous person', and who was to achieve the distinction of being placed on the agenda of a meeting of Lord Protector Cromwell's Council of State.[19] Boswell was sent into England by Prince Charles in June with instructions 'to repair immediately to Mr Denham and to acquaint him with his employment', which was to contact certain prominent royalists and Presbyterians, 'and proceed in all things by his advice'.[20] That an experienced agent like Boswell was expected to defer to Denham's advice shows the extent to which Denham was still highly regarded in royal circles.

The one notable triumph of royalist agents during the dreary months that Charles I was penned up in Carisbrooke and Denham remained in London was the escape of the king's second son James, Duke of York, from St. James's Palace in April 1648. John Aubrey, in his *Brief Lives*, claimed that Denham 'conveyed, or stole away the two Dukes of Yorke and Glocester from St James's (the Tuition of the Earle of Northumberland) and conveyed them into France to the Prince of Wales and Queen-mother'.[21] Although Anthony Wood essentially asserted the same claim that Denham contrived the duke's escape from St. James, there is unfortunately no truth in it.[22] The escape was organised and successfully accomplished by another royalist agent, a highly dubious figure, Colonel Joseph Bampfield, assisted by his companion and possibly mistress, the adventurous Anne Murray.[23] Being in London at the time, Denham may possibly have heard in royalist underground circles that something was being planned, but essentially he had nothing to do with it.

During his months in London, Denham continued to receive and pass on royalist correspondence between England, Ireland, and the queen's court in Paris. In the complex and sensitive diplomatic negotiations to bring together various Irish magnates in a royalist alliance that recognised the leadership of the Marquess of Ormond, it was claimed that Lord Inchiquin 'would trust nobody in the affair

18 Berkeley, *Memoirs*, p. 93.
19 For Humphrey Boswell, see Geoffrey Smith, *Royalist Agents, Conspirators and Spies: Their Role in the British Civil Wars* (Farnham: Ashgate, 2011), pp. 100–03, 117, 121, 157, 171, 192.
20 HMC, Pepys MSS (London, 1911), pp. 211, 279.
21 John Aubrey, *Aubrey's Brief Lives*, ed. Oliver Lawson Dick (London: Peregrine Books, 1962), p. 183.
22 Anthony Wood, *Athenae Oxoniensis*, 2 vols (London, 1721), ii, p. 423, cited in Banks, *PW*, p. 13.
23 Joseph Bampfield, *Colonel Joseph Bampfield's Apology: 'Written by Himself and Printed at His Desire' 1685*, ed. John Loftis and Paul Hardacre (London: Associated University Presses,1993), pp. 22, 26–27, 69–70; *Halkett* [Anne Murray] *and Fanshawe Memoirs*, pp. 23–26; Smith, *Royalist Agents*, pp. 105–06; John Miller, *James II: A Study in Kingship* (London: Wayland, 1978), pp. 4–5.

but the marquis of Ormonde and his friend Mr. Denham, who carried on the correspondence between them'.[24] It seems to have been during this period that he first developed his lasting friendship with Ormond, who was about to return to Ireland from exile to attempt the thankless task of reconciling the various, at least nominally royalist, factions, then to defeat the parliamentarian forces and win control of that distracted kingdom for the king. Writing to Ormond on 28 February 1648, Denham concluded with the promise that if he 'may bee in any way serviceable to your Lordship here, you cannot lay your Commands upon any man that is more ready to obey them than ... Your Lordships most humble and faithfull servant. MK' (Denham's code-initials).[25]Among Denham's other correspondents in exile was Abraham Cowley, secretary to Lord Jermyn, the queen's favourite. Intercepted letters from Cowley led to the end of Denham's career as an intelligencer in London. 'After being discovered by their knowledge of Mr. Cowleys hand, I happily escaped both for myself, and those that had correspondence with me'.[26] In August Denham made a hasty return to the continent.

Once again a fugitive in exile, Denham journeyed not to Queen Henrietta Maria at St. Germain but to Prince Charles at The Hague. At first sight he can have had little positive to report to justify his year in England. Indeed, O Hehir concluded that 'as a counsellor to the King, Denham apparently must take some blame for the disastrous flight that ended in "Carisbrook's narrow" case, particularly for his faulty estimate of Governor Hammond's character'.[27] So it seems likely that by returning to The Hague and not to Paris Denham wanted to distance himself in all senses from his connections with Ashburnham and Berkeley, in particular with what Hyde in his *History of the Rebellion* was to condemn as a 'weakly contrived' design which had the 'non-excusable' result of 'putting the King into Hammond's hands without his leave'.[28] But Denham's apparent ties with the 'Louvrian' faction around the queen were not to be forgotten.

There were lasting results of Denham's year in England, in particular his involvement in the underground workings of the royalist party and the links he established with prominent royalist activists, notably with Ormond and some of his entourage, if Isabella Thynne can be included in that category. Indeed, he seems to have developed a taste for this world of sudden journeys, of ciphers and secret meetings, although whether he could move in it as easily and effectively as agents like the ex-officers Bampfield and Boswell remained to be seen. So, despite his involvement in the flight from Hampton Court disaster, he clearly continued to be highly regarded by his Stuart employers, if not by all their senior advisors, notably Sir Edward Hyde.

24  Kelliher, 'Denham: Letters and Documents', p. 5.
25  Ibid., p. 5.
26  'To the King', Banks, *PW*, p. 60.
27  O Hehir, *HD*, p. 80.
28  Edward, Earl of Clarendon, *The History of the Rebellion and Civil Wars in England*, ed. W.D. Macray, 6 vols (Oxford: Clarendon Press, 1888), iv, pp. 264–67.

## II

Denham was to remain in uninterrupted exile from August 1648 until March 1653. During this period he was employed by both the queen and Charles as a courier and diplomat, employments that involved considerable travelling. Between missions he seems to have preferred the court of King Charles II, as he was recognised by royalists on the execution of his father, and the company of the various 'good fellows' attracted to that impoverished, raffish but lively Stuart household. His year in England as an emissary of the queen meant that he had principally been in the circle dominated by Ashburnham and Berkeley, apart from his time in London, when he had established links with prominent royalist leaders like Ormond and cloak-and-dagger agents like Humphrey Boswell. The circles in which Denham moved on his return into exile were now widened.

The continued high regard for Denham by the Prince of Wales's advisors is shown by their willingness to dispatch him on another mission within a few weeks of his arrival at The Hague. On 11 September Robert Long, Secretary to the Council, drew up 'Instructions for Mr. Denham' and two days later Denham received letters to the Scots Committee of Estates, by this time dominated by Covenanters, and to the Earl of Lanark. Denham was to encourage Lanark 'to continue his endeavours notwithstanding the late misfortune of the Scotch army in England'.[29] In fact, it is practically certain that Denham never went to Scotland for there seems to be no record of any appearance in Edinburgh. The consequences of the total defeat of Hamilton's army by Cromwell at Preston in August were not yet fully appreciated at The Hague. Hamilton was a prisoner, his 'Engager' regime had collapsed and the Covenanters led by the Marquess of Argyll had seized power in Edinburgh. Hamilton's brother Lanark was himself in the process of a hasty flight into exile, as were the king's two principal agents in Edinburgh at this time, Sir William Fleming and Denham's friend Will Murray.[30] For the six months following the battle of Preston royalist traffic between Scotland and the continent was one way.

For the exiled royalists the winter of 1648–49 was a time of grief at the news from England of the execution not only of Charles I but also of Hamilton and of several of the leaders of the different risings that had constituted the second civil war in England. Against a background of bitterness and increasing poverty, intrigues swirled through the households of the queen mother, of Charles, and of his brother James, Duke of York, as counsellors like Jermyn, Berkeley, Hyde, Henry Percy, Sir George Radcliffe, and more peripheral figures like Will Murray and even Joseph Bampfield sought to establish their influence over one or other of the Stuarts.[31] Denham was not a significant figure in these sterile intrigues, being

---

29  HMC, *Pepys MSS*, 70, pp. 226–27; *CCISP*, i, p. 459; O Hehir, *HD*, pp. 83–84.
30  Kelliher, 'Denham: Letters and Documents', p. 7; Smith, *Royalist Agents*, pp. 106–07.
31  Clarendon, *History*, iv, pp. 407, 141; v, pp. 162–65; Ronald Hutton, *Charles the Second, King of England, Scotland and Ireland* (Oxford: Clarendon Press, 1989), pp. 24, 40–42; Miller, *James II*, pp. 12–13.

still employed essentially as a courier in journeys between Paris and The Hague. In May 1649 he received 'Instructions for Mr. Denham' from the queen, written out by Abraham Cowley, whom Denham may have met during his time in Paris. The document conveyed the queen's support for Charles's plan to go to Ireland, while at the same time pointing out that her own 'pressing wants' necessitated the withdrawal of any previous offers of financial support for the expedition. The instructions directed that Charles immediately send Denham back to Paris with replies to the queen's various requests. In fact, in June Charles himself left The Hague, to the undisguised relief of his Dutch hosts, and returned to Paris, with Denham sent ahead to give advance notice of his coming.[32]

In September Charles escaped from the poverty and factional quarrels of the different Stuart households in Paris and moved to Jersey as a step towards his intended expedition to Ireland. Before he left Paris he appointed William Crofts and Denham as envoys to Poland to raise money from the Scottish merchants in that country, who were hopefully believed to be well affected to the king. Denham's companion William Crofts was a controversial figure who enjoyed the friendship and patronage of both Charles II and Henrietta Maria, although he was intensely disliked by some other royalists. Ronald Hutton's description of him as a 'wild young courtier' associated with the 'Louvre' faction is milder than that of some of his contemporaries. To James Hamilton in the *Memoirs of Count Grammont* he was 'that mad fellow Crofts', an 'insipid buffoon'. Hyde referred to him at different times as vain, vicious, and insolent, undeservedly a favourite of both Henrietta Maria and Charles II by whom he was 'too much favoured' at court. For Crofts had enjoyed various court appointments in Oxford during the civil war, but does not seem to have seen much in the way of active service, before going into exile and joining the queen in Paris, where he was captain of her guards.[33]

Clarendon's account of the money-raising embassies in 1650 relates only that Charles sent 'the lord Culpeper into Mosco [*sic*], to borrow money from that duke; and into Poland he sent Mr. Crofts upon the same errand'. Significantly, it makes no mention of Denham.[34] Perhaps surprisingly, the mission was extremely successful. The Polish Diet responded sympathetically to Crofts's eloquent appeal, the initial reluctance of the Scottish merchants to contribute was overruled, and according to Crofts's accounts 66,959 florins were obtained in Poland, 24,693 from Danzig, 2,000 from Konigsberg, and 10,292 from Lithuania and Prussia.

---

32  *The Nicholas Papers: Correspondence of Sir Edward Nicholas, Secretary of State*, ed. G.F. Warner, 4 vols (London: Printed for the Camden Society, 1886–1920), i, pp. 128–29.

33  Stephen Porter, 'Crofts, William, Baron Crofts', *ODNB*; Sir Walter Scott, *Memoirs of the Court of Charles the Second by Count Grammont* (London: Henry G. Bohn, 1853), p. 308; *State Papers Collected by Edward, Earl of Clarendon*, ed. R. Scrope and T. Monkhouse, 3 vols. (Oxford, 1767–86), iii, p. 59; Richard Ollard (ed.), *Clarendon's Four Portraits: George Digby, John Berkeley, Henry Jermyn, Henry Bennett, from the Supplement to the Clarendon State Papers Vol. III (1786)* (London: Hamish Hamilton, 1989), pp. 53, 137; Hutton, *Charles the Second*, p. 73. Hester Chapman, *The Tragedy of Charles II* (London: Jonathan Cape, 1964), p. 237.

34  Clarendon, *History*, v, p. 233.

Denham recorded his role in the embassy in his verses 'On My Lord Croft's and my Journey into Poland from whence we brought 10000L for His Majesty'.[35]

According to Clarendon, the envoys returned from the Baltic with the money 'about the time that the King made his escape from Worcester'.[36] Having been on the run for six weeks after the disastrous battle of Worcester, Charles finally reached Paris at the end of October. Although Crofts joined the court that was gradually reconstituted around the king, Denham for much of the time seems to have remained at The Hague.[37] His absence from Paris illustrates his lack of influence in the disposal of the money collected, a process which was very much controlled by the queen's 'Louvrian' followers, notably Jermyn. Clearly Denham was regarded as a junior partner in the embassy, a fact confirmed by the grant, to the intense annoyance of Hyde, of a respected place in the royal household to Crofts in April. 'Oh! Mr. Secretary', Hyde bewailed to Sir Edward Nicholas, 'this last act of the King's, in making Mr. Crofts a gentleman of the bedchamber, so contrary to what he assured me, makes me mad and weary of my life'.[38] No court appointment came Denham's way.

## III

Denham remained in exile until the early spring of 1653, a period of frustration, idleness, and general demoralisation for the Stuart cause. The surviving strong-points of royalist resistance in England, Scotland, and Ireland were one by one subdued, and the various islands and colonies that had remained loyal to the king were progressively forced to recognise the authority of the Commonwealth. All possible measures to reverse the result of the civil war had apparently been tried and all had failed. During these months Denham seems to have spent some time in Paris and some at The Hague, but as no serious projects required his services as a courier his movements are difficult to trace. According to O Hehir it was during this depressing phase in royalist fortunes that Denham 'returned to his old vices and may also have indulged in vices that perhaps were new', although he really only mentions two, gambling and the 'besetting vice of Charles's court; venery'.[39]

Denham's principal companions during this period can be identified from several literary sources but especially from certain of his occasional verses. The principal friends and acquaintances who joined with him in these more or less dubious activities were the experienced royalist naval commander Sir John Mennes, the courtier and agent John Poley (spelled Pooley by Denham), the

---

35  Figures cited in Helliher, 'Denham: Letters and Documents', pp. 13–14; Banks, *PW*, pp. 107–10. See also Clarendon, *History*, v, p. 233; O Hehir, *HD*, pp. 88–90, notes, 16, 17.
36  Clarendon, *History*, v, p. 133.
37  Geoffrey Smith, *The Cavaliers in Exile, 1640–1660* (Basingstoke: Palgrave Macmillan, 2003), pp. 68–69.
38  *State Papers Collected by Edward, Earl of Clarendon*, iii, pp. 58–59.
39  O Hehir, *HD*, pp. 90–91.

courtier, playwright, and expelled ambassador to Venice, Tom Killigrew, who was also Crofts's brother-in-law, and the Scot William Murray, Earl of Dysart, who acquired a shady reputation for intrigue and double-dealing. To this group of companions should be added a very different character, the woman whose friendship with Denham comes through very strongly in their correspondence, Lady Isabella Thynne.

Denham's letters from The Hague on 27 December 1651 and 8 February 1652 to Thynne in Paris reveal something of his attitudes and feelings during this phase of his time in exile. The letters repeatedly stress Denham's admiration for and friendship with both Lord and Lady Ormond, being 'so particularly a servant of them both', and his dependence on Thynne to present his good offices to them, to do with them 'the Office of a friend'. In contrast, references to Crofts, who 'pretends to bee so much their [the Ormonds's] servant', are disparaging, assuming that he will submit a generous estimate of his expenses incurred on the Polish mission, from which Denham himself had derived no financial benefit.[40]

Despite the tone of his verses on the Polish mission, Denham's friendship with Crofts was superficial and essentially insincere, while his affection for the Ormonds and for Isabella Thynne was clearly genuine. His other friendships operated on a different level. One source for identifying Denham's friends is the reference in Thomas Killigrew's play *Thomaso, or, the Wanderer*, to a gathering of exiles for a convivial pig roast at the St. John's Head in Rotterdam 'where we met Embassador *Will*, and Resident *Tom*, with M. Sheriffs Secretary, *John* the Poet, with the Nose, all *Gondiberts* dire Foes'. Marginal notes identify these persons as Will Crofts, Killigrew himself, Denham, who was possessed of a nose unlike William Davenant, the author of *Gondibert*, who had lost his as an effect of venereal disease.[41] The authors of *Certain Verses Written by Severall of the Authors Friends*, which ridiculed *Gondibert*, has been debated by scholars but there is general agreement that Denham certainly and Crofts probably were two of them.[42]

The doggerel verses that best illustrate the nature of Denham's friendships, pastimes, and activities are, first, 'On My Lord Croft's and my Journey into Poland', referred to above. The second is a crude verse in ballad form to Sir John Mennes on the dubious delights of riding with him and other companions, including '*Aubrey* count of *Oxon*', in other words Aubrey de Vere, 20th Earl of

---

40  Letters printed in Helliher, 'Denham: Letters and Documents', pp. 9–12, 14. Ormond had left Ireland to return to exile in France in December 1650. Despite her youthful liaison with the Marquess, Isabella Thynne seems to have been on good terms with the tolerant Lady Ormond.

41  *Thomaso, or, The Wanderer*, in Thomas Killigrew's *Comedies and Tragedies* (London, 1664), Part II, Act V, scene 7, p. 456; Timothy Raylor, *Cavaliers, Clubs and Literary Culture: Sir John Mennes, James Smith and the Order of the Fancy* (Newark: University of Delaware Press, 1994), p. 198; Alfred Harbage, *Thomas Killigrew: Cavalier Dramatist, 1612–83* (Philadelphia: University of Pennsylvania Press, 1930), pp. 99–100; O Hehir, *HD*, p. 94, n. 25.

42  *Aubrey's Brief Lives*, p. 184; Raylor, *Cavaliers, Clubs and Literary Culture*, p. 198; O Hehir, *HD*, pp. 93, 95–96.

Oxford, in a cart from 'Calice [Calais] to Boulogne to eat a Pig'.[43] The questionable delights included the company of a fat and flatulent Dutch woman and an uncomfortable journey in a cart with inadequate protection from the rain. This primitive conveyance illustrated the poverty of the passengers, encouraging Denham to make unpleasant comparisons with the cart that carried condemned felons to Tyburn.

> For Thief without grace,
> That goes to make a wry-mouth.[44]

The third verse that illuminates the activities of Denham's friends in exile is 'A Dialogue between Sir John Pooley and Mr. Thomas Killigrew', which reflects fairly crudely on the consequences of Poley's too indiscriminate sexual activities. Having 'been an old Fornicator' with a 'Female of Malignant Quality', Poley was now 'shot twixt wind and water' with venereal disease, a condition for which Killigrew suggests various remedies.[45] By contrast the fourth poem, 'On Mr. Tho. Killigrew's return from his Embassie from Venice, and Mr. William Murray's from Scotland', is somewhat superior to the doggerel level of the others, and celebrates more positive qualities of the exiled cavaliers, in particular their cheerfulness in adversity and their refusal to be defeated by morbid thoughts:

> Of Banishment, Debts or dying?
> Not old with their years,
> Not cold with their fears,
> But their angry Stars still defying.

This poem celebrates the capacity of the exiles, whether in Paris, Rome, Venice, or The Hague, despite the hardships of their condition, to enjoy the pleasures of good fellowship to the accompaniment of plenty of wine, for of 'Sobriety' they 'are seldom in danger'.[46]

A superficial reading of these verses tends to support the puritan caricature of the exiled cavaliers as a bunch of impoverished, licentious, foul-mouthed, pox-ridden drunks; a closer examination of the subjects of Denham's poems reveals a more complex picture. Mennes, Poley, Killigrew, and Murray were all significant figures, both as royalist activists and as men of culture and education. Mennes had extensive naval experience from before the civil war, before serving under Prince

---

43 Aubrey de Vere, Earl of Oxford, lacked an estate adequate to sustain his ancient title. In consequence, he spent much of his time in the Dutch service in the Netherlands, where he presumably met Denham. Oxford returned to England in the early 1650s and became involved in royalist conspiracy, where he encountered Denham again. See Victor Stater, 'Vere, Aubrey de, twentieth earl of Oxford (1627–1703)', *ODNB*.

44 Denham's verses composed in exile are all printed in Banks, *PW*, pp. 100–12.

45 Ibid., pp. 103–06. Poley's knighthood did not come until the Restoration.

46 Ibid., pp. 111–12.

Rupert, first as a soldier in England and then at sea in the Mediterranean in 1650. In London before the civil war he had been a member of the social and literary club, the Order of the Fancy, a club to which Denham also possibly belonged.[47] Mennes was a practitioner of the burlesque ballad, a popular genre among the exiled courtiers, and Samuel Pepys, his colleague in the Navy Office after the Restoration, although increasingly critical of his incompetence in financial matters, found him 'a fine gentleman and a very good scholler', and in general 'most excellent company'.[48] Pepys also acknowledged Mennes's friendship with Denham, and recorded Mennes's claim, although he had no medical training, of having great success with his cures during his years in exile, especially of the pox. 'And among others, Sir J. Denham he told me he had cured after it was come to an ulcer all over his face to a miracle'.[49]

Despite his shared experience with Denham of a bout of venereal disease, John Poley was not merely a pox-ridden rake. A member of a prominent Suffolk family, he was a Cambridge fellow, whose proficiency in Latin and Greek is acknowledged by Denham in his poem, while pointing out its current uselessness. Although a courtier, Poley's main employment, for which his scholarly background would have been useful, was as an envoy on a series of missions to different European countries that began in the late 1620s and continued until May 1650, when he made the dangerous journey, evading the Commonwealth's naval patrols, to carry letters from Charles II in Scotland to Paris.[50] The careers of William Murray, Earl of Dysart, and of Thomas Killigrew have some similarities with Poley's. 'Resident *Tom*' Killigrew's period as ambassador to Venice in 1650–51 was short-lived and ended in disgrace when the Venetian government expelled him.[51] Murray's diplomatic career was much longer and at times extremely complex, even controversial. For at least ten years he was employed on missions on behalf of Charles I, Henrietta Maria, and Charles II, partly to English parliamentarians but principally to Scottish politicians of different stamps, from royalists like Montrose to hardline Covenanters like Argyll and more moderate Presbyterian 'Engagers' like Hamilton. This was a career marked by devious intrigues and shifting positions

---

47  For Mennes see Raylor, *Cavaliers, Clubs and Literary Culture*, passim; for Denham's possible membership of the Order see ibid., p. 94.

48  Samuel Pepys, *The Diary of Samuel Pepys*, ed. Robert Latham and William Matthews, 11 vols (Berkeley: University of California Press, 1970–83), ii, p. 210; iii, p. 112. See also Pepys's epitaph for Mennes: 'a very good, harmless, honest gentleman, though not fit for the business'; ibid., vii, p. 255.

49  Ibid., iv, pp. 436–37; v, p. 242.

50  John P. Ferris and Simon Healy, 'Poley, John (1603–1664), of Boxted, Suff. and Pembroke Coll. Cambridge', *The History of Parliament: The House of Commons, 1604–1629*, ed. Andrew Thrush and John P. Ferris (Cambridge, 2010), online edition; Smith, *Royalist Agents*, pp. 61–62, 74, 79, 96, 149, 155; *Nicholas Papers*, i, pp. 254–55.

51  For Killigrew's Venetian embassy, see Philip Major, 'Introduction', in Philip Major (ed.), *Thomas Killigrew and the Seventeenth-Century English Stage* (Farnham: Ashgate, 2013), pp. 1–20 (pp. 3–6).

that led ultimately to his dismissal from royal service.[52] There are both common elements and significant disparities in the attitudes and interests of Denham's friends Crofts, his brother-in-law Killigrew, Mennes, Poley, and Murray during their years in exile. First, they were all courtiers and, with the exception of Denham and Mennes, in the 1640s and 1650s had places in the households of Charles I or Charles II, or both: Crofts as a gentleman of the bedchamber, Killigrew and Murray as grooms of the bedchamber, Poley as a gentleman usher of the privy chamber.[53] They all possessed the cavaliers' traditional fondness for wine, women, and song but, with the possible exception of Crofts, were also cultured men of letters: Denham and Mennes the poets, Killigrew the dramatist, Poley the scholar, and Murray, in the 'halcyon days' before the civil war, a prominent member of the circle of artists and patrons at the court of Charles I.[54] Their personal courage and loyalty to the Stuart cause was demonstrated by their different war services and their willingness both to accept the hardships of exile and to undertake often arduous and dangerous missions as envoys and couriers.

Where Denham's friends in some cases diverged from each other was in their factional allegiances. Crofts was a 'Louvrian', captain of Henrietta Maria's guards, but also, to the despair and disapproval of Hyde, a personal friend of the king. Will Murray served for some years as a kind of unofficial envoy for Charles I, who granted him the earldom of Dysart, then acted as an emissary between the king and Henrietta Maria when the queen went into exile in Paris and was finally employed on missions to Scotland. But his Louvrian associations, his ill-fated advice for an alliance with the Covenanter regime dominated by Argyll and his friendship with the treacherous double-agent Joseph Bampfield led to his repudiation by Charles II and his advisors, who, as Ormond expressed it, now dismissed Murray as 'a creature of 'Argyll's'.[55] Although not a Louvrian like Crofts and Murray, Killigrew also was no friend of the chancellor, who made no secret for his disdain for the 'men of pleasure' who surrounded the king. In his *Life* Clarendon describes how Killigrew was 'compelled to leave the Republick, for his vicious behaviour, of which the Venetian Ambassador complained to the King', although he should have known there were also more pragmatic reasons for Killigrew's expulsion by the hard-headed government of La Serenissima.[56] By contrast, Mennes was devotedly loyal to the chancellor, who much admired his 'clear

52 Cited in Smith, *Royalist Agents*, p. 165. For Murray's career see also R. Malcolm Smuts, 'Murray, William, first earl of Dysart (d. 1655)', *ODNB*; Bruce, *Charles I in 1646*, pp. 6, 12–13, 63–67, 75; David Laing (ed.), *The Letters and Journals of Robert Baillie*, 3 vols (Edinburgh: Robert Ogle, 1841–42), i, p. 393; ii, pp. 48, 277, 394–96, 401; Smith, *Royalist Agents*, pp. 32–33, 75, 93–94, 107, 165, 144, 156, 198.

53 Denham received his long-promised appointment as surveyor of the works and Mennes as a gentleman of the privy chamber and comptroller of the navy at the Restoration.

54 For Murray's artistic and architectural interests, see entry in *ODNB* and *Ham House* (London: National Trust, 2005).

55 *CCISP*, ii, pp. 142, 157, 188, 205, 286, 301; *ODNB*.

56 Hyde, Edward, *The Life of Edward Earl of Clarendon*, 3 vols (Oxford, 1749), i, p. 229; Major, *Killigrew*, pp. 3–6.

and unalterable affection [to the Crown] which appeared on all occasions' and regarded him highly. This friendship lasted. On 24 June 1663 Pepys recorded a conversation with William Coventry who referred to 'Sir J. Mennes, who is great with the Chancellor'.[57] By striking contrast Poley seems to have belonged to no faction and not to have aroused the intense feelings that swirled around Crofts, Murray, and Killigrew.

Although Denham obviously had other friends and acquaintances during his years in exile, for example the members of the Ormond circle and the Earl of Oxford, Mennes, Poley, Killigrew, Murray, and perhaps Crofts seem to have been most important to him. For the most part they were attached to the wandering court of Charles II and not to the Louvre, although Crofts moved between both and Murray had Louvrian associations. By contrast, Denham had little contact with his former companions of the Hampton Court days, for Ashburnham remained in England after the Isle of Wight disaster while Berkeley avoided the king's court and instead established himself firmly in the households both of the queen and of the Duke of York.[58] His fellow poets also saw little of Denham. Fanshawe was largely employed in diplomatic missions to Ireland, Spain, and then to Scotland, from where he accompanied Charles II on his invasion in 1651, was captured after Worcester, and remained in England for the next seven years.[59] Davenant, whose *Gondibert* had been travestied by Denham and others in the *Certain Verses*, set sail for America in 1650 but his ship was intercepted and he got no further than the Tower of London.[60] Waller's sentence of banishment was revoked in November 1651 and he promptly returned to England to devote his literary talents to praising the legitimacy of the Cromwellian regime.[61] With Cowley, who was based in Paris until he too returned to England, and whose poetry Denham much admired, there were occasional civil mentions in correspondence but no significant contact.[62]

Despite his early attachment to the queen's service, Denham by 1649 was essentially a follower of the king. But he cannot be slotted into any one faction and in any case royalist factions, whether the queen's 'Louvrians', Prince Rupert's 'Swordsmen', or the traditional Anglican 'Old Royalists' led by Hyde and Ormond, were fluid and ill-defined.[63] Denham's friendships, for example,

57  Clarendon, *Rebellion*, ii, p. 218, n.1; Pepys, *Diary*, iv, p. 196; Raylor, *Cavaliers, Clubs and Literary Culture*, pp. 199–201, 208.

58  Hutton, *Charles the Second*, pp. 41, 120, 122; Miller, *James II*, pp. 16–22.

59  *Halkett and Fanshawe Memoirs*, pp. 122–30, 133–37.

60  *Aubrey's Brief Lives*, pp. 178–79; John Stubbs, *Reprobates: The Cavaliers of the English Civil Wars* (London: Penguin, 2012), pp. 396–400, 426–27.

61  Warren Chernaik 'Waller, Edmund (1606–1687)', *ODNB*.

62  See, for example, Cowley's postscript to a letter of 3 September 1650 from Jermyn to Lord Culpepper, who had encountered Crofts and Denham in Danzig. Cited in Kelliher, 'Denham: Letters and Documents', p. 12.

63  David Underdown, *Royalist Conspiracy in England, 1649–1660* (New Haven: Yale University Press, 1960), pp. 10–13; Hutton, *Charles the Second*, pp. 72–74; Smith, *Cavaliers in Exile*, pp. 115–32.

cut across factional divisions. Although he had close and lasting friendships with the 'Old Royalists' Ormond and Mennes, he was always 'coldly regarded' by the chancellor himself. It is remarkable that in Clarendon's *History of the Rebellion*, Denham is never mentioned, even when events in which he participated are described, such as the capture of Farnham Castle, of which he was governor, and which 'was taken with less resistance than was fit', the negotiations with Charles I and the king's flight from Hampton Court, the money-raising mission to Poland, or the course of royalist conspiracy in the 1650s.[64] Certainly, Hyde would have disapproved strongly of Denham's friendship with Will Murray. In Denham's poem on the return of Killigrew and Murray from their respective embassies in 1651, his friendly references to Murray ('Though he chang'd face [by growing a beard] and name [to Earl of Dysart], / Old *Will* was the same',) are remarkable in the context of the failure of Murray's mission to Scotland, the widespread suspicion of his treachery and double-dealing, and his total loss of favour at the royal court.[65] As his friendship with the disgraced Murray illustrates, Denham maintained an impressive independence from the factions and allegiances in the Stuart courts.

For all his independence from the factions, Denham was not immune from the other disabilities of life in exile or of the consequences of his own weaknesses, especially his love of gambling. According to Aubrey, Denham was first attracted to gambling in his undergraduate days at Oxford, 'when he would Game extremely', and although 'he was much rooked by Gamesters', was unable to abandon the habit. It is ironic that Denham's anti-gambling tract, composed in 1638–39, presumably to appease his father, should have been first published as *The Anatomy of Play* in 1651, when gambling was once more coming to obsess him.[66] On 13 May 1652 Nicholas wrote from The Hague to Lord Hatton in Paris that 'Mr Denham hath lately had very ill luck at play, which hath made him (I am told) in great want at present. He talks of going for England, but it is thought intends not to adventure it, most for fear what his creditors than the rebels there will do against him'.[67] In fact, during the bleak years after Worcester, many exiles were talking of 'going for England'. Nicholas, in The Hague, had already commented on 'the abundance of royalists gone for England from these parts [...] as having little hopes left them'.[68] Among this 'abundance' of royalists who returned to England from exile during the two years or so after Worcester were the poets Waller and Cowley, a number of courtiers including Poley, and Isabella Thynne, while the disgraced Murray returned to Edinburgh.[69] The settlement of Denham's petition to compound in April 1650 made it possible for Denham to return also,

64  Clarendon, *History*, ii, p. 405; iv, pp. 262–67; v, p. 233, O Hehir, *HD*, p. 96.
65  Banks, *PW*, p. 112.
66  *Aubrey's Brief Lives*, p. 182; O Hehir, *HD*, pp. 8–11.
67  *Nicholas Papers*, i, p. 300.
68  Ibid., i, p. 276.
69  Entries in *ODNB* for Waller, Cowley, and Murray; in *History of Parliament* entry for Poley; in Kelliher, 'Denham: Letters and Documents', p. 16 for Thynne.

although the complicated processes of composition, sequestrations, and land sales continued into 1654.[70] By December 1652 Denham had dropped from the sight of his fellow exiles, who expressed ignorance of his whereabouts. He reappeared before a committee of the Council of State on 1 March 1653, appointed 'to examine Mr Denham, lately come from France, and to report his examination'.[71] The examination was favourable, the years of exile were over, and Denham was now a free man in England.

## IV

Denham's return to England coincided almost exactly with an intelligence-gathering mission by the Irish cavalier Daniel O'Neill, a resourceful follower and friend of Ormond, and an escape artist with a history of plotting dating back to his involvement in the army plots in 1641.[72] Unlike Denham, O'Neill soon returned into exile with a report for Hyde, 'A brief Relation of the Affairs of England as they stand at present', that drew a totally pessimistic picture of the absence of loyalist feeling, there being 'no talk of Presbyterian nor royalist at present'.[73] Seven months later Major Nicholas Armorer, another exiled ex-soldier from the king's armies, but with his career as a plotter still in front of him, arrived in London. In the cipher key issued to him by Nicholas on 8 October, Denham featured as 'Mr Dunton'.[74]

Armorer's secret mission to England, which lasted from October until the summer of 1654, saw a revival of royalist conspiracy, especially the creation of the Sealed Knot, with the responsibility to organise a widespread rising against the newly established Cromwellian Protectorate. From the time of Armorer's mission until the very eve of the Restoration a succession of royalist conspiracies repeatedly staggered, collapsed, and recovered under the weight of a series of bungled schemes, failed plots, mass arrests, and suppressed risings. The six ultra-cautious 'wary gentlemen' of the Sealed Knot saw their authority to direct conspiracy undermined by other more energetic, or at times reckless, groups of plotters, including a 'new council' or 'Action' party, and various other short-lived circles of 'small factors', as Armorer contemptuously dismissed them. The hare-brained schemes of the 'small factors' only intensified the government's persecution and

70  O Hehir, *HD*, pp. 96–98.
71  *CCISP*, ii, p. 160; *Calendar of State Papers, Domestic Series, 1640–1665*, ed. M.A.E. Green (London, 1875–86), 1652–53, p. 193.
72  For O'Neill see J.I. Casway, 'O'Neill, Daniel (c. 1612–1664), *ODNB*; Geoffrey Smith, 'Royalists in Exile: The Experience of Daniel O'Neill', in Jason McElligott and David L. Smith (eds), *Royalists and Royalism during the Interregnum* (Manchester: Manchester University Press, 2010), pp. 106–23.
73  'A Brief Relation of the Affairs of England', ed. C.H. Firth, *English Historical Review*, viii (1893), 529–32.
74  BL Egerton MS 2550, fols 14–15. For Armorer, see Geoffrey Smith, 'Armorer, Nicholas (c. 1620–1686)', *ODNB*.

surveillance of all royalists, including those who just wished to be left alone to live a quiet life.[75]

Denham's involvement in the complex history of royalist conspiracy was serious in intent but ultimately ineffectual in result. It is significant that during Armorer's almost twelve months in England, travelling widely from London, and sending back a series of reports to Nicholas and Hyde that list a number of royalists potentially prepared to join a rising against the government, he never mentions Denham.[76] Of course, it was during this period that Denham, 'being in some straights', enjoyed the hospitality of Philip Herbert, Earl of Pembroke at Wilton, where Aubrey first met him, and where in rural seclusion he could devote himself to poetry and translating some of the *Aeneid*.[77] Denham was certainly back in London in late 1654, when, thanks largely to the vigilance of Cromwell's energetic and efficient secretary of state John Thurloe, the government was well aware of the plans for a rising and was rounding up notorious Malignants. When Penruddock's rising finally broke out in March 1655, it was inevitably and swiftly suppressed, but the arrests of royalists continued into the summer.[78] Henry Manning, Thurloe's vindictive spy at the court of Charles II, kept his employer supplied with lists of royalists to be rounded up. 'I am glad to heare you lay about you', he congratulated Thurloe in a letter in May, that urged the secretary to 'remember Denham, the Lady Isabella', and other named royalists. In another letter a month later, he was still urging Thurloe to 'remember the Colonells Francis Lovelace, Edward Villars [Villiers, a member of the Sealed Knot] & one Mr. John Denham'.[79] In fact, on 8 June, Denham was arrested, one of a group of ten royalists rounded up 'in and around London'; but whereas the others, a mixture of country gentry and previously returned exiles, were committed by the Council of State either to the Tower or to the care of the serjeant-at-arms, it was ordered that 'John Denham be confined to a place chosen by himself not within 20 miles of London'.[80] Possible reasons for Denham's lenient treatment include the intervention on his behalf of influential friends, Pembroke, for example, and the government's awareness that he had not been seriously involved in the March rising.[81]

75  For royalist conspiracy, the most detailed and thorough study remains Underdown, *Royalist Conspiracy*. See also Smith, *Royalist Agents, Conspirators and Spies*; Stephen K. Roberts, 'Sealed Knot (act. 1653–1659)', *ODNB*; Hutton, *Charles the Second*, pp. 81–82, 88, 93–95, 110–11, 114–06.

76  For examples, see BL, Add. MS 4180, fol. 104; *CCISP*, ii, pp. 334–36, 340, 356, 440; *Nicholas Papers*, ii, pp. 22, 30, 60.

77  *Aubrey's Brief Lives*, p. 183; O Hehir, *HD*, pp. 101–12.

78  The rising is generally known as Penruddock's Rising after its only success, the brief occupation of Salisbury by a small force under Colonel John Penruddock.

79  *CSPD, 1655*, pp. 192–93, 204.

80  Ibid., p. 204. Most of the royalists arrested after Penruddock's rising were resident in England, although they included a number who had previously returned from exile. The 'professional' agents who had slipped into England from exile to take part in the rising, like Armorer and O'Neill, almost all escaped back to the continent. See Smith, *Royalist Agents*, pp. 195–96.

81  For a discussion of the reasons why Denham escaped imprisonment, see O Hehir, *HD*, pp. 115–16.

After the suppression of Penruddock's rising, both royalist conspiracy and the career of Denham as a conspirator lapsed into at least two years of inactivity. Although he had only been on the periphery of planning the March rising, from 1657 onwards Denham became increasingly involved in the complex intrigues to control the direction of revived conspiracy in the vacuum created by the gradual erosion of the Sealed Knot's authority. Denham's attempts to build up his own network of plotters brought him into contact with diverse and, at least to the king's principal advisers like Hyde and Ormond, not always congenial company. In June 1657 Denham briefly returned to Charles's court in Brussels, from where Joseph Bampfield, now one of Thurloe's spies, reported the return of the Duke of Buckingham to England with a scheme either for a rising in London or to assassinate the Protector, and that 'the design is known to Mr Denham, who is here'.[82] Denham's contacts with Buckingham, who was promptly arrested and imprisoned after his marriage to Lord Fairfax's daughter Mary, remained tenuous, but with his old friend the disorderly Earl of Oxford, they were renewed.[83] O'Neill, back in England to help organise a new rising, reported to Hyde on 3 March 1658 that Denham 'has much interest with lord Oxford unto whome hee is now goeing [...] with some foolish design from [...] Buckingham'.[84] More serious connections were also established with new figures like Sir Allen Apsley, a hard-drinking cavalier who had served in the west under Berkeley in the civil war, and with Alan Brodrick, secretary to the Sealed Knot, and another cavalier not in much danger of sobriety.[85] Both Apsley and Brodrick were allies of Hyde, now lord chancellor, to whom they were distantly related through Hyde's first marriage, and they were at first disposed to be suspicious of Denham, whose alleged Louvrian connections, his being 'too much of the Queene's faction', in Brodrick's words, continued to haunt him.[86]

The situation changed from mid-1658 after the suppression of royalist plans for another rising. The usual wave of arrests and a few executions were perhaps one reason for Denham's fourth passage across the Channel into exile, although this time with the sanction of an official pass for 'William, Lord Herbert [a son of Denham's patron, Pembroke], John Denham, and five servants to go beyond seas'. By mid-November Denham was back in England and, according to Herbert Price, one of Hyde's regular intelligencers, wishing 'that the King in his letter to him had mentioned something of grace to [Richard] Cromwell'.[87] Any schemes to approach Cromwell were soon abandoned in the light of the king's decision to replace the moribund Knot with a more energetic and efficient organisation,

82  *CSPD, 1657–8*, p. 6.
83  For examples of Oxford's disorderly lifestyle, see *Pepys's Diary 1663*, iv, p. 136; *1665*, vi, p. 3.
84  *CCISP*, iv, p. 21. See also O Hehir, *HD*, p. 126 and n. 25.
85  For Apsley, see Paul Seaward, 'Apsley, Sir Allen (1616–1683)', *ODNB*, 2004. For Brodrick, see Paul Seaward, 'Brodrick, Sir Allen (1623–1680)', *ODNB*. For the incident of their both being drunk in the Commons, see *Pepys's Diary 1666*, vii, p. 416 and n. 3.
86  *State Papers Collected by Edward, Earl of Clarendon*, iii, p. 406.
87  *CSPD, 1658*, p. 580; *CCISP*, iv, p. 111; O Hehir, *HD*, pp. 128–29.

the Great Trust and Commission, under the authoritarian leadership of Lord Mordaunt, a younger brother of the Earl of Peterborough and one of the rising generation of 'new cavaliers'.

Mordaunt's energy and drive revitalised many demoralised royalists, but his prickly and arrogant manner alienated others, causing Denham and associates like Oxford, Apsley, and Brodrick, who disliked Mordaunt intensely, to try and create a rival to the Great Trust.[88] The suppression of the royalist rising in August 1659 weakened Mordaunt's status and intensified the bitter squabbling among several different factions, of which Denham's was only one. By the early months of 1660, Brodrick was moving closer to Denham, claiming to Hyde that 'of Mr Denham there is at this time an universal good opinion, and if your Lordship would engage him by a letter, or induce his Majesty to write, I know not anything in your own power so advantageous'.[89] Although Denham's status among some prominent royalists was rising, Hyde remained essentially unconvinced. The evidence that Denham had been in touch with a noted Louvrian like Ashburnham, his friendship with Buckingham, and his apparent involvement in last-minute schemes to ease the king's restoration by persuading Hyde to resign his lord chancellorship, would not have persuaded him to change his mind.[90] In any case, events were soon out of the hands of the factious groups of royalist plotters. In the events leading to General Monck's occupation of London, the summoning of a free Parliament and the invitation to Charles II to return to England, the royalist conspirator who played the most important role was the Cornish magnate Sir John Grenville, not a particular friend of Denham.[91] When the rewards were handed out to royalist conspirators in the Restoration settlement, Grenville did extremely well, as to a lesser extent did clients of Hyde like Apsley and Brodrick, and clients of Ormond like O'Neill and Armorer. Denham received his reward, the 'signal honour' of being created a knight of the honourable Order of the Bath, royal recognition of his long years of service to the Stuart cause rather than a particular acknowledgement of his role as a conspirator.[92]

## V

In his introduction to Denham's *Poetical Works*, T.H. Banks claimed that, despite his fame among contemporaries, Denham 'has become for us a curiously indistinct figure', a situation which this volume of essays is intended to correct.[93] One

---

88  Ibid., pp. 131–34; Underdown, *Royalist Conspiracy*, pp. 301, 305
89  *State Papers Collected by Edward, Earl of Clarendon*, iii, pp. 644–46. Cited in Banks, *PW*, pp. 17–18.
90  Ibid., pp. 150–51.
91  Underdown, *Royalist Conspiracy*, pp. 300, 312–13.
92  O Hehir, *HD*, pp. 162–63. Denham's office of surveyor general of the works, which was bestowed after the Restoration, was promised by Charles II in September 1649. It had nothing to do with Denham's career as a royalist conspirator. Banks, *PW*, p. 60.
93  Ibid., p. 1.

reason for this lack of distinctiveness is the impossibility of pinning Denham down to a fixed position among the clientage networks and factions that were such an essential element within the royalist party. Although suspected of being a Louvrian, Denham in exile was not constrained by any factional allegiances, numbering among his friends such diverse figures as Killigrew, Will Murray, and Hyde's friend Mennes, but not particularly his fellow poets. Although on friendly terms with some prominent nobles, in particular with Ormond, Pembroke, and, probably briefly, Buckingham, Denham never established a close, lasting client-patron relationship with any of them. Certainly, some friendships lasted. On 19 October 1664 Sir Charles Lyttelton reported to Hatton that Ormond, having arrived in London from Ireland, 'lodges now in Sr. John Denham's house in Scott-land yard'.[94] But this friendship cannot be compared with that of O'Neill, who, according to Fanshawe, was so devoted to Ormond that he showed 'himself at every turn passionately your Excellency's'.[95] One consequence of this lack of a document-preserving patron or employer is that so little of Denham's correspondence has survived. The voluminous papers of Ormond (Carte MSS), Nicholas and Hyde (Clarendon MSS) are literally full of letters to and from clients, friends, intelligencers, and agents, including large numbers from, for example, Brodrick, O'Neill, Mordaunt, and Armorer, but effectively nothing to or from Denham.

If during his years in exile Denham's factional allegiances cannot be pinned down, this is also the case with his involvement in royalist conspiracy in England. Until possibly the very eve of the Restoration, he was not seen as a seriously important plotter, certainly not by the various Commonwealth regimes that treated him with conspicuous leniency. Unlike Brodrick, he was not a member of the Sealed Knot, while his hostility to Mordaunt meant that he was not invited to join the Great Trust either. Nor was he a 'professional' agent like Humphrey Boswell or, more importantly, O'Neill and Armorer, who developed close connections to patrons like Hyde, Ormond, Nicholas, and Mordaunt.[96] Denham worked on the edges of the main centres of conspiracy, trying to establish his own circle, with essentially unproductive associations with men like Buckingham and Oxford and with only gradual and conditional support from Apsley and Brodrick, his influence undermined always by Hyde's lack of trust in him.

So the picture of Sir John Denham during the years of exile and conspiracy is complex rather than indistinct. In some ways he was the stereotype of the cavalier, fond of company, gambling, wine, and women; the women ranging from Lady Isabella Thynne to the anonymous whore who gave him the dose of the clap from which Mennes allegedly cured him. He combined significant achievement in poetry and translating with bawdy and crude burlesque ballads. He was energetic and widely travelled, making several Channel crossings and, when on the continent, frequently travelling between France and the Netherlands, not to mention

94  BL, Add. MS 29577, fol. 44b. Cited in Kelliher, 'Denham: Letters and Documents', p. 17.
95  *Letters and Papers*, ed. Carte, ii, p. 32 (Fanshawe to Ormond, 21 June 1651).
96  For discussion of these client connections, see Smith, *Royalist Agents*, pp. 231, 240–41.

the mission to Poland. He was ambitious but his schemes were unfocused and, from Charles I's flight from Hampton Court to the suppression of a series of royalist plots, were also largely unsuccessful. At the Restoration he received rewards for his loyal services, the surveyorship and the Order of the Bath, but perhaps not recognition and status to the extent he desired. Although in congenial company Sir John Denham was 'no where a stranger', he was never a major figure at the centre of events either.

# 3 Restoration Theatre and Interregnum Royalism

## The Cavalier Rivalry of John Denham and William Davenant

*Marcus Nevitt*

## I

In August 1642 the London bookseller Thomas Walkley brought out a small folio of John Denham's tragedy of ambition and jealousy at the court of Shah Abbas, *The Sophy*. Walkley evidently considered that there was a market for such expensive editions of cavalier Persian plays, as witnessed by his publication of Sir John Suckling's *Aglaura* in exactly the same format in 1638. With Denham, though, Walkley was taking something of a gamble, as he proclaimed from the title page that *The Sophy* had 'been acted at the Private House in Blackfriars by his Majesties Servants'. Martin Butler and Brendan O Hehir have each convincingly argued that there was, in all likelihood, no such performance, whether at Blackfriars or elsewhere.[1] Even though the play was granted a theatrical license by Sir Henry Herbert early in 1642, and whilst Denham wrote a prologue for it which clearly envisaged professional production, it was not included in the list of plays in their repertoire which the King's Men sought to protect from the encroachment of printers and publishers in July 1641 (which suggests that it was unperformed or valued slightly by the company).[2] Unlike Suckling's *Aglaura*, which we know was acted on at least three occasions at court and Blackfriars in the February and April of

---

1 Martin Butler, *Theatre and Crisis, 1632–1642* (Cambridge: Cambridge University Press, 1984), p. 82; O Hehir, *HD*, p. 389. Contrast their view with those of Sidney Lee in the *DNB* and William Kelliher in the *ODNB*, who in their entries on Denham assert, without supplying evidence, that the play was acted 'with success'. This assumption probably originated with Gerard Langbaine, who contended 'that it was acted at the Blackfriars with good applause'; *An Account of the English Dramatick Poets* (London, 1691), p. 128. G.E. Bentley, whilst pointing out that there is no extant evidence for performance, remains open to its possibility; G.E. Bentley, *The Jacobean and Caroline Stage: Plays and Playwrights*, 7 vols (Oxford: Clarendon Press, 1956), iii, pp. 277–78.
2 N.W. Bawcutt, *The Control and Censorship of Caroline Drama: The Records of Sir Henry Herbert, Master of the Revels, 1623–73* (Oxford: Clarendon Press, 1996), p. 210; Bentley, *Jacobean and Caroline Stage*, pp. 277–78. Denham's prologue makes reference to the playwright's payment from the proceeds of the third-night performance: 'Gentlemen, if yee dislike the Play,/ Pray make no words on't till the second day, / Or third be past: For we would have you know it,/ The losse with fall on us, not on the Poet:/ For he writes not for money'; John Denham, *The Sophy* (London, 1642), sig. A2r.

1638, first as a tragedy and then a tragicomedy with a radically transformed final act, there are no textual traces of a staging of Denham's play in the early 1640s. Whether this title-page advertisement is a canny attempt to increase the desirability of a new but unperformed play to a market transformed by the conflict of civil war and already nostalgic for theatre in the capital is as uncertain as O Hehir's claim that all of this is just 'an implausible lie'.[3]

I begin with the obscure stage life of *The Sophy* in order to reframe one of the most famous documents in Restoration theatre history and shed some light on the conflicts and collaborations which helped shape the theatre of the early 1660s. The document in question is the Lord Chamberlain's order of December 1660 granting Sir William Davenant and the Duke's Company exclusive performance rights to a limited number of sixteenth- and seventeenth-century plays; at the centre of this article, and crucial to my interpretation of the Lord Chamberlain's order, is Davenant's relationship with John Denham, who Charles II controversially appointed Surveyor of the Works in May 1660 as a reward for his loyalty as a royalist plotter during the Protectorate. Davenant's theatrical practices in the early years of the Restoration, I will suggest, owe a great deal to his experiences as a controversial and politically engaged artist-entrepreneur during the 1650s, one whose early allegiance to royalism and the Stuart dynasty was tested and found malleable by periods of imprisonment and relative favour under the Commonwealth and Protectorate. My argument will involve more than tracing the now familiar suggestion that some of the arresting novelties of Restoration theatre, such as the introduction of the actress, the proscenium stage, and moveable scenery to professional drama, owed much to the inventiveness of Davenant's masque-like Protectoral operas.[4] Rather, it demands that we look afresh at the ways in which Davenant and his royalist contemporaries remembered his involvement in the cultural and political upheavals of the previous decades and consider how the rivalries experienced during that period might have played out once the nation, its politics, and its theatre were reconfigured with the return of Charles II.[5] In the autumn of 1660, Davenant and the Duke's Company he managed were

3  O Hehir, *HD*, p. 39.

4  See Dawn Lewcock, *Sir William Davenant, the Court Masque and the English Seventeenth-Century Scenic Stage, c. 1605–1700* (Amherst, NY: Cambria Press, 2008); Richard Kroll, *Restoration Drama and 'The Circle of Commerce'* (Cambridge: Cambridge University Press, 2007), pp. 103–05, 188–204; Nancy Klein Maguire, *Regicide and Restoration: English Tragicomedy, 1660–1671* (Cambridge: Cambridge University Press, 1992), pp. 88–90.

5  For recent studies of the relationships between royalist writers in the Interregnum, see John Stubbs, *Reprobates: The Cavaliers of the English Civil War* (London:, 2011); Jason McElligott and David L. Smith (eds), *Royalists and Royalism during the Interregnum* (Manchester: Manchester University Press, 2010); Marcus Nevitt, 'The Insults of Defeat: Royalist Responses to William Davenant's *Gondibert* (1651)', *Seventeenth Century*, 25 (2009), 287–304; Nicholas McDowell, *Poetry and Allegiance in the English Civil War: Marvell and the Cause of Wit* (Oxford: Oxford University Press, 2008); Jeffrey R. Collins, *The Allegiance of Thomas Hobbes* (Oxford: Oxford University Press, 2007); Jason McElligott and David L. Smith (eds), *Royalists and Royalism during the English Civil Wars* (Cambridge: Cambridge University Press, 2007); Jerome De Groot, *Royalist*

in the direst of straits; starved of a repertory by Thomas Killigrew and the King's Company, who had laid claim to practically all extant English drama that had ever been performed by reason of their historic connections to the King's Men, they were forced to turn to a play with a meagre stage history by a bitter rival just to make theatrical ends meet. The rival in question was John Denham and the play, *The Sophy*, deserves a higher billing in the history of Restoration theatre than it has hitherto been accorded.

## II

That Denham and *The Sophy* might have any noteworthy part to play in the history of Restoration theatre will come as a surprise to most students of the subject. This is because Denham's place in any narrative of the re-establishment of theatre in the capital after 1660 has been consistently underplayed.[6] However, as Charles II's surveyor, he did have a key role in determining the venues and sites where the new Restoration theatre companies might establish themselves; the original warrant enshrining the Killigrew-Davenant monopoly of London's public theatre clearly indicated their powers were circumscribed to some degree by Denham's. Both theatre managers were told that they could hire who they wanted, build whatever kind of theatre they desired, and perform without fear of rival companies (which 'shall be absolutely suppressed'), but that they could only do this 'in such convenient places as shall be thought fit by the Surveyor of the works'.[7] As Surveyor General, Denham was also intimately involved in the construction, design, and management of new court theatre venues deemed appropriate for the restored regime. All warrants for work on these venues—ranging from the alteration of individual scenes, to the construction of temporary dance floors, to the repositioning of entire boxes—were addressed to Denham by the Lord Chamberlain,

*Identities* (Basingstoke: Palgrave, 2004); James Loxley, *Royalism and Poetry in the English Civil Wars: The Drawn Sword* (Basingstoke: Palgrave, 1997); Timothy Raylor, *Cavaliers, Clubs and Literary Culture: Sir John Mennes, James Smith, and the Order of the Fancy* (Newark: University of Delaware Press, 1994); Lois Potter, *Secret Rites and Secret Writing: Royalist Literature, 1641–1660* (Cambridge: Cambridge University Press, 1989).

6  Denham is only mentioned incidentally (or not at all) in the following seminal surveys of the Restoration stage: Deborah Payne Fisk (ed.), *The Cambridge Companion to Restoration Theatre* (Cambridge: Cambridge University Press, 2000); Derek Hughes, *English Drama, 1660–1700* (Oxford: Clarendon Press, 1996); Richard Bevis, *English Drama: Restoration and Eighteenth Century, 1660–1789* (London and New York: Longman, 1988); Robert D. Hume, *The Development of English Drama in the Late Seventeenth Century* (Oxford: Clarendon Press, 1976); Allardyce Nicoll, *A History of Restoration Drama* (Cambridge: Cambridge University Press, 1940); Montague Summers, *The Restoration Theatre* (London, 1934); Leslie Hotson, *The Commonwealth and Restoration Stage* (Cambridge, MA: Harvard University Press, 1928).

7  London, National Archives, Secretaries of State: State Papers Domestic, Charles II, SP 29/8, no.1; reprinted in Hotson, *Commonwealth and Restoration Stage*, pp. 199–200. This may in practice have only meant that Denham had the final say on where entertainment venues could be sited on crown land but it was a significant power nonetheless. I am grateful to Robert Hume for this point.

the Earl of Arlington.[8] That this was a demanding role requiring considerable technical and theatrical expertise is evident from a communication between John Carew, Yeoman of the Revels, and the Lord Chamberlain concerning the best way to appoint the tiring room at the Hall Theatre in Whitehall. With abrupt clarity Arlington ordered Carew to 'repaire vnto S$^r$ John Dinham [...] and to advise with him [...] and that you follow and take his directions [...] till it be finished'.[9] Denham's judgment was also respected in the equally fraught matter of theatrical hermeneutics. In March 1663 Charles II personally requested that he take a lead in the regulation of Restoration drama when he demanded that Thomas Killigrew and the King's Company suspend performances of John Wilson's comedy *The Cheats* until Denham and Edmund Waller had analysed the nature and targets of the play's topical humour.[10] If this intervention is 'odd', as one recent assessment has it, it is also testament to the faith that the king put in Denham's judgement in matters theatrical.[11] The connection between Denham and the king's theatrical preferences was perhaps most flamboyantly displayed at court on February 4 1668 with a performance of Katherine Phillips's unfinished translation of Corneille's *Horace*. Denham, knowing something of Charles II's fondness for French drama and the popularity of Corneille translations in cavalier circles, supplied the missing fifth act for the play, which was performed by eminent courtiers including the king's mistress, Lady Castlemaine, playing the part of Camilla in royal jewellery costing somewhere between £40,000 and £200,000, according to contemporary reports.[12] That Denham was a member of the exclusive audience who witnessed this performance seems very likely, since his pre-eminence in

8  Summaries of the warrants are reproduced in Eleanore Boswell, *The Restoration Court Stage, 1670–1702* (Cambridge, MA: Harvard University Press, 1932), pp. 235–38.

9  Ibid., p. 75.

10  William Van Lennep, Emmett L. Avery, and Arthur H. Scouten (eds), *The London Stage, 1660–1800: A Calendar of Plays*, 5 parts in 11 vols, Part I: 1660–1700 (Carbondale: Southern Illinois University Press, 1965), p. 63; Bawcutt, *Henry Herbert*, p. 102.

11  Matthew J. Kinservik, 'Theatrical Regulation during the Restoration Period', in Susan J. Owen (ed.), *A Companion to Restoration Drama* (Oxford: Blackwell, 2001), pp. 36–52 (p. 41).

12  Close friends of Denham, including Edmund Waller, Charles Sedley, and Sidney Godolphin, translated Corneille into heroic couplets in *Pompey the Great* (London, 1664). Though Philips died before her own translation was completed, she did present sections of it to the Duchess of York and Charles II in December or January 1662/3; see Catherine Cole Mambretti 'Orinda on the Restoration Stage', *Comparative Literature*, 37.3 (1985), 233–51 (pp. 243, 245). The decision to stage an elaborate production of *Horace* may have been prompted in part by the impact of Henry Herringman's authorised folio edition of Philips's *Poems* in 1667. Even though Denham's additional final act of the translation was not printed until 1678, his connection with this exclusive project was being noted well before then. One contemporary remarked upon the first performance of the play as well as its co-authorship: 'There are none but the Nobility admitted to see it. The play is Madam Philips's translation of Corneille's Horace, finished by Sir John Denham'; BL, Add. MS 36916, fol. 62. On Charles II's fondness for French theatre, see Tifanny Stern, *Rehearsal from Shakespeare to Sheridan* (Oxford: Clarendon Press, 2000), pp. 133–35; Maguire, *Regicide and Restoration*, pp. 53–5; Sybil Marion Rosenfeld, 'Foreign Theatrical Companies in Great Britain in the Seventeenth and Eighteenth Centuries', *Society for Theatre Research Pamphlet*, series no. 4 (1955).

Restoration theatre circles was still being recalled in the early eighteenth century. In *The Causes of the Decay and Defects of Dramatick Poetry* (1725), John Dennis described him as one of a select group of courtiers and aristocrats—including Rochester, Waller, and the Duke of Buckingham—who exercised an overbearing influence on theatrical tastes. He was one of 'several extraordinary men at Court who wanted neither Zeal nor Capacity, nor Authority to sett the audiences right again; [...] the town fell immediately in with them' in their assessment of plays.[13]

Given Denham's involvement in the composition, location, regulation, and reception of Restoration drama, then, it is extremely surprising that nobody has scrutinised his place in one of the core documents for any account of its history. On the 12 December 1660, three months after the establishment of the theatre monopolies, the following order was issued from the Lord Chamberlain's office:

> Whereas S[r] William Davenant, Knight, hath humbly p[r]sented to us a proposition of reformeinge some of the most ancient Playes that were playd at Blackfriers and of makeinge them, fitt, for the Company of Actors appointed under his direction and Comand, Viz: the playes called the Tempest, measures, for measures, much adoe about nothinge, Rome and Juliet, Twelfe night, the Life of King Henry the Eyght, the sophy, King Lear, the Tragedy of Mackbeth, the Tragedy of Hamlet prince of Denmarke, and the Dutchess of Malfy, Therefore wee have granted unto the sayd S[r] William Davenant, liberty to represent the playes above named by the Actors under his comand, notwithstandinge any Warrant to the contrary formerly granted, And it is our will and pleasure and we comand that noe person or persons upon what p[r]tence soever, shall act or cause to be acted any of those above named Eleven playes.[14]

Thanks to important work by John Freehafer, Robert D. Hume, Judith Milhous, and Gunnar Sorelius, we now have an acute sense of how this document worked in the 'scramble' for rights to old plays in 1660.[15] One thing that has become apparent is just how poorly Davenant's Duke's Company were served by it; their repertory was initially restricted to those plays listed—the majority of which had long fallen from critical favour—plus anything Davenant had written himself, and two months' worth of rights to six other plays. Killigrew's King's Company,

---

13  John Dennis, *The Critical Works of John Dennis: Volume II, 1711–1729*, ed. Edward Niles Hooker (Baltimore: Johns Hopkins University Press, 1943), p. 277.

14  London, National Archives, Lord Chamberlain's Department: Miscellaneous Records, LC 5/137. Reprinted in Allardyce Nicoll, *A History of English Drama, 1660–1900*, rev. edn, 6 vols (Cambridge: Cambridge University Press, 1952–1959), i, pp. 352–53.

15  John Freehafer, 'The Formation of the London Patent Companies in 1660', *Theatre Notebook*, 20 (1965), 6–30; Robert D. Hume, 'Securing a Repertory: Plays on the London Stage 1660–5', in *Poetry and Drama, 1570–1700: Essays in Honour of Harold F. Brooks*, ed. Antony Coleman and Antony Hammond (London: Methuen, 1981), pp. 156–72; Judith Milhous, *Thomas Betterton and the Management of Lincoln's Inn Fields, 1695–1708* (Carbondale: Southern Illinois University Press, 1979), pp. 15–17; Gunnar Sorelius, 'The Rights of Restoration Theatre Companies in the Older Drama', *Studia Neophilologica*, 37 (1965), 174–89.

meanwhile, cornered the market to the vast majority of the performable and still popular Beaumont and Fletcher canon as well as a significant number of plays by Shakespeare and Jonson. If Davenant was one of the great innovators of Restoration theatre, pioneering the introduction of moveable scenery, operatic motifs, and the witty couple into English theatre, he was so because of the lack of raw material afforded by this play list; his innovations were, in other words, partly an imaginative response to scarcity. But for all of the insights afforded by recent research into the Lord Chamberlain's Order, it has focussed almost exclusively on the Shakespeare titles listed in it, in order to examine the role that Davenant and his company played in the making of the national poet after the return of Charles II.[16] What has gone almost completely unremarked is that included in Davenant's astonishingly modest list of plays, alongside a group of largely old-fashioned Elizabethan and Jacobean classics, is Denham's *The Sophy*.[17]

The peculiarity of *The Sophy*'s inclusion in this list is only partly down to what we have already seen: the play's obscure stage history. It had never been the theatrical hit that the Elizabethan and Jacobean plays had been fifty years or so previously; it may not even have been performed, and on that basis alone its presence requires some explanation. But the need to account for Davenant's acquisition of rights to *The Sophy* increases still further once we recognise that of the eleven 'old plays' to which he acquired rights there is only one for which there is no recorded performance in his lifetime. So, whilst every one of the Shakespeare titles was staged in either original or adapted form by the Duke's Company between August 1661 and November 1667, and whilst we know that *The Duchess of Malfi* had a very successful eight-day run in September 1662, it is possible that *The Sophy*'s spectacularly unexciting stage life continued unabated until 12 January 1670 when *The London Stage* notes its performance before Charles II at Lincoln's Inn Fields.[18] By this point both Davenant and Denham were dead and the management of the Duke's Company had passed into different hands. However, owing to the incomplete nature of the performance records for Restoration drama—only approximately one-tenth of performances are recorded—it is entirely possible, too, that *The Sophy* was performed at Lincoln's Inn Fields at some time during this period.[19] I will return to this intriguing possibility in due

---

16  For studies of this process, see Michael Dobson, *The Making of the National Poet: Shakespeare, Adaptation and Authorship, 1660–1769* (Oxford: Clarendon Press, 1992); Paulina Kewes, *Authorship and Appropriation: Writing for the Stage in England, 1660–1710* (Oxford: Clarendon Press, 1998), pp. 180–224; Gary Taylor, *Reinventing Shakespeare: A Cultural History from the Restoration to the Present* (New York, 1989), pp. 27–33.

17  Matthew Birchwood is one of the few critics who has noted 'that Davenant's petition for exclusive rights to perform certain plays specified *The Sophy* alongside his own and seven of Shakespeare's works'; Matthew Birchwood, *Staging Islam in England: Drama and Culture, 1640–1685* (Cambridge: Cambridge University Press, 2007), pp. 104–05.

18  Van Lennep et al., *The London Stage, Part I*, pp. 32, 47, 56, 72–75, 85, 123, 168.

19  Robert D. Hume argues that the performance calendar, before the introduction of newspaper advertisements, 'remains 90% incomplete'; Robert D. Hume 'English Drama and Theatre: New Directions and Research', *Theatre Survey*, 23 (1982), 71–100 (p. 77).

course; suffice it to say here that Davenant's decision to a select a play which had never been a stage success reveals much about his desperate need for a repertory of producible work during his earliest months as a Restoration theatre manager and demands much further scrutiny than it has hitherto received.

This puzzle is further complicated by *The Sophy*'s publication history. It is striking that, even after the closure of the theatres in 1642, and the accompanying expansion of the market for printed drama during the rest of the revolutionary decades, no publisher thought it worth their while to bring out another edition of *The Sophy* until after the Restoration with Henry Herringman's edition of Denham's collected works, the *Poems and Translations* (1668). Indeed, even though Humphrey Moseley acquired rights to the play from Walkley in 1650, he seems never to have published his own version of it, continuing to advertise what was presumably the unsold stock of Walkley's printing for the remainder of the decade.[20] This is not only in marked contrast to Suckling's *Aglaura*, which was printed throughout the civil war and Interregnum in the multiple editions of the extremely successful *Fragmenta Aurea*, but also to Denham's most celebrated work of the early 1640s, *Coopers Hill*, which remained so much in print during the revolutionary decades as to become a bibliographer's brightest joy or darkest nightmare, as Brendan O Hehir's work attests.[21] Yet despite the paucity of printed editions and the likely absence of any theatrical performance, somehow or other *The Sophy* did attain a certain popularity in the period. Anthony Wood's remembrance of Denham and his play best indicates this: 'In the latter end of the year, 1641, he published the tragedy called *The Sophy*, which took extremely much and was admired by all ingenious men, particularly by Edmund Waller of Beaconsfield, who then said of the author, that he broke out like the Irish rebellion, three score thousand strong, when no body was aware, or in the least suspected it'.[22] Critics and literary historians have rarely considered why Wood's recollection of *The Sophy's* favourable reception amongst 'ingenious' men appears to contradict the play's performance and publication history.[23] The contradiction is resolved, however, if we interpret these remarks as evidence of the fairly limited circulation of the printed text of Denham's play amongst influential cavalier circles (populated

20  See W.W. Greg, *A Bibliography of the English Drama Printed to the Restoration*, 4 vols. (London: Bibliographical Society, 1939–1959), ii, p. 752; O Hehir, *HD*, p. 40. Francis Kirkman was still advertising an edition of the play for sale in 1661, although he attributed it to 'Tho. Denham'; *A True, perfect and Exact Catalogue of all the Comedies, Tragedies and Tragicomedies, Pastorals, Masques and Interludes* (London, 1661). Edward Phillips hinted that there was only one printing of *The Sophy* before the *Poems and Translations of 1668*, noting that it had 'been long since published' but then 'came forth a few years since, joyn'd with the rest of his poeticall works'; Edward Phillips, *Theatrum Poetarum* (London, 1675), p. 106.

21  O Hehir, *EH*.

22  Anthony Wood, *Athenae Oxoniensis*, 2 vols (London, 1721), ii, p. 423.

23  O Hehir speculates that it may have been a closet drama, but acknowledges that 'even for reading purposes, the play does [not] appear to have sold very well'; *HD*, p. 40. This is very unlikely since Denham makes explicit reference to the payment of the actors in the prologue to the play; Denham, *The Sophy*, sig. A2r.

by writers like Waller) whose 'ingenious[ness]' was as much an expression of noble social standing as penetrating critical acumen.[24] As both of these meanings were current in the word's seventeenth-century usage, this interpretation also helps illuminate the reasons behind Davenant's determination to secure rights to the text at the Restoration. What Davenant was asserting with Lord Chamberlain's order of 1660—in the face of the King's Company's "ownership" of the most performable pieces of Elizabethan, Jacobean, and Caroline theatre—was his company's right to perform a text which had been read and enjoyed by a select group of Caroline courtiers shortly before the outbreak of hostilities. Even if *The Sophy* had never taken the professional stage by storm, the order shows Davenant, therefore, building a new theatrical culture not only on the durable foundations of Renaissance drama but also out of the formative memories of civil war and Interregnum royalism, a culture in which both he and Denham had prominent, if conflicting, roles.

## III

If Davenant's inclusion of *The Sophy* in the December warrant summoned memories of pre-war court culture, many contemporaries—John Denham prominent among them—were well aware that Davenant had been significantly less than loyal to the Stuart court and its values in the intervening period. Denham was, as we shall see, a close watcher of Davenant's allegiance switches in the mid-century and would surely have recognised in the monopolistic theatrical settlement of 1660 more than a hint of Davenant's work for different political masters during the Interregnum. Davenant (named Charles I's poet laureate in 1638 after the death of Jonson) had produced an astonishing variety of professional and court drama for the Stuarts during the 1630s and early 1640s; he wrote and appeared in court masques and gave much to the royalist war cause throughout the wars, eventually being imprisoned by Commonwealth authorities as a notorious delinquent in 1651.[25] However, the mid-1650s saw Davenant writing operas and works of dramatic theory favourable to the Protectorate, and even hinting to Cromwell's spymaster, John Thurloe, that he was willing to gather intelligence amongst exiled royalist communities in France on his behalf.[26] It was this defection, as much as

24 Whilst the dominant meaning of 'ingenious' as 'Having high intellectual capacity' dates from the fifteenth century, from the 1630s it could also mean 'Well born or bred'; 'ingenious, adj'.; senses 1 and 5a, *OED Online*, June 2014, Oxford University Press <http://www.oed.com.eresources.shef.ac.uk/view/Entry/95751?redirectedFrom=ingenious> [accessed 21 June 2014].

25 Davenant appeared at court as the character of 'the Poet' in his own masques *Luminalia* (1638) and *Salmacida Spolia* (1640); Stephen Orgel and Roy Strong, *Inigo Jones: The Theatre of the Stuart Court*, 2 vols (Berkeley: University of California Press, 1973), ii, p. 87.

26 Davenant wrote to Thurloe in June 1655 asking leave to go to France and promised to 'dedicate my service to you during my short abode there'; Thomas Birch (ed.), 'State Papers, 1655: June (4 of 7)', *A Collection of the State Papers of John Thurloe, Volume 3: December 1654–August 1655*, *British History Online* <http://www.british history.ac.uk/report.aspx?compid=55390&strquery=davenant> [accessed 11 July 2014]; Nevitt, 'The Insults of Defeat', pp. 291–92.

any loss of revenue, authority, or court standing, which Sir Henry Herbert, Master of the Revels, claimed had provoked his objections to the monopolistic terms of the Restoration theatrical settlement. On 4 August 1660 Herbert petitioned the king asserting his own rights above those of Davenant and Killigrew in the business of theatrical regulation, offering a reading of recent theatre history in which his own devotion to monarchy was opposed to the exceptional cupidity of Davenant and his Protectoral entertainments:

> no person or persons haue erected any Playhouses, or raised any Company of Players, without Licence from your petitioner's said Predecessors or from your petitioner. But Sir William Davenant, Knight, who obtained Leaue of Oliver and Richard Cromwell to vent his Operas, in a time when your petitioner owned not their Authority.

In a less-guarded letter to Edward Hyde, Earl of Clarendon, he referred to Davenant as 'Master of the Reuells to Oliuer the Tyrant'.[27] Herbert's pleas were, however, ignored by the king: he upheld Davenant's right to his share in the patent monopoly and allowed him to resume the laureateship conferred by his father in 1638.

That Herbert was unsuccessful in wresting control of the theatres back from Davenant by exposing the provisional nature of his allegiance to the king surely owes much to the fact the latter never attempted to conceal the nature of his Interregnum theatricals. The chief legacy of Davenant's work in the 1650s is extremely familiar: the runaway success of his Protectorate opera *The Siege of Rhodes* (1656) after the Restoration. Davenant reworked and extended his original entertainment into two parts for the opening of his new theatre at Lincoln's Inn Fields in June 1661, thrilling his audiences with the novelty of moving painted scenery and actresses as both subjects and objects of homoerotic desire.[28] The play was not only Pepys's favourite—John Hayls's portrait at the National Portrait Gallery shows Pepys holding a copy of a setting of the song 'Beauty Retire'—but it also virtually emptied Killigrew's rival venue at Vere Street during the opening twelve-day run.[29] When Davenant dedicated the printed quarto of the enlarged edition of *The Siege of Rhodes* (1663) to Clarendon, he was frank about how much he relied upon his powerful old acquaintance for his present rehabilitation:

27  Bawcutt, *Henry Herbert*, pp. 223, 264.
28  In Act IV, Roxalana transported by Ianthe's beauty, fails to murder her love rival and instead gives her a lingering kiss. Hester Davenport played the role of Roxalana whilst the celebrated Mary Saunderson, future wife of Thomas Betterton, took the part of Ianthe; *The Siege of Rhodes: The First and Second Part* (London, 1663), p. 39; Van. Lennep et al., *The London Stage*, p. 29.
29  Having already been to *The Siege of Rhodes*, on 4 July 1661 Pepys went to Vere Street to see Killigrew's *Claracilla* and thought it 'strange to see this house, that used to be so thronged, now empty since the Opera begun; and so will continue for a while, I believe'; *The Diary of Samuel Pepys*, ed. Robert Latham and William Matthews, 11 vols (Berkeley and Los Angeles: University of California Press, 1970–83), ii, p. 132.

'I cannot be safe unless I am sheltered behind your lordship', he remarked, and he tried to distinguish his dedication from others the Lord Chancellor received:

> If I should proceed, and tell your Lordship of what use theatres have anciently been, and may be now, by heightening the characters of valour, temperance, natural justice, and complacency to Government, I should fall into the ill manners and indiscretion of ordinary Dedicators, who go about to instruct those from whose abilities they expect protection.[30]

The syntactical ambiguity at the end of this sentence, whereby the guarantor of protection is also an overbearing influence to be protected from, comes at a particularly revealing moment. Clarendon's power is asserted at exactly the same time as Davenant alludes to another of his Interregnum works, one whose influence on Restoration theatre is rarely traced, and one which told a very different group of powerful men 'what use theatres have anciently been' in securing 'complacency to Government'.

That work was the first of Davenant's entrepreneurial efforts to establish an acceptable form of commercial dramatic entertainment under Cromwell. The pamphlet appeared anonymously as *A Proposition for Advancement of Moralitie* in 1653 and, having offered a historical survey of the social function of drama, reworked arguments from Davenant's preface to *Gondibert* (1651)—a text Denham knew very well—to make a case for a reformed theatre which might find favour with a Puritan regime.[31] It was probably written shortly after Davenant's release from his imprisonment in the Tower and, like the preface to *Gondibert*, is best read as evidence that Davenant was willing to renegotiate his old royalist allegiances and serve new political masters.[32] A summary of the pamphlet was requested by influential members of the Hartlib circle after Davenant had first presented it to Parliament and then the Council of State, some of whose members must have found the strident anti-populism of its arguments provoking:

> There hath not been found a perfect meanes to retaine the people in quiet (they being naturally passionate and turbulent and yet reducible) [...] Perswasion must be joyn'd to Force [...] if the peoples senses were charm'd and entertain'd with things familiar to them, they would easily follow the voices of their shepherds; especially if there were set up some Entertainment, where

---

30  William Davenant, *Siege of Rhodes* (1663), sigs A2v, A3v. Clarendon and Dryden had been friends since the 1620s. Clarendon wrote a commendatory poem to Davenant's *Albovine* confessing the 'fond ambition of a friend', and wondered 'can ought of mine/ Inrich thy volume?'; William Davenant, *The Tragedy of Albovine, first King of the Lombards* (London, 1629), sig. A2v.

31  Even though the title page of *A Proposition* is dated 1654, James R. Jacob and Timothy Raylor have convincingly argued that it appeared in 1653; James R. Jacob and Timothy Raylor, 'Opera and Obedience: Thomas Hobbes and *A Proposition for Advancement of Moralitie* by Sir William Davenant', *Seventeenth Century*, 6 (1991), 205–50.

32  Nevitt, 'The Insults of Defeat', p. 292.

their eyes might be subdu'd with Heroicall Pictures and change of Scenes, their Eares civiliz'd with Musick and wholesome discourses, but some Academie where may be presented in a Theater severall ingenious Mecanicks, as Motion and Transposition of Lights [...] without any scandalous disguising of men in womens habits, as have bin us'd in Playes.[33]

The Protectorate did not implement Davenant's plans for another two years when, through the intercession of John Thurloe (who Davenant briefed on this subject), they permitted him to stage two hours' worth of public declamations interspersed with music, *The First Days Entertainment at Rutland House* (1656), a private entertainment which acted as a forerunner to the production of *The Siege of Rhodes* later that year.[34] Even so, the manuscript précis of *A Proposition* that Davenant wrote for the Hartlib circle reveals that he had determined upon the practicalities of his scheme of moral theatrical entertainment at a very early stage:

[His entertainments] Shall breed in the Spectators courage [...] diverting the people from Vices and Mischiefe; and instructing them (as in a School of Morality) to Virtue, and to quiet and cheerfull behaviour towards the present Government.

In order to which, tis humbly desird, that the Councill of State would please to give a Licence for publick Representations; and that they would authorize those to whome that Grant is directed, to suppresse all other publike Presentments; least scandalous arguments may be againe introduced. And those so authorizd' [*sic*], shall give security to the State that nothing by them represented shall be scandalous to Religion and manners, or prejudiciall to Government.

And likewise, tis humbly desired that they would please to allow them a Guard (which shall be difrayd by the Undertakers) to preserve the publick Peace during the foresaid Morall Presentments.[35]

33  *A Proposition for Advancement of Moralitie By a New Way of Entertainment of the People* (London, 1654), pp. 11, 13, 15. Hartlib noted that John Pell gave him a copy of *A Proposition* 'which was given to the Council of State and Parliament' in 1653; Sheffield, Sheffield University Library, Hartlib Papers 28/2/81A.

34  In the first months of 1656, Davenant wrote a briefing document for Thurloe on the political and social benefits of reformed drama for the Protectorate. Replaying some of the arguments of *A Proposition*, he told Thurloe that 'the city hath occasion of divertisements; not only to recreate those who will too much apprehend the absence of the adverse party, but allsoe entertain a new generation of youth uningag'd in the late differences; of which there is a numerous growth since the beginning of the warre, who should be withdrawne from licentiousnesse, gaming and discontent [...] If morall representations may be allow'd (being without profaneness and scandall) the first arguments may consist of the Spaniards' barbarous conquests in the West Indies [...] of which some use may be made; 'Some Observations Concerning the People of this Nation', Oxford, Bodl., Rawlinson MS A. xlvi, fol. 293. The briefing document is reproduced in full in C.H. Firth, 'Sir William Davenant and the Revival of Drama during the Protectorate', *English Historical Review*, 18 (1903), 319–21.

35  Sheffield, Sheffield University Library, Hartlib Papers, 50H 53/4/1.

Balancing the humility topoi of the petitioner with the confident imperatives and low-risk assurances of the entrepreneur, Davenant not only formulated the ideas he would bring to Clarendon's attention a decade later in the dedication to the expanded edition of *The Siege of Rhodes*; he also devised a blueprint for a monopolistic system of theatre which would dominate English dramatic culture for the rest of the century.

Davenant's arguments in *A Proposition* about the vital interconnections between moral entertainment, state security, monopoly, and hired muscle at theatre doors received their most enduring expression in the warrants inaugurating the Restoration theatrical settlement. Even though he already possessed an old, unused patent from 1639 in which Charles I allowed him to establish a new company at a supersized venue, it was to his 1650s theatre practices that he returned when repositioning himself in the changed circumstances of 1660.[36] By early July that year, Davenant had been forgiven by the king for his Protectorate disloyalty and was, like Killigrew, invited to dictate the terms of the Restoration theatre monopoly, as evidenced by the existence of two draft orders in his hand. One of these, dated 20th August, and addressed to Denham (as Surveyor of the Works) plus several other recipients, combines the circumlocutionary authority of the legislator with the hauteur of a regal register to command all unlicensed performance to cease, arraigning it as morally corrupting:

> Forasmuch, as wee are advertis'd that divers persons [...] doe [...] act, performe and shew in publique, Comedies, Tragedies, and other Entertainments of the Stage, therein publishing much prophaness, scurrility, obsceneness, and other abuses tending to the great Scandall of Religion, corruption of Manners, and ill example of our loving subjects: for the future prevention, therefore, of these and such like abuses and enormities Wee doe hereby command, impower, authorise, and strictly enjoine you, and every [one] of you, from time to time, from and after the Date of this our Warrant, to forwarne and forbid all and every such person and persons, Assemblies in Publique, such or any other Entertainments of the Stage [...] upon paine of our high displeasure, and such other penaltie as shall fall thereon. And wee doe hereby further command and authorise you, and every [one] of you to suppresse, and disperse, and cause to be suppressed and dispersed all and every such Assemblies, Companies and meetings; and for the better effecting hereof, Wee doe hereby enjoine, authorise and command all Constables, and other Officers of the Peace [...] to be ayding and assisting to you and every [one] of you (upon sight hereof) for the performance of this our will and pleasure herein.[37]

36 On the 1639 patent, see Joseph Quincy Adams, *Shakespearean Playhouses: A History of English Theatres from the Beginning to the Restoration* (Boston: Houghton Mifflin, 1917), pp. 425–27.

37 London, National Archives, Secretaries of State: State Papers Domestic, Charles II, SP 20/10, no. 169. The text is reprinted in full in Hotson, *Commonwealth and Restoration Stage*, pp. 201–02.

In seeking to extirpate all competition from actors at the Red Bull, Cockpit, and Salisbury Court theatres, Davenant demonstrated a loyalty to monopoly which, unlike his allegiance to the Stuarts or Cromwell, remained untouched by the tumults of the mid-seventeenth century.[38] Whatever the obscure transmission history of this document—which has meant that only a draft order in Davenant's hand without any official signature survives in the State Papers—when Denham and the other addressees received it they might have noticed that Davenant had, despite his earlier proximity to John Thurloe, now learned to command like a king.

## IV

John Denham moved in a similar orbit to Davenant during this period, albeit in the opposite direction. He, too, associated with members of the Hartlib circle in the 1650s. He was 'well acquainted' with the physician Thomas Coxe, trustee of Hartlib's proposed intelligence office, the Office of Address, and was much closer than Davenant to Hartlib himself, who regarded him as 'a mighty ingenious man' obsessed with the latest technologies such as waterworks and double-writing instruments.[39] Another of Davenant's acquaintances, John Thurloe, was also aware of Denham's activities at this time, though for very different reasons. Thurloe probably knew that Denham had gone to Poland in 1650 to raise money for Charles II, and was later informed that his London lodgings were a congregation point for a 'gang' of disaffected royalists seeking to traffic political dissidents in and out of France and who threatened to 'embroyle the nation'.[40] Throughout 1655, therefore, a year when the Protectorate authorities were intensely concerned about the possibility of royalist insurrection, Denham (who had been one of the principal conduits for Charles I's correspondence with royalist forces during the 1640s) was placed on Thurloe's watch list and was seen to be 'play[ing] the courtier' from his lavish accommodation at the Savoy.[41] By 1657 he was being singled

---

38  On the effects of drama monopolies in the period, see Debora C. Payne, 'Patronage and the Dramatic Marketplace under Charles I and II', *Yearbook of English Studies*, 21 (1991), 137–52.

39  Sheffield, Sheffield University Library, Hartlib Papers, 28/2/81A. In a revealing slip, Hartlib at one stage refers to Davenant as 'Sir Iohn Davenant'; Sheffield, Sheffield University Library, Hartlib Papers, 29/5/62A.

40  Thomas Birch (ed.), 'State Papers, 1655: April (1 of 6)', *A Collection of the State Papers of John Thurloe, Volume 3: December 1654–August 1655* (1742), pp. 332–48, British History Online <http://www.british-history.ac.uk/report.aspx?compid=55376&strquery=embroyle> [accessed 11 July 2014]. On Denham's journey to Poland, see his poem 'On My Lord Croft's and My Journey into Poland, from Whence we brought 10000 L. For his Majesty by the Decimation of His Scottish Subjects There'; John Denham, *Poems and Translations* (1668), pp. 67–70.

41  Birch (ed.), 'State Papers, 1655: April (2 of 6)', *A Collection of the State Papers of John Thurloe, Volume 3: December 1654–August 1655* (1742), pp. 349–63, British History Online <http://www.british-history.ac.uk/report.aspx?compid=55377&strquery=denham> [accessed 11 July 2014].

out as a key player in 'some desperate design, [...] some attempt against the Protector's person' which never came to fruition.[42]

Given their contrasting involvement in Interregnum politics, it is perhaps unsurprising, then, that Denham and Davenant should have had such very different views of theatre's political role. Whereas Davenant regarded his theatrical practice throughout this period as a means of allying himself with sovereign power, whether monarchical or protectoral, Denham, by contrast, saw cavalier allegiance and the business of drama as indissolubly connected. Unlike Davenant, in 1647 he contributed a commendatory poem to Humphrey Moseley's Beaumont and Fletcher folio, an important book, as critics have long recognised, for the assertion of a collective royalist identity during the civil war.[43] Included in a roster of thirty-four of the most eminent royalist writers of the day (including John Berkenhead, Robert Herrick, Roger L'Estrange, Richard Lovelace, and Thomas Stanley), all of whom commended Beaumont and Fletcher as masterful proponents of the cavalier ethos of wit, Denham lauded Fletcher's ability to outstrip even Shakespeare and Jonson and be effortlessly witty:

> I need not raise
> Trophies to thee from other Mens dispraise;
> Nor is thy fame on lesser Ruines built,
> Nor needs thy juster title the foul guilt
> Of Easterne Kings, who to secure their Raigne,
> Must have their Brothers, Sonnes, and Kindred slaine.
> [...] When Johnson, Shakespeare, and thy self did sift,
> And sway'd in the Triumvirate of wit –
> Yet what from Johnsons oyle and sweat did flow,
> Or what more easie nature did bestow
> On Shakespeares gentler Muse, in thee full growne
> Their Graces both appear, yet so, that none
> Can say here Nature ends, and Art begins
> But mix like th'Elements are borne like twins,
> So interweav'd, so like, so much the same,
> None this mere Nature, that mere Art can name
> Twas this the Ancients meant, Nature and Skill
> Are the two tops of their Pernassus Hill.[44]

42   Idem, 'State Papers, 1657: June (4 of 4)', *A Collection of the State Papers of John Thurloe, Volume 6: January 1657–March 1658* (1742), 362–75, *British History Online* <http://www.british-history.ac.uk/report.aspx?compid=55603&strquery=denham> [accessed 11 July 2014].

43   McDowell, *Poetry and Allegiance in the English Civil Wars*, pp. 80, 114, 188–89; Potter, *Secret Rites and Secret Writing,* pp. 21–22; Louis B. Wright, 'The Reading of Plays during the Puritan Revolution', *Huntington Library Bulletin,* 6 (1934), 73–108.

44   Francis Beaumont and John Fletcher, *Comedies and Tragedies Never Printed Before And Now Published by the Authors Original Copies* (London, 1647), sig. bv.

As Denham hymned the unity of art and nature in Fletcher's oeuvre, he also reminded readers of his own creative capacities. With the final couplet echoing the famous Parnassus-driven opening to *Coopers Hill*, and the pointed reference to Eastern tyrants who destroy their families to preserve their throne acutely summarising the plot of *The Sophy*, Denham connected his own recent work with nostalgia for a theatrical culture which had vanished with the outbreak of hostilities against the Stuarts. One contributor to another key text for mid-century royalism, William Cartwright's *Comedies, Tragi-comedies with other Poems* (1651), also made this connection, situating Denham's play in select and witty royalist company. Declaring his own allegiance in forthright terms, Joseph Leigh reflected upon the consolations of verbal art in the wake of political exile and Parliament's sequestration of his estates:

> I that have undergone the common Fate
> In making shift to lose my own Estate,
> Have felt that which did Thousands more befall,
> Thrice in a Siedge, and once in Goldsmiths-Hall;
> Return'd with much adoe to my own Clime,
> Am now just strong enough to make a Rime:
> Not to write Wit, which I pretend not to,
> But to admire those Noble Souls that do:
> Thou rais'd brave Suckling, gav'st him all his own,
> *Aglaura* else had not been waited on:
> [...] Beaumont and Fletchers Volume then stood forth,
> And taught the World what English Wits are Worth:
> Then came *The Sophy* deck'd by Denham's Quill
> With Flowers as Fresh as those on *Coopers Hill*
> [...] Then *Madagascar* fill'd our British Isle
> With *Love and Honour*, wrought by Davenants stile.[45]

With wit thus figured as an oppositional aesthetic it fell to a restricted group of cavalier poet-dramatists, including Davenant and Denham, to serve as guardians of established theatrical forms and values. Thomas Pastell claimed that many saw the situation in even starker terms; in a commendatory poem to Edward Benlowes's *Theophila* (1652), he suggested that some believed that only the wit of Denham and Davenant had pulled seventeenth-century English drama back from the brink:

> Beaumont and Fletcher coyn'd a golden way,
> T'expresse, suspend, and passionate a Play.
> Nimble and pleasant are all Motions there,
> For two Intelligences rul'd the Sphere.

---

45  William Cartwright, *Comedies, Tragi-comedies with other Poems* (London, 1651), sigs *r-*v.

Both Sock and Buskin sunk with them and then
Davenant and Denham Bouy'd them up agen.
Beyond these Pillars some think nothing is:
Great Britains Wit stands in a Precipice.[46]

Though Denham and Davenant may both have baulked at the idea that they were, together, a Beaumont and Fletcher for revolutionary times, twin defenders of English theatrical culture from the depredations of Puritanism, they would have concurred with Pastell's assessment of their evaluation of wit. In the preface to *Gondibert*, Davenant defined wit—as opposed to 'inspiration', which was tainted for him by its association with radical Puritanism—as 'the Soules powder', a refined mixture of instinct and reason and the chief driver of the creative process.[47] Denham, too, self-consciously situated himself in witty company by regularly writing occasional verses to William Crofts, Sir John Mennes, and other members in and around the cavalier drinking club, The Order of the Fancy.[48] He also sought to emulate dramatists like Fletcher and Shakespeare—descendants both, he averred, of 'Old Mother Wit'—by putting wit at the centre of his own tragedy, *The Sophy*.[49]

It was probably this quality which guaranteed the play's popularity amongst a restricted group of royalist readers, and which Davenant sought to capitalise on with his Restoration order by securing rights to it. However, the tempering of tragedy with wit also harmed *The Sophy*'s chances of ever being a stage hit, since even a cursory analysis of Denham's text reveals what unpromising material it made for theatrical success. As a play recounting Abbas, King of Persia's jealousy of his virtuous son Mirza, at first glance it seems to fit the pattern of a number of a royalist Ottaman-Persian tragedies written by people Denham and Davenant knew very well, Fulke Greville's *Mustapha* and Suckling's *Aglaura* amongst them. However, despite labelling his work a tragedy, and giving his plot line an unmistakably tragic arc—the king is haunted by the ghost of his usurped and murdered brother, the unjust and the righteous-mad die in the play's last scene—Denham too frequently pitches the drama on the border of witty comedy for it to sit comfortably in the genre. If the play was multiply plotted, we would have little trouble in seeing it as Fletcherian tragicomedy or as the direct descendent of the Jacobean tragedies of a dramatist like Cyril Tourneur. But as the action revolves around a single plot, it struggles to balance the mix of generic codes it voices.

---

46  Given that Davenant himself contributed one of the commendatory poems to this volume and signed it from the 'Tower, May 13th 1652', where he was imprisoned as a royalist delinquent, perhaps the crisis was more acute than Pestill realised; Edward Benlowes, *Theophila, Or Loves Sacrifice. A Divine Poem* (London, 1652), sigs B6r, dv.

47  William Davenant, *Gondibert*, ed. David Gladish (Oxford: Oxford University Press, 1971), p. 18.

48  See Denham, *Poems and Translations*, pp. 65, 75. On Denham's association with members of the Order of the Fancy, see Raylor, *Cavalier Clubs and Literary Culture*, p. 94.

49  John Denham, *On Mr. Abraham Cowley His Death and Burial Amongst the Ancient Poets* (London, 1667), p. 2.

This is most obvious in the play's prologue, which is much more eager to exhibit the sprezzatura flashes of the genteel amateur than darken anyone's mood with intimations of the tragic action to come:

> But Gentlemen, if yee dislike the Play,
> Pray make no words on't till the second day,
> Or the third be past: For we would have you know t,
> The losse will fall on us, not on the Poet:
> For he writes not for money, nor for praise,
> Nor to be call'd a Wit, nor to weare Bayes:
> Cares not for frownes or smiles: for now you'll say,
> Then why (the Devill) did he write a Play?
> He says, 'twas then with him, as now with you,
> He did it when he had nothing else to doe.[50]

Similarly, Denham altered his source material—Thomas Herbert's *Travels into Divers Parts of Asia and Afrique* (1638)—to prevent the desolation of any tragedy he does offer from being too much to bear. Unlike the source, the innocent Fatyma is spared death at her father's hands and is allowed to escape his clutches. Most radically an entirely new character, Solyman, is created, 'a foolish courtier' who is a favourite of the king, plagued with debts, and a notorious lover of women and wine. This distinctly cavalier Persian is also ineptly embroiled in a political conspiracy, imprisoned, and tortured for information about it. In case we should be too concerned about Solyman's fate—or too bound up in the play's tragic momentum—Denham reintroduces him in the concluding moments of a final scene which heralds the establishment of a new Persian order:

> Enter Solyman, as from the Rack
> Sophy: Alas poore Solyman, how is he altered?
> Solyman: I know not, Sir, it is an art your Grandfather had to make
> Me grow, I think he took me for some crooked Lady,
> I'm sure the engine is better for the purpose, than
> Steele bodies or bolsters […]
> Morat: I think they have stretcht his wit too.
> Solyman: This is your fathers love that lyes thus in my joints,
> I might have lov'd all the pockie whores in Persia, and
> Have felt it lesse in my bones […]
> Friend, I pray thee tell me whereabout my knees are,
> I would faine kneele to thank his Majestie. [51]

---

50  Denham, *The Sophy*, sig. A2r.
51  Ibid., p. 52.

The resurgence of hope and justice at the end of Denham's tragedy is closely allied to the renewal of a commitment to monarchy and the determination to re-sound comic notes in inappropriate places; cavalier wit can, it would seem, triumph over the pain of torture and even the most rigid of genre requirements.[52]

Quite what is being laughed at here is uncertain. It is tempting to suggest that Denham's introduction of Solyman, as well as being a structural challenge to the high seriousness of tragedy (and the historico-cultural verisimilitude which underwrites it), is also a form of gentle, topical humour. If this is the case, it is perhaps the figure of William Davenant who best unlocks it: Davenant was, after all, by 1642 a favourite of the king, plagued by debts, a notorious lover of women and wine who, famously disfigured by venereal infection since the 1630s, knew much about the pains conferred by 'pockie' bodies. He had also recently been imprisoned, threatened with death, and released for his own inept involvement in a political conspiracy (the army plot of 1641).[53] This suggestion is less fanciful than it might initially appear, since Denham's identity as a royalist writer in London and exiled court circles relied in good measure on his ability to make jokes at Davenant's expense. It could be that Denham's Solyman is a benign precursor to the anti-Davenant poems he plied with increasing bitterness after the publication of Davenant's epic *Gondibert*, and which were eventually published as a group of raucous printed satires called *Certain Verses Written by Several of Authors Friends; To be Reprinted with the Second Edition of Gondibert* (1651). The verses which Denham wrote and compiled for this volume mercilessly ridiculed Davenant's war service, his disfigured face, his meagre intellectual abilities and the social snobbery which saw him add an apostrophe to his surname. Such poems were so popular—there are more scribal copies of these works than *Coopers Hill*—that Denham continued to ply this trade in witty Davenant insults post-Restoration, even after his rival's death.[54] Thus his 1668 manuscript elegy for Davenant is obsessed with sounding intertextual echoes of the *Certain Verses* satires when it might more appropriately have been expected to summon airbrushed memories of the recently deceased:

> Though he is dead th'Imortall name
> Of William who from Avenant came,
> Who mixt with English Lombard Flame,

52  On *The Sophy*'s royalist commitments, see Amin Momeni's essay in this volume.

53  Mary Edmond, 'Davenant, Sir William (1606–1668)', *ODNB*; online edn, October 2009 <http://www.oxforddnb.com/view/article/7197> [accessed 12 July 2014]; Alfred Harbage, *William Davenant, Poet Venturer, 1608–1668* (Philadelphia: University of Pennsylvania Press, 1935), pp. 80–82; Arthur Nethercot, *Sir William D'Avenant: Poet Laureate and Playwright Manager* (Chicago: University of Chicago Press, 1938), pp. 182–99.

54  A search of the Union First-Line Index suggests that, on the evidence of survival rates of manuscript scribal copies, Denham's anti-Davenant poems proved even more popular than *Coopers Hill* during this period.

Shall live in the records of Fame
… [Cowley] His Friend hee to the Ancients shows;
Their former Feuds hee doth compose.
To show they are no longer Foes
Naso has lent him halfe his Nose.
In Poetry he raised a Scisme
Gainst the old Bards of Paganisme,
Styled by the Modernes D'avenantisme,
Condemn'd for want of Syllogisme.[55]

In harping on Davenant's obscure origins, his diseased nose, and the punctuation of his surname in singly-rhymed bathetic quatrains, Denham intimates that his death perhaps is not something to be lamented after all, even if he shall 'live in the record of Fame'. The parvenu's apostrophe signals utter nonsense rather than aristocratic mystique—'avenant' is no place, merely the French adjective for 'welcoming' or 'pleasant'—just as his passing produces self-consciously execrable verse. The uncertainty in John Aubrey's account of Davenant's funeral is perhaps related to this posthumous hostility. Pausing to admire the quality of Davenant's walnut coffin, Aubrey turned to his neighbour and found Denham, who either said that the coffin was the 'best' he ever saw or, if we take Aubrey's manuscript correction to be the accurate record of Denham's remark, the 'finest'. It could be, though, that the substitution is a polite veiling of what was actually said, and the distinction is telling: 'best coffin' condenses the callous wit of the rival courtier conscious of both his place at a grand state occasion and his enmity for the deceased; 'finest coffin', though hardly grief-stricken, suggests instead the more sensitive, discriminating judgement of the aesthete with an eye for expensive materials.[56]

## V

Davenant and Denham were not, therefore, the most likely friends or collaborators when Davenant moved to secure exclusive rights to *The Sophy* in December 1660. In fact, throughout the Interregnum and Restoration, all available evidence indicates that Denham was much closer to Davenant's great theatrical rival, Thomas Killigrew. The two poems Denham wrote about Killigrew in the 1650s were both printed in his collected works of 1668 and indicate the warmth of their relationship at every turn. In 'On Mr. Tho. Killigrew's Return from Venice', Killigrew is the embodiment of everything that is good about cavalier sociability; he is what

---

55  John Denham, 'Elegy on S^r William Davenant' in John Denham, *Poems and Translations* (1668), Yale University Beinecke Library, Osborn Collection, pb53, pp. 26–28.
56  Bod. MS Aubr. 6, fol. 47v; John Aubrey, *'Brief Lives', Chiefly of Contemporaries, Set Down by John Aubrey, between the Years 1669 & 1696*, ed. Andrew Clark, 2 vols (Oxford: Clarendon Press, 1898), i, p. 208.

Denham terms 'the good Fellow [who] is no where a stranger'.[57] In 'A Dialogue between Sir John Pooley and Mr Thomas Killigrew', it is Pooley who is the object of the biting satire, whilst Killigrew emerges as an advocate of witty, plain English which cuts through the baffling malapropisms of his cousin.[58] Killigrew was capable of returning Denham's affectionate humour. For instance, the final act of his semi-autobiographical two-part play, *Thomaso*—printed for the first time in the folio edition of Killigrew's works in 1664—describes a particularly convivial meeting between 'Embassadour Will, Resident Tom and John the Poet with the nose', who are glossed in the margin as Killigrew, Will Crofts, and John Denham. It is telling that the men are described as 'all Gondibert's dire foes' with the reference to Denham as 'the poet with the nose' situating him in direct opposition to Davenant, a pre-eminent rival without one.[59]

Killigrew and Denham's relationship after the Restoration intensified to such a degree that it could border on the corrupt—as in 1667 where there is evidence of their having begged estates together, a particularly sharp practice involving the appropriation of prisoners' property for the exclusive use of certain courtiers.[60] Their involvement and collaboration in a piece of professional court theatre gave added piquancy to Davenant's acquisition of rights to *The Sophy* as part of his desperate scramble to assemble a repertory of performable work to match that of the King's Company in late 1660. Part of the function of the 1660 order was that it allowed Davenant to reclaim exclusive rights to his own plays, an important intervention since we know that Killigrew's company had already staged *The Unfortunate Lovers* at Vere Street on 19 November. Davenant's dismay that his work was being performed by a rival company (who claimed rights to it, like so many other plays in the repertoire, on the grounds that they were direct descendants of the King's Men) may well have been compounded by the knowledge that he had already been outmanoeuvred for the first court performance before Charles II, which was to take place at the private Cockpit theatre on the very same day. The honour on that grand occasion went instead to Killigrew's company who offered the king a version of Jonson's *Epicoene* complete with a new prologue by Denham, who had also recently organised the king's coronation ceremony. (Revealingly, both Leslie Hotson and Alfred Harbage incorrectly attributed the prologue to Davenant, assuming erroneously that both patentees and their companies would have collaborated at the first court performance.)[61] Whether or not he attended

57  Denham, *Poems and Translations*, p. 72.
58  Ibid., pp. 122–26.
59  Thomas Killigrew, *Comedies and Tragedies Written by Thomas Killigrew* (London, 1664), p. 456
60  On Denham and Killigrew begging estates, see Alfred Harbage, *Thomas Killigrew: Cavalier Dramatist, 1612–1683* (Philadelphia: University of Pennsylvania Press, 1930), pp. 112–13.
61  The Thomason copy of the prologue which Hotson used does not indicate authorship, but another printing of the text annotated by a contemporary suggests that it was 'By Sir Jo: Denham'. See Bodl., Wood 398 (16); Hotson, *Commonwealth and Restoration Stage*, p. 208; Harbage, *Thomas Killigrew*, p. 118; W.H. Kelliher, 'Denham, Sir John (1614/15–1669)', *ODNB*; online edn, January 2008 <http://www.oxforddnb.com/view/article/7481> [accessed 12 July 2014].

the performance, when Denham's prologue was published as a single-sheet folio within a matter of days, Davenant would have felt its opening exploration of the relationships between Interregnum disloyalty, royal favour, and re-established court theatre especially keenly. It is tempting, too, to hear an exultant anti-Davenant note in its claim that theatrical success only comes with unswerving devotion to monarchy:

> Greatest of Monarchs, welcome to this place
> Which Majesty so oft was wont to grace
> Before our Exile, to divert the Court,
> And balance weighty Cares with harmless sport.
> This truth we can to our advantage say,
> They that would have no King, would have no play [62]

If we recall that Denham's appointment as Surveyor of the Works in June 1660 was particularly controversial, since he was appointed ahead of the widely favoured candidate, John Webb, the man who worked so closely with Davenant to give his Protectorate operas their scenery, we can see that Davenant's place at the Restoration court was not a straightforwardly comfortable one.[63] Even if he did have the security of one-half of a stage monopoly, he was still working in a theatrical culture alongside a number of intensely hostile rivals—such as Denham and Sir Henry Herbert—who were closer than he was to the king and who still harboured grudges about his relationships with Commonwealth and Protectorate administrations. The Lord Chamberlain's order of December 1660 giving Davenant exclusive rights to eleven old plays should, I am arguing, be read in relationship to all of these circumstances.

Acquiring rights to *The Sophy* was, then, a product of Davenant's embittered and embattled position in this period, some kind of manoeuvre on his part made in direct relation to John Denham. The precise nature of this manoeuvre is unclear. If the play remained unperformed until after Davenant and Denham's death, then it might have been some kind of blocking strategy which sought to limit the possibility of a bitter adversary's success in the re-established theatres. Davenant and the Duke's Company were, however, so desperate for repertory in the early 1660s that this seems extremely unlikely.[64] If, though, the play was indeed performed during this period, and the gap in the performance records really is a lacuna, then a series of plausible alternative explanations emerge. Davenant knew that *The Sophy* had been printed and had gained some popularity in cavalier circles in the 1640s, but also realised that, owing to its sprezzatura qualities and over-reliance on wit, the tragedy had never been performed and was still unclaimed by

---

62 *A Prologue to his Majestie at the First Play Presented at the Cockpit in Whitehall* (London, 1660).
63 On Webb's working relationship with Davenant, see Kroll, *Restoration Drama*, pp. 93–122.
64 Milhous, *Thomas Betterton*, p. 15.

Killigrew and the King's Company. In urgent need of stageable material, he may thus have requested rights to the play knowing he could profit from a rival's work whilst simultaneously trading on nostalgia for pre-war cavalier culture and serving an emerging Restoration vogue for witty drama by genteel amateurs like Denham.[65] Equally suggestive is the possibility that his company rehearsed this play alongside the expanded, two-part version of Davenant's own version of a drama about the political ramifications of jealousy in the Muslim world, *The Siege of Rhodes*, which opened to such applause at their new home at Lincoln's Inn Fields at the end of June 1661.[66] If the Duke's Company were indeed switching between the imaginative recreation of Persia and Turkey in some of their early work at this venue, between Denham's cavalier Solyman and Davenant's much-celebrated Solyman the Magnificent, it might be thought to prefigure their practice later in the decade when they presented Roger Boyle, Earl of Orrery's *The Tragedy of Mustapha, Son of Solyman the Magnificent* (1665), as a companion piece to Davenant's Islamic blockbuster.[67]

## VI

Though literary scholars and theatre historians have largely failed to notice it, Davenant's insistence on the right to produce a play by Denham, hostile though he may have been, says much about his awareness of the urgent need and commercial advantages of getting work by living writers into his company's repertoire (and into an industry decimated and starved of fresh writing talent for a generation following the closure of the theatres in 1642). It is plausible, then, that *The Sophy* helped to fill a gap between the Duke's Company's production of Davenant's own work in the first months after the opening of Lincoln's Inn Fields—the *Siege of Rhodes, The Wits,* and *Love and Honour* all played repeatedly during this period—and their subsequent staging of plays by Abraham Cowley, Thomas Porter, James Shirley, and Sir Robert Stapylton later in the 1661–62 season.[68] Whether or not this was the case, putting Denham's play back

---

65  On genteel amateurs and the early Restoration stage, see Kewes, *Authorship and Appropriation*, pp. 132–42, 191–98.

66  This necessarily remains conjectural. John Downes recorded that both parts of *The Siege of Rhodes* were performed alongside Davenant's *The Wits* in the opening fortnight at the new site. He does not list *The Sophy* amongst the Duke's Company's principal old 'stock plays' performed at Lincoln's Inn Fields between spring 1662 and May 1665. Downes's record is, though, notoriously incomplete, his first modern editor drawing attention to 'its brevities and blunders, its deficiencies and its omissions'; Montague Summers (ed.), *Roscius Anglicanus by John Downes* (London, 1929), pp. vii, 20–26.

67  John Downes remembered that Davenant's involvement in the production of *Mustapha* was particularly intense, Davenant taking 'great care of having it perfect and exactly performed'; *Roscius Anglicanus*, p. 28. On *Mustapha* as a self-conscious sequel to *The Siege of Rhodes* see Birchwood, *Staging Islam*, pp. 129–41.

68  Edward Browne reported having seen Stapylton's *The Step Mother* and *The Slighted Maid* as well as Shirley's *Gratefull Servant* and Porter's *The Villain* at Lincoln's Inn Fields between early 1661

into the December order, and looking precisely at what was being restored to the arts with the return of Charles II, shows how one of the most important documents for Restoration theatre history not only preserved Shakespeare for a new age and a different stage but was also haunted by the spectres of civil war and Interregnum royalism and, more specifically, by the intense rivalry of William Davenant and John Denham.

---

and 1663. Cowley's *The Cutter of Coleman Street* played to a packed house for an entire week in December 1661; Van Lennep et al., *The London Stage, Part I*, pp. 36, 44.

# 4 John Denham's *The Sophy* and Anglo-Persian Political Parallels

*Amin Momeni*

## I

Towards the end of Charles I's reign, representations of Islamic Persia and Persians held an increasingly important place in English drama. Surviving play texts show that Persian characters appeared in plays more frequently in this period than previously in Tudor-Stuart English drama, and Persian dramatis personae became more fully realised. The playwrights achieved the latter in part by dramatising real historical figures, and by employing characters such as Sophy, Mirza, and Shah Abbas I (d. 1629), who were known to English audiences through popular works such as the two travel narratives of Thomas Herbert's (1606–1682), a first and 'expanded' second edition which were published in 1634 and 1638 respectively: *A Relation of some Yeares Travaile* [...] *into Afrique and the Greater Asia, Especially the Territories of the Persian Monarchie* (1634) and *Some Yeares Travels into Divers Parts* [...] *Especially the two Famous Empires, the Persian, and the Great Mogull* (1638).[1] In his narratives, Herbert provided detailed accounts of diplomatic encounters with Shah Abbas I, and, thereby, familiarised readers with contemporary Islamic Persian figures. Herbert had been part of the ill-fated journey of Sir Dodmore Cotton, Charles I's official ambassador to Safavid Persia in 1627–28, who died in Persia in July 1628 after suffering from 'severe dysentery', leaving the mission incomplete.[2] In conjuring up Safavid Persian dramatis personae on stage, playwrights such as John Denham, in 1642, and Robert Baron, possibly in 1647, were therefore dramatising characters who would be recognised by the audiences and readers of their plays. Given the tense political climate of the English Civil War, it is also likely that the audiences would have been sensitive to parallels, more or less forcefully implied in the plays, between the Persian

1 Thomas Herbert, *A Relation of some Yeares Travaile, Begunne Anno 1626* (London: Printed by William Stansby, and Jacob Bloome, 1634), sigs E2v, Q3r, S1r; idem, *Some Yeares Travels into Divers Parts of Asia and Afrique* (London: R. Bi. for Iacob Blome and Richard Bishop, 1638), sigs Ii3r, Oo1v, Oo2r, Z2v; see also Ronald H. Fritze, 'Herbert, Sir Thomas, first baronet (1606–1682)', *ODNB*.
2 Cyrus Ghani, *Shakespeare, Persia, and the East* (Washington, DC: Mage, 2008), p. 89; William Foster, *Thomas Herbert Travels in Persia, 1627–1629* (London: Routledge, 1928), p. xvi.

and English monarchies. The royalist playwrights of the late Caroline period, in other words, engaged and intersected with Caroline policies by casting Safavid Persia and Persians. In this chapter, I argue that Denham and Baron used Persian analogies in the period in an attempt to criticise, warn, and preserve the English monarchy; in effect, to influence England's domestic policy.

Thirteen years after the death of Shah Abbas I in 1629, Denham put on the English stage this most potent Persian king, 'who re-established the frontiers of his kingdom, a good deal of the territory of which had been lost to foreign invaders […], and to whom much of the credit for the architectural glories of his new capital, Isfahan, is attributed'.[3] The title page of *The Sophy* states that it was published in 1642, and that it had been 'acted at the Private House in Black Friars by his Majesties Servants'.[4] Critics argue that the play, a verse tragedy, was issued anonymously along with Denham's *Coopers Hill* on the very eve of the civil war; it is also speculated that, despite its title-page advertisement, *The Sophy* had remained unperformed in the early 1640s, as there exist 'no textual traces' of its being staged in this period.[5] The title of *The Sophy* projects the title of the ruler of Persia during the Safavid period (1502–1736). The drama features the Persian court, including the king's grandson, Soffy, who would become the Persian monarch towards the end of the play. *The Sophy* contains detailed depictions of Persian figures such as Shah Abbas I, and to this end appears thorough in terms of dramatising Safavid Persians. Denham used Safavid Persian dramatis personae during a time when England was about to undergo a devastating internal turbulence and instability. *The Sophy* was an attempt to subdue or, perhaps, decelerate the course of such devastation through theatre.

The following is a synopsis of the tragedy. While at the battle frontiers with the Ottoman Turks, Mirza, Shah Abbas's 'brave sonne', whose 'glory like high *Phoebus* shine[s]', falls victim to the conspiracy of the royal counsellors, Haly and Caliph. These plotters, who 'shew [the king] nothing / But in the glasse of flatterie', betray the king and Mirza, the general of the Persian army. Turned against Mirza by the conspirators, the Shah blinds and incarcerates the prince for fear of Mirza's alleged attempts to usurp his throne. Without the king's knowledge, Haly then poisons the blinded, incarcerated prince. The prince dies powerless, begging 'for an houre of life', and forced to 'leave to heaven […] revenge and justice'. Abbas, now delusional and overwhelmed by 'some fearfull dreame', regrets blinding and imprisoning his noble Mirza. The desperate king dies shortly after his son, crying 'sure one hell's / Too little to contain me, and too narrow / For all my crimes'. Soffy ascends the throne, and starts his 'raigne in bloud' by sacrificing Haly's and Caliph's lives as a sign of the new king's 'dutie and justice'.[6]

---

3  David Morgan, 'After Abbas', *Times Literary Supplement*, 7 December 2012, 9.
4  Title page of John Denham, *The Sophy* (London: Richard Hearne for Thomas Walkley, 1642).
5  W.H. Kelliher, 'Denham, Sir John (1614/15–1669)', *ODNB*; Marcus Nevitt's chapter in this volume, p. 53.
6  *The Sophy*, sigs B3r, B1v, G4r, H1r, H3r.

## II

In her analysis of *The Sophy*, Parvin Loloi argues that 'the idea that Abbas does in any way represent Charles [I], or Denham's views on Charles, is dismissed (surely correctly) by O Hehir as fantastically improbable'.[7] My reading of the play, by contrast, adheres more closely to John M. Wallace's and Robert Wilcher's notion that the play does comment, directly and indirectly, on contemporary affairs. A direct parallel between Shah Abbas I and Charles I may not exist, but there are references in the play which remind us of Charles, namely, the 'mistakes made by Denham's "arbitrary ruler" and "good prince"—one by letting too much power fall into the hands of evil counsellors, the other by absenting himself from the capital at the crucial moment'.[8] At the beginning of the civil war, then, *The Sophy* may well have been read as offering a warning counsel to the king, operating as an Anglo-Persian analogy. From the standpoint of such analogy, I aim to build on Wallace's and Wilcher's arguments on the play's contemporary significance by examining the representations of Islamic Persia in the play and their topical resonance in 1640s England.

*The Sophy* begins, in fact, with a warning. At the outset of the tragedy the Ottoman Turks pose an evident threat to the English and the world of Christendom on the one hand, and to the Persians on the other. In the opening lines, Morat, a loyal Persian courtier, addresses Abdall, a lord and friend of Prince Mirza's, and warns of the great number of the Ottoman military: 'We know not their designe: But for their strength / The disproportion is so great, we cannot, but / Expect a fatall consequence'.[9] By the time *The Sophy* was written, the Persians had been intermittently at war with the Ottoman Turks for more than a century. Denham's dramatic representation of the Turks in this tragedy conforms to the persistently negative contemporary British and European perceptions of the Ottomans. Indeed, it is true to say that

> many writers, theatre-goers, and sailors conflated Muslims with Turks, and the repeated confusion of terms, led to a superimposition of the Ottomans' imperial danger onto religion so that Islam became synonymous with Ottoman military expansion. [...] Such confusion had a lasting effect on British perceptions of Islam, since this association of a religious creed with an empire cemented the identification of faith with military conquest.[10]

---

7  Parvin Loloi, *Two Seventeenth-Century Plays* (Salzburg; Oxford: University of Salzburg, 1998), p. lxiv; O Hehir, *HD*, p. 43.

8  John M. Wallace, '"Examples Are Best Precepts": Readers and Meanings in Seventeenth-Century Poetry', *Critical Inquiry*, 1 (1974), 273–90 (p. 274); see also Robert Wilcher, *The Writing of Royalism, 1628–1660* (Cambridge: Cambridge University Press, 2001), p. 118.

9  *The Sophy*, sig. B1r.

10  Gerald Maclean and Nabil Matar, *Britain and the Islamic World* (New York: Oxford University Press, 2011), p. 32.

Such perceptions are evident in dramatic representations of Islamic Persians; Abbas is presented as a powerful Muslim ruler who, due to a tragic flaw, fails in wisdom and kingship and dies. Denham, however, establishes a Persian-Ottoman military confrontation in the play by opposing the Turks to the Safavids, introducing the former as 'fatall' to the latter. Additionally, the fact that both the English and the Persians were enemies of the Ottomans meant that Denham could present the two nations, England and Persia, as sharing common ground.

Denham's attempt to draw political parallels also has a cultural dimension. In a conversation between Abbas's favourite courtier, Haly, whose name is the English distortion of Ali—the fourth Muslim Caliph who ruled after the death of Muhammad—and his confidant, Mirvan, Haly describes his relationship with the prince as follows: 'Have I not found him out as many dangers / As *Iuno* did for *Hercules*: yet he returns / Like *Hercules*, doubled in strength and honour'.[11] Haly complains that his evil plots, or 'dangers', to trap the prince so far have proved futile and have only made Mirza stronger and more worthy of 'honour'. By comparing Mirza with Hercules and Juno with himself, Haly draws a parallel between figures from Islamic Shi'ism and Roman and Greek mythology. By so doing, Denham makes the world of the play explicable to the English audiences and by such comparisons finds a way to enlarge these characters. It would have been usual for the audiences to think of Juno as jealous and vengeful towards Jupiter's lovers and offspring, including Hercules, who were inordinately powerful and heroic mythological figures. It is possible that the play intended to portray Haly and Mirza in the same light, associating them with '*Iuno*' and '*Hercules*' respectively.

Throughout *The Sophy*, Denham characterises figures such as Mirza in relation both to classical Persian and classical Roman and Greek mythology. Political and cultural analogies are thus intertwined and made inseparable. For example, when Haly and Abbas are speaking of Mirza, Haly asserts: 'I'me sure hee's honoured, and lov'd by all; / The Souldiers god, the peoples Idoll'. The king replies: 'I *Haly*, / The Persians still worship the rising sunne'.[12] This dialogue is significant in several ways. Metaphorically, 'the rising sunne' refers to the heir apparent, or monarch-in-waiting, by whose rise Abbas is frightened. Abbas's allusion to the 'rising sunne' is a commonplace phrase, certainly, but one that held additional significance in classical Persian culture—light in general had been a holy element for the Zoroastrians of Persia for centuries, as is particularly evident during the Achaemenid and Sassanian Empires. At this stage, through Persian cultural features, the dramatist differentiates the two major clashing parties in the Persian court. On one side stand the king and those who intend to abuse royal power to eliminate the prince; on the other, Mirza and his affiliates, including his son, Soffy, dramatised by the playwright through classical entities such as '*Hercules*'.

11  *The Sophy*, sig. B4v.
12  Ibid., sig. C3v.

Denham's usage of classical elements becomes increasingly visible throughout the play. Elsewhere in the tragedy the princess, Mirza's wife, addresses him thus:

> Waking I know no cause, but in my sleepe
> My fancy still presents such dreames, the terrors,
> As did *Andromache's* the night before
> Her *Hector* fell; but sure 'tis more then fancie.
> Either our guardian Angels, or the Gods
> Inspire us, or some naturall instinct,
> Fore-tells approaching dangers.[13]

Here, the princess draws on a shared European culture, from Homer's *Iliad*, to further familiarise the audiences with herself and Mirza. She also suggests that there exists a warlike condition from which she struggles, like Andromache, to save the couple. She fails, and the prince is detained and blinded. Immediately after being blinded, in his long soliloquy, Mirza points to another classical mythological figure:

> Death, and what followes death, 'twas that that stamp't
> A terrour on the brow of Kings; that gave
> Fortune her deity, and Jove his thunder.
> Banish but fear of death, those Gyant names
> Of Majestie, Power, Empire, finding nothing
> To be their object, will be nothing too:
> Then he dares yet be free that dares to die,
> May laugh at the grim face of law and scorne,
> The cruell wrinkle of a Tyrants brow.[14]

By presenting Mirza's speech in this style, Denham tries to accommodate Persian dramatis personae to Caroline English audiences by making the Persians speak like Shakespeareans. Men's fear of death, Mirza implies, is what makes cowards of us all: this fear of death makes a goddess of Fortune—because men are afraid that, if she turns against them, they might die—and fuels Jove's thunder, as men who fear death cower before his anger. By contrast, when men are unafraid of death, then 'Majestie, Power [and] Empire', which depend upon men's fear of death for their high status in the world, lose that status.

In contrast, Abbas, Mirza's father, is associated with Islamic prophecy rather than ancient and classical features. Having manipulated Abbas and persuaded him to turn against his son, Haly and Caliph now, ironically, become the reluctant instruments of the Shah's anger against his son. The tyrant Abbas orders Caliph

---

13  Ibid., sig. D4v.
14  Ibid., sig. E3v.

to be absolutely obedient to his will, and when necessary to 'varnish' his 'actions' with an appearance of religiosity:

> We but advance you to advance our purposes:
> Nay, even in all religions
> Their learnedst, and their seeming holiest men, but serve
> To worke their masters ends; and varnish o're
> Their actions, with some specious pious colour.
> No scruples; doo't, or by our holy Prophet,
> The death my rage intends to him [Mirza], is thine.[15]

Abbas threatens Caliph that his disobedience may lead to his death, and swears to it 'by our holy Prophet', implying, at the same time, that the blinding and death he intends for Mirza is also sanctioned or endorsed 'by our holy Prophet'. But courtiers loyal to Mirza are well aware of Haly's and Caliph's evil conspiracy. In their dialogue, Abdall and Morat condemn Caliph's religious hypocrisy. Morat exclaims, 'But oh this Saint-like Devill! / This damned Caliph, to make the King beleeve / To kill his sonne's religion'. Morat means that Caliph has made the king believe that killing Mirza is a religious deed. Abdall replies

> Poor Princes, how are they mis-led,
> While they, whose sacred office 'tis to bring
> Kings to obey their God, and men their King,
> By these mysterious linkes to fixe and tye
> Them to the foot-stoole of Deity:
> Even by these men, Religion, that should be
> The curbe, is made the spurre to tyrannie.[16]

The 'Religion', here, is clearly meant to be Islam, and the context is the Persian court. Religion is compared to a curb that is meant to control the horse of tyranny. On the contrary, it functions as a spur to provoke the tyrannical horse of the Islamic Persian court. The 'tyrannie' that Abdall refers to is that of the princes and kings, driven on by evil counsellors. 'Princes' in its plural form suggests that the victims of such counsellors are not confined to Islamic Persia. Perhaps, the playwright intends to imply how other princes of the Islamic world, particularly those of the Ottomans, are also 'mis-led' by the same unscrupulous clerical advisors who induce a monarch, or prince, to take a pernicious religious path. But this may have been understood by Caroline English audiences in a different way. Outside the context of the Persian court, Abdall's lines apply to any princes, 'sacred office[s]', kings, and religions. Those who possess such offices are responsible for guiding monarchs and men towards the right way. But with their failure, religious leaders such as William Laud are left to feel Abdall's lashing criticism.

15  Ibid., sig. D1v.
16  Ibid., sig. E1v.

At this stage, Denham's attempt is to emphasise further the differences between various clashing attitudes in the Persian court which he established earlier in the play. In addition, the playwright, by implication, intends to leave Caroline English readers/audiences to draw their own conclusions with regards to contemporary England, allowing them to create dramatic parallels with opposing strands of English political thought in the period, including the fundamental divide between parliamentarians and royalists. By the time the tragedy comes to an end, we see that one of the members of Mirza's family, his son Soffy, ascends the throne, and continues the Persian monarchy. All other characters—including Abbas, Haly, and Caliph—associated with Islamic elements are destined to die. Soffy starts his reign by sacrificing Haly and Caliph as an attempt to revive justice, and by doing so symbolically purges the state.

Haly's representation is multidimensional: first, his name has religious connotations; secondly, he is dramatised as an evil plotter; and lastly, he is an influential court favourite. He succeeds in manipulating the Persian king, and to this end uses his authority to persuade Abbas towards tragic purposes. In this regard, Haly could quite conceivably gesture towards Thomas Wentworth (1593–1641), the first Earl of Strafford, whose 'radicalism […] recommended him to the king as chief councillor when Charles realized that the very foundations of his monarchy were about to crumble in the summer of 1639'.[17] O Hehir's observation that 'those so minded could see in the intriguing favorite, Haly, a representation either of Strafford, or of all the "evil councillors" about King Charles' is persuasive, though as he also observes, *direct* parallels with Strafford 'are unlikely in the extreme'.[18] A combination of religious authority and evil, however, is more fully realised in one of Denham's other characters. Caliph, as the name immediately suggests, is the religious leader in the tragedy, and the one who believes Mirza's 'Ambition, [is] the disease of Vertue, bred / Like surfets from an undigested fullness, / [and which] Meets death in that which is the meanes of life'.[19] Caliph goes further in raising his own status, claiming divine authority for his words in declaring that

> Great *Mahomet*, to whom our Soveraigne life,
> And Empire is most deare, appearing, thus
> Advis'd me in a vision: Tell the King,
> The Prince his sonne attempts his life and Crowne.

and that these 'are the Prophets revelations'.[20] Caliph accuses Mirza of having an intention towards the throne while his father still reigns. Only an apparently religiously inspired man, informed by the revelation of 'Great *Mahomet*', could hope to persuade the Lords of the Council of Mirza's alleged treason. Suggesting that he is an imam, Caliph issues a fatwa, a holy order given by a religious

---

17 Ronald G. Asch, 'Wentworth, Thomas, first earl of Strafford (1593–1641)', *ODNB*.
18 O Hehir, *HD*, p. 42.
19 *The Sophy*, sig. D1v.
20 Ibid., sig. D1v.

authority, in order to eliminate Mirza. In fact, he attempts to persuade by intimating that his information comes from a divine vision, from the prophet's revelation, and that these must not be slighted or disregarded. In such a seemingly holy decision, however, lies Caliph's and Haly's personal achievement in ruining the prince, and thus in violating the Persian monarchy.

Like that of Haly, the figure that Caliph represents would have been familiar to theatre audiences during the civil war. The 'grand *Caliph* shall set a grave religious face / Upon the businesse' of conspiracy against the royal family.[21] 'The evil Caliph, who cloaks with religion the sins of the Shah', and the powerful religious figure in the Caroline High Church 'could be identified with Archbishop [William] Laud', albeit in a qualified way.[22] At the same time, from the royalists' perspective, the general religious prejudice suggested by the person of Caliph could be interpreted as criticism of Puritan attributes, showing that the dramatist intended to tread a middle path between extremes.[23] Their 'religious face[s]' hide a sinister intention beneath what is apparent; they intend to dethrone royalty by means of the 'cloaks' of religious authority. Some of Denham's poetry also reflect his hostility towards religious zeal. For example, in 'The True Presbyterian' (1661) he refers to a '*Presbyter*' as a 'Monstrous thing' who lies 'for gain unto the Holy-Ghost'.[24] In 'The Progress of Learning' (1668), Denham praises 'the Sun of knowledge' and human intellect, while creating a sharp contrast between religious prejudice and intellectual reasoning.[25] In *The Sophy*, the playwright criticises religious fraud in the state represented—obliquely—by politicians and religious leaders such as Strafford and Laud. By depicting Anglo-Persian religious parallels on stage, Denham prepares the audience for an even more politically sensitive analogy involving the English monarch. However, this ultimate parallel—between Charles I and his Persian counterpart—differs from those previously discussed.

O Hehir rejects the idea 'that Abbas does in any way represent Charles, or Denham's views on Charles'. I argue that political parallels do exist between Persian figures in the play and Charles, and are certainly not 'fantastically improbable'. Such comparisons are, however, of a different kind to the one-to-one analogies between Haly and Strafford, or Caliph and Laud. Instead, Denham attempts to gesture towards Charles's errors via two different dramatised royal figures, Abbas and Mirza. In other words, these two royal Persians embody, in combination,

21 Ibid., sig. C4r.
22 O Hehir, *HD*, p. 42.
23 I am aware that, when writing about 'The Puritan Revolution', John Morrill considers numerous types of puritan opposition to 'Anglicanism' during 1640–60, such as the 'Presbyterians' and 'Independents'. But in this chapter, I simply use the term 'puritan' in its general sense, i.e., in opposition to the high church Anglican party of William Laud. See Morrill, 'The Puritan Revolution', in John Coffey and Paul C.H. Lim (eds), *The Cambridge Companion to Puritanism* (Cambridge: Cambridge University Press, 2008), pp. 67–88; O Hehir, *HD*, p. 43.
24 John Denham, 'The True Presbyterian without Disguise' (London, 1661), sig. A2r.
25 Robert Anderson, MD (ed.), *A Complete Edition of the Poets of Great Britain*, 13 vols (London: John and Arthur Arch, Bell and Bradfute and I. Mundell and Co., 1792–95), v, p. 687.

some of the mistakes Charles has hitherto made during his reign, particularly during the civil war.[26] One side of this analogy, the Mirza-Charles parallel, would be reinforced by Robert Baron a couple of years later in the dedicatory poem of his tragedy, *Mirza* (1647). But what links Mirza and Abbas to Charles I in Denham's tragedy?

As outlined above, there exists a palpable difference between Denham's presentation of the religious approaches taken by Mirza and Abbas. While he depicts Mirza and his followers as classical Persians with no inclination to Islamic thought, Abbas is portrayed as a man who sees himself as a transcendental agent on earth whose presence and empire is protected by the holy prophet Muhammad. Mirza refers to numerous classical mythological gods in his speech, whereas Abbas repeatedly uses Islamic terms.[27] This kind of religious distinction between the two royal characters mirrors, I wish to argue, the broad distinction that existed between Anglicans and Puritans. The tyrant Abbas and the courtiers around him may well have evoked Puritan parliamentarians in the audiences' mind. The common ground between Abbas and his courtiers, and the Puritan parliamentarians, is that they both employ an overt religious ideology to advance their own purposes. At the same time, a directly political parallel exists between Mirza and Charles, in that both leave 'the capital at the crucial moment', one in the play and the other in reality.[28] 'Charles's decision-making in early January 1642 may have been rational, but this did not make it any less disastrous. [...]. He had surrendered control of London to his enemies [...] by withdrawing from' the city'.[29] Perhaps from the English royalists' perspective in 1650s, the way in which Abbas uses Caliph to maintain the crown by the help of religious authority would hint at the way Cromwell exploited religious piety to become the Protector of the Commonwealth. Denham repeatedly and explicitly describes Abbas as a tyrant king. Such a characteristic conforms to 'the concept of parliamentary tyranny' on the side of Cromwell and other Puritan forces under his command during the civil war.[30] Abbas is not successful in winning any kind of war against his son although his emphasised characteristics, such as tyranny, match those of his contemporary Puritan counterpart.

In a conversation between the king and his lords, and in response to an attack by the Turkish army, whose 'numbers [are] five times' more than theirs, Abbas orders

---

26  It is equally possible that Denham is critiquing the bad advice that Charles has received from his advisors, including Strafford and Laud, during the eleven years of Charles's Personal Rule. See Richard Cust's discussion on 'Laudianism and the Personal Rule' in Richard Cust, *Charles I: A Political Life* (Harlow: Pearson, 2005), pp. 133–48.

27  *The Sophy*, sigs C4r, D1v, E3v.

28  Wallace, ' "Examples Are Best Precepts" ', p. 274.

29  Cust, *Charles I*, pp. 326–27. We also see that Denham favours Mirza's party, as one would expect from a royalist writer, by showing Soffy ascend the throne at the end of the play to continue the royal order despite all disruptions and devastations caused in the royal family. This, in 1642, may have seemed the most encouraging part of a bitter story.

30  Richard Cust and Ann Hughes (eds), *The English Civil War* (London: Arrowsmith, 1997), p. 16.

his lords to 'let twenty thousand men be raised'. But the king is soon informed by the lords that his 'Treasures / Are quite exhausted' and 'the Exchequer's empty'. Abbas replies, 'talke not to me of Treasures, or Exchequers, / Send for five hundred of the wealthiest Burgers, / Their shops and ships are my Exchequer'. Abdall, following an aside which reads ''twere better you you [*sic*] could say their hearts', continues 'Sir upon your late demands / They answered they were poor', to which, unconvinced, Abbas replies,

> Sure the villaines hold a correspondence
> With the enemy, and thus they would betray us:
> First give us up to want, then to contempt,
> And then to ruine; but tell those sonnes of earth
> Ile have their money, or their heads.
> 'Tis my command, when such occasions are,
> No Plea must serve, 'tis cruelty to spare.[31]

In the light of the Ottoman military attack the king orders an additional increase in the number of troops, despite a lack of financial resources. In an act of tyranny, Abbas officially taxes 'five hundred of the wealthiest Burgers', or citizens, in order to supply the money required for military reinforcements. He particularly refers to 'their shops and ships' from which money is to be provided by the lords of the Persian court. Abdall's aside shows his resentment for the king's order to extract more money from people who are already poor. Now delusional, the tyrant Abbas accuses the poor of being in league with the Turks in order to betray the Persian monarchy. Abbas also suggests that he himself is possessed of a godlike transcendental status, far above the ordinary 'sonnes of earth'. But more importantly, Abbas's reference to 'shops and ships' as the king's 'Exchequer' is likely to have struck a resonant contemporary note in 1642. The mention of ships reminds the audiences of Charles's fiscal expedients with Ship Money, funds from which financed a fleet of ships launched by Charles in the summer of 1635, to give England 'renewed credibility as a military force'.[32] Denham dramatises Abbas as an analogy for Charles in order to warn, indirectly, about the English monarch's resented policy. Delusional and desperate Abbas dies at the end regretting his past decisions, and thus leaves a powerful, tragic message. The royalist playwright is, however, aware of the dangers in suggesting death for the English monarch as a result of his controversial policy. The parallel between Charles and the Persian Abbas is sufficiently diffuse,

---

31   *The Sophy*, sigs B2r-v.
32   Cust, *Charles I*, p. 128; Cust & Hughes (eds), *The English Civil War*, p. 162. Ship Money was the most controversial of the financial devices during Charles's Personal Rule (1629–40). It had 'ancient origins, for since Plantagenet times the crown had occasionally, in times of special need, required the ports and maritime countries to furnish ships for the navy or money in lieu'. For the first time, Charles extended ship money to the whole country in 1628 in an attempt to increase the government's revenue. See Austin Woolrych, *Britain in Revolution, 1625–1660* (Oxford: Oxford University Press, 2002), p. 67.

and mitigated by the Persian setting, to avoid any danger of reprisal against Denham by more zealous, hardline members of the king's party.

## III

Anglo-Persian parallels were not confined to Denham's tragedy in the drama of the late Caroline period. Five years after *The Sophy*, Robert Baron's *Mirza* would also suggest parallels between Persian and English royalty. McJannet observes that

> if, as Baron claims in his preface to the reader, he had already written three acts of his play before Denham's *The Sophy* appeared, he may have meant these words for the king's eyes, and the work might even have been published and read by Charles or other members of the court before his defeat in 1646 and his death in 1649.[33]

Baron's dedicatory poem, along with McJannet's speculation, supports the idea that the play was *meant* to be presented to the English monarch, whether in fact it was presented or not. The very opening lines suggest Mirza as a Persian model: 'To wait on *YOU*, the Persian *MIRZAS* come / From the fair shades of his *Elizium*'.[34] Here, Mirza is depicted as a royal Persian prince whose experience can help Charles to avoid monarchic ruin and downfall.

*The Sophy* and *Mirza* are very similar in terms of plot, genre, and theme. There are, however, differences in the number of characters employed by the two writers. Baron's dramatis personae outnumber those of Denham's. *Mirza* attempts to introduce more Islamic Persian characters to English readers, and in this regard is more educational and didactic than Denham's tragedy. Baron explains other key plot differences in his tragedy in an epistle to the reader:

> In his [Denham's *The Sophy*] neither doth the Prince kill any of his *Torturers*; Nor doth *FATYMA* die, which I take to be one of the most important parts of the story, and the compleatest Conquest that ever Revenge obtained over Vertue. In that King ABBAS dies too [...].[35]

Baron also replied to allegations accusing him of plagiarising Denham's work.[36] In addressing the reader, he claims that 'I had finished three compleat Acts of this Tragedy before I saw that [Denham's *The Sophy*], nor was I then discouraged

---

33  Linda McJannet, 'Bringing in a Persian', *Medieval and Renaissance Drama in England: An Annual Gathering of Research, Criticism and Reviews*, 12 (1999), 236–67 (p. 259).

34  Robert Baron, *Mirza. A tragedie, really acted in Persia, in the last age. Illustrated with historicall annotations* (London: Humphrey Moseley, T. Dring, 1647), sig. A2r.

35  Ibid., sig. A5v.

36  These allegations include, for example, the charge that *Mirza* is based heavily on Ben Jonson's *Catiline*. See Jesse Franklin Bradley, 'Robert Baron's Tragedy of *Mirza*', *Modern Language Notes*, 34 (1919), 402–08 (p. 402).

from proceeding, seeing the most ingenious Author of that has made his seem quite another story from this'.[37] There are, however, similar notions in *Mirza* and *The Sophy*. Baron seems to have borrowed from Denham's work or used shared sources. His wording 'what cares the Sea how great the Rivers Swell, / Since all their pride flow into her?' adapts Denham's lines on the same theme:

> Your fame
> Already fils the world, and what is infinite
> Cannot receive degrees, but will swallow
> All that is added, as our Caspian sea
> Receives our rivers, and yet seemes not fuller:
> And if you tempt her more, the winde of fortune
> May come about, and take another point
> And blast your glories.[38]

Baron's and Denham's conceits are both meant to praise: the former celebrates Abbas's fame, and the latter glorifies Mirza. Haly, in the latter extract, compares Mirza's fame to the enormity of the Caspian Sea, which, though filled with great rivers, 'yet seemes not fuller', since the sea is perfect as it stands. In *Mirza*, the same imagery is used in asking why the sea should care 'how great the Rivers Swell' into it, for 'all their pride' is, ultimately, hers. Significantly, Baron's clear echo and reworking of Denham's lines here comes in the first few pages of Act I. This suggests, *pace* Baron's claim that he 'had finished three compleat Acts of this Tragedy' before seeing *The Sophy*, that Baron likely owed a great deal to Denham's ideas while writing *Mirza*. Nonetheless, there exist two unique features of Baron's work. The first is the playwright's employment of the Shi'a term '*Mortys Ally*' (Mortus Ali), Muhammad's cousin and son-in-law, once in his play, for which Baron provides an elaborate annotation at the end of his work.[39] In Shi'a belief, Mortus Ali is held to be the first legitimate successor of Muhammad after his death. The Shi'a belief is in contrast to Sunni ideology, which considers '*Mortys Ally*' the fourth caliph and not the first. While both *The Sophy* and *Mirza* are set in a Shi'a Safavid Persia, *Mirza* is the only work that refers to Shi'a terms.[40] The second unique characteristic of Baron's *Mirza* is the bulky set of annotations

---

37  Ibid.

38  *The Sophy*, sig. C2r; Baron, *Mirza*, sig. B4r.

39  It should be noted, however, that despite being so detailed the annotation does include incorrect information. For instance, after introducing '*Mortys Ally*', Baron notes that '*Ossan* or *Hussan* his Son was proclaimed, but resisted by *Mavius*, and by him poisoned, about the year 657. He had twelve Sons, eleven whereof were murdered with him'. See Baron, *Mirza*, sig. M4v.

40  Later on Baron narrates that Persians 'honour [...] *Hussan*, whose death they yearly celebrate with many ceremonies, nine severall daies, in great multitudes, in the streets altogether, crying out *Hussan! Hussan!*'. By '*Hussan*' Baron probably means Ali's younger son, who was not poisoned as Baron says, but killed in a battle with Yazid's troops. See Baron, *Mirza*, sig. M4v; Brian R. Farmer, *Understanding Radical Islam: Medieval Ideology in the Twenty-First Century* (New York: Peter Lang Publishing, 2006), p. 13.

at the end of the play, reflecting Baron's wish to educate his reader through such a detailed appendix.[41]

## IV

By adopting the story of a tyrannical king preyed upon by an evil counsellor, Baron follows Denham's pattern in order to warn and criticise. His clear analogy in the dedicated lines to Charles I suggests Mirza as one of the parallels to the English monarch.[42] Baron, like Denham, projects Abbas in different ways. By emphasising the negative perceptions of Islam in the work, Baron presents a Muslim tyrant who can be compared with the English Puritans. But Abbas also shows a respect for the nobility of royalty, and seeks to make amends for his past misdeeds. In contrast to Denham's Abbas, the Persian king does not die at the end of the play, but becomes a forgiving, repentant figure. The king intends to purge his court from evil politicians by reallocating courtly positions; in one instance, he addresses Methiculi, Mirza's friend and an officer in the army, and notes 'the Treasurer-ship / We do conferr on you, *METHICULI*'.[43] In other words, Baron's Abbas does not tragically fall; unlike Denham's Persian king he remains alive, and submits to reformation rather than death. It appears that Abbas attempts to respond to social turbulence and discontent by replacing important positions such as the treasurer. Baron reiterates Denham's warnings, but supplements the play with an elaborate annotated bibliography describing Safavid Persian figures such as Shah Abbas I—an attempt to educate English readers in the absence of stage performance during the civil war.[44] John Denham and Robert Baron, therefore, used Safavid Persian dramatis personae for theatrical and nontheatrical purposes during a time when England was in a fraught political condition as a result of internal turbulence and instability. Baron's re-practicing of Denham's work shows that representations of Islamic Persia and Persians were subject to revision for the needs of the English audiences and readers.

41  For the detailed appendix, see Baron, *Mirza*, sigs L8v-S4v.
42  From a broader political perspective, it is true to say that Baron's *Mirza* 'would impinge on the world of Charles II' too, encouraging, from a royalist point of view, the revival of monarchy in the Interregnum and beyond. See Dale B.J. Randall, *Winter Fruit: English Drama, 1642–1660* (Lexington: University Press of Kentucky, 1995), pp. 133–34.
43  Baron, *Mirza*, sig. K6v.
44  John D. Cox, *The Devil and the Sacred in English Drama, 1350–1642* (Cambridge: Cambridge University Press, 2000), p. i.

# 5   Sir John Denham the Political Satirist, 1642–46

*Victoria Anker*

## I

On 22 August 1642, Charles I raised the royal standard at Nottingham, signalling the formal opening of the English Civil War.[1] More significantly, the event also marked the end of the king's reign as a figure above political division. The raising of the standard refashioned Charles as a partisan leader of a political and military faction, even though he remained the head of government. By entering into war against his parliament, Charles reduced the spectre of royal authority; in taking a side, there emerged a possibility that the power and institution of monarchy might be flawed.

Despite the flourishing print war, the burgeoning parliamentary-centric newsbook trade did not capitalise on this event. The raising of the standard represented 'a secure political basis for overt propaganda, but the newsbooks resisted such interventionism'.[2] Other literary forms were not so reticent. Parliamentarian pamphlets were keen to undermine the size of the king's army, whilst the fall of the standard a few days later was interpreted as an omen of royalist doom. One writer remarked that despite the grandeur of the occasion, 'there is no considerable [royalist] party at *Nottingham*'.[3] Such texts sought to boost morale among their faction, to enforce the righteousness of their cause, and to dishearten the enemy. In contrast to parliamentary-endorsed texts (which clearly proclaimed their authorisation), royalist texts often circulated without official approval. As Rory Tanner argues in the next chapter, Charles was initially suspicious of political rhetoric and disinclined to engage in public political discourse.

---

1 I use 'English' here rather than 'British', as the focus of this essay is specifically on the conflict between Charles, as King of England, and the English Parliament at Westminster during the First Civil War (1642–46). This is not to deny the wider importance of rebellions within Scotland and Ireland in bringing about and contributing to the conflict within England, as argued in Conrad Russell, *The Fall of the British Monarchies, 1637–1642* (Oxford: Clarendon Press, 1991).

2 Joad Raymond, *The Invention of the Newspaper: English Newsbooks, 1641–1649* (Oxford: Clarendon Press, 2005), p. 25.

3 *Remarkable passages from Nottingham, Lichfield, Leicester, and Cambridge* (London, 1642).

It is within this context that Sir John Denham wrote 'A Western Wonder' and 'A Second Western Wonder'. Utilising 'popular verse-forms', these verses enabled Denham to enter into a dialogue with both fellow royalists and the parliamentarian opposition.[4] Although Denham follows ballad procedure in the use of narrative, lyricism, and ballad metre, the Western Wonders should—in the satirical imitation of form and exaggeration of parliamentarian claims—be more accurately termed mock-ballads.[5] Whilst the royalist line evident in earlier works never wavers, these mock-ballads affect an artlessness and lower register that played into the broad royalist culture, and which is more prominently expressed in Denham's mock-ballads and satirical verses of the 1650s. These verses—with their negative emphasis on the 'other' rather than the shared values of the royalists—were designed 'more as a way to rally and entertain those already committed' than 'convert the politically ambivalent'. In contextualising 'A Western Wonder' and 'A Second Western Wonder' within the military and literary context of their production, this reading will demonstrate Denham's understanding of contemporary events and his successful challenge to parliamentary interpretation of the victories and defeats in the West Country.[6]

## II

The first major battle of the civil war, the Battle of Edgehill, occurred on Sunday 23 October 1642. The battle proved indecisive, although both sides claimed victory; by evening the following day, the Earl of Essex's parliamentarian army had withdrawn, providing the king with a clear road to London. Despite the joyful exclamations in *Happy news to England sent from Oxford* calling on London's citizens, 'to prepare to entertain him with hearty affections' as 'provision is made for his comming unto White Hall', and indeed, despite Charles's own belief that after three weeks on campaign he would go back to London, he was in fact forced to return.[7] Frustrated by Essex's army, 'the king settled his garrison, court and executive in Oxford, and the city became a symbolic locus for the royalist contingent'.[8] Symbols of royal authority were transferred (the Great Seal), established (the Oxford mint), or refashioned (the Privy Council and Council of War) as a challenge to the financial, legislative, and jurisdictional powers of Parliament.[9]

---

4  Robert Wilcher, *The Writing of Royalism, 1628–1660* (Cambridge: Cambridge University Press, 2001), p. 160.
5  Ballad metre is 'based on a quatrain of lines each having 4 stresses (or 3) rhyming *abcb* or *abab*'; Alex Perringer and T.V.F. Brogan, 'Ballad Meter', in *The New Princeton Encyclopaedia of Poetry and Poetics* (Princeton: Princeton University Press, 1993), pp. 118–20 (p. 119).
6  Mark R. Blackwell, 'Bestial Metaphors: John Birkenhead and Satiric Royalist Propaganda of the 1640s and 50s', *Modern Language Studies*, 29.2 (Autumn 1999), 21–48 (p. 23).
7  *Happy news to England sent from Oxford* ([London,] 1643), sig. A2v.
8  Jerome de Groot, 'Space, Patronage, Procedure: The Court at Oxford, 1642–46', *English Historical Review*, 117.474 (November 2002), 1204–27 (p. 1206).
9  Russell, *Fall of British Monarchies*; R.D. Beresford-Jones, 'The Oxford Mint and the Triple Unites of Charles I', *British Numismatic Journal*, 27 (1952), 334–44 (p. 339): the Oxford mint was

By spring 1643, Charles had the upper (military) hand. Although Parliament controlled London and much of the south-east of England, the West Country had largely turned out for the king, thanks to the popularity of the royalist commander Bevil Grenville amongst the Cornish. Royalists held most of the Midlands, of which Oxford was the most important stronghold, but Parliament's control of East Anglia effectively cut Charles off from northern England, itself an intensely divided area. The queen's arrival in Yorkshire in February 1643 provoked fierce fighting in the north, as too would competition for Gloucester (a staunch parliamentarian city) later that year.

It is important to note the realities of war, because news reports greatly exaggerate the defeats and victories on both sides. Predominantly published in London, the newsbooks largely championed Parliament's position, until the establishment of the *Mercurius aulicus* in Oxford in January 1643.[10] Its creation focused the anti-royal sentiment of London newsbooks, leading to a very public and partisan print war in which newsbooks attacked oppositional reporting, mocked editors, refuted facts and figures, (mis)quoted, and parodied in order to criticise and mock.[11] The verbal sparring between *Mercurius aulicus* and both the *Kingdoms Weekly Intelligencer* and *Mercurius Civicus* is well documented. In seeking to legitimise its stance, *Mercurius aulicus* was not adverse to quoting and referencing other rival newsbooks. Following Lord Francis Willoughby's defeat at Ancaster (11 April 1643), *Mercurius aulicus* scorned the parliamentarian report 'of a great battell fought in this very place, (when non such was fought)' and the misreporting of the death of royalist commander Colonel Charles Cavendish.[12] A few months later, it incorporated a quote from *The Scottish Dove* (a Covenanting newsbook) in relaying the story of a parliamentarian solder caught buggering a mare. The inclusion of a rival newsbook's report of the same story helped to legitimise *Mercurius aulicus*'s claim, despite the attempts of the London newsbooks to refute the story.[13]

The prominence of *Mercurius aulicus* is noteworthy, for the king—throughout much of his reign—had been notably cold towards printed news.[14] Tanner (in this volume) explores Charles's antipathy in the early 1640s, along with royalist concern over the parliamentary rhetoric that dominated Westminster's printed interactions with the public. Despite this concern, as the war progressed, rhetoric

---

established 3 January 1642, having transferred from Aberystwyth to Shrewsbury to Oxford; Ian Roy, 'The Royalist Council of War, 1642–6', *Bulletin of the Institute of Historical Research*, 35 (1962), 150–68 (p. 154).

10  *Mercurius aulicus*, first week (8 January 1643).

11  Raymond, *Invention of the Newspaper*, pp. 25–26.

12  *Mercurius aulicus*, sixteenth week (22 April 1643) p. 195.

13  Blackwell, 'Bestial Metaphors', pp. 24–28.

14  For Charles I's attitude towards the press, see Thomas Cogswell, 'The Politics of Propaganda: Charles and the People in the 1620s', *Journal of British Studies*, 29 (1990), 187–215; Richard Cust, 'News and Politics in Early Seventeenth-Century England', *Past and Present*, 112 (1986), 60–90.

became strategically important for royalist polemicists, enabling them to stereotype the rebels as base and unruly, and present the royalist cause as a defence of England's laws and liberties. Rhetoric was thus an important tool in managing the production of royalist texts. Furthermore, the writers of these texts wrote and published strategically, displaying 'a striking understanding of what one might call 'news management' techniques. They knew how to exaggerate the successes of the king's armies, and to minimize those of their opponents'.[15] Thus it is no surprise that *Mercurius aulicus* glosses over the embarrassing routing of royalist troops at Sourton Down, near Okehampton, Devon (25 April 1643), the event which prompted Denham's 'A Western Wonder'.

The paper war was not confined to newsbooks. Pamphlets, broadsheets, and ballads commented on, and contradicted, both parliamentarian and royalist newsbooks. Edward Bowles saw fit to publish a letter in defence of Essex's actions before Reading, 'not onely for your own satisfaction, but to prevent *Mercurius aulicus*, who I doubt not will tell you strange stories shortly'.[16] Stephen Marshall, in defending himself from accusations of indifference and inconstancy to Parliament's cause, dubbed the newsbook in his subtitle, 'Mendacium aulicum'—the lying courtier.[17] His letter was rebuffed at length by Edward Symmons, whose own letter was in turn promoted by the royalist *Mercurius rusticus* as 'a Solid and satisfactory answer', simultaneously denouncing Marshall as 'a Cauterized Schismatique'.[18] Ballads also fed on the content of newsbooks, as writers 'invariably used public pronouncements for inspiration'.[19] Not just a poetic genre, the ballads offered an alternative form of news, one that circulated via oral—as well as written—dissemination to a broad audience. Ballad writers, however, did not necessarily see themselves as polemicists—with the possible exception of Martin Parker and John Taylor.[20] Rather, these royalist writers were complex, capable of penning ballads and political allegory (as in the case of Denham) alongside a variety of other genres.

## III

By the time Denham wrote 'A Western Wonder' and 'A Second Western Wonder', he had experienced war first-hand at Farnham Castle (26 November 1643), if not

---

15 Jason McElligott, *Royalism, Print and Censorship in Revolutionary England* (Woodbridge: Boydell Press, 2007), p. 10.
16 Edward Bowels, *A letter from a minister in His Excellence his army, to a brother of his in London* (London, 1643), p. 6.
17 Stephen Marshall, *A plea for defensive arms, or, A copy of a letter written by Mr. Stephen Marshall ...* (London, 1642, repr. 1643).
18 Edward Symmons, *A loyall subjects beliefe* (Oxford, 1643); *Mercurius rusticus* second week (27 May 1643), p. 16.
19 Angela McShane, 'Recruiting Citizens for Soldiers in Seventeenth-Century English Ballads', *Journal of Early Modern History*, 15 (2011), 105–37 (p. 115).
20 Martin Parker and John Taylor were staunch royalists and prolific popularist writers in the king's defence. Parker is best known as a professional balladeer, whilst Taylor wrote the well-known *Mad Verse, Sad Verse, Glad Verse and Bad Verse* (London, n.d.).

earlier.[21] Denham's position as poet-cum-soldier was not unusual: Thomas Carew, Richard Lovelace, and John Suckling were active in the Bishops' Wars; Lovelace financially assisted the royalist cause (although he did not fight); William Davenant aided Henrietta Maria's fundraising efforts and served as General of the Ordnance; and William Cartwright sat on Charles's Council of War. This list is far from exhaustive. Although Denham's position as a courtier was comparatively inferior, his recruitment by Charles should not come as a surprise, given his poetical support for the royalist cause. Farnham was a strategically important town, situated on the south-westerly road to London. Royalist strongholds in the south-east were isolated—although Basing House held out until October 1645— and Denham, when faced with a parliamentary attack quickly surrendered, much to the dismay of his royalist allies and the glee of his parliamentarian critics. The castle was 'taken with less resistance than was fit', wrote Clarendon, whilst vicars mocked the royalists' unsoldierly behaviour.[22]

Denham subsequently spent time in prison, although the date of his release is somewhat contentious. Internal dating of *Mr. Hampdens speech* points to the poem's composition in winter 1642–43, when Denham is presumed to have been behind bars. On the premise that Thomason's copy of *Mr. Hampdens speech* is dated 23 March, Brendan O Hehir suggests Denham was at liberty prior to this date.[23] However, the argument that the text's publication necessitates Denham's freedom seems flawed: Sir Francis Wortley and Sir Roger L'Estrange were two of many royalists whose works were published whilst in prison. Herbert Berry, on the other hand, argues for Denham's release in June or July, basing his conclusion on a letter of 11 May beginning 'Whereas I am disabled by my pᵣsent troubles', which implies his continued presence in London.[24] The uncertainty here is twofold: whether Denham's presence in London equates to his continued imprisonment, and why, if the letter is datable to May, it took Denham two months (on Berry's outside estimate) to reach Oxford. Although Berry may be overstating Denham's spell in prison, it is possible, on the basis of his argument, that Denham was still incarcerated—or at least not at Oxford—when 'A Western Wonder' was written. Whilst evidence for Denham's involvement in the 1643 edition of *Coopers Hill* is compelling, the question of Denham's precise date of release from prison and removal from London to Oxford remains unanswered.

On his eventual arrival in Oxford, Denham was fortunate to avoid a court martial: not all commanders who surrendered too easily were so lucky. On 5 May 1643, Colonel Richard Fielding was court-martialled for surrendering Reading to Essex

21 O Hehir, *HD*, pp. 55, 58: O Hehir suggests Denham did not actively participate in war before this date, despite being pricked as sheriff in winter 1642.
22 Quoted in O Hehir, *HD*, p. 61.
23 Ibid., pp. 61–62. O Hehir further argues that Denham must have been released by April 1643, when the Oxford edition of *Coopers Hill* was published, because the revised edition shows clear signs of his involvement.
24 Quoted in Herbert Berry, 'Sir John Denham at Law', *Modern Philology*, 71.3 (February 1974), 266–76 (p. 271).

nine days earlier. Condemned to death, his sentence was later revoked. Two years later, on 3 May 1645, Colonel Francis Windebank (son of the former secretary of state) was shot in Merton College gardens, following a court martial for his surrender of Bletchington House to Oliver Cromwell ten days earlier.[25] Not even Prince Rupert, the king's own nephew, was immune from such procedures: following the surrender of Bristol to Sir Thomas Fairfax (11 September 1645), Rupert was forced to defend his actions before the Council of War at Newark, which—after five days of deliberation—finally pardoned him.[26] Perhaps Denham escaped such an action on account of his imprisonment, but it is also true that by late spring 1643, Charles, having failed to negotiate a suitable peace settlement, was preoccupied with co-ordinating Henrietta Maria's arrival at Oxford and preventing a Covenanter-Westminster alliance. Thus Denham's surrender of an isolated royalist holding went unpunished, and his career as an active soldier came to an end.

The impact of the experience of war on Denham's writing is, like so much of his career, debatable. 'A Western Wonder' and 'A Second Western Wonder' display a marked change in register from early poems; however (as Tanner explores), Denham had already tried his hand at political satire, the results of which (based on known manuscript circulation) were arguably a success.[27] Both Western Wonders are a very specific satirical reaction to a series of battles which took place between April and July 1643. On 25 April, a detachment of parliamentary cavalry headed by Major-General Chudleigh ambushed and routed Sir Ralph Hopton and the royalist army at Sourton Down. This attack took place three days after a local truce in the West Country ended, for which Parliament blamed the Cornish, whilst the royalists blamed the Devonians. *Mercurius aulicus* darkly predicted, 'the warre [is] like to be renewed', and, sure enough, two days after the treaty ended, Chudleigh led a parliamentarian attack on Hopton's army at Launceston.[28]

Chudleigh's success at Sourton Down was impressive: the cavalry fought alone for much of the day before one thousand foot arrived as reinforcements late on. The surprise nature of the attack spread confusion among the royalist army, which abandoned gunpowder, munitions, and stores in their retreat. The parliamentarians also succeeded in capturing letters from the king to Hopton detailing royalist strategy, the revelation of which 'reportedly caused the Earl of Stamford, stricken with gout, to "leap out his Chair for joy"'.[29] Parliamentarian polemicists una-

25  Patrick Morrah, *Prince Rupert of the Rhine* (London: Constable, 1976), p. 176.

26  Ibid., p. 203.

27  Although not exhaustive, the Catalogue of English Literary Manuscripts, 1450–1700, and Union First-Line Index of English Verse between them list the following manuscript copies (some of which post-date Denham's printed edition of 1668): twenty-three copies of 'On the Earl of Strafford's Tryal and Death', twelve copies of 'A Speech against Peace at the Close Committee', and six copies of 'To the Five Members of the Honourable House of Commons'.

28  *Mercurius aulicus*, seventeenth week (29 April 1643), p. 213.

29  Quoted in John Barratt, *Cavalier Generals: King Charles I and His Commanders in the English Civil War, 1642–1646* (Barnsley: Leo Cooper, 2004), p. 84.

shamedly capitalised on the victory: in under a week, three different pamphlets appeared, one of which carried authorisation from the House of Commons.[30] *Certaine informations* believed the victory sufficiently newsworthy to carry the story across three issues.[31]

'A Western Wonder' is a direct response to the inaccuracies and exaggeration of these reports. Denham deliberately overstates the numbers slain ('five thousand men') to emphasise the conflicting statistics described in the parliamentarian reports. *Certaine informations* counted 'at the least 5000 men' in Hopton's army prior to the battle, whilst *Happy Victory* reckoned five thousand fled the battlefield, leaving behind numerous fatalities and prisoners. Denham also mocks reports of Hopton's death:

> There *Hopton* was slain, again and again,
> Or else my Author did lye[32]

The most contemporary report of Hopton's death appeared in *Mercurius Civicus*: 'News also this day came of Sir *Ralph Hoptons* death, and that he died of his wound being shot in his back in his flight'. In the same breath, the newsbook also brands Hopton a coward by implying he had abandoned his troops and turned away from the battlefield.[33] However, Denham's repetition of 'again and again' suggests he had read other reports of Hopton's death, including one which dated it to the collapse of the royalist siege on Plymouth.[34]

In the first stanza, Denham acknowledges the freak weather conditions that contributed to Chudleigh's victory:

> Do you not know, not a fortnight ago,
> How they brag'd of a Western wonder?
> When a hundred and ten, slew five thousand men,
> With the help of Lightning and Thunder.[35]

30  *A most miraculous and happy victory obtained by James Chudleigh Serjeant Major Generall of the forces under the E. of Stamford, against Sir Ralph Hopton and his Forces …* (London, 29 April 1643); *A most true Relation of divers notable passages of divine providence in the great deliverance and wonderfull victory obtained by the Parliament forces under the command of the Earle of Stamford* (London, 1643); *Exploits discovered, in a declaration of some more proceedings of Serjeant Major Chudley, generall of the forces under the Earle of Stamford: against Sir Ralph Hopton* (London, 2 May 1643); for the Commons authorisation on 1 May, see *Journals of the House of Commons*, 3 (1642–44), 65.

31  *Certaine informations*, 15 (24 April–1 May 1643) –17 (8–15 May 1643).

32  John Denham, 'A Western Wonder', ll. 5–6, in *Poems and Translations* (London, 1668), pp. 105–07.

33  *Mercurius Civicus*, 1 (4–11 May 1643), sig. A3v.

34  *Good Newes from Plymouth* (London, 20 February 1643).

35  Denham, 'A Western Wonder', ll. 1–4.

Yet his concern is not to refute the extremities of the weather; that three different reports print a variation of this implies an element of truth.[36] Instead, the emphasis is on 'brag'd' and 'help': the implication is that the parliamentarians could not have achieved the victory without the intervention of nature. By pricking their pride, Denham argues that they are mistaken in thanking God 'and his Servant *Chidleigh*'.[37] The providential emphasis on weather, which dominates *A perfect diurnall*, is here belittled and cast aside.[38]

The parliamentary practice of Thanksgiving also comes under Denham's scrutiny. Days of Thanksgiving were, by 1643, an established ritual that enabled Parliament to tie its military victories to divine providence. The ritual, often observed in conjunction with a fast, offered a puritan replacement of more popish celebrations, which England's citizens (in particular those in London) were expected to observe.[39] Although Parliament did not order a Day of Thanksgiving in response to the victory at Sourton Down, the Commons ordered one on 29 April to celebrate Essex's victory at Reading.[40] Denham ridicules the excesses of such a practice—'a new *Thanksgiving*' hints at the proliferation of thanks already proclaimed—as well as the strict observance of the ritual by the preachers Hugh Peters and Thomas Case, to whom he advises, 'in your Prayer and Grace |Remember the new *Thanksgiving*'.[41]

The puritanism of these prominent figures, along with the Lord Mayor of London, Isaac Pennington, is the subject of Denham's ridicule in his last stanza. However, the issue of religion does not dominate 'A Western Wonder'; it is the silliness of war and the men who lead the battles that are the focus. There is a sense of glee in Denham's caricature of the Earl of Stamford, the parliamentarian commander who, despite possessing Hopton's letters, was later unable to inflict defeat at the Battle of Stratton (16 May). After initial parliamentarian success, the royalists, although outnumbered two to one, succeeded in capturing Chudleigh and gaining the field. The victory consolidated the king's position in the West Country, drastically reducing parliamentary presence in the area and leading *Mercurius aulicus* to proclaim the battle a 'signall victory'.[42] The significance of this victory was

36  *Exploits discovered*, p. 6; *A most true Relation*, pp. 5–6; *Certaine informations*, 17 (8–15 May 1643), p. 131.
37  Denham, 'A Western Wonder', l. 8.
38  John Grismond (ed.), *A perfect diurnall*, 48 (1–8 May 1643), sig. A2: 'this overthrow was so wonderfull and miraculous, that I cannot but remember the words of the sacred History, I will worke a worke in your daies, that those that see it will not believe it'. See King James Bible, Habakkuk 1:5: 'Behold ye among the heathen, and regard, and wonder marvellously: for I will work a work in your days which ye will not believe, though it be told you'.
39  For the puritan co-opting of Fast Days, see Hugh Trevor-Roper. *Religion, the Reformation and Social Change* (Basingstoke: Macmillan, 1972).
40  *Commons Journal*, 3, p. 63.
41  Denham, 'A Western Wonder', ll. 7, ll. 25–26.
42  *Mercurius aulicus*, twentieth week (20 May 1643), p. 262.

not lost on Denham, who advises Stamford that his best route to safety is to flee at Plymouth, before the royalists catch him.[43]

The battle also won Charles a new general in the figure of Chudleigh, who defected whilst prisoner, and subsequently sought to explain his reasons and rebut Stamford's accusations of treachery, in print.[44] Although undated, the pamphlet was likely written before July: Chudleigh praises his captor, 'I received so much humanity and noble favour from Sir *Bevill Gren-vile*', but Grenville died on 5 July and Chudleigh does not offer up any respect of the deceased.[45] Accepting that Chudleigh defected at some point in late May or June—and that the pamphlet was written at a similar time—raises the question of whether Denham knew of Chudleigh's change of heart. That another royalist satire chose to include a par-liamentarian letter acknowledging 'Major Chudleigh is turned against us', sug-gests it was no secret.[46] This satire also references the Common's impeachment of Henrietta Maria (23 May), making it a contemporary of Denham's mock-ballad.[47] Like 'A Western Wonder', *The Round-head remembrancer* reverses the charges of treachery Stamford levelled at Chudleigh whilst also poking fun at Essex: '*Stamford* marched out of *Exeter* with almost as much pomp and vainglory as his *Excellence*'.[48] Denham goes further, linking gout—a condition that caused swelling—to the inflation of Stamford's honour:

And now *Stamford* came, for his Honour was lame
Of the Gout three months together;
But it prov'd when they fought, but a running Gout,
For his heels were lighter then ever.[49]

Denham's suggestion that Stamford had been suffering for three months might indicate the mock-ballad was composed in late June: in mid-April, Stamford's sickness had already forced him to hand control of his forces to Chudleigh. The pun on 'running'—used here as both an adjective (an ongoing condition) and a verb (to run)—mockingly casts doubt on both the seriousness of Stamford's illness and the cowardice he displayed in hastily abandoning the battlefield. Unsurprisingly, parliamentarian newsbooks gloss over the defeat, blaming the Devonians for cowardly running away whilst simultaneously projecting a swift recovery of their position.[50] One was even so bold to claim, 'The Poore Cavaliers

43  Denham, 'A Western Wonder', ll. 20–21. Stamford fled to Exeter, which in turn was besieged by Prince Maurice later in the summer; Stamford was forced to surrender on 4 September 1643.
44  James Chudleigh, *Serjeant Major Iames Chudleigh his declaration to his country-men* (1643).
45  Ibid., p. 2.
46  *The Round-head remembrancer* ([Oxford,] 1643), p. 5.
47  *Journals of the House of Commons*, 3, p. 98.
48  *The Round-head remembrancer*, p. 2.
49  Denham, 'A Western Wonder', ll. 13–16.
50  *Certaine informations*, 19 (22–29 May 1643), p. 14; Grismond (ed.), *A perfect diurnall*, 51 (22–29 May 1643), unpag.

are so beset now, that they have sent for another Treaty, but it will not be granted them'.[51] Such news manipulation did not escape the attention of *The Round-head remembrancer*, which dryly remarked, 'If they fight and are beaten, then either they deny it, and *give thanks for a victory*; or else confesse some small losse, which God sent to them by his *speciall Providence to draw the Cavaliers into further destruction*'.[52] It is not providence but rather luck that Denham suggests the parliamentarians now need. In the closing lines of 'A Western Wonder', he hints at further royalist victories ('now dig for your life'), jovially threatening London's safety and questioning the strength of the city's earthwork defence.[53]

The royalist victory at Stratton, although strategically significant, did not end the conflict in the West Country. Skirmishes continued throughout June 1643, Hopton's army now reinforced by that of Prince Maurice and the Marquis of Hertford. In 'A Second Western Wonder', written in the summer of 1643, Denham continues the themes laid out in the first, drawing upon the royalist victories at the Battle of Lansdowne (5 July) and the Battle of Roundway Down (13 July). In his opening line, Denham presumes a familiarity with both newsbook reports as well as his first mock-ballad:

> You heard of that wonder, of the *Lightning* and *Thunder*,
> Which made the lye so much the louder;[54]

Beyond the obvious play on words—thunder is loud—the 'lye' in question is in fact plural, referring to both the number of lies and their embellishment. Once again, newsbooks carefully sidestepped the issue of defeat and Denham enjoins the reader to 'list[en] to another' of their lies.[55] Following Lansdowne, in which the royalists marginally succeeded in defeating Sir William Waller, the central story was of an accidental gunpowder explosion that temporarily blinded and badly burnt Hopton. The swelling of his head features prominently in three reports, with *Certaine informations* claiming 'that his eyes are burnt out'.[56] There can be no doubt as to the seriousness of the injuries—Hopton was out of action for several months—but this did not prevent Denham from making light of the newsbooks' reporting:

> Oh what a damp, struck through the Camp!
> But as for honest Sir *Ralph,*
> It blew him to the *Vies,* without beard, or eyes,
> But at least three heads and a half.[57]

51 Pecke (ed.), *A perfect diurnall*, 49 (15–22 May 1643), unpag.
52 *The Round-head remembrancer*, p. 1.
53 Denham, 'A Western Wonder', ll. 27.
54 Denham, 'A Second Western Wonder', l. 1 in *Poems and Translations*, pp. 107–09.
55 Ibid., l. 3.
56 Pecke (ed.), *A perfect diurnall*, 3 (10–17 July 1643), p. 21; *Mercurius Civicus*, 7 (6–13 July 1643), p. 50; *Certaine informations*, 26 (10–17 July 1643), p. 204.
57 Denham, 'A Second Western Wonder', ll. 4–8.

Waller pursued the royalists to Devizes (Vies), besieging the town for four days before an approaching royalist relief forced him to lift the siege and engage them at Roundway Down. The battle resulted in another substantial royalist victory, as Waller and his troops were forced to flee for Bristol, abandoning ammunition, munitions, and provisions in the process. The victory was equal, if not superior, to that at Stratton, eliminating Parliament's army in the west and isolating the five remaining parliamentarian garrisons.[58] *Mercurius aulicus* proclaimed, 'this was a most absolute victory', whilst cheerily noting that Waller fled, 'with as much diligence and speed as could be'.[59] In 'A Second Western Wonder', Denham is more scathing of Waller's retreat:

> But now without lying, you may paint him flying,
> At *Bristol* they say you may find him
> Great *William* the *Con* so fast he did run,
> That he left half his name behind him.[60]

In just four lines, Denham challenges the newsbooks to call him out as a liar ('without lying'), links Waller's retreat with that of Stamford ('so fast he did run'), and simultaneously exposes Waller as a cowardly fraud ('*Con*'), whilst proving him unworthy of his historical eponym, William the Conqueror. It is the subject of misreporting, however, that Denham takes most issue with:

> And now came the Post, saves all that was lost,
> But alas, we are past deceiving,
> By a trick so stale, or else such a tale
> Might mount for a new *Thanksgiving*.[61]

The newsbooks' attempts to save face, to redeem the reputation of Parliament and its army, are here exposed. Denham suggests their tricks no longer work, possibly because they frequently contradicted themselves and each other, thus exposing their lies. The reader of *Mercurius Civicus* would learn that Waller 'lost not in all 200 of his men, and not any Commander of note', whilst a glance at *A perfect diurnall* might instil more concern: 'The Court is turned into an *Academy* of Try-umph, for since Sir *William Waller* is de-feated, and the Queene safe come to the King, they cannot be now lesse then all Con-querors'.[62] *Certaine informations* however, avoids any mention of Roundway Down, commenting only that 'The

---

58  Barnstable, Bideford, Dartmouth, Exeter, and Plymouth.
59  *Mercurius aulicus*, twenty-eighth week (15 July 1643), p. 371.
60  Denham, 'A Second Western Wonder', ll. 13–16.
61  Ibid., ll. 17–20.
62  *Mercurius Civicus*, 8 (13–20 July 1643) p. 59; Pecke (ed.), *A perfect diurnall*, no. 4 (17–24 July 1643), p. 26.

Parliament hath taken care, specially to provide moneys for *Sir William Waller*'.[63] There is great irony in the notion that the newsbooks' success in duping their readers could prompt a Commons' order for a Day of Thanksgiving—unwittingly leading parliamentarians to praise God for the victories of their enemy. This possibility was not as absurd as might first appear. On the departure of the royalist relief force from Oxford, *Mercurius Civicus* sniggered to see royalists 'ring their Bels and make Bonefires at *Oxford* (as they did for their former overthrow) mistaking it (poor souls) for a second victory obtained against Sir *William Waller*'.[64] The joke was on the other foot and *Mercurius aulicus* lost no time informing its readers, ''tis worth your notice, that on *Thursday* last, when God granted His Majesty this exceeding great victory, [Roundway Down] on that very day (and the same houre too) these Legislative Hypocrites were at the height of their *Thanksgiving*'.[65] In 'A Second Western Wonder', Denham displays awareness of, and is keen to expose, the association of political lies with religious polemic. The realisation that the newsbooks do deceive causes the Presbyterian Case to 'fall a weeping', even as he continues to distort the truth from his pulpit.[66]

As with 'A Western Wonder', Denham ends the second mock-ballad on a note of faux-casual warning:

> Lest *Essex* should start, and play the *Second part*,
> Of *Worshipful* Sir *John Hotham*.

Within these lines, Denham plays on two contemporary concerns: the arrest of Sir John Hotham and his son, in June, on account of their secret negotiations with the royalists, and the growing uncertainty over Essex's competency and leadership. Already, Essex had been warned that 'if he had a minde to lay down Armes, hee should let them know it, and they would find men of as great abilities to pursue the warre'.[67] In both Western Wonders, Denham is primarily concerned with the absurdity of war, and the idolisation and idleness of parliamentarian commanders. In expressing this concern, he emphasises the ridiculous and inaccurate nature of parliamentary reports, which jarred with their apparent desire 'to undeceive the people'.[68]

## IV

The above reading closely demonstrates Denham's awareness of contemporary newsbooks and pamphlets, both parliamentarian and royalist. In this he was not

63 *Certaine informations*, no. 27 (17–24 July 1643), 214; *Commons Journal*, 3, p. 163; the Commons resolved to raise £10,000.
64 *Mercurius Civicus*, 7 (6–13 July), p. 56.
65 *Mercurius aulicus*, twenty-eighth week (15 July 1643), p. 372.
66 Denham, 'A Second Western Wonder', ll. 17–20.
67 Quoted in *Mercurius aulicus*, twenty-ninth week (22 July 1643), p. 375.
68 *Mercurius Civicus*, 1 (4–11 May), sig. A2.

alone. The spring and summer of 1643 had been a 'good year' for royalists. This goes some way to explaining the number of royalist ballads and poems that take their inspiration from specific events of this time, although not all were so light-hearted in their celebration of royalist victories. Denham's mock-ballads stand in stark contrast to *Verses on the Death of Sr Bevill Grenville*, a collective production by royalist writers at Oxford in honour of the commander (who died at Lans-downe). Although styled as a volume of university verse (the 1684 reprint credits the University of Oxford), in a similar manner to *Musarum Oxoniensium*, the volume celebrating Henrietta Maria's return, not all contributors were university figures. The primary focus was 'in configuring a poetics of elegy to represent the dead hero'.[69] The valorising of Grenville thus dominates the volume, although this did not prevent the poets from attacking Parliament (for prolonging the rebel-lion and the politicised practice of Thanksgiving) or London (for its continued support of Parliament).

Within the volume, John Birkenhead is one of the few writers to recognise Grenville's wider military career beyond Lansdowne: 'So as loose *Stamford* frighted left the stake' recalls the commander's cowardly actions in the West Country, whilst 'Thus *Bodmin, Stratton* felt thy influence' reminds readers of Grenville's (and by extension the royalist party's) victories earlier in the year.[70] It is also implied that even Parliament's deceased commanders should fear for their well-being: '*Brooke* and *Hampden* quake / To find themselves not safe'.[71] There is a unifying emphasis on constructing Grenville as a martyr-like figure, heroically dying for the king's cause, and the description of this and the battle scene is remi-niscent at times of the 1643 Oxford edition of *Coopers Hill*.[72] In the same way that Denham's stag seeks safety among his friends but is shunned and left alone, so Granville fights alone: '*Granvil* against an Army He being one: / Cannon, Horse, Foot Himself'.[73] The stag 'disdaines to die / By vulgar hands' whilst Granville stands unequalled 'against whole Troops of foes', namely, the 'Sergeant-Major Cobler' and 'Mechanick Colonell' (a parodying of London's tradesmen within the city's Trained Bands).[74] William Cartwright denounces these tradesmen collec-tively as 'th' incensed Rebell' who enjoys 'undeserv'd success.[75] Whilst the stag is 'glad and proud to dye' by Charles's hand, so Grenville is praised for 'Dying truly in the Kings defence'.[76] The implication is that the king's cause is greater

69   Jerome de Groot, *Royalist Identities* (Basingstoke: Palgrave Macmillan, 2004), p. 152.
70   J[ohn]. B[erkenhead]., 'The Villains now are ripe', ll.22, 31, in *Verses on the death of the right valiant Sr Bevill Grenvill* (Oxford, 1643), pp. 15–17.
71   W[illiam]. C[reed]., 'Hallow my temples', ll.22–23, in *Verses on Grenvill*, pp. 18–19.
72   De Groot, *Royalist Identities*, pp. 152–53.
73   Denham, *Coopers Hill* ([Oxford,] 1643), ll. 270–73; T[homas]. M[asters]., 'It is not He', ll.25–26, in *Verses on Grenvill*, pp. 1–2.
74   Denham, *Coopers Hill*, ll. 291–92; W[illiam]. B[arker]., 'What We have Lost in Thee ', l. 28, D[udley]. D[igges]., 'Thou Name of Valour!', ll.18–19, in *Verses on Grenvill*, pp. 12–13, 13–15.
75   W[illiam]. C[artwright]., 'Not to be wrought Malice', ll.51, 53, in *Verses on Grenvill*, pp. 8–11.
76   Denham, *Coopers Hill*, l. 298; Creed, 'Hallow my temples', l. 28.

than any one individual, bringing to mind a line from Denham's elegy on Strafford, 'yᵉ glory of thy fall / oute weighes yᵉ cause'.[77] Likewise there are echoes of Denham's 'Dying he [the stag] dies, purples with his bloud' in the closing line, 'Till all His Purple Current dry'd and spent'.[78]

The eulogising of Grenville allowed the poets to overlook the more serious strategic problems generated by his death. Grenville was 'a thoroughgoing professional soldier who also had a huge influence in his native Cornwall', a characteristic both Birkenhead ('they [Cornish Army] made vast Devon quake') and Creed ('*Granvill*! The Cornish *Paen* it shall be',) acknowledged.[79] 'Although the Cornish could be formidable fighters, their obedience could never be taken for granted', a worry that became increasingly problematic after Grenville's death as subsequent Cornish royalists failed to emulate his success.[80] Whereas Denham chooses to overlook Grenville's death, unable to incorporate it within his irreverent verse, collectively the verses in this volume seek (not always successfully) to mourn Grenville's physical death whilst maintaining his continued existence as an idealised royalist hero. Thus he also appears in a list of victorious royalist generals—all very much still alive—in Birkenhead's contribution to *Musarum Oxoniensium*.[81]

The writers of *Verses on Sir Grenville* and *Musarum Oxoniensium* were no doubt aware of the propagandistic impact of these volumes: they functioned not only to celebrate the intended recipient, but as a reinforcement of a broad royalist identity, and an opportunity for poetic exchange. The diversity of the contributors emphasises the 'paratactic and porous groupings of acquaintance and affiliation' that constituted the contemporary literary scene.[82] In contrast to the print circulation of these volumes—which makes identifying its reception an easier task—it is only through speculation that the reception of Denham's Western Wonders can be traced. He might have had similar intentions, but the lack of documentation makes this difficult to discern. The lyrical quality of the Western Wonders is suggestive of their dissemination in oral—as well as manuscript—form. This is supported by the occasional transcription error that affects the meaning and interpretation of these verses. The most notable of these errors concerns the final stanza of 'A Second Western Wonder'. Rather than 'For the Laws of your Cause, you that loath 'um', the transcribed copy reads, 'For your Cause & your Lawes you that love

---

77 Denham, 'Vpon my Lo Straford', ll. 17–18, in BL Egerton MS 2421, fol. 39r.
78 Denham, *Coopers Hill*, l. 300; M[artin]. L[lewellin]., 'The Close', l. 5, in *Verses on Grenvill*, p. 22.
79 Barratt, *Cavalier Generals*, p. 2; Birkenhead, 'The Villains now are ripe', l. 21; Creed, 'Hallow my temples', l. 7.
80 Ibid., p. 82. See also: Mark J. Stoyle, '"Pagans or Paragons?': Images of the Cornish during the English Civil War', *English Historical Review*, 111.441 (April 1996), 229–323.
81 Berkenhead, 'Now let them vote, declare, contrive' in *Musarum Oxoniensium* (Oxford, 1643), sig. Aa r-Aa v.
82 James Loxley, 'Echoes as Evidence in the Poetry of Andrew Marvell', *Studies in English Literature*, 5.1 (2012), 165–85 (p. 172).

them'.[83] Although inverting Laws and Cause is questionable, it is the substitution of 'loath 'um' for 'love them' that strongly suggests the possibility of oral transmission. However, it is difficult to determine the extent to which Denham's mock-ballads enjoyed truly popular oral transmission. Blackwell proposes that Birkenhead's use of these lower literary forms represents an act of 'deliberate slumming', 'perhaps to amuse a more learned royalist coterie among whom the poem first circulated'.[84] Similarly, it has also been suggested that 'confidence in, and enfranchisement of, the popular reader is anathema to royalist writers'.[85] Considering the prominence of ballads within drinking culture, and the prominence of drinking within royalist culture (both at Oxford and in exile), it is highly likely that Denham's fellow royalists at Oxford were the primary audience for his Western Wonders. However, the possibility of transmission further down the social spectrum remains high. Civil war Oxford was a social melting pot; soldiers were drawn from all walks of life (even though senior positions remained resolutely elitist), townsfolk jostled shoulders with courtiers, many university members still resided in the city. The displaced geography of the Oxford court made it impossible to avoid intermingling with these people: as de Groot's description of a drunken Rupert singing and stumbling down the streets with his friends demonstrates.[86] The very nature of the (mock-) ballad form made oral circulation highly effective yet difficult to control.

## V

As with his movements, sure knowledge of Denham's works in the remaining years of war is slim. It is, however, possible to discern in 'A Western Wonder' and 'A Second Western Wonder' the beginnings of the bald humour that dominated Denham's verse satires during his exile. More importantly, the satires preached the royalist cause of loyalty, community, and order which many still thought attainable. Whilst the language becomes cruder, the irreverent tone and lower register are evidence of continuity in Denham's work. As with the Western Wonders, in these verses, Denham continues to delight in ridiculing subjects; although now it is his fellow exiled royalists rather than Parliament's military leaders that are the focus of his mockery. The need to expose the lies of Parliament has quietened, the fear that exaggeration and rumour could lead to drastic action proven by the execution of the king. Yet the air of disregard and irreverence evident in the Western Wonders still clearly runs throughout.

In satirising his mission to Poland with William Crofts, Denham directs his satiric gaze towards the Scots, emphasising their stubbornness, whilst implying

---

83   Denham, 'A Second Western Wonder', l. 26; Denham, 'The 2$^d$ Part of a Western Wonder', l. 26 in National Library of Scotland, Adv. MSS 19.3.4., fol. 30r.
84   Blackwell, 'Bestial Metaphors', p. 29.
85   De Groot, *Royalist Identities*, p. 74.
86   Quoted in de Groot, 'Space, Patronage, Procedure', p. 1214.

they are reluctant to part with their money or openly support the king: 'They must give word and oath, / Though they will forfeit both'.[87] Denham ridicules their unwillingness to support their new king, 'Nor assist our affairs / ... But only with their prayers', and accuses John Mollesson of resorting to lies in much the same way as did the author of *A Most Miraculous and Happy Victory* back in 1643.[88] In two other contemporary verses, Denham jocularly mocks his fellow royalist exiles: Viscount Ascot is 'That tender stripling', while John Mennis is but a 'Little admiral'.[89] Thomas Killigrew receives the most sustained mockery, albeit in a convivial manner, following his dismissal from Venice.[90] Denham acknowledges the trumped up reasons for his expulsion, 'The farce of his negotiation' but suggests that despite this he is smarter than his detractors gave him credit for: 'But who says he was not / A man of much plot, / May repent that false accusation'.[91] These lines further suggest Denham's criticism of those who criticised Killigrew (notably the Earl of Clarendon, which did not prevent his secretary from making a manuscript copy of the poem): their criticism is here a form of slander, which Denham criticises even as he mocks his friend's leisurely pursuits during his residency.

These verses served as a form of entertainment emphasising the bonds tying royalist exiles together. This was especially important when the royalist court was more susceptible to division.[92] 'Warmly mocking his friends, he [Denham] pictured their little group as a typical band of merry Cavaliers, drinking their way through exile'.[93] This sense of loyalty to his fellow royalists is evident in the 'them versus us' mentality of the Western Wonders. Although both poems lack the drinking associations that permeate the later satires, the satirical sending up of prominent parliamentarian figures defines the royalists by what they are not. As readers of the Western Wonders would be able to identify against and laugh at the dishonourable Stamford, the zealous Isaac, the cunning (and conning) Waller, and the Presbyterian Case, so they could identify and laugh with Croft, Mennis, Killigrew, William Murray, and Denham himself. In 1643 the mocking of parliamentarians in a period of conflict draws the royalists together; now, the mocking of royalists in a time of exile does the same.

---

87  Denham, 'On My Lord Crofts and My Journey into Poland', ll. 30–31, in *Poems and Translations*, pp. 67–70.

88  Ibid., ll. 16, 18.

89  Denham, 'To Sir John Mennis Being Invited form Calice to Bologne to Eat a Pig', ll. 27, 3, in *Poems and Translations*, pp. 73–76.

90  Denham, 'On Mr. Tho. Killigrew's Return from his Embassie from Venice, and Mr. William Murray's from Scotland', in *Poems and Translations*, pp. 70–72.

91  Ibid., ll. 12, 7–9.

92  For a balanced overview of the culture of exiled royalists: Geoffrey Smith, 'Long, Dangerous and Expensive Journeys: The Grooms of the Bedchamber at Charles II's Court in Exile', *Early Modern Literary Studies*, Special Issue 15 (August 2007).

93  Marika Keblusek, 'Wine for Comfort: Drinking and the Royalist Exile Experience, 1642–1660', in Adam Smyth (ed.), *Pleasing Sinne* (Cambridge: D.S. Brewer, 2004), pp. 55–68 (p. 67).

In the 1668 publication, these verses were not set to tunes (although two manuscript copies assign the tune 'First came my Lord Scroope' to 'Killigrew's Return').[94] A later satire, 'News from Colchester' was however set to the tune of 'Tom of Bedlam'.[95] This piece ridicules Quakers in Essex, much as the Western Wonders had ridiculed London's puritan faction. The 'zealous' Quaker Green is accused of bestiality, a popular contemporary association that other royalist writers, most notably Birkenhead, eagerly exploited.[96] Both Denham's and Birkenhead's bestial satires can be seen as part of 'the transformation of an accusation standard to the anti-popery rhetoric of the period into propaganda against Parliamentarians, Presbyterians and Quakers'.[97] Although less biting than Birkenhead, Denham mocks the Quaker's theological position: ''Twas but an insurrection / Of the Canal part, / For a Quaker in heart / Can never lose perfection', and their disapproval of festive events such as Christmas, 'Which though our saints have damn'd all', in the same way that he sent up Parliament's Thanksgiving celebrations and sermons.[98] He even jovially mocks the 'damn'd cavalier', thus once again drawing together those who do identify as royalists and did enjoy such seasonal festivities.[99] These verses, despite their obvious bias, were a form of news, even though circulation was limited to manuscript copies. The humour and banding together of exiles evident in these poems can also be seen as a reaction against the 'retirement' genre. Whilst the royalists might be in a literal exile—be it 'At Paris, at Rome, / At the Hague', this didn't necessarily translate to a metaphorical exile.[100]

## VI

Denham's use of mock-ballads and satirical verse forms in 1643 can be seen as a mirror of the realities of war. The lofty elevation of *Coopers Hill* is replaced by verses that lack finesse, despite the sustained attack on Parliament and its puritan allies. The language of 'A Western Wonder' and 'A Second Western Wonder' is deliberately simplistic in its attempt to captivate the broad membership of the royalist cause. Rather than a defence of kingship and power (as in *Coopers Hill*), the mock-ballads are centred on battles and personalities. Denham—like Charles—had entered the fray; the verses are a deliberate response to and provocation of the parliamentary newsbooks and pamphlets that misreported the events. Hence

94  Bodl., MS Clarendon 43, f.236r; Yale, Osborn MS fb.228, p. 55.
95  Denham, 'News from Colchester', in *Poems and Translations*, pp. 109–15.
96  Ibid., l. 2. Other Quaker satires: *The Quakers Shaken, or, A Warning Against Quaking* (London, 1655); Birkenhead, *The Four-Legg'd Elder* (London, 1647); idem, 'The four-legg'd Quaker', in *The Rump, or Collections of Songs and Ballads* (London, 1660), 358–62.
97  Blackwell, 'Bestial Metaphors', p. 22.
98  Denham, 'News from Colchester', ll. 57–60, 17.
99  Ibid., l. 19
100  Denham, 'On Mr. Tho. Killigrew's Return', ll. 34–35.

the Western Wonders reveal the intertextuality of news and literary forms during the civil war.

Far from a text-focused approach, however, this chapter has sought to recontextualise Denham's works within the society (military, cultural, and political) from which they emerged. The importance of context to text should not be underestimated, as evidenced by Denham's detailed parodying of contemporary newsbook reports. The mockery and jibes directed towards Parliament's military figures and puritan zealots would be turned inwards during the 1650s. The humorous taunting now aimed at fellow royalists functioned 'as a celebration of the cavalier ethos', despite (or perhaps because of) exile.[101] Like Brome and Birkenhead, the scandalous, borderline obscene content of Denham's verses offered both amusement and—more importantly—validation of their continued commitment to the royalist cause.

101 Nigel Smith, *Literature and Revolution in England, 1640–1660* (New Haven: Yale University Press, 1994), p. 312.

# 6 Political Authority, Discourse, and Tumult in the Revolutionary Writing of John Denham

*Rory Tanner*

## I

The assembly of Parliament in 1640 marked an end to Charles I's decade-long personal rule. It marked also a beginning to a most active and deeply divisive debate among the gathered MPs about their responsibilities as contributing members of a deliberative political assembly. Journals and proceedings in both the Short and Long Parliaments witness how these MPs' deliberate attention to matters of debate, rhetoric, and decision-making brought into relief a distinct line between those among them who sought to support deliberation as parliamentary privilege and those who wished to prevent any delay of legislative work. From the debate between them emerged many of the patterns of representation that came to define the popular political literature of England's revolutionary decade. Preoccupation at Westminster with rhetorical concerns came to provoke in popular writing a much broader discussion among those who sought to assess the reliability of discourse, whether it occurred in Parliament or in public, as a driving force within the English political sphere.

The writing of Sir John Denham features prominently in this body of texts, which itself came to surround, and sometimes also intrude inside, the political centre at Westminster. This chapter identifies Denham as an early and committed cavalier respondent to the parliamentary political culture that emerged in the early 1640s. His early writing gives clear expression to the prevailing themes of royalist messaging that issued in the crucial years after the personal rule and before the outbreak of civil wars. He pays special attention, however, to one particular element of Charles's emerging political platform: a deep suspicion of political rhetoric. This preoccupation defines Denham's poems on parliamentary occurrences in that period, including his elegy on Thomas Wentworth, Earl of Strafford, 'The Humble Petition of the Poets' and 'A Speech against Peace at the Close Committee'. These works offer much more than the typical fare of contemporary royalist writing, which could be relied upon to provide praise of the monarch and condemnation of his opponents. As a loyalist in a political environment where the monarch—and the monarchy itself—was called into question, Denham sought also to cast into doubt that prevailing parliamentary view that popular representation through political discourse—whether at Westminster or farther afield—could be a reliable means of directing the affairs of state.

From within the sphere of political representation in the early 1640s, Charles's own public relations acknowledged the importance of his subjects but not of public discourse or deliberation. He addressed his subjects in print and in person, but treated them more often than not as an audience or as spectators rather than as participants in a deliberative political forum. The response from Charles and his close advisors to parliamentary activities and ambitions has since been characterised as having a pacific theme, and aiming to promote 'unity and peace, rather than division and discord'.[1] In contrast were the reform-minded MPs whose progress in debates could indeed seem to the outside observer very much like disorder; Archbishop Laud described the Commons's debates as 'that noise'.[2] However, it was owing at least in part to the early successes of the proponents of such 'noise' at Westminster—which group was then not yet properly a *party*—that England's Parliament so successfully transformed itself, as one historian has put it, 'from an event to an institution'.[3] A broader coming to terms with dissent accompanied this political development. For Denham, however, the loyal poet remains as a sceptical voice to question the use of oppositional discourse and the facility of those who claimed to wield it for the nation's sake.

During an era in which England was fully 'intoxicated with language',[4] and where politicians, preachers, and authors all strove variously to determine and prove its capabilities, shortcomings, and failures, such scepticism was well justified. If the main front of the 'war of words'[5] said to have accompanied the English Civil Wars was that between textual representations promoting the authority either of the king or of Parliament, then the second front was that which saw the dispute over the capacities of discourse, whether as it issued among MPs in the Commons, or as encountered in writing through scribal or print publication. Denham's political writing within its wider context invites its study not only as a vehicle for promoting or refuting various political positions but also as a commentary on the aims and achievements of language used in political discussion. As a critic, he concerned himself with issues of discourse relating to miscommunication and misrepresentation. This required him to answer specific parliamentary poems— once they were available—as well as the parliamentary ideals and objections to Charles that were expressed in the Short and Long Parliaments.

It is right to observe, as Bruce Boeckel has done, that the 'pacific topography' of *Coopers Hill* is at odds with 'the bellicose mental landscape of the poem's

1  David Como, 'Predestination and Conflict in Laud's London', *Historical Journal*, 52.2 (June 2013), 263–94 (p. 263).
2  Quoted in Hugh Trevor-Roper, *Religion, the Reformation and Social Change* (London: Macmillan, 1972), p. 346.
3  Michael Braddick, *God's Fury, England's Fire* (London: Allen Lane, 2008), p. 56. See also Conrad Russell, *Parliaments and English Politics, 1621–1629* (Oxford: Clarendon Press, 1979), p. 3.
4  Thomas Kranidas, *Milton and the Rhetoric of Zeal* (Pittsburgh: Duquesne University Press, 2005), p. 1.
5  Elizabeth Sauer, *'Paper-contestations' and Textual Communities in England, 1640–1675* (Toronto: University of Toronto Press, 2005), p. 10.

original audience'.[6] A major feature of that landscape was the ongoing debate about the use and misuse of political language. Whatever the tone of *Coopers Hill* might suggest, Denham's potent adversarial poems on parliamentary occurrences show how cutting he could be in political controversy. The latter work circulated widely in print and manuscript, competing with pieces in the same literary culture that Denham condemned in his own writing. But Denham proves himself capable of making also the more decisive literary move, stepping away from a culture where a confusion of terms and styles seemed to preclude any real debate between political opponents. By the time Denham wrote his 'Western Wonders', as Victoria Anker concludes in her contribution to this volume, he may have been writing for fellow royalists rather than participating in a literary sphere that, for Denham, seemed to yield ever diminishing returns. Denham could also retreat to an even more distanced and abstracted register: *Coopers Hill* may be shown to reflect a limit to its author's engagement with contemporary political writing, constituting in those terms a properly royalist corrective to wayward political and literary activity.

## II

The royalist line that found such clear expression in Denham's writing was put through its paces in the Short Parliament, which was called in mid-April 1640, and dissolved a mere three weeks later. A unique case study in political tumult, that assembly doubtless confirmed in Charles both his deep dislike for political disorder and his 'suspicion of novelty'.[7] Debates among the gathered MPs in that session were interpreted by him as an unnecessary 'delay' that was 'worse than denial'.[8] Some such delay was owing to practicalities rather than spite: the Commons featured a seating arrangement that marginalised some of those present and privileged others;[9] the language of debate often tended to the baroque;[10] and the many newly elected members in the Short Parliament had yet to accustom themselves to the formalities of Commons's business.[11] However, by its bitter end the

---

6  Bruce Boeckel, 'Landscaping the Field of Discourse: Political Slant and Poetic Slope in Sir John Denham's "Coopers Hill" ', *Papers on Language and Literature*, 34.1 (Winter 1998), 57–93 (p. 37).

7  L.J. Reeve, *Charles I and the Road to Personal Rule* (Cambridge: Cambridge University Press, 2003), p. 23.

8  Esther Cope (ed.), *Proceedings of the Short Parliament of 1640* (London: Offices of the Royal Historical Society, 1977), p. 114.

9  As Aston records in one instance, the matter of choosing 'the committee of privileges of elections' degenerated into a shouting match, 'so those next the chair name most of the committee'; Thomas Aston, *The Short Parliament Diary of Sir Thomas Aston*, ed. Judith Maltby (London: Offices of the Royal Historical Society, 1988), p. 3.

10  Orlando Bridgeman urges his fellow MPs 'to speak short & to speak plain English'. Aston, *Diary*, ed. Maltby, p. 123.

11  Newly elected members made up a considerable proportion of the House in April 1640, and their influence was duly noted. In response to a colleague's objections about the 'indecency' of

session would seem to have removed from the Commons any claim to Charles's good graces; and had he succeeded later that year in the second Bishops' War it might 'have meant the end of Parliament altogether'.[12] The events of the next twelve months proved further to Charles that disorder at Westminster could lead to much wider consequences.

Key speeches that bookended the Short Parliament, as well as the printed *Declaration* that followed it, all attest to how far Charles centred his messaging on order, and—more specifically—order in the House of Commons. Early passages in Lord Keeper Finch's opening speech before the Commons and the Lords on behalf of Charles offer a passive version of political participation and representation. 'By you', Finch addresses the Lords and Commons, 'as by a select choice and abstract of the whole kingdom is presented to his majesty's royal view, and made happy in your beholding of his most excellent and sacred person'.[13] The Lord Keeper's rhetoric casts 'participation' as gazing upon, or 'beholding', the royal person. His address on this opening day seeks to set the stage for subsequent relations between the Commons and the king in these terms. He later offers at least some suggestion of a properly representative government, where 'even the meanest of his Majesty's subjects are graciously allowed to participate and share in the honor and in the councils that concern the great and weighty affaires of king and kingdom'.[14] Yet his following allusions to Uzzah, who touched the Ark of the Covenant despite instruction otherwise and was killed by God as a result,[15] and to Phaeton, who took the reins of his father's chariot and so set the world on fire,[16] both emphasise their sharing in 'honor' more than sharing in 'councils'.[17] These twin cautionary stories demand of the newly gathered MPs a hands-off approach to government. History attests to their reluctance to follow that suggestion.

The Short Parliament offers a prelude to the grand political contest that was to come in the years that followed. It insisted upon a reconsideration of political debate, demonstrated the permeability of Westminster through crossings-over of political rhetoric from the Commons chamber to a public audience, and proved the great depth of the impasse that existed between Parliament and Crown. That parliamentary spring of 1640 witnessed early forms of political practice that later came into much wider use during the revolutionary period, beginning the process whereby parliamentary concerns regarding dissent and discourse found expression in political writing and so became public concerns.

---

members' humming during debate, Sir Henry Vane 'excused the humming saying so many young men being of the House were ignorant of the indecency of it as yet'; Ibid., p. 143.

12 Trevor-Roper, *Religion, the Reformation and Social Change*, p. 237.
13 Cope, *Proceedings of the Short Parliament*, p. 115.
14 Ibid., p. 115.
15 See II Samuel 6.
16 See Ovid, *Metamorphoses*, trans. A.D. Elmville (Oxford: Oxford University Press, 2008), Books I–II.
17 Cope, *Proceedings of the Short Parliament*, p. 116.

Charles faced this wider audience after dissolving the Short Parliament. In *His Majesty's Declaration: to All His Loving Subjects, of the Causes Which Moved Him to Dissolve the Last Parliament* (1640), Charles deliberately offered an authoritative public record of the late parliamentary session in response to a rise in public political dissemination so great that it required a royally approved corrective. Never before had Charles in his printed declarations acknowledged public opinion so deliberately. The *Declaration* describes in unprecedented detail the proceedings in the Lower House, surpassing the treatments that appear in previous declarations.[18] The earlier *Declaration* that had followed the dissolution of 1629, by contrast, recorded a relatively narrow assortment of parliamentary occurrences that took place over a three-year period. These were cited in support of that *Declaration*'s argument for the king's right in dissolving Parliament. Unlike that of 1629, whose author had selected various events in the Commons as emblematic of parliamentary provocation, the *Declaration* of 1640 offers a record that in its breadth appears to make some concession to the significance of public opinion. With such fuller reference to the goings-on inside Westminster, citizens might do more than simply take the king at his word,[19] but could more reasonably feel able to judge for themselves the session and its outcome. Such an attempt at public relations—even if unsuccessful[20]—shows Charles's active interest in controlling the political narrative. To that end Charles's messaging throughout the Short Parliament was thorough and deliberate, and it can be read productively as presenting an opening position within the image wars of England's revolutionary decade.

> The increasing visibility of public opinion in the wake of the Short Parliament demanded new responses also from other political authorities who sought to manage and to influence it. Although some months passed before a distinctly parliamentarian literary voice emerged in popular political writing, the Short Parliament would seem to have done much to lay the groundwork for its expression. Upon the dissolution, MP Thomas Peyton observed that now some say, we are where we were; but I think we are worse, for what grievances soever the subjects thought themselves molested with and therefore would resist 'em, this striving with the king could be thought but

18  Strictly speaking, the level of detail may have raised questions of parliamentary privilege. Mr St John: refers to 'an Act in H. 4 not printed; That no man should speak to the King or any other of what passeth in the house'. Cope, *Proceedings of the Short Parliament*, p. 179.

19  John Rous readily accepted the king's account in 1629: 'This parliament was dissolved, March 2, by proclamation. See the book of the king's declaration, made to his subjects, of the causes why he dissolved it'. John Rous, *Diary of John Rous*, ed. Mary Green (London: Camden society, 1856), p. 36.

20  See Esther Cope, 'The King's Declaration Concerning the Dissolution of the Short Parliament of 1640: An Unsuccessful Attempt at Public Relations', *Huntington Library Quarterly*, 40 (1977), 325–31.

the act of private men, 'til now in Parliament it is made the act of the third estate.[21]

Despite such broad invitation, no significant concentration of parliamentarian poetry written directly in response to the failure at Westminster has survived in the extant manuscript miscellanies. Parliamentary publication did not begin in earnest until over a year after the publication of Charles's *Declaration*.[22] Statements of dissatisfaction with the failure at Westminster issued after the dissolution of the Short Parliament in riot rather than poetry or other forms of writing.[23] In the near term, parliamentary occurrences rather than parliamentary poetry provided sufficient grist for mills loyal to Charles.

One such occurrence was the trial and execution just one year later of Thomas Wentworth, Earl of Strafford, which provoked Denham's twinned political and literary interests. His elegy, 'On the Earl of Strafford's Trial and Death', was read widely; its presence in so many contemporary manuscript miscellanies confirms that Denham's poem was among the most popular of those touching on Strafford's death, second only to an epitaph that has been attributed to John Cleveland (*beg.* 'Here lies Wise and Valiant Dust'). Denham's proves the more sympathetic of the two. Even so, both poems equivocate between pity and judgement. Cleveland describes Strafford as 'the Prop and the Ruin of State; The People's violent Love, and Hate: / One in extremes loved and abhorred';[24] for his part, Denham sees Strafford similarly as 'The Enemy & Martyr of the State, / Our Nations glory, & our Nations hate'.[25] Resort to this divided sentiment reflects a climate where 'aesthetics and politics became indistinguishable and political turmoil rendered inherently unstable any personal or public stance'.[26] A later version of this poem that appears in Denham's *Poems and Translations* (1668) replaces this ambivalence with a more steady complaint against the convicting Parliament and its 'Legislative Frenzy'.[27]

But already in the earlier version of his elegy on Strafford, Denham undertakes deliberate and distinctly royalist poetic work. The central passage of the poem

---

21  Cope, *Proceedings of the Short Parliament*, p. 8.

22  Sheila Lambert, *Printing for Parliament, 1641–1700* (London: List and Index Society, 1984), p. i.

23  John Rous, *Diary*, ed. Green, pp. 88–90: 'Much discontent. Insurrections at London. Insolences by soldiers [...] Ship money exacted, and in diverse places diversely refused [...] Upon the dissolving of the parliament, presently were two insurrections in one week, at Southwark and Lambeth; in the first the White Lion prison was broken and prisoners set free, &c.; in the second, Lambeth House in hazard, &c. One man was taken and hanged and quartered; see a proclamation about it'.

24  John Cleveland, 'Epitaph of the Earl of Strafford', l. 8–9, in Gerald Hammond, *Fleeting Things: English Poets and Poems, 1616–1660* (Cambridge: Harvard University Press, 1990), pp. 47–48.

25  John Denham, 'On the Earl of Strafford's Trial and Death', ll. 19–20, in Bodl. MS Douce 357, fol. 8r.

26  Tanya Caldwell, 'John Dryden and John Denham', *Texas Studies in Literature and Language*, 46.1 (2004), 49–72 (p. 50).

27  Denham, 'On the Earl of Strafford's Trial and Death', l. 25, in *Poems and Translations* (1668), p. 66.

reveals Denham's characteristic suspicion of parliamentary speech, and it is there that the poet reiterates and further amplifies Charles's own dark view of political rhetoric at Westminster. As Denham writes, Strafford's wisdom 'did appeare / Three kingdoms wonder, & 3 Kingdoms feare', and was further

> Joyn'd with an eloquence, so great to make
> us hear with greater passion then he spake
> That wee forc'd him to pittie us while hee
> Seem'd, more unmov'd & and unconcearn'd, then wee.[28]

The passage represents in detail the effects of sophistry, casting Denham as a capable manipulator who can excite his audience's passion and persuade his opponents to overturn their belief in his guilt. Through it all he remains the controlled centre, 'unmov'd and unconcearn'd'. But Strafford's distinction here as an orator leads to his downfall: the talent is so terrible that his accusers 'feare to lett him live'.[29] Parliamentary diaries attest to Strafford's eloquence during his trial, which was held in the upper house and superseded all other business at Westminster for its duration. Denham's elegy shares Charles's own scepticism about rhetorical work at Westminster, and it also anticipates the broadening of that concern to include public deliberative work in England's nascent public sphere through the 1640s.

Extant manuscript records reveal the response to Denham's poem as well as its reach within the context of scribal publication: in two miscellanies it is accompanied by an answer, 'Wentworth's Fatal Fall'.[30] This rejoinder to Denham's elegy follows the original line by line, resolving its equivocations through slight rewriting to deliver a more fully negative view of Strafford. 'Great Strafford' there becomes 'Poor Strafford', whose 'Ruin' was 'just' rather than 'hard', and whose reputation stands as the 'Monster'—not 'Martyr'—'of the state'. However, the satirist did agree with Denham on one point: Strafford's 'eloquence', he conceded, 'was great indeed'.

That such a poem was written is not surprising. 'Answer poetry' is a familiar feature of English miscellanies dating to the sixteenth and early seventeenth century. However, the practice took on an overtly political aspect during the civil wars[31] within the literary culture of animadversion that grew up surrounding the division between king and parliament. A later miscellany, for example, casts in adjacent poems the death of John Lilburne as twice 'untimely'—in one epitaph

---

28  Denham, 'On the Earl of Straford's Trial and Death', ll. 9–12, Bodl. MS Douce 357, fol. 8r. In that manuscript the poem is given the title 'Wentworth's Triumph Over All'.

29  Ibid., l. 16.

30  Miscellanies in Bodl. MS Douce 357 and Yale MS fb.106(9) contain both poems.

31  See Arthur Marotti, *Manuscript, Print, and the English Renaissance Lyric* (Ithaca: Cornell University Press, 1995), pp. 159–71; among the examples cited there, one 'witty exchange […] concern[s]' an unreturned borrowed cloak' (p. 160), while others engage in 'poetic competition' (p. 161), or issue in 'class antagonism' (p. 163).

'too soon', and another, too 'late'.[32] Additional examples abound of political verses that appear to have been matched with opposite, answering claims by miscellany makers.[33] Overall, these instances suggest that Parliament was, for the committed royalist, by no means the only site of problematic political discourse. The rise to prominence of that 'third estate', as Payton observed, brought with it a new kind of disorder, one given very clear expression through an emerging literary culture of public poetic critique. Diarists and miscellany compilers recorded numerous instances of poems that were posted on the doors at Westminster, 'dropped' within the Commons chamber,[34] and 'affixed' in public places.[35] Inasmuch as they focused public attention on the Commons, such writings at times served a parallel function to the formal genres of public petition and of published parliamentary speech. But taken as a whole by contemporary readers— royalist or otherwise—these materials point towards disorder as a defining feature of that emerging literary public sphere. Already in the year that followed the end of Charles's personal rule were this sphere's activities active enough to prompt the concern of the king's party.

## III

Denham's subsequent work responds further to problematic political speech, sounding a warning about unchecked representation in the literary political sphere. As Strafford's death 'tipped the scales toward a new surge of Parliamentary government and the decline of benevolent despotism',[36] Denham's aim shifted accordingly to address directly the MPs who gathered in what came to be known as the Long Parliament. In a pair of poems set directly at Westminster, 'To the Five Members of the Honourable House of Commons: the Humble Petition of the Poets' and 'A Speech against Peace at the Close Committee',[37] Denham shows how that earlier royalist concern about political speech came to include both parliamentary and public forums. These Parliament-focused poems demonstrate how little difference there might be between actual and perceived power, and lament the effects of unchecked talk on England's citizens and monarch.

Like his elegy on Strafford, Denham's poem 'To the Five Members' was prompted by political controversy: Charles's failed attempt to arrest the MPs

---

32  Both sides of this debate appear in Bodl. MS Ashmole 36, 37, fol. 126r.

33  See Bodl. MS Rawl Poet 26, fols 96r & 98r for a ballad and a 'counter-ballad' (fol. 99r) 'upon the Parliament'; Princeton MS Taylor 34: 'Upon the parliament' (p. 74), 'The Answer' (p. 85).

34  Cope, *Proceedings of the Short Parliament*, p. 242: 'These verses were dropped in the Parliament house'; see also Worcester College MS 216, fol. 4r, 'A copy of verses dropped in Westminster hall, in the city, and other places of the kingdom'.

35  Bodl. MS Tanner 52, fol. 13r, 'Verses affixed to a picture of Cromwell set up on the Exchange'.

36  John Milton, *The Complete Prose Works of John Milton*, gen. ed. D.M. Wolfe, 8 vols (New Haven: Yale University Press, 1953–82), i, p. 92.

37  These poems circulated widely in manuscript. Two miscellanies collect them both: Bodl. MS Ashmole 36, 37 and Bodl. MS Douce 357. They appear adjacent to each other in Denham's *Poems and Translations* (1668).

Holles, Pym, Haslerig, Hampden, and Strode on 4 January 1642. The operation was met with widespread condemnation as a breach of parliamentary privilege. As such, it provided an inviting opening for Denham to pen an apology in the king's defence. But even with this aim in view, he addressed somewhat equivocally in this poem the merit and use of public writing on state affairs. On the one hand condemning the influence of political poetry and on the other confirming the influence of such public writing, he strikes a satirical tone in describing state poets but restrained himself from absolute irony. The 'Humble Petition of the Poets' suggests Denham's own reluctant acknowledgement of the power that public discourse—whether in the form of poetry or of rhetoric—appeared to have on contemporary political process.

In keeping with its imagined speaker, 'The Humble Petition of the Poets' suggests at its outset that poems are more suitable than traditional petitions as expressions of public opinion. Denham laments in the poem's opening section that although 'set forms of prayer be an abomination / set forms of petitions find great approbation'.[38] His answer is instead to offer a petition in verse. But the appeal in the poem to the higher possibilities of poetry—'a privilege ancient and native'[39]— is overshadowed by the reality of poets who speak too freely. Such complaints were often made in poetic satires against the MPs gathered at Westminster during the political uncertainty at Westminster, and Denham turns that association to account here:

> For all these pretty knacks you compose
> alas; what are they but poems in prose
> and between them and ours is no difference
> but that yours want the rhyme and the wit and the sense
> but for lying the most noble part of a poet
> you have it abundantly and yourselves know it.[40]

As 'The Humble Petition' continues, Denham's description of the claimants strengthens connections between MPs and poets, inasmuch as they both prove antagonists to the king. The failings of one party are made to emphasise those of the other, whether ill-considered speech—'to speak what ever we please / without fear of prison or pursuivant fees'[41]—or simple misrepresentation:

> an old custom our fathers did name it
> Poetical License & always did claim it
> by this we have power to change age into youth

---

38  Denham, 'The Humble Petition of the Poets', ll. 7–8, in Bodl. MS Rawl D. 398, fol. 233r. Quotations from this text are drawn from the copy in Bodl. Library MS Rawl. D. 398, fols 233r-v, unless noted otherwise.

39  Ibid., l. 19.

40  Ibid., ll. 43–48.

41  Ibid., ll. 21–22.

turn nonsense to sense & falsehood to truth
in brief to make good whatsoever is faulty
(this art some poet or the devil hath taught ye).[42]

'Some poet or the devil'—Denham seems unable to decide whose sins are greater. While other contemporary verse satires of political figures represent failed speech acts, here the representations turn more adversarial. In this case, the criticised speakers are more than inept and now have pointedly dishonest aims.

How does this derision of poets complicate Denham's own ethos as a writer of political verse? Denham's poetic aim in this poem remains difficult to discern, shifting between critique and lament. The former mood acknowledges the power of political poetry and political rhetoric. Denham warns the reader that he ought not to trust what he reads, whether penned by poets or MPs. What then ought he to make of Denham's own writing? 'The Humble Petition of the Poets' wavers between outright satire of unrestrained political discourse and Denham's uncomfortable acceptance of the need to resort to the same ways and means he finds so disagreeable. Even as Denham's poem highlights royalist fears of unchecked political discourse, whether in Parliament or outside, it adds mass and hence momentum to 'the proliferation of printed materials' that itself 'legitimized public opinion' in the period.[43] Such provoking material did not only invite a response—it demanded it. Behind the unflattering scene of literary and political misrepresentations may lay the poet's own acknowledgement—however grudging—of 'that trust above all others in poets reposed / that kings by them only are made and deposed'.[44]

That Denham's claims against public poetry echoed royalist critiques of parliamentary discourse suggests some wider acknowledgement that the two deliberative forums were more similar than not. Throughout the early 1640s, royalist scepticism of political discourse shifted readily from Parliament to a wider sphere of political discussion. To this end, the theme that Denham developed in 'To the Five Members' is amplified further in a second parliamentary poem, 'A Speech against Peace at the Close Committee'.[45] That poem is dated to early 1643, by which time the civil war had begun and Denham himself had taken up arms for the king's cause.[46] At the centre of this poem is the MP John Hampden, framed there as 'the begetter of the war' and a 'fanatic enemy of the Church'.[47]

In Denham's view, Hampden's power is the same as that of Strafford and the petitioning poets: it derives from speech. Against a troubled backdrop of political

42  Ibid., ll. 25–30.
43  Elizabeth Sauer, *'Paper-contestations' and Textual Communities in England, 1640–1675* (Toronto: University of Toronto Press, 2005), p. 7. According to the Union First-Line Index of English Verse, 'The Humble Petition' appears in six separate manuscripts and in three printed pamphlets.
44  Denham, 'The Poets Petition', ll. 33–34, in Bodl. MS Rawl D. 398, fol. 233r.
45  In some miscellanies, the same poem is titled 'Mr Hampden's Speech Against Peace, 23 March 1643'. This detail is omitted in Denham's *Poems and Translations* (1668).
46  O Hehir, *HD*, p. 51.
47  Ibid., p. 53.

116    *Rory Tanner*

reform, rhetorical persuasion, and executive action at Westminster, the satiric
'Speech' builds on Denham's earlier work in its accounting of sophistry and its
effects. The poem centres on a dramatic attribution to Hampden of a wide-ranging
and disruptive communications campaign that has thrown England into disarray:

> Did I for this take pains to teach
> Our zealous Ignorants to Preach,
> And did their Lungs inspire,
> Gave them their Text, shew'd them their Parts,
> And taught them all their little Arts,
> To fling abroad the Fire?[48]

The scene confirms the fears of a world subject to discussion, and thereby turned
upside down by a third estate too fragmented, unruly, and susceptible to the 'Arts'
of rhetoric. Hampden, in this representation, is made to play the part of the arch
sophist, who teaches his pupils

> Sometimes to beg, sometimes to threaten,
> And say the Cavaliers are beaten,
> To stroke the Peoples ears;
> Then straight when Victory grows cheap,
> And will no more advance the heap,
> To raise the price of Fears.[49]

The irony of 'The Humble Petition of the Poets' gives way to a much more cynical view in Hampden's imagined 'Speech Against Peace'. In this later vision it is
not just the MPs who offend by speaking improperly; those 'zealous Ignorants'
who learned their trade from Hampden also contribute to the tumult that provoked
Denham's own response. Denham's own wide reading of 'contemporary newsbooks and pamphlets, both parliamentarian and royalist', which Victoria Anker
identifies above (p. 99), only fuelled his scepticism further.

Opposite Denham were those among his contemporaries who imagined much
greater possibilities for political discourse, promoting the abilities of readers
to discern the ill effects of sophistry. Some of these politically minded authors
undertook with care to instruct their readers, and to support 'people's public use
of their reason'[50]—that criterion which Habermas identifies as crucially supporting public sphere formation. Their efforts proceeded in various ways: some

---

48  Denham, 'A Speech Against Peace at the Close Committee', ll. 55–60, in *Poems and Translations*,
    p. 98.
49  Ibid., ll. 61–66.
50  Jürgen Habermas, *The Structural Transformation of the Public Sphere* (Cambridge: MIT Press,
    1991), p. 27. Habermas writes of reason (*Räsonnement*) that it 'In our [German] usage [...] unmis-
    takably preserves the polemical nuances of both sides: simultaneously the invocation of reason
    and its disdainful disparagement as merely malcontent griping'.

directed attention to the problems of representation, exhorting readers to 'invert the terms'[51] of propaganda they encounter; while others developed formal structures that brought into relief the problematic aspects of partisan culture. In a notably early example, George Wither's pamphlet *Letters of Advice* (1644) instructed readers how best to withstand aspiring political candidates' attempts at persuasion. Such writing brought greater purpose, if not greater order, to the 'Babel' of political discourse that circulated during the civil war;[52] it aimed ultimately to establish a model of rhetorically driven citizenship where reading could be a crucial support to political participation. That lofty goal proved for some to be well worth fighting and writing for; from the perspective of one such as Denham, however, it promised only discord.

## IV

The context and content of Denham's Westminster poems inform his best-known work, *Coopers Hill*, which itself surely surpasses all of the poet's earlier efforts in its thorough and confident support of the monarch. First written in 1641, Denham's masterpiece was frequently revised, and occasionally printed, although modern scholarship distinguishes chiefly versions early (1641/2; the 'A' text) and late (1655; the 'B' text).[53] In his *Index of English Literary Manuscripts*, Peter Beal adds that the poem was 'transcribed repeatedly', and prompted 'widespread manuscript circulation'.[54] This dissemination strongly favours the 'A' text of *Coopers Hill*,[55] which itself appeared in print in 1642. Having been present at the proceedings against Strafford (in which trial he served as witness), Denham wrote the poem in part to caution Parliament 'against provoking the dormant strength of the King'.[56] The poem is known for its expression of this political sentiment, and for its innovative form, which pioneers the 'topographical reflective' genre. Yet the poem follows Denham's Westminster poems by commenting as directly on the nature of public political language as it does on that of kingship. Here, Denham argues conclusively for the king's status as a subject that defies discourse, and whose authority exceeds poetic representation.

*Coopers Hill* deliberately casts a shadow upon the growing contemporary interest in the potential of political discourse. Here Denham presents the proliferation of royal representations in public poetry as unnecessary and inadequate responses to their subject. Such reservations about the efficacy and use of state poetry follow

51 See E.P., 'Charles the 2d. after he was crowned King of Scotland, was proclaimed Traytor, & all his Adherents Rebells: by the Rump-Parliament', l. 9, in Bodl. MS Rawl. Poet. 26, fol. 163r.
52 The image of 'Babel' was cited often by royalists 'to register horror at the fact of political disagreement'. See Sharon Achinstein, *Milton and the Revolutionary Reader* (Princeton: Princeton University Press, 1994), p. 73.
53 O Hehir, *EH*, p. ix.
54 Peter Beal, *Index of English Literary Manuscripts*, 2 vols (London: Mansell, 1980), i, p. 331.
55 O Hehir, *EH*, p. ix.
56 Ibid., p. 35.

closely that prevailing royalist scepticism about the effectiveness of rhetorical debate in Parliament. Denham emphasises the king's primacy early in the poem, writing that 'Courts make not Kings, but Kings the Court'.[57] Later in the poem he observes another thing that a king 'needs not':

> He, who not needs that Emblem which we paint,
> But is himself the Soldier and the Saint.
> Here should my wonder dwell, and here my praise,
> But my fixed thoughts my wandering eye betrays.[58]

Here, secondary representation—the 'Emblem'—is unnecessary. These remarks may stand as a rejoinder in earnest to the satiric construction in 'The Humble Petition of the Poets' that 'kings by [poets] only are made and deposed'. A prefatory note to the 1655 edition of *Coopers Hill* shares this scepticism about representation: the poet John Birkenhead compliments Denham's allegory as one 'skillfully mantain'd without dragging or haling in Words and Metaphors'.[59] Denham imagines and characterises a world in which monarchical authority is self-evident, capable of touching citizens with a sense of awe yet not dependent on any labour of attendant poets beyond their 'wonder' and 'praise'—such registers as Milton perhaps imagined in his condemnation of 'flattery' in *Animadversions upon The Remonstrants Defence Against Smectymnuus* (1641).[60]

Denham's own rhetorical thrust in *Coopers Hill* points to an arrangement between a king and his subjects not mediated by discourse. In the poem, Denham described ties between citizens and monarch that are not rhetorical, but filial:

> That blood, which thou and thy great Grandsire shed,
> And all that since these sister Nations bled,
> Had bin unspilt, had happy *Edward* known
> That all the blood he spilt, had been his own.[61]

This relationship was represented as natural, or intrinsic, rather than one open to question or reconsideration. The poem's penultimate passage (celebrating *Magna Carta*) frames a similar relation between 'King and subject', where the former

---

57  John Denham, *Coopers Hill* (1642), p. 1.
58  Ibid., p. 6.
59  Denham, *Coopers Hill* (1655), sig. A2v.
60  Milton persistently and 'plainly' addressed the 'ingenious' readers in *Animadversions*, in part because the moment at which he wrote—'our time of Parliament, the very jubilee, and resurrection of the State'—required an open political discourse to oppose 'that deceitful, and close couched evil of flattery that ever attends them'. See Milton, *The Complete Prose Works of John Milton*, ed. Wolfe, i, p. 663.
61  Denham, *Coopers Hill* (1642), p. 7. The figure of 'Edward' here is 'Presumably Edward III's grandfather, Edward I, rather than his great-grandfather, the ineffective Henry III'; see O Hehir, *EH*, p. 117.

'give[s] liberty' and the latter 'love'. Political dissent voiced in response amounts to empty words that fail to describe the truth of the arrangement: 'Tyrant and Slave, those names of hate and fear, / The happier style of King and Subject bear'.[62] Denham's imagined public bears resemblance to the scene described in Martin Parker's broadside upon the assembly of the Short Parliament[63] of a group unified by their beholding the royal person, as well as by their positive response to royal display.

What of those citizens who might respond differently? From his political milieu, Denham could not overlook the issue of dissent. His model of representation and discourse presupposed that 'discord' exists but that it did not necessitate expressions of opposition. In *Coopers Hill*, the poet lamented the political tumults that had overtaken England: 'is there no temperate region [that] can be known?'[64] While Denham suggested that difference and 'discord' were inevitable, as 'the harmony of things, as well as that of sounds, from discords springs', it remained for 'Nature' to 'unite [...] such huge extremes'.[65] Political intervention was not a sure means of such resolution. O Hehir observes the influence on *Coopers Hill* of a particular world view: 'that least understood classical and Renaissance cosmological principle of "balanced opposition" or *concors discordia*'.[66] The doctrine posits that 'the most usual method of effecting a net balance of the opposites is that of alternation. Day and night follow each other successively, as do winter and summer'. Thus, in that which 'may be termed [...] God's system',[67] politics was subject to such a higher, universal power. This assumption marginalised the scope for alternative political arrangements that reflected immediate expressions of public will rather than the ebb and flow of natural, or universal law. Denham's musings on 'discord' and 'harmony' promoted to his readers a conservative way of thinking about themselves and the state, accepting the already existing settlement between 'King and Subject'.

The recourse to natural order that issues in the final passage of *Coopers Hill* evokes a common vocabulary in contemporary political writing that linked political pressure on the king—what might be termed 'public' political pressure, even if only by way of representatives—with images of flooding. Denham describes the recklessness of 'Husbandmen' who with 'high rais'd banks' would 'strive to force, / His channel to a new, or narrow course'. Such 'striving' likely referred to recent exercises in parliamentary authority, which Denham saw as a dangerous provocation of Charles. *Coopers Hill* promised a swift response:

> No longer then within his banks he dwells,
> First to a Torrent, then a Deluge swells

---

62  Denham, *Coopers Hill* (1642), p. 17.
63  See Martin Parker, *An Exact Description of the manner how His Majesty and his nobles went to Parliament* (London, 1640).
64  Denham, *Coopers Hill* (1642), p. 8.
65  Ibid., pp. 12–13.
66  O Hehir, *EH*, p. 165.
67  Ibid., p. 168.

Stronger, and fiercer by restraint he roars,
And knows no bound.[68]

When cast in these terms, challenges to royal prerogative are shown to risk a dangerous reaction. Similar images of embankment and overflow appeared in Charles's *Answer to the Nineteen Propositions* (1642). In their attempts to regulate royal practice, the provoking propositions plainly constituted a 'restraint' along the lines of that imagined by Denham. According to Charles's *Answer*, these incursions on royal prerogative risked disrupting the existing 'Balance [...] between the three Estates', whereby each may 'run jointly on in their proper Channel (begetting Verdure and Fertility in the Meadows on both sides) and the overflowing of either on either side raise not Deluge or Inundation'.[69] As in Denham, attempts to restrain the 'channel' result in danger, disorder, and 'Deluge'. A later poem, extant only in manuscript, applies the same vocabulary to Cromwell, who 'with odds of number and of fate / Removed this bulwark of the ~~King~~ Church and state'. Here the anonymous royalist poet observes much the same consequences as were feared in *Coopers Hill* and in Charles's *Answer*: 'For when the bank's neglected or overthrown / The boundless torrent does the country drown'.[70]

## V

Denham's writing in the years that followed Charles's personal rule takes part in a much broader effort to represent oppositional politics as 'tumult'—first among 'the ills of Democracy' listed in Charles's *Answer to the Nineteen Propositions*.[71] Beyond the royalist statement in that document and in parliamentary-focused poems from Denham, many other authors expressed reservations about the threat of revolutionary rhetoric and politics. Although Parliament was imagined by many as the source of such expression, it was seen also as an increasingly common motivator for public writing. But at least one undeterred author downplayed the threat of clamorous, revolutionary rhetoric. The anonymous poem 'To the house of Commons', which circulated widely after the dissolution of the Short Parliament, also framed anti-royalist sentiment in terms of a flood, although more

---

68  Denham, *Coopers Hill* (1642), p. 18.
69  Charles Stuart, *His Majesties Answer to the Nineteen Propositions of both Houses of Parliament* (Cambridge, 1642), p. 12.
70  BL, MS Harley 6947, fol. 229r. The second half of this paragraph replicates a paragraph in my chapter 'An Appleton Psalter: The Shared Devotions of Thomas Fairfax and Andrew Marvell', in Andrew Hopper and Philip Major (eds), *England's Fortress: New Perspectives on Thomas, 3rd Lord Fairfax* (Farnham: Ashgate, 2014), pp. 213–34 (p. 227).
71  See Charles Stuart, *Answer*, p. 12: 'The ill of absolute Monarchy is Tyranny, The ill of Aristocracy is Faction and Division, The ills of Democracy are Tumults, Violence and Licentiousness. The good of monarchy is the uniting a nation under one head to resist invasion from abroad and insurrection at home; the good of aristocracy is the conjunction of council in the ablest persons of a state for the public benefit; the good of democracy is liberty, and the courage and industry which liberty begets'.

optimistically than others: 'Kings like Noah's ark are nearer to the skies / The more the billows under each them rise'.[72] There was some truth to this image, for the agitations in subsequent years obtained for Charles a similarly elevated place: to a generation of his followers Charles's most enduring image was that of the *Eikon Basilike* (1649), whose frontispiece was graced by the late king in a martyr's pose.[73]

In that longer view, the preoccupations of public political writing at the outset of England's revolutionary decade proved prescient. It took less than a year for the Long Parliament to provoke one wit to create a series of critical 'Anagrams of the PARLIAMENT'; in these he uncovered such truths about the assembly as 'I part al men', 'I trap al men', and 'Lay-men prate'.[74] Denham's own writings from this period reflect the concern of those who believed already in the years immediately following Charles's personal rule that such 'prating' could lead easily to something much more consequential. The Long Parliament soon showed itself ready to make that leap, however uncertain, from rhetorical debate to executive action. And already in 1642, the ultimate end of that effort could well be imagined:

> Is there no Church? Wee'le put it to the vote.
> Is there no God? Some fooles say so by rote.
> Is there no King, but Pimme, to rule us sent?
> That shall be try'd by vote of Parliament.
> No Church? No God? No King? t'were very well;
> could they but make an Act, there were no Hell.[75]

The capacity of rhetoric to remake the world was plain enough to see for cavalier and roundhead alike. For Denham, that prospect offered little more than a threat to the nation's peace, order, and good government. The risk of what might be lost through the reformative zeal of an ascendant Parliament and its attendant public was great enough to prompt his sustained response in verse, and to confirm his commitment to the royalist line in England's 'war of words and paper bullets'.[76]

---

72  Bodl. MS Tanner 306, fol. 290v.
73  Charles Stuart, *Eikon Basilike: The Pourtrature of His Sacred Majestie in His Solitudes and Sufferings* (1649).
74  See Anon., 'Anagrams of the PARLIAMENT, 1642', in Bodl. MS Rawl Poet 26, fol. 137v.
75  Anon., 'Upon the Parliamentary Occurrents, &c., 1641', ll. 5–10, in Bodl. MS Rawl Poet 26, fol. 133r.
76  Kevin Sharpe, *Image Wars: Promoting Kings and Commonwealths in England, 1603–1660* (New Haven: Yale University Press, 2010), p. 285.

# 7    Sir John Denham's *A Version of the Psalms of David* (1714)

*Philip Major*

## I

Even by the standards of the seventeenth-century courtly elite, Sir John Denham's life and career render him an impressively protean figure—Lincoln's Inn lawyer, poet, playwright, translator, wit, courtier, exile, diplomat, politician, and Surveyor of the King's Works. Through it all, his dedication and service to the House of Stuart remained strong and unquestionable. Yet, in an age when royalism and Anglicanism were virtually synonymous, a strong sense of Denham's religion has remained strangely elusive. We search mainly in vain the foundational source text of Denham literary criticism, his *Poems and Translations*, for signs of Christian literary allusion, much less conviction. His modern editor, T.H. Banks, divided Denham's poetic oeuvre into 'Miscellaneous', 'Political', 'Elegies and Eulogies', and 'Translations'; not unreasonably, he saw no need for a section marked 'Devotional'.[1] For what religion there is in Denham's verse is—it would seem—overwhelmingly classical. Line 2 of 'Coopers Hill' invokes Parnassus, signalling from the outset the literary and mythological impulse we find infusing several other poems, too, such as 'A Song', with its supplication to Morpheus, and 'Friendship Against Love', saturated in the imagery of Troy, and of a Phoebus who 'resigns his Darts, and *Jove* / His Thunder to the God of Love'.[2]

Even the elegies seem to eschew orthodox religion: 'On Mr. Abraham Cowley His Death and Burial amongst the Ancient Poets' privileges kudos-carrying associations with Chaucer, Shakespeare, Horace, Virgil, and Pindar, whom (with Cowley) 'Heroes, Gods, or God-like Kings / They praise, on their exalted wings' (152). The classical imperative is maintained in all of Denham's translations, including Books 2–6 of Virgil's *Aeneid*, while *The Sophy*, Denham's single play, is set in Muslim Safavid Persia. Explicit references to Christianity in *Poems and Translations* are exiguous and peripheral—and sometimes knowingly trivial. However, they at least provide apercus into Denham's antipathy towards religious

---

1 Banks, *PW*, pp. ix–x.
2 Ibid., p. 98. All quotations from Denham's poetry to this source.

enthusiasm: 'When nothing, but the Name of Zeal, appears / 'Twixt our best actions and the worst of theirs' informs an unflattering account of the Reformation in *Coopers Hill*;[3] 'News from Colchester' mocks a 'Zealous' parliamentarian town at a time (1644) when Christmas celebrations had been banned; the same location is used in a bawdy satire on Quakers, whose first verse gives a flavour of the whole:

> ALL in the Land of *Essex*,
> Near *Colchester* the Zealous,
>> On the side of a bank,
>> Was play'd such a prank,
> As would make a Stone-horse jealous.[4]

We can also identify a sense of *contemptus mundi* in 'Of Prudence':

> What's Time, when on Eternity we think?
> A thousand Ages in that Sea must sink;
> Time's nothing but a word, a million
> Is full as far from Infinite as one.
> To whom thou much dost owe, thou much must pay,
> Think on the Debt against th' accompting day;
> God, who to thee, Reason and Knowledge lent,
> Will ask how these two Talents have been spent.[5]

Like 'The Progress of Learning', 'The True Presbyterian without Disguise' is another merciless invective against zeal, though its attribution to Denham is doubted by Banks,[6] while 'A Speech Against Peace at the close Committee' lampoons John Hampden as the archetypal puritan opponent of Charles I who 'would not Monarchy destroy, / But as the only way to enjoy / The ruine of the Church' (122). As for the designedly nugatory, in 'On My Lord Croft's and my Journey into Poland', a successful mission to raise money for Prince Charles's exiled and attenuated court, the moment of decision is wryly bathetic:

> For when
> It was mov'd there and then
> They should pay one in ten,
> The Dyet said Amen.[7]

---

3  Ibid., p. 73.
4  *A relation of a Quaker, that to the shame of his profession, attempted to bugger a mare near Colchester* (London, s.n., 1659).
5  Banks, *PW*, p. 194.
6  Ibid., p. 325.
7  Ibid., p. 109.

One other poem is worthy of mention—a previously unpublished work held in Surrey Archives, ostensibly written by Denham's father on the occasion of the almshouses he founded for five poor women in Egham, Surrey, in 1637. It is quite conceivable that the seventy-seven-year-old Judge John Denham (1559–1639) was assisted (at least) in the composition of 'The Founder to his Work' by his twenty-one-year-old son, which if true would make it Denham's earliest known poem.

> Here as a steward have I spent
> Part of what God my Master lent
> Then say not mine the Fabric is
> For its not mine but his
> Least praise or vain applause prophane
> The work and my intentions stain
> For that a present Garden were
> But my reward I seek not here
> Not Builders nor Dwellers sloth
> This Pile intends, but that from both
> God may have glory in the loan
> Of those his goods which are his own
> God is the widows House and Livery
> Where widowed from the world they may
> Contemplate Heaven and to him pray
> That they and we and all may come
> To praise him in a larger roome.[8]

Essentially, though, there seems little evidence of a sustained engagement with the Christian religion in Denham's poetry and translations.[9] In consequence, for most observers the abiding impression of Denham's religion is, according to one's perspective, either a comically or poignantly delusional one: his bizarre claim to Charles II, during his temporary madness (widely thought to be induced by the open affair between his second wife and the Duke of York), to be the Holy Ghost.[10] According to Sir Stephen Fox, 'Sir John Denham, that great master of

---

8  Surrey History Centre, 2118/2/5 ('Denham's Almshouses').

9  Denham's treatise against gaming, *The Anatomy of Play* (1651), has a section on 'how heinously it is offensive to God' (p. 25), though as illustrated in Geoffrey Smith's chapter in this book the author's actions on this matter fell someway short of his rhetoric; *The Anatomy of Play: Written by a worthy and Learned Gent.: Dedicated to his Father, to shew his detestation of it* (London: G.P. for Nicholas Bourne, 1651). The situation is also ambiguous regarding Denham's long career as Surveyor General (1660–68): he was a prominent member of the commission for the repair of St. Paul's Cathedral prior to the Great Fire of 1666; however, this was a position for which (albeit legitimately) he received an additional salary; H.M. Colvin et al., *The History of the King's Works*, 6 vols, v, 1660–1782 (London: HMSO, 1976), pp. 6, 9.

10  John Aubrey, *'Brief Lives', Chiefly of Contemporaries*, ed. Andrew Clark, 2 vols (Oxford: Clarendon Press, 1898), i, p. 219.

wit and reason, is fallen quite mad, and he who despised religion, now in his distraction raves of nothing else'.[11] Only marginally more credible, in fact, is the friendship Denham, the 'bon viveur and prankster'[12] and irreverent royalist writer of squibs and satires, struck up with the firebrand parliamentarian preacher Hugh Peters, after being captured at Dartmouth, in April 1646.[13] His reputation for irreligiousness persisted: a fashionable nineteenth-century magazine doubts that Denham, who 'had passed his youth in the indulgence of every licentious pleasure without restraint', murdered his second wife but cautions, 'it was not likely he would be withheld by those religious principles, which would have made any other man shudder at so horrible an act, and which principles he had been known to ridicule'.[14]

Yet despite the apparent dearth of the devotional in Denham's poetry, Fox's assertion that he 'despised religion', and his posthumous reputation, Samuel Johnson wrote that Denham 'appears, whenever any serious question comes before him, to have been a man of piety', since he 'consecrated his poetical powers to religion, and made a metrical version of the psalms of David'.[15] Denham's posthumously published *A Version of the Psalms of David, Fitted to the Tunes used in Churches* (1714),[16] composed in 1667 or 1668, has attracted remarkably little critical attention since Johnson. Banks contents himself with reproducing Denham's version of the twenty-third Psalm, since

> The task of writing good poetry that was at the same time fitted to church tunes proved too much even for Milton. This being the case, it seems unprofitable to attempt a detailed comparison of Denham's work with that of his rivals.[17]

O Hehir, Denham's modern biographer, though not reproducing any of Denham's versions of the Psalms, provides more detail as to their publication; even so, further scrutiny he sees as redundant, since they 'are not to be judged by the ordinary

11  HMC, *Ormonde Manuscripts*, n.s. (1904), iii, p. 217.
12  Timothy Raylor, *Cavaliers, Clubs and Literary Culture: Sir John Mennes, James Smith, and the Order of the Fancy* (Newark: University of Delaware Press, 1994), p. 94.
13  'After the delivery of your Royal Father's Person into the hands of the Army, I undertaking to the Queen Mother, that I would find some means to get access to him, she was pleased to send me, and by the help of Hugh Peters'. From the Dedication to the King', in *Poems and Translations*. Peters was executed at the Restoration for having pressed for the execution of Charles I. See O Hehir, *HD*, p. 68.
14  'Biographical Sketches of Illustrious and Distinguished Characters: Lady Denham', in *La Belle Assemblée; or, Bell's Court and Fashionable Magazine* (London, England), issue 141, 1 October 1820.
15  Samuel Johnson, *The Lives of the Most Eminent English Poets: With Critical Observations on Their Works*, 2 vols (London: John Sharpe, 1805), i, p. 67.
16  John Denham, *A Version of the Psalms of David, Fitted to the Tunes used in Churches, By the Honourable Sir John Denham, Knight of the Bath* (London: Jonah Bowyer, 1714); hereafter Denham, *Version*.
17  Banks, *PW*, p. 44.

canons of poetry.[18] Johnson himself wrote of Denham's Psalms that 'he has failed; but in sacred poetry who has succeeded?'.[19] The critical reception of Denham's *A Version of the Psalms* before Johnson is, at first glance, equally cool: neither Aubrey, in *'Brief Lives'*, nor Langbaine, in *An Account of the Dramatick Poets*, deems the work worthy of mention,[20] while the approbation of Isaac Watts, a prominent figure—with Charles Wesley—in the rise of eighteenth-century Protestant hymnody, is equivocal:

> I resign to Sir *John Denham* the honour of the best Poet, if he has given his Genius but a liberty; yet his Work will ever shine brightest among those that have confined themselves to a meer Translation. But that close Confinement has often forbid the Freedom and the Glory of Verse, and by cramping his Sense has render'd it sometimes too obscure for a plain Reader and the publick Worship, even tho' we lived in the Days of *David* and *Judaism*.[21]

However, other sources present a radically different picture and run counter to the critical neglect into which the text has subsequently fallen. Samuel Woodford's poem 'To the Honourable Sir John Denham, upon his new Version of the Psalms' (1668), and Woodford's influential role in Denham's translation, will be discussed in further detail below. The other contemporary—and equally effusive—response comes from the royalist poet and dramatist, Jasper Mayne (1604–1672). Echoing a lament for the state of metrical Psalm translations voiced (as we will see) by Denham and Woodford, though employing more piquant language, Mayne brackets previous writers with 'those dark Ages when the World was blind', where attempts to English the Psalms resembled primitive drawers wont to 'Leaving it doubtfull by their want of skills, / Whether Man were not an Ape drawn ill'. The pervasive and enduring Sternhold and Hopkins Psalm translation, 'a kind of classical pop music to thousands upon thousands',[22] takes the brunt of Mayne's ire.

> So, though our English Psalms be David call'd,
> They by Translation are grown flat and pall'd:
> And lost much of that native height and fire,
> Which did the first Original enspire.
> Dull Sternhold Phoebus and John Hopkins muse,
> Our Parish Clerks do now for phlegm refuse:
> And will not grant their Meeter to be Psalms,
> But Rustick Numbers born of zealous qualms:
> Scarce worthy to be read …

18  O Hehir, *HD*, p. 250.
19  *The Lives*, i, p. 75.
20  Gerard Langbaine, *An Account of the English Dramatick Poets* (Oxford, 1691), pp. 125–29.
21  Isaac Watts, *The Psalms of David imitated in the language of the New Testament* (London, 1719), p. xxv.
22  David Norton, *A History of the Bible as Literature*, 2 vols (Cambridge: Cambridge University Press, 1993), ii, p. 47.

Denham's decorous language and faithfulness to the Hebrew text has, however, changed the landscape, restoring the original royal author, no less, to his former glory:

> Your noble Muse doth more decorum keep,
> Than make him sing as when he sang to Sheep:
> Or cloath him in a poor course Shephers weed,
> And change his Harp into an Oaten Reed.
> Your English sparkles like the Hebrew flame,
> The Garment's divers, but the Heat the Same.
> In his new Robes, attir'd by you he Sings,
> As Psalms of Poets, and as best of Kings.
> Two Crowns do now his sacred head infold,
> Yours made of Laurel, and his own of Gold.

Mayne is keen to praise Denham's accommodation of the Psalms' many moods and registers, 'High without swelling, low and yet not weak, / Nothing to Strein'd as doth in streining break', concluding that

> By your Translation are confuted, who
> With Davids Psalms translate his Spirit too:
> And his rich Piety by you is sung,
> So like to him, that tis his Harp new strung.[23]

The first post-publication appraisal of Denham's *Version* was made by the clergyman and academic, Henry Felton (1679–1740), in the second and enlarged edition of his *A Dissertation on Reading the Classics, and Forming a Just Style*, published in 1718. Writing to advise a young nobleman in social affairs, Felton lauds the 'excellent' Psalms which Denham, 'by a noble Simplicity of Style, by a Clearness and Easiness of Expression, by an Exactness and Harmony of Numbers, hath made […] so delightful to the Ear'. Denham's adroit adaptability to the devotional material at hand is particularly meritorious: our satisfaction is 'vastly rais'd'

> when we consider the Subject Matter various as the several Occasions, and devout Passions of the Psalmist, and observe the Translator varying his Style, and every where forming himself to the Spirit of the Original, sometimes in humble Acknowledgements of a repenting Sinner, sometimes in the chearful Voice of Praise and Thanksgiving.

Denham has successfully married content to form, 'delivering Divine Precepts with all the Plainness, Simplicity, and Majesty of Verse', and 'in the sublimest

---

23  Bodl. MS. Eng. poet. e. 4, 1r-4v.

Strains, above the Reach of all mortal Eloquence'. Felton concludes with the striking claim that in this final work the poet has surpassed himself: 'In his other Pieces this honourable Bard rose above most others, in an Age that most abounded with good Poets; but much more in this Translation, by which he hath not only rais'd his Fame, but Himself, to Heaven'.[24]

John Holland, in his roll-call of British Psalm translators and translations, accords Denham the honour of his own entry, alongside his Psalm 145, 'O Lord my God, my Songs to thee', noting that 'some portions of his translation […] have been highly and deservedly praised'. In turn, he quotes William Tattershall's view, stated in the latter's Preface to his edition of James Merrick (1797), 'that none of his predecessors or contemporaries have ever come near him, and that few of his successors have equalled, scarcely one surpassed him'. He adds, 'what height of devotion, what elegance of diction, do we meet with from the beginning to the conclusion of this author's work, wherein there is nothing too difficult for meaner capacities, nothing foreign to, or incoherent with the Scriptural sense of the Psalmist!'.[25]

In concurring with Herrick's epithet of 'rare Denham',[26] but linking it to a work of devotion, Mayne doubtless strayed into the realm of formulaic flattery; the latter was, after all, praising a fellow alumnus—and royalist—in a poem located in a late seventeenth-century Oxford University poetic miscellany.[27] Nevertheless, together with the subsequent praise Denham's translation received from Felton, Holland, and Tattersall, it shows that while this work has not gone unnoticed it has failed to influence his fundamental reputation. Whatever its aesthetic merits, Denham's *Version* was a considerable literary undertaking—at 152 quarto pages, only 35 shorter than *Poems and Translations*. Effectively providing us with 150 additional poems, as well as a revealing dedication and Preface, it offers fresh insight into a Denham self-fashioning himself as a literary figure in the Restoration. It also opens up a religious vista—including, as we will see, a network of clerical friends—usually eclipsed, if not occluded, by a secular and satirical outlook traditionally emanating from a pervasively present-day, worldly viewpoint.[28]

24  Henry Felton, *A Dissertation on Reading the Classics, and Forming a Just Style* (London: Jonah Bowyer, 1718), pp. 219–21.
25  John Holland, *Psalmists of Britain: Records of Upwards of One Hundred and Fifty Authors, Who Have Rendered the Whole or Parts of the Book of Psalms, into English Verse*, 2 vols (London, 1843), ii, pp. 113–14. The author claims that 'In order to give every advantage to this Version, it was accompanied with music composed by Andrew Roner, the friend of Handel'.
26  From Herrick's poem, 'To Mr Denham, on his Prospective Poem'.
27  Mayne's poem is placed first in a 248-page quarto volume also featuring (in the same neat hand) poems by Waller, Cowley, Marvell, and Dryden.
28  In Bonamy Dobrée's spoof account by Denham of a conversation between Bishop King and Edmund Waller, Waller observes, 'It was not his [Denhams's] nature to suffer idleness, and where gentle Mr. Cowley could be happy in contemplation, he could only rage in impotence'. Bonamy Dobrée, *Sir John Denham: A Conversation between Bishop Henry King and Edmund Waller, at the Palace, Chichester, March, 1669* (Kensington: Cayme Press, 1927), p. 9.

**II**

In a sense, despite the paucity of devotional material identified above, it should come as no great surprise that Denham made a translation of the Psalms. For any self-respecting man of letters, the literary environment for doing so in the seventeenth century remained as propitious as it had been in the sixteenth. In a post-Reformation confessional landscape where 'the singing of hymns and psalms [...] played a profound part in inculcating a sense of loyalty and identification with the new worship',[29] metrical Psalms were of particular moment: the task of replacing Sternhold and Hopkins, as Hannibal Hamlin has shown, 'attracted a huge diversity of translators, representing a startling range of aesthetic, doctrinal, ecclesiastical, and political positions'.[30] Publication figures help bear this out: the period between 1600 and 1653 witnessed 206 new complete metrical versions.[31] More widely, the Book of Psalms was revered by contemporaries, for whom it was 'the epitome of the entire scripture, the compendium of all theological, doctrinal and moral knowledge'.[32] Moreover, writers of the Renaissance 'remained convinced that the Psalms were indeed poems'.[33] Their poetic properties, enhanced by the metaphorical richness of the original Hebrew text, strengthened the musical associations with the 'songs' of David, inspiring memorable English metrical translations from the 1530s onwards. Thus the cultural, not just religious, freight of the Psalms is clear: for Denham's literary contemporaries the Psalms represented 'the highest matter in the noblest form'.[34] The Psalm paraphrases of Sir Thomas Wyatt, the Earl of Surrey, Sir Philip Sidney, and the Countess of Pembroke, among others, had brought the devotional verse of the Psalms firmly into the English literary canon; so much so that Sidney claims in his *Defence of Poesy* (1590) that the poetic charge of the Psalms is sufficient justification for assigning poetry a privileged position in the minds of his contemporaries, for 'what else is the awaking his musical instrument [...] but a heavenly poesy?'[35]

---

29  Andrew Pettegree, *Reformation and the Culture of Persuasion* (Cambridge: Cambridge University Press, 2005), p. 40. In the event, *The Whole Booke of Psalmes, collected into Englysh metre by T. Starnhold, T. Hopkins & others* ... (London, 1562) proved exceptionally hard to dislodge: approximately 819 editions were published between 1562 and 1729; Beth Quitslund, *The Reformation in Rhyme: Sternhold, Hopkins and the English Metrical Psalter, 1547–1603* (Aldershot: Ashgate, 2008), p. 1, n. 1.

30  Hannibal Hamlin, *Psalm Culture and Early Modern English Literature* (Cambridge: Cambridge University Press, 2004), p. 51.

31  Banks, *PW*, p. 44, n. 184.

32  Barbara Lewalski, *Protestant Poetics and the Seventeenth-Century Religious Lyric* (Princeton: Princeton University Press, 1979), p. 41.

33  Hamlin, *Psalm Culture*, p. 6.

34  From 'Upon the Translation of the Psalms by Sir Philip Sidney, and the Countess of Pembroke, his sister', in *John Donne: The Complete English Poems*, ed. A.J. Smith (London: Allen Lane, 1971), p. 333

35  *Sir Philip Sidney's Defence of Poesy*, ed. Lewis Soens (Lincoln: Nebraska University Press, 1970), p. 8. This paragraph has been adapted from Philip Major, *Writings of Exile in the English Revolution and Restoration* (Farnham: Ashgate, 2013), p. 35.

And the pervasive influence of the Psalms can be seen also in the vogue for new religious lyrics, evidenced pre-eminently in *Paradise Lost*, 'perhaps the most lyrical of epics, and a poem steeped in the Psalms'.[36] For these reasons Denham's 'professional' and 'amateur' literary peers from both sides of the mid-century political divide, Cowley and Milton, Hyde and Fairfax, had been able to establish, cement, or self-fashion their place as men of letters by composing works on the Psalms.[37] It was with this established literary milieu and tradition, which included a specific subset of royalist writers, that Denham identified himself in composing his translation.

Though the precise circumstances behind the timing of its publication remain unclear, Denham's *A Version of the Psalms* owes much to the author's friendship with the religious poet Samuel Woodford (1636–1700), a fellow alumnus of Wadham College, Oxford, who in 1667 had cemented a growing poetic reputation with his popular *A Paraphrase upon the Psalms of David*, dedicated to Denham's cousin, George Morley, Bishop of Winchester.[38] In an extensive Preface, the author acknowledges (as Denham was to do) the influence of Cowley's version of Psalm 114, as well as works on the Psalms by George Buchanan, George Sandys, Henry King, Sir Philip Sidney, and John Wilkins. He also issues a challenge which, as we will see, Denham responds to in his own Preface.

36  Cowley translated Psalm 114 as part of his unfinished epic, *Davideis*; Milton, in 1648 and 1653, Psalms 80–88 and 1–8, respectively, and Psalms 114 and 136 as a schoolboy; Hyde wrote the posthumously published *Contemplations and Reflections on the Psalms of David* while in exile on Jersey, in Madrid and Antwerp. It features in *A Collection of Several Tracts of the Right Honourable Edward, Earl of Clarendon* (London: T. Woodward and J. Peele, 1727). For a recent study of *Contemplations*, see Major, *Writings of Exile*, pp. 27–65. Fairfax composed his complete translation in retirement at Nun Appleton in the 1650s or 1660s. It occupies 388 of the 551 folio pages of devotional writing in Fairfax's unpublished 'The Imployement of my Solitude', in Bodl. MS Fairfax 40. For a recent study of which, see Rory Tanner, 'An Appleton Psalter: The Shared Devotions of Thomas Fairfax and Andrew Marvell', in Andrew Hopper and Philip Major (eds), *England's Fortress: New Perspectives on Thomas, 3rd Lord Fairfax* (Farnham: Ashgate, 2014), pp. 213–34.
37  Hamlin, *Psalm Culture*, p. 213. The close link between the Psalms and *Paradise Lost* may add a kernel of supporting evidence to the anecdote stemming from Jonathan Richardson's *Explanatory Notes and Remarks on Milton's Paradise Lost* (London, 1734), that Denham 'came into the House one morning with a sheet, wet from the press, in his hand. What have you there, Sir John? Part of the noblest poem that ever was wrote in any language, or in any age. This was Paradise Lost'. Finding the book in a bookshop, Denham had been 'surprised with some passages he struck upon dipping here and there, and bought it. The bookseller begged him to speak in its favour if he liked it, for that it lay on his hands as waste paper'. The story has been delineated and its possible veracity defended by Banks (*PW*, pp. 32–35) and O Hehir (*HD*, pp. 239–42), and opposed by Hilton Kelliher, in his review of O Hehir's *Harmony from Discords*, in the *Review of English Studies*, new series, 22. 85 (February 1971), 79–81 (p. 80). It has yet to be pointed out, however, that the publication of *Paradise Lost*, in August 1667, was coterminous with Denham's planning or composing his *Version*, and hence that the Psalms-inspired religious language of the 'passages he struck upon' would indeed have resonated strongly with him.
38  Samuel Woodford, *A Paraphrase upon the Psalms of David* (London, 1667). For Woodford, see *ODNB*.

A complete edition of Woodford's works was published in 1713, the year before Denham's *Version*. This edition reprinted his flattering sixteen-quatrain poem, dated 1668, 'To the Honourable Sir John Denham, upon his New Version of the Psalms', first published in *A Paraphrase upon the Canticles* (1679).[39] The existence of the poem means that Woodford must have had access to Denham's manuscript some forty-six years before it was published. His praise for Denham is fulsome, and while the pre-existing friendship between them makes Woodford a more partial critic than Johnson, his own well-received work on the Psalms also makes him a more informed one. Thus, while the hyperbole is sometimes painful to behold, the poem cannot simply be dismissed as a formulaic encomium.

Its most striking feature is its focus on poetry rather than on the sacred content or import of the Psalms. Because of Denham's Version, 'Verse, which had many Ages been a slave; / Regain'd its freedom'. What is more, it did so, patriotically enough, 'in our Northern [Protestant] Clime'. Poetry was

> Fetter'd before in gross Impertinence,
> And by strange Monsters forc'd, it Pris'ner lay;
> Whose Strength was big swoln Words, and empty sense,
> And all the Cheats, which Ignorance betray.
>
> To make Vile Anagrams, was its best Art
> And lewdly then to descant on the Text;
> Whose Gloss was evermore the dullest part,
> And all the Wits to seem, and be perplext. (ll. 5–12)

Denham has ridden to the rescue of devotional poetry, belying his reputation solely for wit, and eschewing the convention of rhyme.

> 'Twas you, great Sir, who like the Redcross Knight,
> To save the Damsel Poesy, arose;
> Like him did with th'Enchanted Dragon fight,
> And made her Reign a Queen, amidst her Foes.
>
> Wit from your Pen, was quite another thing,
> Than what the Ignorant imagin'd it;
> And in your manner skilfully to Sing,
> More than to make rich Rimes, and Noises hit. (ll. 25–32)

In Denham's hands the Psalms have been reinvigorated, their divinity replenished by a 'Worthy' poet to 'whom all did look', who has successfully straddled the divide between secular and sacred poetry. The praise is all the higher coming from

---

39  Idem, *A Paraphrase upon the Canticles, and some select hymns of the New and Old Testament* (London, 1679), pp. 146–49. All quotations to this source.

a devotional poet and prebendary of Chichester who 'must have needed consider-able persuasion on the part of his publishers before he allowed his secular to be included in his book'.[40]

> From you the Jewish Psalmist has receiv'd
> The latest Glory, which he could expect;
> And all, who at his barbarous Sufferings griev'd,
> With Pleasure on them thus expir'd reflect.
>
> You were that Worthy, for whom all did look,
> To' attempt, and execute this bold Design;
> Nor was there other Way, than what you took,
> By Humane Poesy, to restore Divine. (ll. 49–56)

Seen through Woodford's eyes, Denham has not only accomplished a radically new (and superior) version of the Psalms, but also fashioned a fresh image as a serious poet. As we shall see, it is an image Denham himself, in his Preface, is not slow to advertise.

## III

The task of editing Denham's Psalms fell not to Woodford himself but to his son, Heighes (1664–1724), alumnus—like his father and Denham—of Wadham College, Canon of Chichester, Vicar of Epsom in Surrey, and domestic chaplain to Lord Anglesey. There is no clear evidence as to why he published Denham's *Version* in 1714. The closest his descendent comes to an answer is to comment that 'This version by Sir John Denham seems to have been mislaid for a time, and after his death it came into the hands of Heighes Woodford, Samuel's eldest son, who edited it, and dedicated it to the Earl of Derby'.[41] However, it seems reasonable to surmise that the publication reflects the high opinion of the work which Samuel Woodford expressed in his poem, and was intended, a year after Samuel's complete works had been posthumously published, as a tribute by Heighes to his late father's friendship with and admiration for Denham. In fact, the Dedication to Lord Derby betrays further, mutual connections between the Woodfords and Denhams. As Heighes remarks near the beginning, Derby was the husband of Denham's granddaughter, the daughter of Sir William Morley, who had married Denham's daughter Anne; he was thus a 'Worthy Patron for this last Performance of so Celebrated a Man'.[42] More so than his father had done, per-haps reflecting his senior clerical status, Heighes is keen to distinguish between

---

40  Dorothy Heighes Woodforde (ed.), *Woodforde Papers and Diaries* (London: Peter Davies, 1932), p. 7.
41  Ibid., p. 7.
42  Denham, *Version*, p. iv.

Denham's former and last work, not to decry the secular poetry but to praise the sacred. 'The Fine Genius of Sir JOHN DENHAM, appears every where in his former Writings; yet in This, the Product of his Piety and retired years, He seems even to have excell'd Himself'.[43] Exceeding even his father's effusiveness, Heighes perceives in Denham's *Version*

> a most devout Elevation of Soul, and wonderful Energy and Beauty of Expression […] So that all his other Monuments, rais'd by Verse to perpetuate his Memory, seem mere Vanity to This, and unworthy to be compar'd with this Excellent Design, which is fitted for the Service of the Church of GOD.[44]

After touching on Denham's stated intention to correct 'the Imperfections of the Version [Sternhold and Hopkins] then, and still continued in Use', Heighes reminds Derby of the immediate circumstances behind the publication. The original manuscript had 'lain a considerable time with the Right Reverend Father in God, GEORGE [Morley] Lord Bishop of *Winton*' before Heighes had returned it to Derby's family.[45] This puts Denham's work in good company, for Morley was also an important literary figure, with an extensive and wide-ranging patronage. He assisted the exiled Clarendon with his *Brief View* (1676), a reply to Hobbes's *Leviathan*, asked Adam Littleton to complete Bishop John Earle's translation of Richard Hooker's *Ecclesiastical Polity* into Latin, and mentored Izaak Walton.[46] It also reflects further familial ties, for Morley and Denham were first cousins, Morley's mother's brother being Denham's father, the judge Sir John Denham.[47] Heighes claims that Denham's grandson William Morley had returned the manuscript to him, 'with Commands to transcribe them for the Press',[48] though from whom those commands originated remains unclear.[49] Since William was Denham's main heir, it was in his gift to execute his grandfather's wishes, hence we may infer that publication was one of them. If true, this makes Denham's *Version*, intriguingly, a form of self-fashioning from beyond the grave.

The diligence with which Denham composed the work, supporting the notion of authorial intent to publish, is attested by Heighes's needing to incorporate 'the numerous Interlinings which were made' to the original text; the editor's own

---

43  Ibid., p. v.

44  Ibid., pp. vi–vii.

45  Ibid., p. viii.

46  Hyde, Edward, *A Brief View and Survey of the dangerous and pernicious errors to Church and State, in Mr. Hobbes's book, entitled Leviathan* (Oxford, 1676).

47  Morley's close links with both Denham and Hyde (during the Interregnum he kept the flame of Anglicanism alive in Hyde's house in Antwerp) appear to have done little to thaw the perennially frosty relations between the two men.

48  Denham, *Version*, p. viii.

49  O Hehir speculates that William's premature death helped cause the delay in publication. If true, it does not explain why Heighes held back for at least another thirteen years; William must have died by 1701, when his sister Mary became sole heir to their father, Sir William Morley; O Hehir, *HD*, pp. 250, n. 68, p. 256, n. 80.

assiduousness reinforced by his having to negotiate 'a Hand not very easy to read'. Completion of the editing process was not solely influenced by Denham's familial request, however, for 'that which more particularly moved me to finish this Work, was a sight of some late Translations of the Psalms, which I perceiv'd to fall as short of Sir JOHN DENHAM'S Spirit, as they exceeded him in Length'.[50] Collaboration was key: if the original manuscript had been examined by an authoritative source, Bishop Morley, the edited draft enjoyed the 'Perusal of several Eminent Judges; among whom was that Great Ornament of the Church of *England*, Dr. SHARPE, the late Archbishop of York, who approv'd of it so far, that he often intimated his earnest Desire to see it Publish'd'.[51] John Sharpe (1644/45–1714) preached at the coronation of Queen Anne and became her closest advisor. It is possible that his death in February 1714 provided the final impetus for Heighes to steer 'This long-conceal'd Manuscript, and most Excellent Piece of Divine Poesy' into print.[52]

## IV

If Heighes Woodford's Dedication reveals the background to its publication, Denham's Preface to his *Version* illuminates the circumstances of composition—and by extension the author's frame of mind in the twilight of his life. His Preface to *Poems and Translations* has been usefully mined by scholars for its autobiographical content, but the far longer Preface to his *Version of the Psalms* has been largely ignored. This neglect is surprising, since the latter Preface represents an important attempt—in hindsight, largely unsuccessful—at a redefinition of Denham's self- and public image as he entered old age, an explicit narrative of the implicit self-transformation communicated by the Psalms themselves. In the process, Denham not so much rejects his former poetry—he likely wrote several more secular and classical pieces between 1667 and 1668, including 'Friendship and Single Life against Love and Marriage' and 'Sarpendon's Speech to Galucus in the 12th of Homer', respectively—as essays an ambitious fusion of it.

From the outset, the author casts himself in the role of a writer serving a 'new Master', David, rather than his 'old Master *Virgil*', echoing the sentiments of his Preface to 'The Progress of Learning':

> *My early Mistress, now my Antient Muse,*
> *That strong Circaean liquor cease to infuse,*

---

50  Denham, *Version*, pp. viii–ix. There are a number of candidates for these 'late' works, including Daniel Burgess's *Psalms, Hymns and Spiritual Songs by the late Daniel Burges* (London: John Clarke, 1714). For other possibilities, see William J. Chamberlin (ed.), *Catalogue of English Bible Translations: A Classified Bibliography of Versions and Editions Including Books, Parts and Old and New Testament Apocrypha and Apocryphal Books* (Westport, CT: Greenwood, 1991), pp. 287–88.

51  Denham, *Version*, p. ix.

52  Ibid., p. x. The absence of an entry (and hence entry date) for Denham's *Version* on the Stationer's Company Register hinders further speculation on this point.

*Wherewith thou didst Intoxicate my youth,*
*Now stoop with dis-inchanted wings to Truth;*[53]

But there remains a crucial link between the two masters, for just as the Roman poet had told of Apollo's pulling him by the ear and 'advising him, That a Shepherd ought to mind his Sheep, and to sing only of low and humble things',[54] so David was himself a shepherd, and (in Psalm 131) 'speaks to the same purpose', though 'from a higher Spirit than *Apollo's*'.[55] Denham's 'bold Undertaking' is mandated by both authors ignoring their own rule, manifested in Virgil's 'proving the highest Poet that ever *Rome* produc'd, and the other not only above him in That, but in Prophecy above All others, before, or since, till the *Messiah*, who was to descend from Him, came into the World'.[56] In this way, Denham can usefully have it both ways, acknowledging the superiority of his new tutor but also reminding readers of the august inspiration for his former writing.[57] The same dual theme is further developed in respect of the immediate incentive for his composition, for Denham was

> far from undertaking this Work upon these, or any Suggestion, or Instigation of my own; being solicited, and almost forc'd to it, by many of my Learned Friends, both of the Clergy and Laity, and some of them as well vers'd in the Art of Poesy as in most of the other Liberal Sciences.[58]

That he had 'many' friends in holy orders is in itself something of a departure from the common perception of Denham as the archetypal bon vivant cavalier, a man who 'despised religion'. Pride of place in the subsequent roll-call of informed 'Commentators' with whom he consulted goes not to Morley but to 'my old Friend', the Anglican divine Henry Hammond (1605–1660), about whom, however, nothing more is said.[59] Hammond was an influential member of the Great Tew circle of the 1630s and chaplain to Charles I; he did more than anyone to shape the theology of the Church of England in the Interregnum and beyond, especially regarding the importance of episcopal authority.[60] Friendship with Hammond therefore gives Denham access to the highest

---

53  Banks, *PW*, p. 114.
54  Taken from Virgil's *Eclogues* 6.3–5.
55  Denham, *Version*, p. xiii.
56  Ibid., pp. xiii–xiv.
57  Hamlin notes a vestigial Homeric-Virgilian epic strain, a strong focus on journeying to the underworld, consonant with an author who had penned *The Destruction of Troy*, in Denham's Psalm 23, where 'To walk in Shades among the Dead / My hopes, not Fears, increase'; Hamlin, *Psalm Culture*, p. 164.
58  Denham, *Version*, p. xiv.
59  Ibid., p. xv.
60  For a recent account of Hammond's prominent role in the English Church of the 1640s and 1650s, see Sarah Mortimer, 'Exile, Apostasy and Anglicanism in the English Revolution', in Philip Major (ed.), *Literatures of Exile in the English Revolution and Its Aftermath, 1640–1690*

circles of the English Church during a formative stage in its history. The work Denham alludes to is Hammond's compendious paraphrase and annotation of the Psalms, published in 1659,[61] which was still being reprinted in the mid-nineteenth century.

Special mention is made by Denham of the Latin version of the Psalms by George Buchanan (1506–1582).[62] Here, in the ongoing navigation between the exigencies of poetry and piety, the pendulum swings back to classical literary aesthetics: Buchanan is 'a most Eloquent Poet, and nearest the Ancients of any that I have seen [...] The Stile of his Version is round and just, and always suted to the Subject', an opinion shared by 'the Learned Pope *Urban* VIII, who was likewise an Excellent Poet'.[63] Samuel Woodford's version is another influence, his paraphrases a 'Pleasure' to read, but there can be no emulation of it here, since 'his Verse is not for Singing, but Reading'.[64] The signal importance of Woodford, however, is that 'by some modest Expressions in his Preface, he seems to invite, or indeed to provoke me to a new Attempt'.[65] In the passage Denham refers to, Woodford's language is formulaically modest; the challenge he sets anything but.

> I know all that has ever yet been assay'd may be infinitely outdone, and I should be so far from grieving at it, though now a little concerned, that I heartily with this way of mine may give the first occasion to some excellent Person to undertake another version, and publish the Book of Psalms with greater beauties than ever it has appeared in, since it left Jerusalem.[66]

George Sandys (1578–1644), whom Samuel Woodward praises, is another author of whom Denham is aware.[67] The contrast between Sandys and Woodford is one of several passages lifting a veil on Denham's views on the ideal characteristics of devotional poetry, which are sufficiently generic to apply also to the

(Farnham: Ashgate, 2011), pp. 91–104. As with his connections with Morley, Hyde's close link to Hammond, via Great Tew, flies in the face of the his apparent antipathy towards Denham.

61  Henry Hammond, *A paraphrase and annotations upon the books of the Psalms briefly explaining the difficulties thereof, by H. Hammond D.D.* (London: R. Norton, for Richard Davis, 1659).

62  Denham, *Version*, p. xv; George Buchanan, *Paraphrasis psalmorum Dauidis poetica multo quam antehac castigatior auctore Georgio Buchanano; adnotata vbique diligenter carminum genera; eiusdem Buchanani tragoedia quae inscribitur Iephthes* (London, 1580). The book was printed by Henry Denham, unrelated to the poet.

63  Denham, *Version*, p. xv.

64  Ibid., pp. xv–xvi. In fact, this is one of the few points in the Preface when song is mentioned, seemingly belying the force of the subtitle, 'Fitted to the Tunes Used in Churches'. There is an important caveat, however: Denham explains that he has not gone beyond the octosyllabic in line length, since decasyllabic verse is 'incapable to be ordinarily sung' (p. xviii).

65  Ibid., p. xvi.

66  Woodford, *A Paraphrase upon the Psalms*, sig. C1v.

67  His *A Paraphrase upon the divine poems* (London, 1638) included a commendatory poem by Edmund Waller, 'To His Worthy Friend, Mr George Sandys on his Sacred Poems'.

secular sphere. They additionally suggest that song is not the sole end of his own Psalms: Woodford's

> Length is only in order to Fluency and Roundness of Expression, and the better to fit his Paraphrase for private Meditation and Delight, which I wou'd not willingly have lost. But Mr. *Sandys*'s Brevity makes him now and then irregular, obscure, and without that agreeable taste which becomes so weighty an Argument.[68]

According to Denham, the verse translation of the Psalms by William Barton (1597/8–1678), first published in 1644,[69] shows him to be 'a great *Hebrician*', who 'brings his Version very near the Original'; but 'either to make the Rhime more easy, or the Sense more plain, [he] has made the whole Work languishing and enervous'. It is better to emulate 'the Design of the first chief Author', who 'when he wrote Psalms of Praise, Thanksgiving, or Rejoicing, uses sprightly and chearful Airs, and the brightest Images', and exhibits a 'fervent, moving, and reconciling Spirit'.[70]

After this canter through the influences on his *Version*, Denham begins a more contemplative, autobiographical section of his Preface. The 'Change which Age and many Infirmitys had made in me', a 'Sense of Age, or Decay of Strength', has brought him to this task of 'restoring the Royal Poet to his first Dignity and Honour'.[71] The wit and invention of his younger years have given way to the judgement and experience necessary for a version of the Psalms. This is the ageing cavalier satirist and poet relinquishing the 'exuberant Excrescences of Youth' to deal with the weightier literary matter now at hand.[72] Still others have played their part, though, for he 'sent forth [the draft] to be fed, fashion'd and educated by others', notably the theologian, natural philosopher, Wadham College Warden, and newly appointed Bishop of Chester, John Wilkins (1614–1672), 'the same Dr. *Wilkins*, whom Dr. *Woodford* mentions in his Preface, as his Encourager, and with whom I have had a long and most friendly Acquaintance'.[73]

As himself a 'Promoter and Incourager of other learned Men to cooperate with him', Wilkins 'took most care of it', and 'was the person most proper to do it'. Here as elsewhere, Denham is anxious to convey an impression of collegiality. This is in part a useful if drily humorous means of spreading the blame for the book's imperfections ('if I have committed an Error, there are so many Accessorys to it, that even those, to whom I appeal'd as my Judges, are in some part

---

68  Denham, *Version*, pp. xvi–xvii.
69  William Barton, *The Book of Psalms in Metre* (London, 1644).
70  Denham, *Version*, pp. xvii–xviii.
71  Ibid., pp. xx, xix.
72  Ibid., p. xxi.
73  Ibid., pp. xxi–xxii. Wilkins had shown Woodford the Sidney Psalter in manuscript form, a Psalter which Denham did not see; Hamlin, *Psalm Culture*, p. 107.

as guilty as my self').[74] But it also, and more so, allows Denham to position his book along a kudos-carrying continuum. Given the subject matter at hand, the axiomatically independent-minded cavalier poet is content to sacrifice a measure of autonomy.

Turning specifically to the English tradition of sung Psalms, the aversion towards religious enthusiasm which we saw in the secular poetry resurfaces. The 'obsolete and unbecoming Dress wherein our singing Psalms have so long been disguis'd [...] embases and depraves the Splendour and Purity of the Original'. Denham concedes that Reformation 'Zeal' was responsible for the first singing of Psalms in the English Church, but this 'cannot justify the Continuance of them without Correction and Amendment'. To the author, 'It looks as if Poesy were so fatally divorc'd not only from good Sense, but from Divinity (tho it was the first Conveyer of it to Mankind) that it were impossible they shou'd ever meet again'. Denham sees his purpose as no less than bridging the gap he has identified between poetry and the devotional, as demonstrating that the two things 'are not utterly inconsistent'. This is something Cowley ('happily seconded' by Woodford) had so memorably achieved in his translation of Psalm 114, in his *Davideis*, thereby redeeming poetry 'from that Slavery, wherein the deprav'd Age has prostituted her to all imaginable Uncleanness'.[75] Thus Denham can claim, on the one hand, 'to shew that I have no other Ambition thro the whole Undertaking, than the Service of God, of this Blessed Church my Mother [the Church of England], and of my Brethren its Members'; and on the other, that if his 'Verse make it not despicable to High Understandings [...] I have both attain'd my own end, and serv'd that of Poesy, Delectare [et] Prodesse, to profit and delight'.[76] The latter half of this equation comes as no surprise, but the powerful endorsement of the Established Church in the former, if taken at face value rather than as affectation, stands athwart the abiding image of Denham the religious sceptic.

For all his at times artful disclaimers, Denham makes a large claim for his translation. No less than the 'Cry of the Nation calls for it', as an antidote to 'that Spirit of Profaneness which is gone out amongst us', the 'making [of] Sport with Scripture, and turning it into Ridicule'.[77] The chief culprit here is the Sternhold and Hopkins version: 'the vulgar Translation of the Psalms, which we keep in use, may have promoted this bold and most profane Licentiousness'. This is a stain both on the original author of the Psalms and on England itself: Denham's achievement will be 'to wipe off the Dirt thrown upon [David]; and no ill Office done to this learned Nation'.[78]

74  Denham, *Version*, pp. xix, xxii.
75  Ibid., pp. xxii–xxiv.
76  Ibid., p. xxvi. From Horace's *Ars Poetica*.
77  Denham, *Version*, p. xxix.
78  Ibid., pp. xxv–xxvi.

**V**

Given the enduring appeal of Sternhold and Hopkins, a work whose 'simple ballad metres imprinted the elements of Protestant spirituality on the hearts and minds of English people',[79] Denham failed in his task. There is little question, however, that he successfully distanced his *Version* linguistically from *The whole booke of Psalmes*. An extract from Psalm 57 will exemplify this. In Sternhold and Hopkins, the Psalm begins

> Take pitie for thy promise sake,
> have mercy Lord on me:
> For why my soule doth her betake
> unto the helpe of thee.
> Within the shadow of thy winges
> I set my selfe full fast:
> Till mischief, malice, and lyke thyngs
> be gon and overpaste.[80]

In Denham, this becomes:

> Extend, Oh Lord, thy Clemency,
> To him whose Trust in Thee is plac'd
> Under thy shad'wing Wings I'll ly.
> Till these Calimitys are past.[81]

Condensation and a concomitant pithiness, complemented by adherence to a uniform metre, characterise Denham's style, here and elsewhere. But the most arresting imagery from the Hebrew—in this case remaining under the shadow of God's wings—is invariably retained, if reformulated; while the diction and syntax seem to have been 'modernised' for seventeenth-century tastes. The abab rhyme scheme mirrors that of Sternhold, but Denham divides this Psalm into verses of six lines, each concluding with a rhyming couplet—in this verse, 'To the Most High my Crys ascend; / To God, who will my Cause defend'. Elsewhere, Denham's rhyme scheme varies considerably, independent of the Sternhold version, while his verse length fluctuates between four, six, and eight lines. Whether or not he consulted the original Hebrew, this is clearly a work on which Denham expended much scholarly energy.

What is harder to demonstrate than linguistic divergence from Sternhold and Hopkins is that Denham's Psalms are of autobiographical moment, betraying salient commentary and rumination either on his sometimes embattled post-Restoration life (encompassing a public cuckolding in his second marriage and,

79  Rivkah Zim, *English Metrical Psalms: Poetry as Praise and Prayer, 1535–1601* (Cambridge: Cambridge University Press, 1987), p. 207.
80  *The Whole Booke of Psalmes*, p. 133.
81  Denham, *Version*, p. 78.

relatedly, temporary madness) or, retrospectively, on the personal and political struggles of the civil war and Interregnum. Speculation on this is, however, perfectly legitimate, since the Psalms were rich matter for public and private reflection during the mid-century; indeed, few of them were refashioned in a disengaged or drily abstract way. It would seem churlish, for example, not to entertain the idea that that quintessential Psalm of displacement, Psalm 137, in which 'the experience of exile is fresh and acutely painful',[82] resonated for Denham with his experiences a decade and more earlier, in France and at The Hague. Though like many royalists he went back and forth to the continent during the 1650s, variously though never permanently reaching an accommodation with the republican regime, and though for some of that time, especially in 1646, it suited him well to escape his creditors, he was also—genuinely—a political fugitive, twice excluded from the king's counsels,[83] with a longest absence from England of four-and-a-half years, from August 1648 to March 1653.[84] What is to say that this seminal period in his life did not haunt him as he described

> WHEN on *Euphrates* Banks we sate,
> Deploring *Sion*'s doleful State;
> Our Harps, to which we lately sang,
> Mute as ourselves, on Willows hang.
>
> …
>
> Oh! How can we our Airs compose,
> And sing of God amongst his Foes!
> When I forget his Sacred Hill,
> May my right Hand forget her Skill![85]

The opening lines of several other Psalms—'LORD, why art thou from us so far' (10), 'AGAINST my Foes, O Lord, most High' (Psalm 56), 'LORD, Save me from my Enemys' (59), 'O God, to whom Revenge belongs' (94)—mobilize a similar hybrid of supplicatory despondency, bewilderment and anger, echoing the reflection on Psalm 6—while in exile on Jersey, between 1646 and 1648—of Edward Hyde: 'How long, O Lord, wilt thou let us lie under this insupportable Oppression? How long shall our enemies triumph in our Griefs, and in our Tears; in our banishment and in our Poverty'.[86] There are further Psalms which register a particularly

---

82  Robert Alter, *The Book of Psalms* (New York: Norton, 2007), p. 473.

83  Banks, *PW*, p. 11.

84  O Hehir, *HD*, p. 98. Displacement overseas was by no means essential for a sense of exile among royalists, or the literary expression of it. See Major, *Writings of Exile*, Chapter 3, 'Royalist Internal Exile', pp. 101–38.

85  Denham, *Version*, p. 203.

86  Edward Hyde, *Contemplations and Reflections on the Psalms of David*, in *A Collection of Several Tracts*, p. 394.

powerful sense of personal predicament, such as 'MY God, why dost thou me forsake' (22), 'LORD, thou my Ways hast search'd and known' (139), and 'WHEN in my sad Distress I cry'd' (120). Equally, we find palpable assertions of personal religious conviction, often mingled with a tone of *contemptus mundi*, such as in Psalm 144:

> GOD is my Rock, my Tow'r, my Shield,
> He taught my Hands the Sword to wield,
> And I, supported by his Power,
> Go forth the Nations Conqueror
> O what is Man, to Thee compar'd,
> That Thou his Offspring dost regard!
> Man of Mere Vanity is made,
> His Days soon vanish like a Shade.[87]

And in Psalm 82, 'GOD sits above the Thrones of Kings', there is—potentially—a rare trace of the limitations Denham places on monarchical authority, where the translator recalls how

> The Mighty once I Gods did call,
> And Sons of the most High,
> Till I beheld how Princes fall,
> And like the Vulgar die.[88]

In the febrile atmosphere of Restoration politics, such sentiments might on their own have precluded publication in Denham's lifetime; here, the discretion with which Denham was occasionally able and willing to express mild censure of the Crown dissolves in the Psalmist's clear-eyed meditation.

Faithfulness to the original is a familiar claim in Psalm translations of the seventeenth century, though whether the translators were working from the Hebrew source text, or from a version already Englished, is often a moot point. Denham insists he has done the former: he has 'kept as near as possibly I cou'd to the Letter, and never willingly vary'd from the Sense, unless it be to make it plainer to *English* Ears than the Original', a claim supported by his contention that 'the *Hebrew* is so short and abstruse a Language, that many single Words of it, to be rightly understood by us, must be turn'd into a kind of Sentences'.[89] If Denham has indeed gone back to the original Hebrew, it reinforces in the reader's mind the idea that his *Version* is no superficial undertaking, but a major linguistic exercise requiring a significant investment of time and intellectual energy. But the pervasive twin focus on piety and poetry remains the outstanding feature of Denham's

87 Ibid., p. 211.
88 Ibid., p. 120.
89 Ibid., pp. xxv–xxvi.

Preface, and it is not without autobiographical poignancy. His *Version* represents a long-delayed maturation of his poetic gifts, which were, he confesses, wasted on him as a youth. Poetry 'came to me by Nature from my Infancy, before Reason cou'd direct [it]: Yet as I came early to it, so I early laid it by in pursuance of other Inclinations'. Denham hopes God will accept this work 'in part of repayment of that Talent which I have so long mispent'.[90]

# VI

Sir John Denham's metrical translation of the Psalms subverts the neat labels of cavalier wastrel and secular poet all too easily attached to seventeenth-century royalist men of letters in general, and to Denham in particular. Its circumstances of production also challenge the perceived composition of the literary and courtly milieu he orbited, revealing a wide and long-lasting network of clerical friend-ships and influences dating back to his Oxford days. His Preface betrays a man self-fashioning a different legacy to the one which has endured, not that he was disavowing poesy, but rather taking it, as Felton believed, to an appositely higher level. Denham's Preface makes clear that his *Version* was not the product of a late conversion, but rather the fruit—and apogee—of long-held Christian conviction. In this context it would be hard—though not entirely implausible—to argue that his translation is a work of distended expiation, bolted on to a fundamentally secular corpus; a literary equivalent to his friend Thomas Killigrew's depiction in visual art, late in life, as a pilgrim of St James.[91] If we take this view, however, it probably says more about our *wanting* to remember Denham as first and fore-most a cavalier, a term which predominantly fails to accommodate—and often represents the antithesis of—a serious religious sensibility.[92] Denham will never be seen as primarily a divine poet, and there is no compelling evidence that he wanted to be. However, his *Versions of the Psalms of David* provides a new—Anglican—critical optic through which to view his final years, at least. Whether the same lens will yield new readings of his earlier poetry remains to be seen.

90  Ibid., pp. xxvii–xxviii.
91  See Philip Major (ed.), *Thomas Killigrew and the Seventeenth-Century English Stage* (Farnham: Ashgate, 2013), 'Introduction', p. 6.
92  See Chapter 1 of this volume, by John Stubbs.

# 8    The Hunting of the Stag

## Denham, Davenant, and a Royalist Dispute over Poetry

*Timothy Raylor*

## I

In his note to the reader of Sir John Denham's *Coopers Hill*, the publisher of the 1655 edition, the elusive 'J. B'., guarantees the superiority of this to earlier editions of the poem by drawing attention, as its major selling point, to 'that excellent Allegory of the *Royall Stag* (which among others was lop't off by the *Transcriber*) skilfully maintain'd without dragging or haling in Words and Metaphors, as the fashion now is with some that cannot write, and cannot but write'.[1] J.B. refers to the expanded version of the celebrated stag hunt incorporated into this new edition. That this expansion was the result of recent authorial revision, rather than the discovery of previously missing material, is clear from the editorial labours of Brendan O Hehir—with the consequent undermining of J.B. and his account of the poem.[2] The recent discovery of a single copy of an edition dated '1653'—substantively the same as that of 1655 (though without the prefatory note)—further undermines the authority of J.B.[3] But neither O Hehir nor any other commentator has, to my knowledge, been able to explain the latter part of J.B'.s cryptic remark: his contrast between Denham's delicately succinct handling of the allegory of the stag with the work of those excessively prolix and incompetent contemporaries who, by implication, and unlike Denham, *do* drag or hale in words and metaphor. It is my contention that, although mistaken about the genesis of the expanded stag hunt, J.B. is correct in his sense that the revised passage stands as a rebuke to contemporary poets who have tried, and failed in the ways he describes, to achieve a similar effect to Denham's allegory: the revised passage is, I suggest, an explicit rebuke to such writers.[4] The identification of the offending authors and the discovery of Denham's motives for the revision shed new light upon a dispute over

---

1  O Hehir, *EH*, p. 137. All quotations from *Coopers Hill* are taken from O Hehir's edition.
2  Ibid., pp. 67–70; O Hehir, *HD*, p. 109.
3  On this edition, see Timothy Raylor, 'The "1653" Copy of Denham's *Coopers Hill*', *Yale University Library Gazette*, 71 (1997), 130–39; *Index of English Literary Manuscripts*, vol. II, 1625–1700, comp. Peter Beal; pt. I, Behn-King (London and New York: Mansell, 1987), pp. 330, 335 (DeJ 9); Bernard Quaritch, *English Poetry before 1701*, catalogue 1027 (London, 1982), no. 55 (pp. 17–18).
4  O Hehir's suggestion that J.B. is merely defending 'by aggression' the additions seems to me unconvincing; *EH*, p. 138.

poetic reform that flourished among erstwhile royalists in exile at the Louvre in the late 1640s and that continued, after their dispersal, into the 1650s. At stake in this debate were fundamental questions about the function and language of poetry, and the direction it ought to take in the wake of the civil war.

## II

Our prime question is: Why did Denham, having promised King Charles I in the late 1640s to abjure poetry as a juvenile and irresponsible activity, return to the stag hunt in the early 1650s, expanding it to such an extent that it risked toppling the whole delicately balanced structure of his poem?[5] There are several possible answers to this question, all of which depend upon our understanding of the nature of the 1653 revisions to *Coopers Hill*. To understand these revisions, we need to look back at the evolution of the poem. In its earliest version (1641?), the stag hunt occupies 38 lines of a 328-line poem. The hunt is introduced when the poet, from his heightened vantage upon the hill, scans Egham Mead below:

> Here have I seene our Charles (when greate affaires
> Give leave to slacken & unbend his Cares)
> Chasing the Royall Stagge, the gallant beast
> Rous'd with the noyse twixt hope & feare distrest,
> Resolves tis better to avoyde, then meete
> His danger, trusting to his winged feete
> But when he sees the doggs now by the view,
> Now by the Sent, his speede with speede pursue:
> He tryes his frends amongst the lesser heard,
> Where he but lately was obey'd & fear'd:
> Safety he seekes, the heard unkindly wise:
> Or chases him from thence, or from him flyes;
> (Like a declying Statesman left forlorne
> To his frinds pitty & pursuers scorne)
> Wearied, forsaken & pursu'd, At last
> All Safety in dispaire of safety plact.
> Courrage he then assumes, resolv'd to beare
> All their assaults, when tis in vayne to feare:
> But when he sees the eager chace renew'd
> Himselfe by doggs, the doggs by men pursu'd;
> When neither speede nor Art, nor frends nor force
> Could helpe him, towards the Streame he bends his course:
> Hoping those lesser beasts would not assay,
> An Element more merciles then they:
> But feareles they pursue, nor can the flood

5  Banks, *PW*, p. 60.

Quench their dire thirst, (Alas) they thirst for blood.
As in a Calme the Oare-fynn'd Galleys creepe,
About a winde bound, & unweildy Shipp;
Which lyes unmov'd, but those that come too neere
Strikes with her thunder, & the rest with feare,
Till through her many leakes the Sea shee drinkes
Nor yealds at last but still resisting sinks:
So stands the stagg among the lesser hounds,
Repells their force & wounds returnes for wounds,
Till Charles from his unerring hand letts fly,
A mortall shaft, then glad & proud to die
By such a wound, he falls. The Cristall flood
Dying he dyes, & purples with his blood. (ll. 243–80)

One of the most remarkable features of this passage is its delicate disposition
of sympathy between royal hunter and noble prey—an effect achieved by sub-
tle shifts of perspective. The expression of sympathy for the stag was a common feature of humanist literature of the hunt, reaching back through Jaques's
lament in *As You Like It* to *The Noble Arte of Venerie or Hunting* (1576), which
includes a poem by George Gascoigne, written from the point of view of the hart
and lamenting the cruelty of humans in hunting.[6] In few cases, however, is the
disposition of sympathy between hunter and prey so deftly balanced as it is in
*Coopers Hill*.[7] Denham's stag hunt begins with the entrance of the royal hunter,
in pursuit of his game, but immediately adopts the perspective of 'the gallant
beast'—a shift announced by the epithet 'Royall', which associates the hunter
with the quarry. The perspective of the hunted stag is maintained as he struggles to
make his escape, and the declining statesman simile of lines 255–56 compounds
his humanisation. But to prepare for the reintroduction of the king, who must kill
the stag without appearing cruel and barbarous, some distancing or dehumanising
of the stag is necessary. This is achieved through the ship simile of lines 269–74,
which associates the stag with an inanimate object.

For our immediate purposes, the more important feature of this passage is the
semiotic status of the hunt. As Denham's editor explains, we lack an adequate
terminology to describe the subtlety of this formulation: 'The events are not

6  George Turberville, *The Noble Arte of Venerie or Hunting* (1576) (Oxford: Clarendon Press, 1908),
   pp. 136–40.
7  The voice of the hart in Gascoigne's poem, for example, is simply pitted against the surrounding
   text, which it decries as 'A looking Glasse of lessons lewde' (p. 137). On the tradition of ambivalence about hunting, see Claus Uhlig, '"The Sobbing Deer": *As You Like It*, II.i.21–66 and the
   Historical Context', *Renaissance Drama*, new series, III (1970), 79–109; Eric Rothstein, 'Discordia
   Non Concors: The Motif of Hunting in Eighteenth-Century Verse', *Journal of English and Germanic Philology*, 83 (1984), 330–54. On the argument over its legitimacy, see Keith Thomas, *Man
   and the Natural World: Changing Attitudes in England, 1500–1800* (London: Allen Lane, 1983),
   pp. 160–65.

allegorical, but quasi-allegorical: they parallel other events, or resemble other events in details, or obliquely refer to them'.[8] Although a general didactic purpose underlies the hunt, the particular focus here seems to be the fall of the Earl of Strafford: rejected by his peers as the deer is by the herd, and executed on the reluctant and tearful approval of the king. The poet's avoidance of a purely allegorical handling of the hunt is apparent in the comparison of the stag to a declining statesman—a move which points from the stag back to its referent; for, as O Hehir points out: 'Strafford was not like a declining statesman; he was one'.[9] There is a blurring of distinctions between tenor and vehicle here; a concern to forge closer and apparently natural connections between them, and to avoid the arbitrary and intrusive effect of naive allegory. Such concerns explain the omission, in the first printed text of the poem (1642), of the ship simile and its replacement with a simile comparing the drowning stag to a hero:

> As some brave *Hero*, whom his baser foes
> In troops surround, now these assaile, now those,
> Though prodigall of life, disdaines to die
> By vulgar hands, but if he can descry
> Some Nobler foe's approach, to him he cals
> And begs his fate, and then contented fals. (ll. 289–94)

The change removes the inanimate object and retains the personification of the stag, intensifying its association with Strafford and his predicament, and preparing the way for the king's coup de grace by making the stag-statesman a willing sacrifice.[10]

Despite the efficacy of his new simile, Denham was evidently unhappy with the complete omission of the ship. In the 1653 edition he restored it in a truncated form, merging it with the hero simile, in order to achieve, at the climax of the passage, an appropriate balance between sympathy and distance:[11]

> So towards a Ship the oarefin'd Gallies ply,
> Which wanting Sea to ride, or wind to fly,
> Stands but to fall reveng'd on those that dare
> Tempt the last fury of extream despair.
> So fares the Stagg among th'enraged Hounds,
> Repels their force, and wounds returns for wounds.
> And as a Hero, whom his baser foes
> In troops surround, now these assails, now those,

---

8  O Hehir, *EH*, p. 203.
9  Ibid., p. 204.
10  Ibid., pp. 223–24.
11  I quote here from O Hehir's text of the 1655 edition, which does not differ, in the passages quoted, from the 1653 edition.

Though prodigal of life, disdains to die
By common hands; but if he can descry
Some nobler foes approach, to him he calls,
And begs his Fate, and then contented falls.
So when the King a mortal shaft lets fly
From his unerring hand, then glad to dy.
Proud of the wound, to it resigns his bloud,
And stains the Crystal with a Purple floud. (ll. 307–22)

The reintroduction of the ship simile was, however, only one part of a massive expansion of the stag hunt episode to a total of eighty-two lines, some thirty of them completely new, in the 1653 edition.[12] Earl Wasserman has suggested that such additions serve merely to flesh out the description of the hunt, and that they blur the political significance of the passage and upset the balance of the poem.[13] O Hehir, however, has shown that the revisions move more in the direction of personification than description, with a human psychological process being attributed to the stag; and that, rather than muddying the political significance of the hunt, the revised version elaborates a new application, in which the demise of the king himself, rather than that of Strafford, becomes its prime referent.[14] While O Hehir's argument is convincing in its broad outlines, a number of questions remain. As O Hehir concedes, the details added to the stag hunt exceed the requirements of the local political application. The introduction of the hunters and the account of the stag's behaviour is especially revealing in this respect:

Here have I seen the King, when great affairs
Give leave to slacken, and unbend his cares,
Attended to the Chase by all the flower
Of youth, whose hopes a Nobler prey devour:
Pleasure with Praise, & danger, they would buy,
And wish a foe that would not only fly.
The stagg now conscious of his fatal Growth,
At once indulgent to his fear and sloth,
To some dark covert his retreat had made,
Where nor mans eye, nor heavens should invade
His soft repose; when th'unexpected sound
Of dogs, and men, his wakeful ear doth wound.
Rouz'd with the noise, he scarce believes his ear,

---

12 In addition to the revived ship simile, the major additions to 1653 fall into four main segments: the replacement of lines 245–50 of the earliest version with a twenty-five-line addition (243–68), thirteen new lines after line 256 (275–88), an additional couplet after line 260 (293–94), and an extra four lines after line 262 (297–300).

13 Earl Wasserman, *The Subtler Language* (Baltimore: Johns Hopkins University Press, 1959), pp. 75–76.

14 O Hehir, *EH*, pp. 244–51.

> Willing to think th'illusions of his fear
> Had given this false Alarm, but straight his view
> Confirms, that more than all he fears is true.
> Betray'd in all his strengths, the wood beset,
> All instruments, all Arts of ruine met;
> He calls to mind his strength, and then his speed,
> His winged heels, and then his armed head;
> With these t'avoid, with that his Fate to meet:
> But fear prevails, and bids him trust his feet.
> So fast he flyes, that his reviewing eye
> Has lost the chasers, and his ear the cry;
> Exulting, till he finds, their Nobler sense
> Their disproportion'd speed does recompense.
> Then curses his conspiring feet, whose scent
> Betrays that safety which their swiftness lent. (ll. 241–68)

Nor can the revision of the final couplet of the stag hunt section, which substitutes a balanced antithesis ('And stains the Crystal with a Purple floud') for a conceited pun ('Dying he dyes, & purples with his blood'), be attributed to this new political imperative. To offer an adequate explanation for these revisions, we need to look outside the allegorical referents of the passage, and attend to the other issues at stake in its expansion: issues which are best approached by way of the circumstances of the revision.

## III

On his return from exile early in 1653, Denham repaired for a year or so to Wilton House, the country seat of Philip Herbert, fifth Earl of Pembroke.[15] Rural retirement was for Denham one of the major desiderata for poetical composition.[16] And what more inspiring a retreat could there be for the pursuit of a major literary project, a translation on new principles of Virgil's *Aeneid*, than the very estate on which Sir Philip Sidney had composed his ground-breaking *Arcadia* some sixty years earlier, during a similar period of enforced retirement—a work for which he received inspiration, according to local legend, while hunting in the surrounding plains?[17] This literary association was not forgotten at Wilton: it was proudly advertised in a series of painted panels illustrating scenes from the *Arcadia,* recently executed by Emanuel de Critz.[18] The revision of *Coopers Hill* was a natural preparation for work on the *Aeneid* because Denham saw it as a georgic

---

15   O Hehir, *HD*, pp. 99–112.
16   Banks, *PW*, p. 60.
17   John Aubrey, *'Brief Lives': Chiefly of Contemporaries, Set Down by John Aubrey, between the Years 1669 & 1696*, ed. Andrew Clark, 2 vols (Oxford: Clarendon Press, 1898), ii, p. 248.
18   Edmund Croft-Murray, *Decorative Painting in England, 1537–1837*, 2 vols (London: Country Life, 1962, 1970), i, pp. 42, 198.

poem—and georgic was, of course, the middle step on the laborious ascent to the epic in Virgil's model career.[19]

While the model of the *rota virgiliana* might explain the return to *Coopers Hill*, there were other reasons why Denham should have focused on the stag hunt while in retirement at Wilton. Prime among these was that the Earls of Pembroke were fanatical huntsmen who took a keen interest in the art and literature of their sport.[20] Shortly before Denham's arrival, the family had, in the process of remodelling the house after a disastrous fire, commissioned from Edward Pierce a series of eighteen panels depicting hunting scenes from Europe, Africa, and Asia. These panels, which now adorn the Hunting Room at Wilton, are copied from engravings by Antonio Tempesta: they depict, alongside domestic scenes of hawking, fowling, and the like, the pursuit of such exotic quarry as monkeys, crocodiles, and leopards. Clearly recognisable among the huntsmen are the figures of the fourth Earl and his son, Denham's patron, who completed the restoration work.[21] It is possible that Pierce was still at work on the paintings during Denham's sojourn at Wilton, for the earliest recorded reference to them is that of John Evelyn, who saw them in July 1654.

The Herberts' interest in the artistic depiction of hunting was not confined to the visual arts. Their library included a rare manuscript of Dame Juliana Berner's seminal English hunting manual, *The Book of St Albans*. This was employed during Denham's residence by Christopher Wase, the family tutor, who was then engaged on his translation of a classical hunting poem, the *Cynegeticon* of Gratius Faliscus—a translation he published in 1654 with a dedication to his tutee, the young William Herbert.[22] Wase, a royalist, had been forced to resign his fellowship at King's College, Cambridge and had fled abroad. He turned up in Paris, where he sought the patronage of Richard Browne, the English Resident there, before returning to England along with Browne's son-in-law, John Evelyn, early in 1652.[23]

Much can be gleaned from Wase's *Cynegeticon* about the ambiance of Wilton in the early 1650s, where topics of conversation evidently included hunting, techniques of translation, and the georgic moralisation of nature. In his 'Preface to the Reader', Wase deploys the standard Renaissance commonplaces in

19 O Hehir, *EH*, pp. 9–15. Denham had drafted part of his translation by 1636 and returned to it in the 1650s. On the development of the translation, see the edition and commentary in *Early Augustan Virgil: Translations by Denham, Godolphin, and Waller*, ed. Robin Sowerby (Lewisburg, Penn.: Bucknell University Press, 2010), pp. 118–30.
20 Edward, Earl of Clarendon, *The History of the Rebellion and Civil Wars in England*, 6 vols (Oxford: Clarendon Press, 1888), i, p. 174.
21 Croft-Murray, i, pp. 41, 201.
22 Aubrey, *'Brief Lives'*, i, pp. 311–12; Gratius Faliscus, *Cynegeticon. Or a Poem of Hunting by Gratius the Faliscian*, trans. Christopher Wase (London, 1654), sig. a2r; pp. 73–74.
23 *The Diary of John Evelyn*, ed. E.S. de Beer, 6 vols (Oxford: Clarendon Press, 1955), iii, p. 55; Richard E. Hodges, 'Wase, Christopher (1627–1690)', *ODNB*. Wase later dedicated his translation of Benjamin Priolo's *History of France under the Ministry of Cardinal Mazarine* (London, 1671) to Browne; sig. A3r.

defence of hunting as a healthy and civilised pastime, admirably 'proportion'd to the spirits of youth', which 'neither remits the mind to sloth and softnesse, nor (if it be us'd with moderation) hardens it to inhumanity; but rather enclines men to acquaintance and sociablenesse' (sig. a8r). Not only is hunting in moderation conducive to the development of robust gentlemen, it is a tonic for the kind of depression to which such gentlemen are prone: 'Nothing does more recreate the mind, strengthen the limbs, whet the stomack, and clear up the spirit when it is overcast with gloomy cares' (sig. a8v). While this defence of hunting no doubt speaks to the views of his patron, Wase's careful definition of his translation as 'a strict Metaphrase' (sig. a11v) responds to Denham's newly developed distinction between such line-for-line redaction and the looser, more liberal method of translation he was currently essaying in his translation of Virgil—a method to which Dryden was later to apply Cowley's term 'imitation'. That Denham, in the theoretical Preface to the 1656 selection of an episode from his *Aeneid*, was to attack such 'Verbal Translation' as 'a vulgar error' does not imply a dispute between himself and Wase over the nature of translation, for he insists merely that such a method is inapt for those dealing with poetical fiction—for 'them who deal in matters of Fact, or matters of Faith' it is entirely appropriate:[24] matters of fact are, as Wase makes clear in his Preface, the prime focus of Gratius's text. Wase explains that, in terms of its scope and subject, Gratius's poem 'may come into comparison with a Georgique of *Virgil*' (sig. a7r). He means by this not only that it is concerned with country matters, but that it is, as the georgics were currently thought to be, an exercise in natural history, in the Baconian sense: for Gratius, writes Wase, 'falls in with the *Novum Organum* and that illustrious *Scheam* of *Philosophia, Instaurata*, for while he reflects on an Harmony of diffus'd Experiments, he seems to write (if I may be allow'd to use that significant term of my Lord *Verulam*) the particular Histories of Hemp, of Dogs, of Horses' (15–16). The *Cynegeticon* is also—like *Coopers Hill*—georgic by virtue of its author's tendency to politicise or moralise his subject: a procedure he undertakes through 'Naturall, and Familiar' metaphors, by carefully-chosen epithets (17–19), and by allegorical application: 'He does almost every were allegorize hunting under Terms of the *Roman Militia*' (19); 'It is wonderfull elegant when he moralizes to precepts of Temperance from the allowance given to dogs that they may be kept to have a quick fine sent' (20). Although such moralising operated, for the most part, on a general level, that Wase sensed a contemporary political application in Gratius's work is, given his earlier, highly politicised translation of Sophocles's *Electra*, quite probable.[25] It is tempting to read a covert allusion to the preparations for Penruddock's rising of early 1654/5, in which both Denham and Pembroke at Wilton were implicated, in

24  Banks, *PW*, p. 159.
25  On Wase's *Electra*, see Lois Potter, *Secret Rites and Secret Writing: Royalist Literature, 1641–1660* (Cambridge: Cambridge University Press, 1989), pp. 53–54.

these lines concerning the need for careful preparation and a delicate sense of occasion in support of one's allies:[26]

> For Huntsman choose some lusty youthfull swaine,
> Who must be skill'd, and a couragious man:
> Knowe where to find the fo, when to fall on,
> And dare to his opprest allyes come in:
> Else they would fly, or bloody conquest win.
> Then heede your worke, and proper armes provide,
> Armes will make way … (sigs B5v, B6v)

The association of hunting with warfare was commonplace, with hunting perceived as a form of training for or surrogate form of warfare.[27] And a sense that important questions of military strategy hover behind Wase's rendition of Gratius is obliquely confirmed by the commendatory poem, 'On my Worthy Friend the Author', provided for the volume by Edmund Waller, who had probably met Wase in France through their mutual friend Evelyn, and who assisted him in his quest for tutoring post back in England.[28] Waller's poem is the product of a clear understanding of the art of the hunt, and displays a close reading of Wase's work.[29] He begins simply enough with a decorous celebration of the excellence and utility of Gratius's work in Wase's translation, but a turn occurs in the poem's pivotal stanza (the sixth), in which he introduces the notion that modern warfare differs substantially from the ancient method by virtue of the invention of gunpowder. The ensuing stanzas develop the argument that because the techniques of hunting have been fundamentally altered by this invention, a new account is called for:

> But, worthy friend! the face of war
> In ancient times doth differ far
> From what our fiery battles are.
>
> Nor is it like, since powder known,
> That man, so cruel to his own,
> Should spare the race of beasts alone.

---

26 O Hehir, *HD*, pp. 113–14.

27 Roger B. Manning, *Hunters and Poachers: A Social and Cultural History of Unlawful Hunting in England, 1485–1640* (Oxford: Clarendon Press, 1993), pp. 4–5, 36–41.

28 See *The Letterbooks of John Evelyn*, ed. Douglas D.C. Chambers and David Galbraith, 2 vols (Toronto: University of Toronto Press, 2014), i, p. 124; *The Poems of Edmund Waller*, ed. George Thorn Drury, 2 vols (London: Bullen, New York: Scribner's, 1901), ii, p. 198 (hereafter 'Waller').

29 Waller's 1645 collection included a celebratory poem on the hunt ('On the head of a stag'), and a love poem which employed the simile of a hunted stag seeking sanctuary in the water which it might be tempting to associate with Denham's stag simile, were this not so conventional a trope in the literature of the hunt; Waller, i, pp. 110, 88. Banks's attempt to find echoes of the former poem in *Coopers Hill* has been dismissed by O Hehir in 'The Early Acquaintance of Denham and Waller', *Notes & Queries*, new series 13 (1966), 19–23 (pp. 19–20).

No quarter now, but with the gun
Men wait in trees from sun to sun,
And all is in a moment done.

And therefore we expect your next
Should be no comment, but a text
To tell how modern beasts are vexed.

Thus would I further yet engage
Your gentle Muse to court the age
With somewhat of your proper rage;

Since none does more to Phoebus owe,
Or in more languages can show
Those arts which you so early know.[30]

The move from hunting to warfare and back again is deftly handled; but the stanza on the cruelty of modern warfare remains resolutely prominent: an unclosed parallel, retrospectively protruding from the argument. For if Wase is to produce an account of modern hunting, who will produce the parallel account of modern warfare—an account which the poet does not suggest has already been supplied? Not, it seems, Wase himself, whose 'gentle Muse' would be unsuited for such a task. In this respect it is significant that in the autumn of 1653—at about the time he was writing his commendatory poem for Wase—Waller was said to have been at work on his own history of the civil war, a work apparently conceived as a romance.[31] Whatever the fate of Waller's romance on the war, the delicate obliquity of his handling of the association of hunting with warfare in the commendatory poem is an extraordinarily apt imitation of the method of Wase's translation.

The georgic moralisation and politicisation of the hunt is, then, the defining feature of the *Cynegeticon*. And if we look back at the expanded text of *Coopers Hill* in light of Wase's translation, it seems reasonable to suggest that Denham's interest in elaborating his account of the hunt may have been prompted by his sojourn with the Pembrokes at Wilton, and that his desire to employ the stag as a vehicle for generalised moralising—quite apart from any desire to associate it with the dead king—may have been inspired by his exposure to Gratius's georgic of the hunt.

## IV

While Denham's reading of Gratius allows us to account in general terms for his expansion of *Coopers Hill*, it does not explain J.B.'s comment that the expanded stag hunt stands as a rebuke to those writers who are guilty of 'dragging or haling in Words and Metaphors, as the fashion now is with some that cannot write,

---

30  Waller, ii, p. 19.
31  Dorothy Osborne, *Letters to Sir William Temple*, ed. Kenneth Parker (Harmondsworth: Penguin, 1987), p. 132 (24 or 25 September 1653).

and cannot but write'. Once again, Wase's Gratius provides us with a vital clue. In his commentary on the text, in the midst of a discussion on the difficulty of rendering terms of art from one language into another, Wase offers the following gloss on the term 'Metagon:' 'a Dog that drawes after a Dear, or Beast, these Metagontes are commended by him, because they did taciti accedere, which quality is describ'd in the heroicall Poem set out by Sir William Davenant. Canto 2. Stanza 30'—a stanza Wase goes on to quote in full (sig. b1r). The recognition that the reading matter at Wilton included Davenant's *Gondibert* provides us with the prime target of Denham's tendentious revisions.

Wase's reference is to the royal stag hunt in the second canto of *Gondibert*—an episode generally thought to be indebted for its narrative structure and its allegorical method to *Coopers Hill*.[32] After a lengthy epic catalogue which establishes the nobility of the hunting party (I.ii.3–22), Davenant cuts to the chase, in which the 'Lime-Hounds' pursue the prey, and the 'Harborers'

> Boast they have lodg'd a Stagg, that all the Race
> Out-runs of *Croton* Horse, or *Regian* Hounds;
> A Stagg made long since Royall in the Chace,
> If Kings can honor give by giving wounds.
>
> …
>
> Now winde they a Recheat, the rows'd Dear's knell;
> And through the Forrest all the Beasts are aw'd;
> Alarm'd by Ecchoe, Nature's Sentinel,
> Which shews that Murdrous Man is come abroad.
>
> Tirranique Man! Thy subjects Enemy!
> And more through wantoness then need or hate;
> From whom the winged to their Coverts flie;
> And to their Dennes even those that lay in waite.
>
> So this (the most successful of his kinde,
> Whose Foreheads force oft his Opposers prest,
> Whose swiftness left Persuers shafts behinde)
> Is now of all the Forrest most distrest![33]

There are a number of obvious similarities between the two accounts: Davenant's stag, like Denham's, is a leader, a royal beast. It initially seeks the protection of

---

32  Georg Gronauer, *Sir William Davenants 'Gondibert'* (Erlangen: von Junge, 1911), pp. 72–74; Alfred Harbage, *Sir William Davenant: Poet Venturer, 1606–1668* (Philadelphia: University of Pennsylvania Press; London: Oxford University Press, 1935), p. 186; Rothstein, pp. 334–35. Other parts of the poem also reveal such a debt: Gladish notes that *Gondibert*, II.i.3–21, comprises a 'prospect poem' after the manner of *Coopers Hill*; *Sir William Davenant's 'Gondibert'*, ed. David F. Gladish (Oxford: Clarendon Press, 1971), p. 299.

33  *Gondibert*, pp. 72–73 (I.ii.32, 37–39), hereafter cited by line number within the text.

the herd and is rejected (I.ii.40); it then takes to the water in hope of losing the dogs, but fails to do so, and is brought down by the hunters, weeping with grief as it dies (I.ii.44–54). Like Denham, Davenant is much concerned with the moralisation and politicisation of the hunt. His procedure, however, is decidedly different from Denham's.

Davenant's lengthy theoretical Preface to *Gondibert* expounded the view that a poem ought to express natural and philosophical truth, and Davenant was concerned to uncover an apt manner of doing so.[34] In his poem, as in his Preface, he was heavily influenced by Hobbes's reservations about language: by the philosopher's concern that in communication a constant vigilance is required to avoid the injuries attendant upon so delusive and unreliable a tool. To the materialist Hobbes, words were merely the names or tokens of corporeal things. It followed, as he noted in *Leviathan*, that the metaphorical use of such tokens—the use of words 'in other sense than that they are ordained for'—was an abuse of language, and a dangerous threat to social order.[35] Although certain abuses might be excused in poetry, the poet was not given carte blanche. In his 'Answer' to Davenant's Preface, Hobbes noted the major pitfalls to which poets were liable:

> There be so many wordes in use at this day in the English tongue, that, though of magnifique sound, yet (like the windy blisters of a troubled water) have no sense at all; and so many others that loose their meaning, by being ill coupled, that it is a hard matter to avoyd them [...]
> To this palpable darknesse, I may also adde the ambitious obscurity of expressing more then is perfectly conceaved; or perfect conception in fewer words then it requires. Which Expressions, though they have had the honor to be called strong lines, are in deed no better then Riddles.[36]

Hobbes's objections to empty grandiloquence, poorly combined terms, and strong-lined, Donnean obscurity, might appear to be self-explanatory; but his conception of them is distinctive and may be clarified by reference to *Leviathan*, where his theory of language and its attendant vices is more amply explained. Hobbes includes in a discussion of '*Words insignificant*' the improper combination of words into self-contradictory strings, such as: 'an *incorporeall body*, or (which is all one) an *incorporeall substance*'—a clear instance of 'ill coupling' (ii, p. 60). Under the heading of '*Inconstant names*', he places 'The names of such things as affect us, that is, which please, and displease us, because all men be not alike affected with the same thing, nor the same man at all times:' these are terms which purport to offer a neutral account of the world, but which are coloured by

34  See Timothy Raylor, 'Hobbes, Davenant, and Disciplinary Tensions in the Preface to *Gondibert*', in *Collaboration and Interdisciplinarity in the Republic of Letters: Essays in Honour of Richard G. Maber*, ed. Paul Scott (Manchester and New York: Manchester University Press, 2010), pp. 59–72 (pp. 63–70).
35  *Leviathan*, ed. Noel Malcolm, 3 vols (Oxford: Clarendon Press, 2012), ii, p. 50 (i.4).
36  *Gondibert*, p. 52.

the vagaries of individual prejudice: 'For one man calleth *Wisdome*, what another calleth *feare*; and one *cruelty*, what another *justice*' (ii, p. 62).

The communication of natural and philosophical truths, unambiguously and disinterestedly, is, then, the goal of the new epic. For Davenant, this necessitated a rejection, on the grounds of its natural philosophical inaccuracy, of the magical world-view of classical epic and modern romance, which saw in the processes of nature the operation of occult or divine forces—the world view which yielded the kind of emblematic reading of nature elaborated by Denham in *Coopers Hill*. Davenant's desire for the poem to embody a philosophically accurate and useful account of the world, on the basis of a constant recourse to the technical expertise of 'men of any science, as well mechanicall, as liberall', is apparent at all levels of the stag hunt episode.[37] At the level of diction, his precise employment of the vocabulary of the hunt—'Relays', 'Harborers', 'Lime-Hounds', 'Recheat', and so forth—was striking enough, in the context of a poem as opposed to a manual, to earn the commendation of Wase. The quest for philosophical truth also determined the moralisation or politicisation of the hunt. Of particular interest is his handling of the standard topos of the rejection of the stag by the herd. Davenant offers a radical, Hobbesian interpretation of the behaviour of the herd, who, following the law of nature, look to their own interests—self-preservation—and reject their erstwhile leader-by-conquest because he is unable to offer them protection:

> The Heard deny him shelter, as if taught
> To know their safety is to yield him lost;
> Which shews they want not the results of thought,
> But speech, by which we ours for reason boast.

> We blush to see our politicks in Beasts,
> Who Many sav'd by this one Sacrifice;
> And since through blood they follow interests,
> Like us when cruel should be counted wise. (I.ii.40–1)

This is applied Hobbism; for although Hobbes did not comment explicitly upon the appropriate action of the subject when the sovereign flees the field, the stag has clearly forfeited any role he might once have had as protector of the herd.[38] Davenant's analysis of the psychology of the deer in I.ii.40 is similarly concerned

---

37 *Gondibert*, p. 22.
38 Thomas Hobbes, *De Cive: The Latin Version*, ed. Howard Warrender (Oxford: Clarendon Press, 1983), p. 117 (iii.26), pp. 158–59 (vii.18); idem, *De Cive: The English Version*, ed. Howard Warrender (Oxford: Clarendon Press, 1983), p. 72 (iii.26), p. 116 (vii.18); *Leviathan*, ii, p. 344 (ii.21). These aspects of Hobbes's thought are neatly summarized in Johann P. Sommerville, *Thomas Hobbes: Political Ideas in Historical Context* (Basingstoke: Macmillan, 1992), pp. 28–51. Niall Allsopp offers a complementary discussion of the Hobbism of Davenant's stage hunt and its influence, in 'Sir Robert Howard, Thomas Hobbes, and the Fall of Clarendon', *Seventeenth Century*, 30 (2015), 75–93 (pp. 78–81, 83–88).

with philosophical accuracy. It seems also to embody the theory of animal reason developed in Paris in the later 1640s by his patron, the Marquess of Newcastle, who disputed the question of animal intelligence with Descartes, and found support in the work of Hobbes for his belief that the absence of language in animals should not be equated with lack of reason.[39]

That Davenant's account operates at a different level of psychological sophistication from the merely poetical humanisation of the deer in *Coopers Hill* is obvious. But it should also be noticed that Davenant, in the concluding lines of the passage offers a direct rebuke to Denham, whose account he subjects to a rigorous philosophical unpacking. Denham had handled the rejection thus:

> He tryes his frends amongst the lesser heard,
> Where he but lately was obey'd & fear'd:
> Safety he seekes, the heard unkindly wise:
> Or chases him from thence, or from him flyes;

In Hobbesian terms the phrase 'unkindly wise' was an outrageous instance of 'ill coupling', the impropriety of which hinges upon the ambiguous use of the adjective 'unkindly'. Either Denham laments the absence in the deer of a sort of moral probity that they cannot possibly, as beasts, possess (*OED*, 1a), or he accuses them of unnaturalness in following their natural instinct for self-preservation (*OED*, 1b, 2, 2c, 4a).[40] Either way, he is guilty of 'ill coupling': of linguistic and logical impropriety. But he is also guilty, in his judgement of the herd's behaviour as unkind, of 'inconstant naming'—of failing to acknowledge the distorting prism of his own self-interest in such a judgement. Davenant corrects him and glosses his error in a Hobbesian fashion, pointing out that, while the behaviour of the deer might look to us like a distressing instance of unkindness or cruelty, it is, from their perspective, natural wisdom:

> We blush to see our politicks in Beasts, […]
> And since through blood they follow interests,
> Like us when cruel should be counted wise.

---

39  *La Méthode Nouvelle et Invention Extraordinaire de Dresser les Chevaux* (Antwerp, 1658), sigs f1v-2r; *Oeuvres de Descartes*, ed. Ch. Adam and P. Tannery, rev. edn, 12 vols (Paris: Vrin, 1964–76), iv, pp. 573–76 (letter to Newcastle, 23 November 1646). There is an English translation of this letter in *The Philosophical Writings of Descartes*, trans. John Cottingham, Robert Stoothoff, Dugald Murdoch, and Anthony Kenny, 3 vols (Cambridge: Cambridge University Press, 1984–91), iii, pp. 302–04. In advancing his argument, the Marquess appears to be making a tendentious use of some of Hobbes's statements from *The Elements of Law*—a work written for and dedicated to him; *The Elements of Law Natural and Political*, ed. J.C.A. Gaskin (Oxford: Oxford University Press, 1994), p. 38 (I.v.13).
40  O Hehir glosses the term by reference to the natural inclination of deer to herd together (*EH*, p. 128); but such an inclination is—in Hobbesian terms—less fundamental than that towards self-preservation.

To put it in Hobbesian terms: one man's cruelty is another man's wisdom.

Davenant's concern to avoid the pitfalls of fictional humanisation and 'inconstant naming' also informs his handling of the problem of perspective in the hunt. Where Denham had negotiated the problem through delicate shifts—moving from stag to hunter—Davenant refuses to sentimentalise the stag to the degree that Denham does, and deploys instead the distancing device of generalised apostrophes on human murderousness and tyranny (I.ii.38, 52–54). Thus, although the stag is, like Denham's, a 'Royall Stagg', the meaning of this phrase is thoroughly demystified in a preparatory gloss which preemptively empties the phrase of the very meaning it might be supposed to possess: Davenant's stag is not innately noble, it is 'made [...] Royall in the Chace' (I.ii.32), as it is hunted by a king. While this is a clear debunking of 'ill coupled' terms, Davenant's perspectival strategy is a little confusing. It looks like an attempt to convert the traditional humanist objections to hunting—a conventional feature of the literature of the chase—into a philosophically accurate account of human political behaviour (the identification of Nimrod the hunter as the original tyrant was a common one); if so, the effect is poorly managed. Such apostrophes are not easily reconciled with the heroic praise of Gondibert and his train that opens the canto. Although Davenant takes pains to dissociate Gondibert himself from any act of barbarism or cruelty (he is—pace Earl Miner—cautiously vague about who actually kills the stag), those apostrophes are too broad and authoritative in their application to allow us to exclude the hero from their compass.[41] Nor do they speak clearly to Gondibert's flaws, which are not those of a Nimrod; pathological lack of ambition is his failing. Such remarks would more aptly apply to Gondibert's rival, the ambitious and bellicose Oswald, whose faction ambushes the hunting party in the latter part of the canto; but if this application is intended, it would have been more appropriate to have Oswald lead the hunt.[42] Perhaps these questions might have been resolved in the completed text of the poem; as it is, the political significance of the hunting passage remains one of the many perplexing features of Davenant's unfinished experiment.

## V

*Gondibert* had been Denham's bête noire since the late 1640s, when Davenant had pursued his fellow exiles down the corridors of the Louvre, pressing upon courtiers, poets, and philosophers—upon anyone, it seems, too slow to escape—his plans for the reform of the epic. Denham had been at the centre of a group of wits who clubbed together to circulate verses mocking Davenant for his social pretensions, his tedious theorising, and his interminable poem. He contributed the lion's

---

41  Earl Miner, *The Restoration Mode from Milton to Dryden* (Princeton, NJ: Princeton University Press, 1974), p. 75.

42  Gladish's suggestion that the nobility of the stag is supposed to 'prefigure symbolically human nobility as represented by Aribert and Gondibert' does not solve the problem (*Gondibert*, p. 295): Gondibert's nobility is already established; and the stag's derives from its being wounded by a king (I.ii.32).

share to a collection of these verses, and may have overseen its printing in London in April 1653 as *Certain Verses Written by severall of the Authors Friends; to be reprinted with the Second Edition of Gondibert.*[43] His concern with *Gondibert* was little short of an obsession: he continued to pen squibs on the poem after the publication of *Certain Verses*, and he carefully transcribed corrected texts of his contributions to that collection and additional poems into his copy of the 1668 edition of his works, from which they had been tactfully omitted.[44]

Why should he have been so grossly irritated by *Gondibert*? Denham, more than *Gondibert*'s other opponents, was enraged by Davenant's glib critique of the ancient epic from the perspective of a nascent modernism that looked to him like an ignorant and self-aggrandising 'D'avenantisme', which attacked the ancients for their 'want of Syllogisme'—for that logical impropriety which Davenant had found in Denham's stag hunt.[45] Denham and his associates scoffed at Davenant's reliance upon the newfangled notions and puffing of Hobbes—a response which probably involved a conservative rejection of the controversial political opinions of the philosopher.[46] Thus, although Christopher Wase approved the accuracy of Davenant's description of the swift and silent hounds, one of the major objections to *Gondibert* was its concern with such technical precision, and its quest for such natural philosophical accuracy. One of the contributions to the *Certain Verses* parodied the literal-minded pedantry of Davenant's new method:

1. Sunk neer his evening Region was the Sun,
(But though the Sun can ne're be said to sink,
Yet when his beams from our dull eyes are run,
He of the Oceans moysture seems to drink.)

(And though the Ocean be as far remote
From his as we, yet such is the false light
Of mortall eye, that though for truth we know't
We yet believe our own deceiving sight.)

(Nor without cause) (for what our eyes behold
Unto our sense most evident hath been;
But still we doubt of things by others told,

43  O Hehir, *HD*, pp. 91–92; Timothy Raylor, *Cavaliers, Clubs, and Literary Culture: Sir John Mennes, James Smith, and the Order of the Fancy* (Newark: University of Delaware Press; London and Toronto: Associated University Presses, 1994), p. 198. Niall Allsopp makes a strong case for associating with him and the circle responsible for *Certain Verses*, a heavily and hostilely annotated copy of *Gondibert* now in the National Library of Scotland: ' "Let none our Lombard author rudely blame for's righteous paine": An Annotated Copy of Sir William Davenant's *Gondibert*', *Library*, seventh series, 16 (2015), 24–50 (pp. 32–37).
44  Denham, Appendix A (pp. 311–25); p. xiii; *Index of English Literary Manuscripts*, p. 332.
45  *Gondibert*, p. 273; cp. Denham, pp. 313, 325. For this and other aspects of the attack on Davenant, see Allsopp, ' "Let none our Lombard author rudely blame" ', 45–46, 49.
46  *Gondibert*, pp. 277, 279, 283, 284; cp. Denham, pp. 319, 320.

(For Faith's the evidence of things not seen.)[47]

This is a brilliant attack on Davenant's self-glossing poetic procedure, and on his concern with optical precision (as, for example, II.i.3): a concern that may have been prompted in part by the optical researches pursued by Newcastle and Hobbes at Paris in the 1640s.[48]

Beyond the general and conventional complaints about poetic incompetence and incontinence, Denham and his associates, in their attacks on *Gondibert*, home in on the points noted by J.B.: the haling and dragging in of words and meta-phors.[49] Such charges are repeated throughout Denham's contributions to the volume, with the former making up the bulk of his parodic 'Canto 2'—a witty collage of Davenant's more mechanical or pretentious epithets, which includes a glance at the stag hunt:

> Then as a pack of *Regian hounds*
> Pursuing o're the *Illyrian grounds*
> *A Tuscan Stag*, if in the wind
> A flock of *Brescian* sheep they find,
> *Calabrian swine*, or *Padan Goats*,
> In blood they bath their *Cannon throats* ...[50]

The pastiche also parodies Davenant's Hobbesian concern with the analysis of power and his cumbersome metaphoric strategy:

> Brave friends, quoth he, *Power is a liquor*,
> Makes hands more bold, and wit more quicker,
> It is a *tree* whose boughes and branches
> Serve us instead of legs and hanches
> *It is a Hill* to whose command,
> Men *walk by Sea* and *sail by Land*.
> But what's our power unlesse we know it?
> And knowledge what? unlesse we shew it[51]

It is in light of Denham's objections to *Gondibert* that his revisions to the text of *Coopers Hill* may best be understood. His rewriting of the final couplet of the passage, replacing a conceited, Donnean pun with a balanced, Latinate antithesis, seems to acknowledge the force of the objections to this kind of wit expressed by Davenant and Hobbes, without endorsing their recommendations for a new poetic.

---

47 *Gondibert*, pp. 281–82.
48 Allsopp furnishes valuable new evidence for the critical focus on Davenant's concern with natural philosophy in " 'Let none our Lombard author rudely blame" ', 47–49.
49 *Gondibert*, pp. 274, 277; cp. Denham, pp. 314, 318–19.
50 *Gondibert*, p. 281; cp. Denham, p. 317.
51 *Gondibert*, p. 280; cp. Denham, p. 317.

Indeed, Denham's major revision is the systematic expansion of the humanised psychology of the stag: the very aspect of his poem which Davenant had rebuked, from a philosophical position which Denham and his associates had systematically parodied. Denham's expansion of this humanisation is a virtuoso restatement of his commitment to the mystical, emblematic reading of nature against Davenant's poetic of natural philosophical literalism.

## VI

The competition between Denham and Davenant for an appropriate means of handling the hunting of the stag—a competition hinted at by J.B. in his prefatory remarks to the 1655 edition—is symptomatic of a poetic dispute among royalists in exile in Paris in the later 1640s: a dispute that continued as such men recalibrated their allegiances and made their way back to England in the mid-1650s. Underlying the dispute was a sense of doubt about the value and proper procedures of poetry—a sense that generated the several proposals by such exiles for its reform, or its renouncement.[52] For Denham and Davenant, the way forward required a rejection of the conceited style of Donne. They were not, however, agreed on the direction in which poetry ought now to move. While Davenant sought to base a new poetic upon the philosophical and political theories of Hobbes, Denham turned back to the model of the ancient poets, accommodated to modern English usage.

The consequences of this dispute were far-reaching, extending well beyond the frequent appearance of the stag-hunt motif in the verse of the following century. For the theories of both Davenant and Denham exerted an enormous influence upon the poet laureate of the next generation and, through him, on the poetry of the next age. In the short term, Davenant's new method seemed to hold sway: Dryden's first major poem, *Annus Mirabilis* (1667), borrowed its stanza form, its definition of wit, and its concern with natural philosophical accuracy and technical precision from *Gondibert*. Over the long term, however, Denham's new theory of translation was to eclipse the influence of *Gondibert*. For it was to Denham's conviction of the aptness of the ancient models, appropriately interpreted, that Dryden would in his maturity turn; and his elaboration of Denham's theory and practice would determine the shape of English poetry for the greater part of the next century.[53]

---

52  For the wider context, see Timothy Raylor, 'Exiles, Expatriates, and Travellers: Towards a Cultural and Intellectual History of the English Abroad, 1640–1660', in *Literatures of Exile in the English Revolution and Its Aftermath, 1640–1690*, ed. Philip Major (Farnham: Ashgate, 2010), pp. 15–43 (pp. 37–42).

53  For a complementary judgement on the longer-term implications, see Allsopp, 'Sir Robert Howard, Thomas Hobbes, and the Fall of Clarendon', pp. 78, 89–90.

# 9  *Cooper's Well* (1767)

## A Forgotten Denham Parody

*J.P. Vander Motten*

## I

In his 'Life of Sir John Denham' (1779), Samuel Johnson famously stated that *Coopers Hill* 'had such reputation as to excite the common artifice by which envy degrades excellence'.[1] Denham's late seventeenth- and eighteenth-century reputation is amply illustrated by the biographical accounts and the various editions of his collected works, and as far as *Coopers Hill* is concerned, its inclusion in numerous collections of British poets, anthologies, and critical essays, in which the poem was almost universally hailed as having set a standard for later Augustan poetry. Johnson's 'common artifice' was probably a glance at the numerous older and contemporary attempts at topographical poetry by a number of (mostly minor) writers, who unashamedly took their cue from Denham's poem. Modern scholarship has lent weight to Johnson's opinion. Robert Arnold Aubin has recorded 315 'English hill-poems' between 1642, when *Coopers Hill* was first published, and 1884. '[B]etween 1650 and 1841', Aubin has pointed out, 'more than two hundred works in verse or prose either referred to (almost always eulogistically) or borrowed slightly from [*Coopers Hill*]'.[2] One such, hitherto ignored, adaptation is *Cooper's Well*, a parody in verse described on the title page of its first, 1767, edition as 'A Fragment, Written by the Honourable Sir John Denham, Knight of the Bath, and Author of the Celebrated Poem of Cooper's Hill, found amongst the Papers of a late Noble Lord. Dated in the Year 1667'.[3] Although Denham's authorship is implicitly contradicted by the title-page announcement that the anonymously published poem had been 'Printed for the Author', the two prefatory documents were evidently designed to advertise it as a long-forgotten,

1 Samuel Johnson, *The Lives of the Most Eminent English Poets; with Critical Observations on Their Works*, ed. Roger Lonsdale, 4 vols (London: Oxford University Press, 2006), i, p. 235 (hereafter 'Johnson').

2 Robert A. Aubin, *Topographical Poetry in XVIII-Century England* (New York: Modern Language Association of America, 1936), pp. 35–36 (hereafter 'Aubin').

3 All in-text references, by page number, will be to this edition. Line numberings are my own. No mention is made of *Cooper's Well* in O Hehir's edition of *Coopers Hill* or in Banks, *PW*, Appendix D ('References to, and Imitations of *Cooper's Hill*'), pp. 333–41.

'rare little poem' (iii). Backdated one hundred years to 'Hampton Court, August 9, 1667', the forged—or spoof—dedication 'To the Right Honourable the Lord Rochester', signed '[Your] most devoted humble Servant, John Denham', was calculated to mark *Cooper's Well* as the centenary celebration of the publication of *Poems and Translations with The Sophy. Written by the Honourable Sir John Denham Knight of the Bath* (London: Henry Herringman, 1668).[4] As much as this dedication, the editor's address to 'The World', dated 'London, 1767' and no doubt the work of the anonymous parodist himself, reveals a great deal about his 'archaeological' intentions. A brief contextual examination of these para-textual materials is indispensable to a correct understanding of the poem they accompany.

## II

The close relationship between Denham and the Earl of Rochester posited by the dedication is an imaginative though not altogether far-fetched interpretation of the literary-historical facts. As opposed to what the dedication implies, Rochester and Denham, who was thirty-two years older, were never in exile together with their 'Royal Master' (i).[5] But the two men did become acquainted after the Restoration. By 1667 Rochester, who had been introduced to the court of Charles II in 1661 or 1662, had made his mark as a notorious member of a 'coterie of rakehells'.[6] 'Denham''s description of him as a man of an 'airy, pleasant disposition' who also possessed 'skill and fame with the Maids of Parnassus' (i), is therefore scarcely an exaggeration. Some of the members of the Buckingham literary circle at court, especially Denham and Edmund Waller, are known to have 'strongly influenced Rochester's early attempts at writing poetry'.[7] There is, on the other hand, no evidence that Denham submitted his poems to Rochester's attention in order to 'amuse' him in his 'own amorous way' (i), or that he would have done so with this type of poem, let alone that he looked upon the Earl as a patron of sorts—the drift of 'Denham''s fulsome address. Professedly begun at Hampton Court, 'the inspiring pigeon-houses of Harry Tudor' (ii), *Cooper's Well* by 'Denham''s own admission was a poem out of his 'common beaten path' (i). In the eyes of the unsuspecting eighteenth-century reader, no dedicatee of this salacious parody could have been more appropriate than the facetious Earl. By way of conclusion 'Denham' invited Rochester to read out these verses unrestrictedly to his 'levee of Beauties' (ii) but kindly asked him never to divulge their true author, arguing that 'I dare not venture to shew the King my sentiments of a Well, he never found me in' (ii). Commenting on this request (of his own making), the editor in his address 'to the World' (see

4   In-text references to the prefatory materials will be to this edition. In 1769 and 1771 two more editions of *Poems and Translations* were to be published, at London and Glasgow respectively.
5   It was the first Earl who shared the future King's exile and performed valuable services for him. See Ronald Hutton, 'Wilmot, Henry, First Earl of Rochester (bap. 1613, d. 1658)', *ODNB*.
6   James W. Johnson, *A Profane Wit. The Life of John Wilmot, Earl of Rochester* (Rochester, NY: University of Rochester Press, 2004), pp. 56, 76.
7   Johnson, p. 82.

below) wondered 'what could make Sir John Denham so diffident [...] when we find up and down his Works, that the King was very fond of him, and often gave him themes to write on' (iv). Like most other historically founded evidence contained in both prefatory documents, this information was drawn from Denham's own *Epistle Dedicatory* to the King in the 1668 *Poems and Translations*.[8]

Denham's account of how Charles II's father, after having inspected some of the poet's recent verse, had in July 1647 advised him no longer to indulge 'the overflowings of [his] Fancy that way' (A2v) is rehearsed in the 1767 dedication's resolve that 'nothing is more dangerous, than giving too loose a run to Poetry' (i). The title of the parody itself may have been suggested by Denham's confession that for some twenty years he had abided by the King's wish, 'till this Summer at the Wells' (A3r),[9] where he had found occasion to divert himself again with his poetry after the fear of a 'Foreign invasion, and domestick discontent' had been dispelled. Closely echoing these circumstances, the composition of *Cooper's Well* is placed in Charles II's reign, at a time when 'no more clouds of discord and rebellion [...] darken and destroy this land' (i). Less explicit references of an autobiographical nature are meant to reinforce the impression of historical *vraisemblance*. The hope that henceforth there will be 'no more reliance on Scotch perfidy, and no more need to try the strength of their arms and purses' (i–ii) harks back to the days when, to secure political, military, and financial support for the young Prince of Wales, Denham had been sent on two separate missions, one to Scotland in September 1648 and another to the Scottish factory in Poland in June 1650.[10]

And although not explicitly modelled on the 1668 address, the self-deprecating hint at the accusation that *Coopers Hill*, 'written when I was not in the best health and spirits', was not Denham's own was a self-revealing touch that readers familiar with Samuel Butler's savage attack on the poet might have readily picked up.[11] For convenience sake, the same reader was kindly expected to disregard the fact that all borrowings from Milton's *Paradise Lost* (1667), Dryden's *Absalom and Achitophel* (1681), and Pope's *The Rape of the Lock* (1712) (see below), in

---

8  Denham testified that while waiting 'upon your Majesty [i.e., Charles II] in Holland and France, you were pleased sometimes to give me arguments to put off the evil hours of our banishment' (*The Epistle Dedicatory*, A3r). The epistle is included in the 1671, 1684, 1703, 1709, and 1719 editions, in all of which *Coopers Hill* was given pride of place, as well as in separate editions of the poem, such as the 1709 and 1751 (Glasgow) ones.

9  The reference, repeated in the Preface to 'Of Prudence', a translation from the Italian (Denham, *Poems and Translations*, pp. 145–46), was to either Epsom or Tunbridge Wells, where Denham stayed in the summer of 1667. See O Hehir, *HD*, p. 210.

10  O Hehir, *HD*, pp. 83–84, 89–90. 'On my Lord Croft's and my Journey into Poland', a record in verse of Denham's second mission, was included in *Poems and Translations*, pp. 67–69.

11  For his most famous poem, the writer is made to confess, he 'acquired praises more than my due', and so '[t]he World with great justice may think I write too well for John Denham; but can I my Lord write amiss when pupil to such a master as Waller' (i–ii). Butler's 'A Panegyric Upon Sir John Denham's Recovery from his Madness', alluding to 'the bought *Coopers Hill*, or borrow'd *Sophy*' (l. 16), had been published in R. Thyer (ed.), *The Genuine Remains in Verse and Prose of Mr. Samuel Butler, Author of Hudibras. In Two Volumes* (London, 1759), i, pp. 155–60.

a poem supposedly composed before 9 August 1667, were patent anachronisms, unless of course s/he was also to assume that these poets belonged to the 'numbers [...] indulged with reading [*Cooper's Well*] in manuscript' (iii).[12] The eighteenth-century author evidently sought to capitalise on the steady interest in Denham's works in general, and the reputation of *Coopers Hill* in particular, as well as on the popularity of Rochester's poetry, which had continued to be published since the Earl's death, both in separate editions and in more extensive collections of verse. The reading public's curiosity about Rochester's literary legacy can be gauged with reference to those editions which professedly performed an act of historical recovery by adding hitherto unknown materials to the Rochester canon. The title page of the 1718 edition of the *Remains of the Right Honourable John, Earl of Rochester* specified that these were based on '*a Manuscript found in a Gentleman's Library that was Cotemporary* [sic] *with him*'.[13] Only six years prior to the publication of *Cooper's Well*, the 1761 edition of *The Poetical Works of that Witty Lord John Earl of Rochester* informed its 'inquisitive Reader' (v) that these poems, '[l]eft in *Ranger's* Lodge in *Woodstock* Park, where his Lordship died, and never before Printed', had narrowly escaped destruction.[14] This '[h]umour of destroying Writings [...] when on the Verge of Dissolution' placed Rochester in the company of distinguished writers such as Sir Philip Sidney, who 'ordered his *Arcadia* to be burnt', and Sir Walter Raleigh, who 'actually burnt himself, the second Part of his *History of the World*' (iv). Rochester's 'very Name', the conclusion confidently went, 'is a sufficient Passport wherever the *English* is spoken or understood' (v). Performing a similar task in honour of 'Denham''s poetical 'remains' while keeping an eye on Rochester's status as a renowned writer, the editor/author of *Cooper's Well* thus cleverly concocted a dedication partly written in extenuation of the prurient poem he purported to have brought to light.

## III

Claiming to have had access to the 'papers' of an 'illustrious person', 'The Editor to the World' emphasised the favour he rendered the public by rescuing from oblivion a poem which had long been circulating in manuscript form and indeed 'deserves the second place in Sir John Denham's compositions' (iii). He tantalisingly went

---

12  A giveaway, line 250, 'Nine times the space which measures day and night', is bodily lifted from Book I of *Paradise Lost* (l. 50), and cited between quotation marks. Milton's epic was first published in October 1667.

13  While the idea of the found manuscript, widespread in eighteenth-century works, cannot be taken at face value, successive editors and publishers did seriously try to make Rochester part of a broad modern British canon; see Howard D. Weinbrot, *Britannia's Issue. The Rise of British Literature from Dryden to Ossian* (Cambridge: Cambridge University Press, 1993; repr. 2006), Chapter 4. The two-volume edition of *The Poetical Works of the Earls of Rochester, Roscomon* [sic], *and Dorset* (London, 1739), for instance, contains no fewer than five 'Memoirs', in addition to a full-page woodcut, of the author.

14  'The Preface', i–v. The collection includes an extensive life account '[e]xtracted from Bishop *Burnet*, and other Eminent Writers' (pp. vi–xxix).

on to reveal that 'Denham''s dedication had elicited a response from Rochester which 'carrie[d] with it so much of his Lordship's indelicate wit, that, I thought proper to omit it' (iii). The work itself he found 'delicately wove, and the allusions and metaphors are so clean and sweet, that it cannot fail to please the most chaste; and pass the judgment of the severest Criticks, without offending their modesty' (iii). Whatever the sensibilities of his readers, such self-congratulating (if slightly diffident) appraisal was as unwarranted as the verdict that '[a]mongst the numbers of amorous Poems thrown out in the reign of that amorous Monarch, none had the ease and delicacy of *Cooper's Well*' (iv). Its target, the author/editor speculated, may have been 'some favourite Lady of the Sh——y family' (iv), a mystifying allusion to a relative or descendant of Anthony Ashley Cooper (1621–1683), first Earl of Shaftesbury, which if well-founded would have made the poem a personal satire rather than a pastiche or a parody.[15] This saucy, eponymous interpretation of the title, which would have tended to thicken the smokescreen even more, was admittedly very 'conjectural' and the poet's 'real intention' remained 'only known to Mr Waller and himself' (iv), an echo of Denham's literary apprentice-ship already acknowledged in the dedication. On the subject of the poem's impact as a type of scribal publication, the author/editor's attempt to throw the reader off the scent was rather more glaring:

> Mr. Armstrong's thoughts, in his incomparable Poem of the *Oeconomy of Love*, are in many parts like it, not that I imagine that Gentleman had an opportunity of borrowing from Cooper's Well; however, if he has seen this piece in manuscript; he has improved upon the thoughts, without being guilty of any plagiarism. (iii)

The half-hearted accusation of literary theft, tempered with praise for the plagia-rist's creativity, unambiguously referred to a work that as late as 1767 was still within the educated reader's ken: *The Oeconomy of Love: A Poetical Essay*, by the Scottish physician Dr John Armstrong (1708/9–1779), first published anony-mously in 1736 and widely read in the eighteenth century. The author of a vari-ety of works, mainly on medical subjects, Armstrong was to gain renown with *A Synopsis of the History and Cure of Venereal Diseases* (1737) and especially his blank-verse georgic, *The Art of Preserving Health* (1744).[16] Alone among his works, *The Oeconomy of Love* 'must have produced among his sobersided Scotch friends and relatives considerable consternation'.[17] Tracing in graphic detail the

---

15  The Shaftesbury identification is explicitly made in the text of *Cooper's Well* (including the prefa-tory materials) as it appeared in *The Court of Cupid. By the Author of the Meretriciad. In Two Volumes* (London, 1770), ii, p. 83. On the poem's authorship, see below.

16  See L.M. Knapp, 'Dr. John Armstrong, Littérateur, and Associate of Smollett, Thomson, Wilkes, and Other Celebrities', *Publications of the Modern Language Association*, 59 (1944), 1019–58.

17  Knapp, p. 1021. Armstrong himself later described it as a 'Parody upon some of the didactic Poets'; see Adam Budd, *John Armstrong's the Art of Preserving Health: Eighteenth-Century Sen-sibility in Practice* (Farnham: Ashgate, 2011), p. 19.

growth of passionate feelings in young maids and boys, Armstrong's erotic poem provided advice on such matters as what sexual pitfalls to avoid, how to build a relationship based on mutual attraction and respect, and how to take care of illegitimate children.[18] Despite the editor's protests, this essentially didactic 'sex manual in blank verse'[19] owed no debt to *Cooper's Well*, which appeared some thirty years later: even a superficial comparison shows that if any debt there was, it was rather in the opposite direction.[20] Perhaps promoting *Cooper's Well* as a work that had furnished some 'thoughts' to an author who by the 1760s had become a literary personality and an authority on medical matters would have seemed a way of stimulating interest in its publication.[21] Whatever the aim of citing Armstrong may have been, with its mixture of sweeping critical judgement, easy surmise, and plausible insinuation, the address to the reader was designed to lend authority to the dedication to Rochester and establish the historical significance of the literary find turned up from the Earl's private papers.

The title-page description of this find as 'A Fragment' was not in itself without significance. Devoid of omissions, gaps, and discontinuities, the text of *Cooper's Well* does not have the makings of a 'fragment' in the manner of more famous contemporary works such as Henry Mackenzie's *The Man of Feeling* (1771). Nor is it presented as part of a longer work. The poem indeed moves towards a lengthy conclusion conveying a distinct sense of finality—the contention that Cooper's Well outdoes all other natural sights and works of art ('Statues, nor Pictures, can such charms excel; / For all who see it sigh for COOPER'S WELL', ll. 321–22). The Latin postscript 'Caetera Desiderantur' ('the rest is lacking'), instead of denoting the incompleteness of the manuscript, is therefore no more than a conventional modesty topos signifying that nothing meaningful could be added, or that nothing more was called for. Taking his cue from the fashionable interest in the fragmentary, which by the mid-eighteenth century had come to be recognised as 'an established mode of literary expression',[22] the author of *Cooper's Well* was out to palm off his forgery as an authentic, rediscovered poem—a 'fragment' of a larger monument—deserving a canonical status legitimated by the unabated interest in Sir John Denham's works. In the absence of contemporary comments, it is impossible to gauge how successful this elaborate exercise in make-believe

---

18   For an extensive summary of the poem's fifteen sections, see Clive Hart and Kay Gilliland Stevenson, 'John Armstrong's *The Oeconomy of Love*: A Critical Edition with Commentary', *Eighteenth-Century Life*, 19 (1995), 38–69.

19   James Sambrook, 'Armstrong, John (1708/9–1779)', *ODNB*.

20   For instance, lines 243–46 in *Cooper's Well*, 'Emollient Baths where mighty Gods and Kings, / Have bath'd their members, and ador'd the springs) / Are dry'd of all, but heavy casual rains: / O! what a yawning chasm alas! Remains!' were definitely inspired by the following lines in Armstrong's poem: 'Perhaps the purple Stream, / Emollient Bath, leaves flexible and lax / The parts it lately wash'd. But hapless he, / In nuptial Night, on whom a horrid Chasm / yawns dreadful, waste and wild' (242–46).

21   Knapp, p. 1044.

22   Sandro Jung, *The Fragmentary Poetic: Eighteenth-Century Uses of an Experimental Mode* (Bethlehem: Lehigh University Press, 2009), p. 18.

actually was, but the poet-editor's ownership of the text and his alleged knowledge of its circumstances of composition made him eminently suitable to carry out, for the benefit of the reading public, what looked like a feat of literary archaeology. In so far as 'eighteenth-century fragments usually refer to a greater framework such as the self, a community, or a work of literature',[23] the use of the term 'fragment' would have hinted that Denham's art could not be fully comprehended without recourse to his own (fake) parody of *Coopers Hill*. Implicitly pretending to shed a new light on the poet, *Cooper's Well* set out to exhibit, in a ribald manner, Sir John Denham's erotic bent of mind.

## IV

Before entering into a critical discussion of *Cooper's Well*, it is necessary to assess its debt to *Coopers Hill*. Close correspondences in such features as diction and word order confirm that the eighteenth-century author used the 1668 edition of the text, the version 'which has continued to represent Denham's poem to posterity'.[24] The verbal parallels are so obvious that one cannot help imagining him working with a copy of this edition before him and systematically marking the passages suitable for mock treatment. Witness the opening lines of *Coopers Hill*,

> Sure there are Poets which did never dream
> Upon *Parnassus*, nor did tast the stream
> Of *Helicon*, we therefore may suppose
> Those made not Poets, but the Poets those,
> And as Courts make not Kings, but Kings the Court,
> So where the Muses & their train resort,
> *Parnassus* stands; if I can be to thee
> A poet, thou *Parnassus* art to me (ll. 1–8)[,]

which the parodist, announcing the sexual interest of his poem, adapted as follows:

> Sure there are Lovers which did never sip
> The stream of VENUS; nor did taste the lip
> Of COOPER'S WELL; we therefore may suppose
> Those made some Lovers, and some Lovers those:
> And as Wells make not Springs, but Springs the Well,
> So, where the GRACES, and the MUSES dwell
> Flows COOPER'S STREAM; if I can be to thee
> A pleasing BARD, thou'rt HELICON to me. (ll. 1–8)

---

23  Jung, p. 136.
24  O Hehir, *EH*, p. 38. This is the so-called B text, which had appeared in a substantially identical version in 1655. All in-text references will be, by line number, to the 1668 version of the poem in the O Hehir edition (pp. 137–62).

But the imitation remained largely confined to the first quarter of the poem. Of *Cooper's Well*'s 322 lines of rhyming decasyllabic couplets, the first seventy-four, a mixture of (primarily) literal quotation, clever paraphrase, and verbal echoes, are nearly all directly inspired by Denham. Of the remaining 248 lines, another twenty-five are borrowed from or contain echoes of the original; all in all some hundred lines have their origin in *Coopers Hill*. The compression of the larger part of this debt in the opening section may suggest that the (more or less) original lines from seventy-five until the end constitute an extensive elaboration of what began as an exercise in wit.

The author drew most emphatically on the first forty-six lines of Denham's poem, dealing with the two awe-inspiring sights traced by the poet's eye, St Paul's and Windsor Castle, and, to a lesser extent, on two further passages from the middle and the conclusion of the poem. The first is the section on 'The Forrest' and 'Narcissus' (ll. 197–240), the latter one of several references to classical myths which is fastened on in the ambiguous hymn on Cooper's Well as a spot to which 'all the horned host resorts / To frisk, to wanton, gambol, bathe and gaze, / And Nature's master-piece sublimely raise' (ll. 56–58). The second is the section on 'Magna Charta' (ll. 333–35) and the need to contain within its proper limits the power of kings and subjects, which is translated rather awkwardly into the image of the well's drowning the ploughman after having been 'swell'd by sudden rains' (l. 71). More selectively used are the important historical-political sections of *Coopers Hill*, especially lines 47–196 and 241–332. Of the first, the lines dealing with Windsor Castle as the seat of English royalty and the 'monstrous dire offence' (l. 117) of Henry VIII are largely ignored. The address to the Thames as the giver of plenty (ll. 159–95), on the other hand, not only supplied a number of lines in virtually unchanged form, including the famous couplet 'O could I flow like thee, and make thy stream / My great example, as it is my theme!' (ll. 189–90), but also provided the inspiration for the long laudation of 'the stream of Venus', the central image in *Cooper's Well*, which will be dealt with below. Of the second section, incorporating the stag hunt as an allegory of the trial and execution of King Charles I, only four or five lines (199–200 and 203–05) found their way into *Cooper's Well*, suggesting that more than a century after the civil wars the political dimension of the original had become irrelevant. If the figure of the king is introduced at all, it is not as the embodiment of monarchy but as a regular visitor of the Well where, 'unfix'd from cares', he would '[e]nraptur'd bathe his sturdy limbs' (ll. 200–01), or as the patron who 'will run to read what Denham writes' (l. 108). And if Denham's 'declining States-man, left forlorn / To his friends pity, and pursuers scorn' (ll. 273–74) could carry associations with both the Earl of Strafford and Charles I, in *Cooper's Well* the allusion to the 'imperious Statesman' who '[b]y one deep motion sunk himself in shame' (l. 62) has become a lubricious rather than a political one.

The sequential borrowings from *Coopers Hill* account for a coherence of sorts in the first 74 lines of the parody, loosely devoted to the announcement of the theme (ll. 1–8), the nature of the 'landscape' taken in by the poet's 'wanton eye' (ll. 9–30), the blessings bestowed by this place of retirement (ll. 31–44), and the Well as an emblem of balance and moderation (ll. 45–74).[25] Owing no more than a minor debt to Denham, the remaining part of *Cooper's Well* (ll. 75–184 and 209–322) lends an epic flavour to what was first conceived as a mock-topographical poem. Five fairly discrete sections can be distinguished: (1) an invocation (ll. 75–98), hailing the Well as the seat of Love and Beauty (two of the Graces alluded to in the opening lines of the poem) and asking that the latter may inspire the writer's 'am'rous tongue' (l. 93); (2) a *praepositio* (ll. 99–128), which epitomises the theme of the poem as '[t]he hidden Mystries of that sacred Well, / Where WILMOT sprung, and oft' where WILMOT dy'd' (l. 118–19) and characterises the writing of such a poem, tongue-in-cheek, as a risky enterprise, especially in an age as 'chaste' (l. 115) as Charles II's; (3) an extended description of the geography of the Well (ll. 129–209), which in all its detailed intricacies must have been aimed at placing the reader quite literally in medias res; (4) a digressive panegyric on the virtues of the stream emanating from the Well (ll. 210–82), which are such as to reduce more famous rivers in classical mythology 'to common jakes' (l. 212); and (5) a conclusion (ll. 283–322) in praise of the Well, whose beauty deserves far greater renown than the bowers of Woodstock and Hampton Court or the 'speaking Pictures' (l. 312) drawn by Raphael.

Sounding a more heroic note than *Coopers Hill*, the first two sections, with their allusions to *The Rape of the Lock* ('BOLD's the attempt', l. 99; and 'BOLD be th' attempt!', l. 105), *Absalom and Achitophel* ('And spread their Sovereign's image thro' the land', l. 84), and Book I of *Paradise Lost* ('A Well, as deep as nine times day and night', l. 121), were meant to underscore the serio-comical nature of the poem.[26] The enumeration of ancient rivers (Alpheus, Scamander, and Styx) and the idealisation of the Well as a Shangri-La of rural happiness in the fourth and fifth sections, on the other hand, offer a direct link with the conventions of topographical poetry, the former looking back to a prototype such as Henry Vaughan's 'To the River Isca' (1651), the latter to the 'retreat urge' which has been identified as an 'outstanding' feature of *Coopers Hill*, an urge here voiced more emphatically in such lines as 'O! could I change my state, and with ye dwell / Within the borders of my COOPER'S WELL' (177–78).[27] Larded with expressions of the persona's feelings of wistfulness, *Cooper's Well* in its less ambiguous passages indeed partakes of the sentimental nature of a type of verse categorised by Aubin as 'river-poetry', in which scenes of natural description served as 'visible

---

25  Typography may offer a clue as to the writer's modus operandi in dealing with his source text, or even the relative haste with which this part of the poem was cobbled together. Each of the three verse paragraphs, separated by a blank space, into which the text in the 1767 edition is divided (ll. 1–30; 31–44; 45–74) ends with one to four lines *not* derived from *Coopers Hill*, evidently passages intended as transitions linking together the densely knit borrowings derived from different sections of the original.

26  See, for comparison's sake, William Godwin's *A Poetical Description of Bristol* (London, 1712), explicitly modelled on *Coopers Hill*, and John Huckell's *Avon. A Poem* (London, 1758), both of which give the Muses short shrift.

27  Aubin, p. 35. Not very surprisingly, the parodist also had an eye to *Windsor Forest*, line 8 of which is echoed thus: 'Inspire my verse, inspire my am'rous tongue, / Till praise, thy due, breathes musical in song!' (ll. 93–94).

expressions of or backgrounds to their poets' own emotions, generally woeful'.[28] Rising beyond the poetical tradition itself, this personal note probably purported to capture the voice (or, one voice) of Sir John Denham himself, of whose authorship the reader must be constantly reminded. As the dedication to Rochester notes in passing, however, the preoccupation of *Cooper's Well* is with 'Denham's' devotion to the cause of 'Love and Venus' (ii). To such diverse ingredients as the heroic couplets (lending an air of dignity to the scurrilous lines), a vaguely epic structure, a lyric impulse, and the trappings of traditional descriptive-topographical verse, *Cooper's Well* adds a curious interest in the vogue for erotica.

# V

If Cooper's Hill, Surrey, was the vantage point from which the seventeenth-century poet had surveyed the surrounding landscape, giving rise to 'historical retrospection, or incidental meditation',[29] Cooper's Well is both the parodist's 'Helicon' and the object of his voyeuristic gaze. An unidentifiable place devoid of historical associations, and therefore a timeless spot, the setting of the Well is a drawn-out metaphor for the female body, and more specifically the genitalia, whose 'geography' the poem ceaselessly explores as the inexhaustible source of love, beauty, and happiness. While several passages masquerade as species of innocuous local-descriptive poetry, the more prurient flights testify to the parodist's familiarity with a body of erotic (often satirical) materials in which features of the natural landscape were invariably paralleled with the female anatomy.[30] In the opening lines, heavily indebted to Denham's prospect of Windsor, St Paul's, and the Thames Valley, the reader is granted a prospect of the Well's location as seen from 'two snowy Mountains' (l. 17):

> Below, a lovely, velvet Valley swells,
> Where STRENGTH with BEAUTY, MARS and VENUS dwells;
> And to the eye it doth itself present,
> With such an easy, and unforc'd descent,
> No horrors there appear to hurt the eye,
> Nor access to the Fair and Young deny:
> But such a gentle slope, as doth invite
> A pleasure, rapture, rev'rence for the sight. (ll. 19–26)

Replacing Denham's 'unforc't ascent' towards Windsor Castle (l. 42) with a (no doubt more pleasurable) 'descent' into a 'velvet Valley', this poem identifies the

---

28  Aubin, Chapter VI, 'Murmuring Waters'.
29  Johnson, p. 238.
30  See Julie Peakman, *Mighty Lewd Books: The Development of Pornography in Eighteenth-Century England* (London: Palgrave, 2003; repr. 2012), passim. I am indebted to Peakman's study for some of the source materials cited below.

location of the Well as a gendered landscape whose various elements the attentive
student schooled in the use of double entendre is expected to puzzle together:

> Seated within a Grot of make divine,
> Built without mortar, chisel, rule, or line:
> Soft moss without; of lively crimson hue
> The canopy …
> High on two alabaster pillars rear'd
> (Which Popes have kiss'd, and Infidels rever'd)
> The grotto was; where men of all degrees
> Present their largest off'rings on their knees …
> Soft, Mossy Grotto, exquisitely fair,
> The work of Jove himself, and man's chief care
> Around grew wanton shrubs, of various hue,
> In wanton tufts; seem'd wanton as they grew
> Luxuriant creeping, and they dangl'd o'er
> To kiss the borders of the flowery shore:
> In this neat Grotto, thro' a dark Alcove,
> Rises the spring of COOPER'S WELL, and Love …
> Which in a gentle rill, runs gently through
> The nether tufts, and wets each pendent bough. (ll. 129–32; 135–38;
> 143–44; 159–64; 167–68)

Part of a concretely imagined but intricate corporeal landscape, the Well springs
in a dark grotto on a 'little snowy hill' (l. 147), only accessible through a narrow entrance wrapped 'in obscurity' (l. 152) and leading to a 'dark Alcove' (l.
163). Unlike man-made grottoes, this one is 'of make divine', a place of worship
for 'men of all degrees', including kings and popes, who present there (in more
senses than one) 'their largest offerings on their knees'. Supported by alabaster
pillars—an echo of the 'Song of Solomon', 5:15—and consecrated to Jove, the
grotto carries both biblical and classical associations, which add to its aura of
time-honoured mystery. With its soft, mossy cave, crimson 'canopy', 'luxuriant'
tufts of 'wanton' shrubs, and 'flowery' shore, the sexualised setting of *Cooper's
Well* transforms the politicised landscape of *Coopers Hill* into an essentially
female space, presented as an awe-inspiring object of desire.[31] As in Denham's

---

31 The parodist has evidently appropriated some of the vocabulary used to describe the nature of
   the 'creature' in Edward Ward's *A Riddle: Or, A Paradoxical Character of a Hairy Monster, often
   found under Holland* (London, 1725; repr. 1737), a raunchy satire lacking the relative sophistication of *Cooper's Well*.

   > The Learn'd, the Wise, the Grave, the Gay,
   > In its Embraces take Delight;
   > Tho' hid, th' adore it in the Day,
   > And often kneel to it at Night.
   > It justly may be stil'd a Well,

poem (and indeed *Windsor Forest*), this space is the home of Mars and Venus (l. 20), an emblem of harmonious balance and moderation, where 'all the rough-ness of the creeping Wood, / Strives with the gentle oozings of the flood' (ll. 45–46). But as a feminised locus, it is given an extra dimension, that of a testing-ground exerting an irresistible attraction on the 'horned host' (l.56) seeking to unveil its hidden Mystries' (l. 118). '[U]nfathom'd by the sons of light' though 'frequented by the brave and great' (ll. 122, 124), the grotto has never surren-dered its secrets, for

> Thousands have toil'd to reach in endless goal,
> And all in striving spent their mighty all;
> Returning faint, without their former might;
> Praising the joys of darkness more than light. (ll. 156–58).

Inscrutable for all their appeal, the cave and the spring hidden inside it are at the origin of the most powerful natural presence in the poem. Extending its use of botanical-geographical metaphors for the female genitalia, *Cooper's Well* depicts the vaginal fluid emanating from the grotto as the 'stream of Venus'—the counter-part of the Thames in *Coopers Hill*. Denham's river, as O Hehir has pointed out, is an emblem of 'harmonious *power*—the power in the state (or in the universe), whatever its particular locus, which guarantees our peace, happiness, and prosper-ity as long as it remains within bounds, but which can destroy us if it runs wildly over its banks'.[32] Although it too is viewed as a life-giving force with a destructive potential, the stream in *Cooper's Well* acquires significance on a level beyond the prosperity of the nation but in a manner that the context at first only articulates by indirection:

> Prolifick stream! which can at once give Breath
> To various Creatures, and eternal death:
> Thrice powerful stream, which can destroy and save,
> And prove at once the cradle and the grave: ...
> All my possessions in this world I'd give,
> To only die, where you are known to live.
> O! Animalcula, was I like you,

---

> At each Spring-Tide it overflows;
> Its Depth no mortal Man can tell;
> That none but he that made it knows.
> It lies obscurely in a Clift,
> That's fenc'd with Brambles round about;
> Yet every Fool can make a Shift,
> Tho' never so dark, to find it out. (ll. 17–28)

32  O Hehir, *EH*, p. 242.

'Twould be my cradle, and my coffin too:
Prolifick stream, and more prolifick fry,
Where myriads quicken, and where myriads die. (ll. 171–74; 179–84)

Just as alluring as the 'joys of darkness' afforded by the grotto, the 'thrice powerful' stream itself has the speaker longing to give up all his possessions and, somewhat counter-intuitively, share the fate of the unidentified 'myriads' who have
found there both a 'cradle' and a 'grave'. Despite the hints at carnal gratification
(as in the verb 'to die'), the real satisfaction to be derived from 'dwelling' (l. 177)
with the river proves to be one for which the lubricious context has not prepared
the reader. The key to a proper understanding of this textual tangle lies in the allusive nature of such terms as 'prolifick fry', 'myriads', and especially 'Animalcula'
(ll. 181, 183–84) or 'little animals'. The latter is the existential condition to which
the speaker, ready to 'change [his] state' (l. 177), aspires in the hope of being not
just *like* the river but *part* of it. Strange as such desire may seem, it does reveal
something about the poet's scientific interests and the nature of the 'mystery' with
which the grotto and the 'stream of Venus' are associated.

The passage strongly suggests that *Cooper's Well* is in parts a satirical response
to recent developments in the study of biology and medicine. Some of these had
come about with the help of new, more sophisticated microscopes, allowing
researchers such as Antony van Leeuwenhoek (1632–1723) to reveal the existence, in various kinds of liquids, including human semen, of tiny organisms,
denoted as *vermiculi* or *animalcula*. These insights had opened up new avenues
of research into the mechanisms of fertility and reproduction but had also given
rise to diverse (often far-fetched) theories about human conception, especially in
relation to the respective role of the male and the female in the process.[33] The specific properties of *animalcula* revealed by microscopic study were their very large
numbers and extraordinarily vital power. In his *Micrographia Nova*, Benjamin
Martin noted that one 'Sort of *Animalculae* [...] of the Maggot-kind'

> are in prodigious Numbers in prepar'd Water, and move with great Celerity
> confusedly among each other [...] They have a surprizing Tenacity of Life;
> for I have put 'em in a Glass Tube in a freezing Mixture [...] yet upon thaw-
> ing the same, [they] soon recover'd Life and Motion, and were as well, to
> Appearance, as before.[34]

Described by some as spider- or eel-like, by others as resembling tadpoles, these
organisms aroused intense curiosity and exercised the imagination of many. One

---

33  For a summary, see Peakman, Chapter 4, 'Erotica and Science'.
34  Benjamin Martin, *Micrographia Nova: Or, A New Treatise on the Microscope, and Microscopic
Objects* (Reading, 1742), pp. 51–53.

theory, reported and debunked in the 'Philosophical Transactions' of the Royal Society, held that *animalcula* were miniature humans originally formed by the Creator:

> a certain Physician [...] while he was attentively observing these *Animalcules*, one of them [...] presented itself, having almost slipped off it's Skin: And then there plainly appeared two naked Thighs and legs, a Breast, and two Arms, above which, the Skin being thrust up, covered the Head as it were a Cap [...] it died in endeavouring to get clear of the Skin.[35]

While granting that '[t]he *Ova* have a principal Part in Propagation', a proponent of the Aristotelian idea of the pre-existence of the 'larger Animal' in the '*Sperm* of the Male' speculated that the countless seeds that do not contribute to fertilisation 'either die [...] (which I can hardly think) or return back from whence they came into the open Atmosphere to go the same Round again'.[36]

Given the fanciful nature of some anatomical disquisitions, one begins to see how an imaginative parodist could flippantly represent the 'stream of Venus' as a primal force capable of giving birth and death to 'myriads' of 'prolific fry', thus outdoing Windsor Castle, which had been a 'Cradle' and a 'Tombe' to only a handful of British kings in *Coopers Hill* (l.76). Nor would it have taken an imaginative leap for the same poet to visualise himself as a homunculus, one of 'various Creatures' living and dying in this stream. However, this apparently grotesque aspiration may reflect the keen awareness, as one contemporary writer put it, of 'how very little we as yet know of the deep Mysteries and secret Recesses of Nature'[37] as well as the subliminal desire to unlock the secrets, if not of Nature as a whole, at least those of the female body. As opposed to the bawdy medical erotica of the period,[38] the aim here was not to titillate the reader's curiosity about a taboo subject so much as to convey the poet's reverence for the hidden power of the female sex. This is why the stream, whose 'milky current' (l. 190) is assimilated with the unexplored regions of the '*Via lactis*' (l. 189), the stars, and 'Jove's abodes' (l. 191), is celebrated as hyperbolically as it is and becomes, within the confines of the poem, '[m]y only pass-time, as it is my theme' (l. 186).

35  John Martyn, *The Philosophical Transactions (From the Year 1732, to the Year 1744) Abridged, and Disposed under General Heads. In Two Volumes* (London, 1747), pp. 123–24.
36  John Cook, *The New Theory of Generation, According to the Best and Latest Discoveries in Anatomy, Farther improved and fully displayed* (London, 1762), pp. 15, 19, 308 (hereafter 'Cook'). The notion of male '"seeds" being propagated by air' (see Peakman, p. 81) probably lay at the back of the parodist's description of the 'nether tufts' by Cooper's stream: 'Oft on these boughs a thousand airy things, / When tir'd with bathing, dry their little wings' (ll. 169–70).
37  Cook, p. 17. Peakman notes that in the 'mechanical philosophy [...] the female body was a mystery to be fathomed' (p. 68).
38  For a brief survey, see Peter Wagner, 'The discourse on sex—or sex as discourse: eighteenth-century medical and paramedical erotica', in G.S. Rousseau and Roy Porter (eds), *Sexual Underworlds of the Enlightenment* (Manchester: Manchester University Press, 1987), pp. 46–68.

The final sections, then, are in praise of those aspects of the stream which are implied to be the components of the mystery it symbolises, more particularly its iridescent 'min'ral tints' (l. 215), inexhaustible fertility, and perennial youth. But the mere articulation of these familiar qualities—representing the cyclical pulses of life—helps to shatter the sense of the ineffable conjured up earlier. And with respect to all three, parody informed by sexual metaphor is largely abandoned in favour of a pastoral vision, initiating a shift of focus and a distinct tonal change which give the poem an oddly disjointed look. The overwhelming emphasis is now on the 'variegated' hues of Cooper's 'tide' (l. 218), which far exceed both the 'various dyes' (l. 221) of New World maps and the rich colours of the Sicilian fountain Arethusa, one of the deities of pastoral poetry.[39] Unlike Scamander, a river on the Trojan plains which is claimed to have 'dry'd up' (l. 238), Cooper's stream is predicted never to lose 'the power of [its] relaxing springs' (l. 236) but to remain a permanent source of enjoyment.[40] Unlike flowers withered with age, the stream will resist the onslaught of time; and when Youth and Beauty will eventually 'quit [its] Grotto Love', 'more religious pastimes' (ll. 264–65) are sure to supplant them. Even the poet's express repudiation of the outworn clichés of topographical poetry[41] and the trappings of 'past'rals and Elysian Bowers' (l. 282) cannot efface the fact that 'the circle' (l. 272) of Cooper's Well (a figure of perfection), initially depicted as a dark and challenging place, has itself been turned into a locus of Arcadian happiness, a world of 'Fancies' and 'Dreams' (l. 292),

> Where blushing flowers are timely seen to blow,
> And seeds prolific most luxuriant grow;
> Where streams meander, and where Fountains play,
> And smiles and sun-shine sport the live-long day …
> Where softest motions, softest musick suit,
> Beyond the GERMAN, or the DORIAN Flute:
> Musick which gives emotion to the heart,
> A fainting flutter, and a pleasing smart. (ll. 273–76; 279–82)

By now, *Cooper's Well* approaches much more nearly the blithe, celebratory spirit of Edmund Waller's 'On St. James's Park' with its

> Lovers walking in that amorous shade,
> The Gallants dancing by the Rivers side,

---

39 'Gage, / The great map-jobber of the present age' (ll. 219–20) refers to Thomas Gage, a contemporary of Denham's and the author of *A New Survey of the West-Indias: Or, The English American his Travail by Sea and Land* (London, 1655; 2nd edn), a work containing maps of the New World.

40 The dried-up current, leaving only 'a yawning chasm' (l. 246) symbolising infertility, is one of two or three links with the sexual metaphors of the previous sections.

41 The final lines explicitly poke fun at platitudinous phrases such as 'rough Cascades', 'tinkling Rills', 'aromatic Shades', all derived from a host of major and minor contemporary poets.

> They bath in Summer, and in Winter slide,
> Me-thinks I hear the Musick in the Boats,
> And the loud Eccho which returns the notes,[42]

than it does the cynical obscenities of 'A Ramble in St. James's Parke' (composed before 1672–73), the mock-topographical version of Waller's poem by Rochester, the supposed recipient of the Denham parody. Admittedly, the 'blushing flowers', the 'seeds prolific', and the closing words of praise, 'Her Grot's more cool, and deeper's her retreat: / Her Arch more conic, and her Well more deep' (ll. 316–17), faintly echo the sexualised landscape that was the tenor of the first half of the poem. But this echo is drowned out by the occasionally moralising but generally exultant tone into which the parody, at the outset directly inspired by *Coopers Hill* and heavily reliant on sexual double entendre, has modulated in its concluding sections. Having all too soon exhausted the erotic potential of his source-text and the sense of mystery that it momentarily engenders, the poet ultimately leaves the reader in a state of bewilderment as to his true intentions.

## VI

Three years after the first appearance of *Cooper's Well*, in 1770, the publisher-bookseller C. Moran brought out a revised version of the poem, now included in *The Court of Cupid*, a two-volume collection of verse 'by the Author of the Meretriciad'.[43] In a footnote introducing the text, Moran (or the poet himself) found it necessary to return to the issue of the poem's authorship that had been such a crucial feature of the first edition:

> I am greatly divided whether this composition is really *Sir John Denham's*, altho' the manuscript strictly declares it such. I should rather conceive it to be some of the salacious Geniuses of that time, who wanted to vex the chaste Knight, by a parody on his *Cooper's-Hill*: but tho' the thought and words have or have not, an obscene tendency, nevertheless they are so neatly rolled up, as to avoid offence to the chastest eye and ear. (p. 85)

Although holding onto the fiction of the found manuscript, the author of this explanatory note would have all too clearly realised that the publication of *Cooper's Well* along with a series of racy satires, including *The Meretriciad* (1761), *The Courtesan* (1765), and *The Demi-Rep* (1756), was a dead giveaway. The last-named items had already figured on a list of books printed for and sold by Moran, appended to

---

42  *Poems, etc. Written upon several Occasions, And to several Persons* (London, 1668; 3rd edn), p. 160.

43  On Moran, see H.R. Plomer, *A Dictionary of the Printers and Booksellers Who Were at Work in England, Scotland and Ireland from 1726 to 1775* (Oxford: Oxford University Press, 1932; repr. 1968), p. 178. *The Court of Cupid* also includes the dedication and address to the reader prefixed to *Cooper's Well* (see vol. 2, pp. 73–104).

the first edition of *Cooper's Well*—a list which also included the second edition of *Sailors Letters, written to his Select Friends in England*, by 'Mr. Thompson'. Published anonymously but known to be the work of Captain Edward Thompson (1738?–1786), a naval officer who carved out a literary career in the 1760s, *The Meretriciad, The Courtesan,* and *The Demi-Rep* proved enormously successful, going through several editions in the space of a few years.[44] Despite the fact that Thompson implicitly acknowledged *Cooper's Well* as his own by allowing it to be included in *The Court of Cupid*, modern bibliographers and literary historians have remained hesitant about ascribing the poem to him.[45] Space does not permit a closer investigation of the correspondences between *Cooper's Well* and the satiric design of Thompson's other poems. But the opening of *The Meretriciad*, a satire on the courtesan Kitty Fisher composed around 1761, which testifies to the author's interest in Denham's 'melodious rhymes' and adduces Rochester as a tutelary spirit, may be regarded as a prelude to his more sustained grapple with *Coopers Hill*:

> Immortal DENHAM in far earlier times,
> Tun'd this soft maxim in melodious rhymes:
> That mild *Parnassus*, nor her milder streams,
> E'er made some poets, or the poets themes;
> For many sure there are, who've sung, and sing,
> Yet never sip'd at the *Castalian* spring …
> How durst you soar so high, kind honour'd Maid?
> Without invoking *Wilmot*'s lathy shade,
> Whose generous soul pursu'd this theme in death,
> And rail'd at lewdness with his parting breath. (ll. 1–6, 46–49)

Thompson's revisions of the 1767 text consist mainly of the substitution of individual words and phrases, the cancellation of a few obscure lines, the addition of footnotes explaining some of the classical references, and the introduction of new verses inspired by sections of *Coopers Hill* originally left untouched. Some of the alterations suggest that, in line with the change of tack already evident in the 1767 version, Thompson had expanded his eulogy on the 'azure stream' (p. 96) while at the same time toning down the sexual innuendo.[46] His revisions may have been guided by a concern to further emphasise the link with *Coopers Hill* and make the text more accessible, but they did not fundamentally alter the heterogeneous nature and the confused effect of the end product. Nor did they herald a further edition of the poem, which after 1770 sank into complete oblivion. In the absence of contemporary readers' comments, it is impossible to gauge how convincing a

---

44  Clive Wilkinson, 'Thompson, Edward (1738?–1786)', *ODNB*, Oxford University Press, 2004.

45  The British Library's *English Short-Title Catalogue* describes it as being 'sometimes attributed to Edward Thompson'.

46  For instance, he cancelled the 'animalcula' reference, thus taking the edge off the sexual-scientific imagery in this passage. And in the lines quoted earlier ('Her Grot […] her Arch […] her Well'), he replaced the possessive pronoun with the article 'the', rendering the phrasing less suggestive.

forgery *Cooper's Well* turned out to be. But the appearance at least of Thompson's poem may be located at the intersection point of various tendencies: the contemporary interest in erotica, which furnished the idea for the sexual parody in the first place; the fashion for imitations and 'discoveries' recently given an added impetus by such collections as James Macpherson's *Fragments of Ancient Poetry* (1760) and Thomas Percy's *Reliques of Ancient English Poetry* (1765); the continuing appeal of the satirical as well as the topographical mode; and the dawn of a more reflective, self-orientated nature poetry. Although an uneasy mixture of all of these, *Cooper's Well* remains of interest not only as a minor literary-historical curiosity but also as a testimony to the high regard in which Sir John Denham's poetry continued to be held in the eighteenth century.

# 10 Cooper's Hill and Runnymede as Sites of Memory

*Naomi Howell and Philip Schwyzer*

## I

Before the 1640s, the name of Cooper's Hill would have been barely known beyond the immediate vicinity of the small town of Egham in Surrey, on whose western side it rises.[1] Nor was the name of the meadow beneath it, Runnymede, much more widely recognised, beyond the circles of antiquaries and legal historians who might recall its association with Magna Carta. That Runnymede is today a toponym recognised throughout and beyond the English-speaking world owes much to one man, Sir John Denham, and one poem, *Coopers Hill*. Situated roughly midway between the baronial conflicts of the early thirteenth century and our own era, Denham's poem marks the emergence of Runnymede as a *lieu de mémoire*, and inaugurates a tradition of landscape poetry and memorialisation in this micro-region that has steadily gathered force over almost four centuries.[2] Not only did *Coopers Hill* play a crucial role in the rise to fame of this strip of Thames floodplain; it has also had an impact on the physical environment itself, which over the last century has been transformed into a memorial park. This chapter situates Denham's poem at the hinge of this landscape's cultural history, glancing both backward and forward to construct a biography of place.

## II

Today, Runnymede is a familiar metonym for Magna Carta and the perceived dawn of various modern freedoms. Phrases such as the 'The Road to [or from] Runnymede' generally serve to indicate passages in the history of constitutional

---

1  The first recorded mention of Cooper's Hill occurs in a survey of 1547–50; the name is thought to derive from the local landowning Cowper family. Richard Williams, *Runnymede: A Pictorial History* (Addlestone, Surrey: Egham-by-Runnymede Historical Society, 1995), p. 6.

2  On *lieux de mémoire,* signifying the crystallisation of cultural memory in a particular location (not necessarily geographical), see Pierre Nora, 'Between Memory and History: *Les Lieux de Mémoire*', *Representations*, 26 (Spring 1989), pp. 7–24. Whilst Nora sees such sites of memory as a product of modernity, the Past in its Place project, from which this chapter emerges, has been seeking to uncover the premodern history of sites of memory in England and Wales. The Past in its Place project is funded by the European Research Council.

liberties, without presuming any reference to that stretch of the motorway A308 running between Egham and Old Windsor.[3] Yet the persistent association of a constitutional watershed with an otherwise obscure water meadow is remarkable. Not to put too fine a point on it, everything happens somewhere; yet only comparatively rarely does the location of a political event become so bound up with our way of conceptualising its significance.[4] There is surely something paradoxical in the persistent tendency to align universal, immaterial notions such as liberty, democracy, and equality before the law, with a particular place on the map. How did this come about?

The name of Runnymede has been thought to derive from the Old English words for counsel [*rune*] and meadow, which could suggest a long-standing history as a meeting place.[5] The name does not occur in Domesday, however, and the first surviving reference to Runnymede occurs no earlier than 1215, in the concluding words of Magna Carta itself. Here King John refers to the charter as being 'given by our hand in the meadow that is called Runnymede, between Windsor and Staines, on the fifteenth day of June in the seventeenth year of our reign'.[6] Talks between the barons and the king's representatives had taken place at or near Runnymede for several days before the sealing of the charter, and the meeting would not break up until 19 June, when a 'firm peace' was declared.[7] This point on the Thames lay roughly equidistant between John's base at Windsor some three miles north-west, and the barons' encampment at Staines, three miles further east (Figure 10.1). The nature of the site as an undeveloped floodplain perhaps enhanced its perception as neutral ground, with no strong associations favourable to either party; the limited points of access from either east or west would also have mitigated a risk of a surprise attack by either side.[8] King John may have found another covert significance in a site subject to semi-annual erasure by the flooding Thames; his undoubted hope was that the Great Charter would prove no more permanent than the dry land on which it was signed. In this he was

---

3  'The road [...] to Runnymede was direct, short and unavoidable'; J.C. Holt, *The Northerners: A Study in the Reign of King John* (Oxford: Clarendon Press, 1992), p. 100; see also the chapter entitled 'The Road to Runnymede' in Richard Huscroft, *Ruling England, 1042–1217* (London: Routledge, 2004), pp. 170–75; Cary J. Nederman, 'The Liberty of the Church and the Road to Runnymede: John of Salisbury and the Intellectual Foundations of the Magna Carta', *PS: Political Science & Politics*, 43 (2010), pp. 457–61; A.E. Dick Howard, *The Road from Runnymede: Magna Carta and Constitutionalism in America* (Charlottesville: University of Virginia Press, 1968).

4  The Putney Debates of 1647 marked a crucial step in the development of the principle of the universal franchise. Yet to speak of the road to Putney fails to take us far beyond the street map of south-west London.

5  See the *OED*, s.v. ROUN, Etymology (sense 3): 'Apparently also attested early (in sense 3) in the place name Runemede, Surrey (1215; now Runnymede), with the original meaning probably being "meadow at the island where councils are held" (the first element reflecting Old English *rūn-īeg, lit. "deliberation island")'.

6  English Translation of Magna Carta, BL, <http://www.bl.uk/magna-carta/articles/magna-carta-english-translation>.

7  Ralph V. Turner, *Magna Carta: Through the Ages* (Harlow: Pearson, 2003), pp. 61–63.

8  J.C. Holt, *Magna Carta* (Cambridge: Cambridge University Press, 1965), pp. 160–61.

*Figure 10.1* Details of John Speed's maps of Berkshire and Surrey, showing the course of the Thames between Reading and London. © The British Library Board; John Speed, *The Theatre of the Empire of Great Britain* (1650), Maps/C.18.C.4, pp. 11–12, 27–28.

justified, for a papal annulment of Magna Carta would reach England by September, well before the Thames had an opportunity to breach its banks.

There is little to indicate that Runnymede as a specific site developed any special notoriety in the aftermath of Magna Carta, though the Close Rolls of 1244 include an interesting reference to the *parleamentum de Rumened* (the Parliament of Runnymede) where the Great Charter was agreed.[9] Yet it is arguable that the immediate region, namely, the southern bank of the Thames stretching between Windsor and Staines, did become charged with associations which might not have been fully speakable. The area is clearly significant in *L'Histoire de Guillaume le Marechal*, a near-hagiographical, verse romance-biography of John's most capable commander, William Marshal (d. 1219). Though the landscape is traversed many times, the narrator brings it into our consideration very delicately, and with many evasions.

The narrator of the *Histoire* expresses reluctance to discuss the events converging on Runnymede in 1215, declaring that it is both ignoble and dangerous to do so.[10] William Marshal's role in the negotiations is minimised and even denied.[11]

---

9  Turner, *Magna Carta*, p. 114.

10  'Quer trop i out des acheisons / Qui ne sunt proz a reconter, / Ains me porreit a mal monter' (15034–36: 'For there are too many events which are ignoble [not edifying] to recount; rather, something bad could happen to me'). Paul Meyer (ed.), *L'Histoire de Guillaume le Marechal, Comte de Striguil et de Pembroke, Règent d'Angleterre de 1216 a 1219* (Paris, 1891).

11  'Mès saciez que de tot cel mal, / Par le conseil del Mar[eschal] / N'i out riens porchacié ne fe[i]t, / Ainz li pesa molt de[l] sorfeit / D'amedeus pars, quant il le sout, / Qu'il nel consenti ne ne volt / Ne par son conseil rien ne firent / Londreis qui a els s'asentirent' (15053–15160: 'But know that of

Instead, his attitude is portrayed as one of deep disapproval for and distance from the 'whole evil business' (15053 'Tot ce mal'). Disassociated from the discord and division caused by 'the excess of both parties' (15056–57), the Marshal's own heart is 'whole and pure' (15123 'Qui out le cœur entier et pur'). Similarly, the role of the Marshal's eldest son in these events goes unmentioned (possibly at his own request). William Marshal the Younger and his brother John were both among the rebel barons at Runnymede, possibly as part of a cunningly crafted diplomatic strategy on the part of the Marshal family.[12] In the poem, the younger William Marshal, who commissioned the *Histoire* after his father's death, is ardently praised for resembling his father; the proverbial 'good fruit of a good tree'.[13]

The road from Reading and Windsor to London—that is, the road past Cooper's Hill through Runnymede—is implicitly negotiated dozens of times in the *Histoire*, and yet the narrator seems reluctant to 'go there'. The description of events surrounding Magna Carta take us no closer than London (15052, 15060, 15064), where the barons assembled in May 1215 before meeting the king in June at Runnymede. In contrast, elsewhere the *Histoire* recounts in great precision the movements of the king, William Marshal, the rebel barons, and Louis of France. After relating the death of the king, the *Histoire* dwells at length on the Marshal's role in securing the Treaty of Kingston after John's death, but omits to mention the initial negotiations which, according to Matthew Paris, took place on an island near Staines—a place of likely symbolic importance for the barons who had encamped there in 1215.[14] We are told rather that the Marshal and his men gathered at Chertsey and then met Louis of France on an island near Kingston. Indeed, Staines is mentioned only once in the *Histoire*, but on this occasion it seems to outweigh even Westminster Abbey in significance and emotional power.

Nowhere is the politic, delicate manoeuvring across this landscape so evident as in the final great occasion of the *Histoire*. The description of the Marshal's funeral procession makes a pronounced if implicit point of recalling the events

---

this evil business nothing was endeavoured or done by the counsel of the Marshal. Rather, he was much saddened by the excess of both parties, when he knew of it, which he had neither counselled nor desired. Nor did the Londoners do anything by his counsel or consent').

12  Suggested in the Worcester Annals, *Annales de Wifornia*, in *Annales Monastici*, iv, ed. H.R. Luard (London: Longman, 1869), p. 406. See also Sidney Painter, *William Marshal: Knight-Errant, Baron, and Regent of England* (Baltimore: Johns Hopkins Press, 1933); David Crouch, *William Marshal: Knighthood, War, and Chivalry, 1147–1219* (Harlow: Pearson, 1990), pp. 121–22.

13  *Histoire*, 14960, 19180; 'de bone arbre vient bon fruit'. Matthew Paris tells us that William Marshal the Younger and his brother John were present at Runnymede on the side of the barons, and appointed to ensure John's adherence to the agreements of Magna Carta; Matthew Paris, *Flores Historiarum*, ed. J.A. Giles (London, 1849), p. 323.

14  Henry Elliot Malden contends that Matthew's phrase 'propre villam de stanes, juxta flumen Thamasiac, in quadam insula' to situate the Treaty of Kingston, has been mistakenly attributed to the events of 1215; Henry Elliot Malden (ed.), *Magna Carta Commemoration Essays* (London: Royal Historical Society, 1917), pp. xxv–xxvi. If this is the case, then the slippages of location and association that we see in the *Histoire*'s depiction of the Thames Valley landscape would be repeated in subsequent centuries. For the nineteenth-century reputation of 'Magna Carta Island', pp. 191–95.

of 1215, serving to re-establish and knit up the relationships whose edges were frayed by the tensions surrounding Magna Carta. The movement of the Marshal's body in its transition from life to death can be seen as a highly symbolic and carefully choreographed set of actions. Beginning in the Tower of London, where he sets his affairs in order, William travels up the Thames to Reading, where the Abbot absolves him and he is made a Templar. After his death, the body travels back along the Thames, again silently passing either by or through Runnymede before halting for a vigil at Staines; finally William returns to London where his body is laid to rest in Temple Church. On the one hand, this movement can be understood as one which relinquishes worldly possessions and political dealings to embark on a more personal, penitential journey to salvation. On the other hand, the vigil over the body in Staines serves as a kind of re-enactment of the highly politicised events that had taken place there almost exactly four years before, with the same bodies—living and dead—criss-crossing the same landscape. Almost all the key participants in the negotiation of Magna Carta seem to travel with William's body or arrive to meet at Staines, where the vivid description of the vigil merges seamlessly into that of the ensuing funeral.[15] The conjunction of this cast of characters with this location on the Thames underlines the implicit recollection of Magna Carta.

The never-named Runnymede landscape of the *Histoire* emerges as a much-trodden, highly charged site of forgetting—and all-too-persistent memory. Yet whatever significance Runnymede and its environs held in the popular imagination in the decades after 1215, it was bound to fade over the course of the later Middle Ages. The Great Charter, revised and reissued on several occasions over the thirteenth century, remained well known. However, later generations of legalists and parliamentarians would look back to that version of the Charter issued by Henry III in 1225 as the cornerstone of English liberties.[16] It is by no means clear that those who celebrated the fundamental freedoms confirmed in the Charter of 1225 were even aware of the Charter of 1215, or the troubled circumstances of its birth.

Even in the sixteenth century, with the rise of antiquarian and topographical literatures, references to Runnymede are comparatively scant. Some mention of the locale might have been expected, for instance, in the scholarly John Leland's *Cygnea Cantio* (1545), which traces the journey of a swan down the Thames past

---

15 From Simon, Abbot of Reading, and his own sons, to the illustrious company which meets the body in Staines (the Earl [William] of Warenne, Earl Robert de Vere, the Earl [now Gilbert de Clare] of Gloucester), to the Archbishop Stephen Langton who orders the vigil and officiates at the funeral service, to Brother Aimery (or Aymeric), Master of the Knights Templar in England, at whose side William Marshal will be laid at their mutual request—all were key figures in the negotiations and sealing of Magna Carta.

16 'By the end of the Middle Ages, John's Charter was largely forgotten, and only Henry III's 1125 version was known'; Turner, *Magna Carta*, p. 87 (see also pp. 105, 141); Herbert Butterfield, *Magna Carta in the Historiography of the Sixteenth and Seventeenth Centuries* (Reading: University of Reading, 1969), p. 9.

sites redolent of royal history (including such locales in the immediate vicinity of Runnymede as Ankerwycke, Staines, and Chertsey). It is possible that Leland was unaware of the meadow's historical significance; more probably, as one of a generation of English reformers who looked to King John as a positive prototype of Henry VIII, he considered the episode too awkward or compromising for mention in a poem in praise of the latter monarch. By contrast, William Lambarde, an antiquary and constitutional historian of the early Elizabethan period, devoted several pages to an entry on Runnymede in his *Dictionarium Angliae Topographicum & Historicum*; whilst mostly concerned with delving to the root of the conflict between John and his Barons (much exacerbated, Lambarde insists, by papal interference), the entry does note that the meadow was 'thought the metest Place' for the meeting because of its location midway between Staines and Windsor, and suggests, if the derivation from Old English *runian* is correct, it probably derived from the 1215 meeting; the pre-eminent Anglo-Saxonist of his generation, Lambarde found it plausible that the old tongue was not completely forgotten in the early thirteenth century.[17]

Lambarde's topographical dictionary remained in manuscript until the eighteenth century, and is unlikely to have been available to Sir John Denham in researching the history of the landscape he celebrated in *Coopers Hill*. Denham could easily have turned, however, to the work of Lambarde's celebrated contemporary, William Camden. Although Camden's *Britannia* mentions Runnymede only briefly, to him belongs the distinction of authoring the first verses on the place; these verses occur in the course of his poem on the marriage of Thames and Isis, from which he quotes liberally at various points in *Britannia*:

> that most famous Medow Runingmead commonly called Renimed: in which the Baronage of England assembled in great number in the yeere 1215 to exact their Liberties of King John. Whereof in the marriage of Tame and Isis the Poet wrote thus, speaking of the Tamis that runneth hard by.

> Subluit hic pratum, quod dixit Renimed Anglus,
> Quo sedere duces armis annísque verendi,
> Regis Joannis cuperent qui vertere sceptrum,
> Edwardi Sancti dum leges juráque vellent
> Principe contempto tenebroso è carcere duci:
> Hinc sonnere tubae plusquam civilia bella,
> Venit & hinc refugus nostras Lodovicus in orat.

> Hence runnes it hard by Medow greene, in English RENIMED,
> Where close in counsell sat the Lords, as well for armour dred
> As ancient yeeres right reverend: who sought their soveraigne King

---

17  William Lambarde, *Dictionarium Angliae Topographicum & Historicum: An Alphabetical Description of the Chief Places in England and Wales* (London, 1730), pp. 303–04.

John to depose from regall Throne: Whiles that they ment to bring
(Contemning Prince) S. Edwards lawes and liberties againe,
Inure, which had long time forlet a quite forgotten laine.
Hence more than civill Warres, aloud the trumpets ganne to sound,
Hence Lewis of France, who soone retir'd, set foot on English ground.[18]

As Camden charts the journey of the Thames, various locales emerge as *lieux de mémoire*, prompting the recollection of different historical events. Just as nearby Hampton Court recalls the pride and downfall of Cardinal Wolsey, so Runnymede is indelibly linked to the events of 1215. For the politically cautious Camden, the barons' intent to revive the laws and liberties of Edward the Confessor may be laudable, yet the main consequence of their actions is the disastrous invasion of England by a foreign power. Indeed, this precipitation of 'more than civil Warres' is the only thing that seems to happen at Runnymede, for Camden skirts over John's granting and subsequent repudiation of the Charter. Like the author of *L'Histoire de Guillaume le Marechal*, Camden seems eager to leave 1215 behind as swiftly as possible in favour of the more clear-cut conflicts of 1216–17. This point is underlined in the English translation's use of the term 'hence' to indicate both movement in space and causation in time, so that Runnymede becomes little more than an arrow pointing downstream to the Treaty of Kingston. As for the field of Runnymede itself, the local landscape is barely pencilled in. (Even the designation of the meadow as 'greene' is merely a device to make up the metre in Philemon Holland's English translation, where Camden's Latin has the bare word 'pratum'.)

We might well expect to find some account of Runnymede in the great topographical poem of the Jacobean era, Michael Drayton's *Poly-Olbion* (1612), a work which undoubtedly lies in the background of *Coopers Hill* in its marriage of landscape description with the celebration of diverse local histories. In fact, the meadow can be found in the book, but not in Drayton's poem (which refers only in a general way to John's conflicts with his barons). The reference occurs rather in the prose annotations supplied by the poet's friend John Selden, who notes that the Great Charter was sealed 'in Ruingned neere Stanes'.[19] That Selden should be drawn to the matter of Magna Carta is hardly surprising. Although still a comparatively young man, he had already authored several works of legal history, drawing attention in his *Englands Epinomis* (1610) to some divergences between the Charter of 1215 and the more well-known version of 1225 (and quoting, by the by, some of Camden's verses on Runnymede). As a Member of Parliament in the 1620s, Selden would draw on Magna Carta as a bulwark against the encroachments of the Crown.[20] Yet for Selden, as for his predecessors

---

18  William Camden, *Britain, or, a Chorographicall Description of the most flourishing Kingdomes, England, Scotland, and Ireland …* trans. Philemon Holland (London, 1610), pp. 419–20.
19  Michael Drayton, *Poly-Olbion* (London, 1612), p. 272.
20  David Sandler Berkowitz, *John Selden's Formative Years: Politics and Society in Seventeenth-Century England* (Cranbury, NJ: Associated University Presses, 1988).

and contemporaries, Runnymede was little more than a footnote to Magna Carta; the meadow by the Thames was not yet, as it would soon become, the byword and pastoral embodiment of 1215.

As this brief survey has gone to show, the century before Denham wrote *Coopers Hill* had seen some strengthening of the association between the legal document Magna Carta and the location Runnymede, thanks partly to the rediscovery of the significance of the original 1215 Charter, and partly to the rise of local antiquarian survey and topographical poetry. Runnymede was itself, however, only in the barest sense a *lieu de mémoire*. It is worth underlining the point that no writer before Denham suggests a specific link between the local conditions and ecosystem of Runnymede and the events that took place there in 1215. In drawing this link, Denham is arguably not only the author of Runnymede as a site of memory, but of a certain way of thinking about the relationship between place, memory, and history.

# III

Runnymede is not named in the actual verses of *Coopers Hill*; yet all early and authoritative texts, both print and manuscript, incorporate a marginal note referring to '*Runny Meade, where the great Charter was first sealed*'.[21] The note occurs at that point where the death of the hunted stag prompts the poet to recall the different 'chase' of 1215, and does not signal an actual shift in location. This is explicitly 'the self-same place' (324) as that 'spacious plain' (223) where the stag and his companions were seen grazing (identified in the 'A' text as '*Egham Meade*'). Readers of the poem are almost bound to be brought up short by the transition from the death of the stag to the sealing of the Great Charter. Variously described as 'a declining States-man' (273), as 'royall' ('A' text 265), and as 'a bold Knight Errant' (281), the stag is often seen to stand in early versions of the poem for the recently executed Earl of Strafford, and in later versions for Charles I himself. In either case, the retrospective designation of its destruction as 'a more Innocent, and happy chase' (323) than that which led to the sealing of Magna Carta, is jarring. Even if, as some critics insist, the stag at this point is again merely a stag, the animal cannot be expected to shed instantly in its death the varied and poignant associations it has accrued in its fight for life.[22] The relationship between the two hunts is made all the murkier when the poem instructs us to identify the hunter with King John (A: 'tyranny'; B: 'lawless power'), and the hunted

---

21  Except where noted, quotations are—by line number—from the 'B' text of the poem as presented in O Hehir, *EH*.

22  For discussion, see Ann Baynes Coiro, 'The Personal Rule of Poets: Cavalier Poetry and the English Revolution', in Laura Lunger Knoppers (ed.), *The Oxford Handbook of Literature and the English Revolution* (Oxford: Oxford University Press, 2012), pp. 206–37 (pp. 214–15); Robert Wilcher, *The Writing of Royalism, 1628–60* (Cambridge: Cambridge University Press, 2001), pp. 86–87; Nigel Smith, *Literature and Revolution in England, 1640–1660* (New Haven: Yale University Press, 1997), p. 323; O Hehir, *EH*, pp. 205–06.

with the baronial party ('Fair liberty'). Not only does this require the reader to imagine a hunt in which the quarry succeeds in overpowering the huntsman, but it conflicts with the panoply of images which have presented the stag as a lone, elite individual, pursued and betrayed by a common multitude (in the two forms of the hounds and his own disloyal herd). Whilst there are sufficient figurative resources in the account of the stag hunt to carry forward into the Magna Carta passage, the reader cannot help but be aware of the metaphorical ground shifting beneath his or her feet.

In the 'A' text, the introduction of Runnymede is immediately followed by six lines in which Denham appears to weigh up the rights and wrongs of the barons' cause.

> For armed subjects can have no pretence
> Against their princes but their just defence;
> And whether then, or no, I leave to them
> To justifie, who else themselves condemne.
> Yet might the fact be just, if we may guesse
> The justness of an action from successe. (A: 307–12)

Though Denham later deleted these lines, finding them manifestly inappropriate in the wake of the civil war, the degree of sympathy for the barons expressed here is in any case very limited. The third couplet makes a show of fence-sitting, but in fact amounts to saying that the Magna Carta barons were justified only if one accepts that the end justifies the means. Not only is this a morally dubious position, but in this case, as the poem goes on to make amply clear, the end was not a happy concord between king and subject. As the fruit of violence, Magna Carta has led only to a perpetual struggle for mastery between monarchs and subjects, in which neither has felt constrained by love, duty, or moderation.

The endless struggle between monarch and people leads to the concluding (in the B-text) image of a river in violent flood.

> When a calm River rais'd with sudden rains,
> Or Snows dissolv'd, oreflows th'adjoyning Plains,
> The Husbandmen with high-rais'd banks secure
> Their greedy hopes, and this he can endure.
> But if with Bays and Dams they strive to force
> His channel to a new, or narrow course;
> No longer then within his banks he dwells,
> First to a Torrent, then a Deluge swells:
> Stronger, and fiercer by restraint he roars,
> And knows no bound, but makes his power his shores. (349–58)

There is an obvious and potentially awkward contrast between the final depiction of a great river in flood and that famous couplet, earlier in the poem, in which the Thames is invoked as an example of moderation, which the poet himself would wish to emulate: 'Though deep, yet clear, though gentle, yet not dull, / Strong without rage, without ore-flowing full' (191–92). In retrospect, these lines were never really appropriate to the poem's location; Runnymede is after all part of a floodplain, where the Thames overflows fairly often. Nor are they appropriate to Denham's practice as a poet, whose metaphors retract, expand, and shift their courses, rather than remaining within fixed bounds. Elsewhere, perhaps, the Thames is capable of serving as a model of moderation to poets and people; but not here.

In short, both the political pessimism of the poem and the style of the poet seem appropriate to the locality of Runnymede, where—in spite of the river being banked by a causeway constructed in the thirteenth century—flooding was a familiar occurrence.[23] In wishing that his poem could flow like a river that respects its shores, Denham is effectively wishing for a different landscape, with different environmental conditions and historical associations, which would allow him, perhaps, to be a different poet. Yet such is not his lot. By attuning his verse and his historical perspective to the nature of the locality, Denham constructs Runnymede as particularly strong kind of *lieu de mémoire*. Its association with Magna Carta is no longer accidental, or contingent upon mere practicalities, but essential. If Denham stops short of saying that Magna Carta worked out badly because it was sealed on a floodplain, he constructs Runnymede as a landscape that both remembers and embodies the lessons of the past. A steady stream of later poets would follow him in this, perpetuating Runnymede as a site of memory, whilst often differing sharply as to what its lessons were.

## IV

The latter half of the seventeenth century saw the movement of Magna Carta beyond English shores. The figurative road from Runnymede now led as far as the New World. The Quaker William Penn had successfully invoked Magna Carta when on trial in 1670, which led to the enshrinement of the principle of the independence of the jury; in 1687, the founder of Pennsylvania arranged for the first American printing of the Great Charter.[24] Paradoxically, this outward movement of Magna Carta was matched by a new fascination with and focus on the specific locale from which it emerged. The centrifugal forces dispersing English constitutional ideas across the globe were matched by a centripetal tendency to look back to Runnymede and its environs, especially in poetry.

Amongst the earliest as well as the most well-known successors to *Coopers Hill* is Alexander's Pope's 'Windsor Forest' (1713). In a homage that is also an act of appropriation, Pope responds to Denham's creation of a site of memory by at once embracing and erasing it, omitting all reference to John and the barons,

---

23  O Hehir, *EH*, pp. xxiv–xxvi.
24  Edwin B. Bronner, 'First Printing of Magna Charta in America, 1687', *American Journal of Legal History*, 7 (1963), 189–97.

and making Cooper's Hill instead a monument to Denham (as well as to Cowley, who died nearby):

> Bear me, oh bear me to sequester'd Scenes,
> The Bow'ry Mazes and surrounding Greens;
> To Thames's banks which fragrant Breezes fill,
> Or where ye Muses sport on Cooper's Hill.
> (On Cooper's hill eternal Wreaths shall grow,
> While lasts the Mountain, or while Thames shall flow)
> I seem thro' consecrated Walks to rove,
> I hear soft Musick dye along the Grove;
> Led by the Sound, I roam from Shade to Shade,
> By God-like Poets Venerable made:
> Here his first Lays Majestick Denham sung;
> There the last Numbers flow'd from Cowley's Tongue.
> O early lost! what Tears the River shed
> When the sad Pomp along his Banks was led?
> His drooping Swans on ev'ry Note expire,
> And on his Willows hung each Muse's Lyre.[25]

Roaming from shade to shade through the groves that edge Runnymede, Pope's trajectory recalls that of the desperate stag who flees 'to the coverts, & the conscious Groves'. Yet in his more sedate wanderings Pope does not seek to escape death, but rather goes in search of the dead whose faintly caught strains lead him on. That Pope never quite succeeds in catching the elusive tune he follows is appropriate, for the work of 'Windsor Forest' is to erase both the political content and the political context of *Coopers Hill*. It is rather as if someone were to declare that Lincoln's spirit hovers over Gettysburg, and the site should be always remembered for his Address. At once acknowledging and overwriting Denham's establishment of Runnymede as a site of memory, Pope transforms the landscape from a theatre of history into a memorial to the poet himself.

Runnymede's associations with Magna Carta are restored in Mark Akenside's (1721–70) poem 'For a Column at Runnymede', one of an intriguing series of 'Inscriptions' for imaginary or unrealised monuments. Despite the locale's now inextricable association with Magna Carta, there was as yet no physical memorial at Runnymede in the eighteenth century.

> Thou, who the verdant plain dost traverse here,
> While Thames among his willows from thy view
> Retires; o stranger, stay thee, and the scene
> Around contemplate well. This is the place

---

25 Alexander Pope, 'Windsor Forest', in *Pastoral Poetry and An Essay on Criticism*, ed. E. Audra and Aubrey Williams (London: Methuen, 1961), ll. 261–76.

> Where England's ancient barons, clad in arms
> And stern with conquest, from their tyrant king
> (Then render'd tame) did challenge and secure
> The charter of thy freedom. Pass not on
> Till thou hast bless'd their memory, and paid
> Those thanks which God appointed the reward
> Of public virtue. And if chance thy home
> Salute thee with a father's honour'd name,
> Go, call thy sons: instruct them what a debt
> They owe their ancestors; and make them swear
> To pay it, by transmitting down intire
> Those sacred rights to which themselves were born.[26]

The description of a king being 'render'd tame' recalls the stag of *Coopers Hill*, ready to acquiesce to death upon sight of the king (whom, in the post-regicide version of the poem, he also represents). Yet while the Thames is an omnipresent if ever-shifting symbol in Denham's poem, Akenside curiously insists upon the river's retirement behind a screen of willows. It is as if the task is precisely to forget the lesson of *Coopers Hill*, embodied in the river, and thus to recover the different lesson of the plain. As Pope made the landscape the site of Denham's remembrance and Magna Carta's forgetting, so Akenside performs the same operation in reverse. Shakespeare, too, is at once recalled and forgotten here, with the injunction to transmit the memory of Magna Carta down the generations, recalling Henry V's Crispin's Day oration: 'This story [of Agincourt] shall the good man teach his son'.[27] Here, however, the conflict celebrated in memory is not a royal conquest but a conquest over royalty.

Akenside may have been the first in the eighteenth century to call for a column at Runnymede, but he would not be the last. In 1788, the Whig Club would vote in favour of the erection of precisely such a monument. The immediate occasion for the proposal was the centennial anniversary of the Glorious Revolution; the pillar at Runnymede would be a shrine to constitutional liberty, drawing an implicit association between the taming of one tyrant and the ejection of another. For Tory observers, this amounted to a political appropriation of the landscape with dangerous future implications for the Hanoverian monarchy.[28] The poet and satirist Anthony Pasquin was the first to respond to the proposal in his poem, 'An Epigram, Written on the 5th of November, 1788'.

26 *The Works of the English Poets: Akenside*, ed. Samuel Johnson (London, 1772), p. 329.
27 William Shakespeare, *Henry V*, in Stephen Greenblatt, et al. (eds), *The Norton Shakespeare* (New York: W.W. Norton, 1997), IV.3.56.
28 *The Civil and the Ecclesiastical Systems of England Defended and Fortified* (London: T. Longman, 1791), p. 21.

The sinister Whigs, in the third George's reign,
Have in general congress agreed,
To erect a huge column to shade the green plain,
In the hamlet of fam'd Runnymede.
What the deuce can they mean by this popular cant?
What end have the caitiffs in sight?
'Tis an emblem of beauty, quoth Truth, they [c]all want,
To make the base varlets upright.
It's rather, said Wit, if we think ere we search,
A symbolical offering to Fate;
That one half may be pillars of Albion's church,
And the rest become pillars of State.[29]

Since Runnymede is already, as the poet insists, 'fam'd', it requires no monument to make it a site of memory; those who advocate the superfluous pillar must have another aim in view. The 'huge column' they propose to 'erect' is not pictured as emerging organically from the 'green plain', but as overshadowing and symbolically violating it. Drawing an opposition between the misguided multitudes ('sinister Whigs', 'general congress', 'popular cant') and authoritative singular entities (George III, Truth, Wit), the epigram conveys a conservative mistrust of the mob which can also be discerned in Denham's depiction of the stag hunt. The fictitious date in the title of Pasquin's poem, November 5th, serves as a pointed reminder of the fate of traitors.[30] An anonymous Tory pamphlet, *The Civil and the Ecclesiastical Systems of England Defended and Fortified*, published in 1789, likewise condemned the proposed Runnymede column which, it asserted, could 'stir no emotion in the breast of a worthy patriot'.[31] In the end, this Whig initiative led to nothing, and no monument would be erected on the plain of Runnymede for another 130 years.

The first decade of the nineteenth century witnessed a further heightening of poetic interest in the landscape around Runnymede, prompted at least in part by the topical resonance of the themes of liberty and tyranny in the wake of the French Revolution and the present context of the Napoleonic Wars. In 1807, William Thomas Fitzgerald celebrated the ancient Ankerwycke Yew (Figure 10.2), which stands near the shore on the opposite side of the Thames from Runnymede:

What scenes have passed since first this ancient Yew
In all the strength of youthful beauty grew!
Here PATRIOT BARONS might have musing stood

---

29  Anthony Pasquin [John Williams], *Poems* (London, 1789), p. 124.
30  The poem was first published in the *Monday Post and Daily Advertiser*, Monday, 20 October 1788 (London), p. 3.
31  *The Civil and the Ecclesiastical Systems of England Defended and Fortified* (London: T. Longman, 1791), p. 22.

*Figure 10.2* The Ankerwycke Yew (photograph by Naomi Howell).

And plann'd the Charter for their country's good;
And here, perhaps, from Runnymede retir'd
The haughty John, with secret vengeance fir'd;
Might curse the day which saw his weakness yield
Extorted rights in yonder tented field![32]

Here the yew seems to stand in for the columns proposed by Akenside and the Whigs. An arboreal monument even older than the events it has come to commemorate, the tree has stored up multiple layers of memories over the centuries. Beginning by recalling the conflict between patriot barons and the haughty king, Fitzgerald shifts forward to the equally polarised pairing of the virtuous Anne Boleyn and the tyrant Henry VIII, who were said to have courted beneath the tree. The poem concludes by wishing that the yew had 'its direst venom shed / Upon the cruel Henry's guilty head' before he could work the death of his innocent queen. Yet unlike Denham's Thames or Akenside's memorial in the meadow, the yew is incapable of imparting moral lessons, despite its advanced age. Instead, it serves as mute witness to the seemingly endless violence of tyrants.[33]

---

32  Dated 25 July 1807, the poem appears in John Evans, *An Excursion to Windsor in July 1810* (London: Sherwood, Neely, and Jones, 1817), p. 285.
33  This poem offers some interesting parallels and divergences from an earlier poem on an ancient yew by the same author. Celebrating the old yew at Himley in Staffordshire, Fitzgerald had imagined the tree having been by 'some Norman Baron planted here, / Who liv'd by rapine, and who ruled by fear'. The contrast between the rapacious baron of the Staffordshire yew and the 'patriot barons' at Ankerwycke is striking, and suggests the tug of Runnymede as a site of memory, shaping perceptions of the past.

The recollection of *Coopers Hill* is much more explicit in a poem of the same decade, Thomas Love Peacock's *The Genius of the Thames* (1810):

> Sweetly, on yon poetic hill,
> Strains of unearthly music breathe
> Where Denham's spirit, hovering still,
> Weaves his wild harp's aerial wreath.
> And sweetly, on the mead below,
> The fragrant gales of summer blow:
> While freedom's pristine fire shall glow,
> That mead shall live in memory,
> Where valor, on the tented field,
> Triumphant raised his patriot shield,
> The voice of truth to kings revealed,
> And broke the chains of tyranny.[34]

Peacock attempts to marry Pope's notion of the landscape as a memorial to the poet Denham with its now established role as a site of Magna Carta memories. Technically, perhaps, it is the hill that honours the poet's memory, whilst Magna Carta is remembered on the plain; yet the clear association of Denham's aerial music with the fragrant gales that warm the plain below make the poet the genius loci of the meadow, and thus involved (if not at the point of origin) in its status as a *lieu de mémoire*. If Denham's spirit still hovered over Runnymede in 1810, one can imagine it would have been appalled by the now inextricable association of Runnymede with the triumph of freedom over tyranny, a far cry from *Coopers Hill*'s more balanced and wary perception of history.

There is no scope here to explore in detail the many literary evocations of Runnymede in the Victorian era, including texts as diverse as William Morris's *News from Nowhere* and Jerome K. Jerome's *Three Men in a Boat*. Maintaining a focus on the poetry landscape, we turn now to what is perhaps the most well-known poem about this locale after *Coopers Hill* itself. Rudyard Kipling, in 'The Reeds of Runnymede' (1911), finds both the memory of conflict and the embodiment of constitutional rule in the local landscape.

> At Runnymede, at Runnymede,
> What say the reeds at Runnymede?
> The lissom reeds that give and take,
> That bend so far, but never break.
> They keep the sleepy Thames awake
> With tales of John at Runnymede.
>
> At Runnymede, at Runnymede,
> Oh hear the reeds at Runnymede:—

---

34  Thomas Love Peacock, *The Genius of the Thames* (London: Hookham, 1810), p. 92.

"You mustn't sell, delay, deny,
A freeman's right or liberty,
It wakes the stubborn Englishry,
We saw 'em roused at Runnymede!

"When through our ranks the Barons came,
With little thought of praise or blame,
But resolute to play the game,
They lumbered up to Runnymede;
And there they launched in solid line,
The first attack on Right Divine—
The curt, uncompromising 'Sign!'
That settled John at Runnymede.

"At Runnymede, at Runnymede,
Your rights were won at Runnymede!
No freeman shall be fined or bound,
Or dispossessed of freehold ground,
Except by lawful judgment found
And passed upon him by his peers!
Forget not, after all these years,
The Charter signed at Runnymede".

And still when Mob or Monarch lays
Too rude a hand on English ways,
The whisper wakes, the shudder plays,
Across the reeds at Runnymede.
And Thames, that knows the moods of kings,
And crowds and priests and suchlike things,
Rolls deep and dreadful as he brings
Their warning down from Runnymede![35]

Although there is no explicit acknowledgement of Denham here, Kipling's even-handed mistrust of 'Mob and Monarch' is closer to the spirit of *Coopers Hill* than many eighteenth- and nineteenth-century effusions on Runnymede and liberty. Like other poets before him, part of Kipling's strategy is to invest an as-yet-unnoticed feature of the Runnymede landscape with the memory of Magna Carta, and then to draw an appropriate lesson from the qualities of his chosen feature. In this case, the reeds embody three valorised qualities, in the form of English stubbornness (they bend but do not break), historical stability (they are the same reeds through whose ranks the barons marched), and loquacity (whispering their stories to the Thames). This final quality, recalling the whispering reeds of Greek myth that betrayed the secrets of King Midas, seems especially significant. As we

35  C.R.L. Fletcher and Rudyard Kipling, *A History of England* (London: Doubleday, 1911), pp. 86–87.

have seen, the poets who followed Denham had either insisted on the landscape's muteness (Fitzgerald's silent yew), or conjured some supplement in the form of an imagined inscription (Akenside) or a poet's music borne upon the breeze (Pope and Peacock). Kipling's poem includes no reference to a breeze, but the reeds move rather of their own volition, making their own whispering music. Here, in other words, memory seems to be crystallised and preserved in the landscape itself, without the need of a tutelary bard or remembrancer.

Yet just around the time that Kipling wrote, Runnymede was ceasing to be a simple water meadow where nature might be imagined to whisper unto itself. It was instead shortly to become home to a cluster of closely adjoining and some-times competing monuments, which have continued to accumulate down to the present day. The first to fulfil the Whiggish wish to see a memorial at Runnymede had been George Simon Harcourt, who built a lodge on so-called Magna Carta Island in 1834, using stone from nearby Marlow church. The lodge featured a refreshment room, open to respectable visitors, in which stood an octagonal table embedded with a stone slab inscribed with the statement that Magna Carta had been signed on the island.[36] The first monument to Magna Carta in the locality was not established by public subscription or an act of government, but by a private individual at the heart of a private dwelling. For most of the ensuing century, the absence of any competing monument on the south bank of the Thames contrib-uted to the perception (also based on a misreading of Matthew Paris's reference to the Treaty of Kingston) that the Charter had in fact been sealed on an island in the stream.

Only in the 1920s, following the threatened sale of Runnymede to a private buyer (an initiative withdrawn after a few days due to public outcry), was the first permanent memorial erected on the mainland. This was sponsored by the local landowner Captain Symons-Jeune—the mid-sized square stone, still standing, but mostly illegible, declaring that 'Very near this spot was sealed MAGNA CARTA confirming rights which were in peril and won from King John by the BISH-OPS AND BARONS for the abiding benefit of the PEOPLE OF ENGLAND and later of the British Dominions and United States of America'.[37] Within a dec-ade Symons-Jeune's initiative was copied and one-upped by Lady Fairhaven, the widow of local MP and landowner Urban Broughton (d. 1929); Edwin Lutyens was commissioned to design matching lodges with inscribed piers on either side of the A308 at the western (Windsor) end of Runnymede, and smaller kiosks with piers at the Egham end. The piers are inscribed on one side with a memorial to Magna Carta—'the earliest of constitutional documents whereunder ancient and cherished customs were confirmed abuses redressed and the administration of jus-tice facilitated new provisions formulated for the preservation of peace and every individual perpetually secured in the free enjoyment of his life and property'— and on the other with a dedication to the perpetual memory of Urban Hanlon

---

36 Edward Wedlake Brayley, *A Topographical History of Surrey, Volume II* (Dorking: Robert Best Ede, 1841), p. 279
37 *Runnymede: A Pictorial History*, p. 50.

Broughton. A few years after the erection of these competing memorials, in 1934, a lavish pageant was held on the fields of Runnymede, celebrating in one of its scenes the sealing of Magna Carta. Other scenes depicted episodes ranging from the Roman invasion to the happy aftermath of Waterloo; here we see Runnymede emerging as a site of national memory.[38] It was around this time that Runnymede ceased to refer specifically to the stretch of meadow nearest Egham, adjoined by Long Mead on the west, but to the whole expanse. Indeed, most of the memorials to Magna Carta erected in the twentieth century are in what was until recently known as Long Mead, rather than Runnymede.

More memorials sprang up in the years after World War II, attracted not only by the site's historical resonance but by one another, as Runnymede and its environs were transformed into a monument park. The American Bar Association sponsored the erection of a classical monument to Magna Carta in the midst of the meadow in 1957. By this time, looming above the meadow was the Commonwealth Air Forces Memorial. The Queen's address at the unveiling of the memorial on 17 October 1953 is now inscribed on a plaque at the entrance:

> It is very fitting that those who rest in nameless graves should be remembered in this place. For it was in those fields of Runnymede seven centuries ago that our forefathers first planted the seed of liberty which helped to spread across the earth the conviction that man should be free and not enslaved. And when the life of this belief was threatened by the iron hand of tyranny, their successors came forward without hesitation to fight and, if it was demanded of them, to die for its salvation.

There is something paradoxical in the linking of a small group of named elite men (the Magna Carta barons) with thousands of obscure individuals whose graves are nameless. Yet the ground has been prepared for this in the poetic tradition, especially perhaps in Kipling's poem, where the reeds of Runnymede in their massed ranks become an embodiment of the freedom-loving folk. In referring to the successors of those 'forefathers' who planted liberty's seed, the speech echoes Akenside's injunction to make Magna Carta a matter of generational memory and duty, transmitted from father to son; now, however, the freedoms embodied in Magna Carta are imagined as the patrimony of the whole earth (or at least the Commonwealth). The Queen's speech then proceeds—inevitably, one might think—to invoke the poetic tradition which has been traced in this article. 'With prophetic insight, Pope wrote of this hill on which we stand: "On Cooper's Hill eternal wreaths shall grow / While lasts the mountain, or while Thames shall flow"'. Where Pope recalled *Coopers Hill* to make the landscape memorialise Denham and erase the memory of Magna Carta, the Queen's speech quotes Pope to reinstall the memory of Magna Carta as part of the ongoing struggle for freedom against tyranny, erasing the memory of Denham.

38  Ibid., pp. 36–48.

Within the memorial we encounter one more contribution to what is now a long tradition of Runnymede poetry. In the glass of a window in the belfry are inscribed these lines by Paul H. Scott (Figure 10.3):

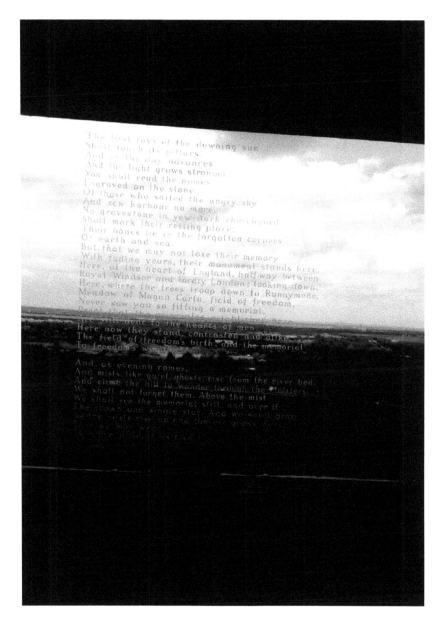

*Figure 10.3* Poem on glass, Commonwealth Air Forces Memorial, Cooper's Hill (photograph by Naomi Howell).

The first rays of the dawning sun
Shall touch its pillars,
And as the day advances
And the light grows stronger,
You shall read the names
Engraved on the stone of those who sailed on the angry sky
And saw harbour no more.
No gravestone in yew-dark churchyard
Shall mark their resting place;
Their bones lie in the forgotten corners of earth and sea.
But, that we may not lose their memory
With fading years, their monuments stand here,
Here, where the trees troop down to Runnymede.
Meadow of Magna Carta, field of freedom,
Never saw you so fitting a memorial,
Proof that the principles established here
Are still dear to the hearts of men.
Here now they stand, contrasted and alike,
The field of freedom's birth, and the memorial
To freedom's winning.
And, as evening comes,
And mists, like quiet ghosts, rise from the river bed,
And climb the hill to wander through the cloisters,
We shall not forget them. Above the mist
We shall see the memorial still, and over it
The crown and single star. And we shall pray
As the mists rise up and the air grows dark
That we may wear
As brave a heart as they.

The contrast between field and hill as birthplace and culmination of the struggle for freedom gives retrospective meaning to Magna Carta. The statement that the 'Meadow of Magna Carta' had never received so fitting a memorial is of course contentious, given the proliferation of poetic and subsequently physical memorials in the centuries since Denham wrote. But the work of the poem is to negotiate the relationship between the new memorial and a landscape that is already one of memory. There is something of Denham's style in the uneasy concluding figure of the mists rising up from the river to envelop the monument, seeming to flicker between ghosts of a consoling past and portents of a threatening future. The poem operates not only textually but materially and spatially, inscribed as it is on glass so that the words literally merge with the landscape in the viewer's perspective. The poem is placed in a position where one may look through it down to the fields of Runnymede and across the river to the Ankerwycke Yew (recalled in the 'yew-dark churchyard').

The steady accumulation of monuments on and around the meadow in the post-war period culminated in 1965 with the construction of the John F. Kennedy Memorial on a wooded rise above the Lutyens lodges. In the years since, Runnymede's status as a site of memory has continued to grow in importance and complexity. Since 2012, the contest over the meaning and ownership of the past in this place has been much enlivened by the presence of an ecovillage on Cooper's Hill, inhabited by a group of modern-day 'Diggers'. Their name suggests associations with nearby St George's Hill, where Gerrard Winstanley and his companions established the original Digger colony in 1649. Yet the added associations of Runnymede, perceived as a site of popular resistance against oppression, have become increasingly important to the Diggers, who have held regular meetings at the foot of the ABA's Magna Carta memorial. As the 2015 anniversary of Magna Carta approached, the encampment became generally known as the 'Runnymede Eco-Village'. We would argue that the ideal of the ecovillage, inhabiting the landscape without leaving a permanent mark, resonates with a long tradition of writing about Runnymede, which has insisted on the superfluity of physical monuments. Through their very ephemerality, the Diggers have written themselves into this *lieu de mémoire*.

In early 2015, competing understandings of Runnymede and the memories it enfolds collided in the public eye. On the 15th of June, Elizabeth II and her family attended a celebration on the floodplain marking the eight-hundredth anniversary of Magna Carta. A thirteen-foot bronze statue of the Queen by the sculptor James Butler, the first new monument at Runnymede in fifty years, had been unveiled the previous day. Speaking at the celebrations, Prime Minister David Cameron took the opportunity to promise the repeal of the Human Rights Act, the legal codification of the European Convention on Human Rights, replacing it with a British bill of rights. The Prime Minister's stance on this matter has been sharply opposed by civil and racial justice organisations including the Runnymede Trust, for whom the Human Rights Act is a direct outcome of the constitutional process begun by Magna Carta.[39] A few hundred yards from the royal festivities, and under close police surveillance, the Diggers at the Runnymede ecovillage held a competing Festival for Democracy. This alternative celebration culminated in a gathering at Ankerwycke Yew, where the participants called for a new constitutional convention and hung handwritten charters of their own from the branches of the ancient tree.[40] On the same day, a district judge in the Guildford Law Courts ordered

---

39 Matthew Weaver, 'Cameron Condemned for "using Magna Carta day to push British bill of rights"', *Guardian*, 15 June 2015 <http://www.theguardian.com/uk-news/2015/jun/15/david-cameron-magna-carta-push-british-bill-of-rights-claim>. The Runnymede Trust, which has campaigned for racial equality in Britain since 1968, looks to Magna Carta as 'the cornerstone of many ensuing historic legal documents, such as the Human Rights Act' <http://www.runnymedetrust.org/about/what-s-in-a-name.html>.

40 'Runnymede "Festival For Democracy" Ends under the Ankerwycke Yew Tree with Call for Citizen-led Constitutional Convention' <http://occupydemocracy.org.uk/2015/06/16/runnymede-festival-for-democracy-ends-under-the-ankerwycke-yew-tree-with-call-for-citizen-led-constitutional-convention/>.

*Figure 10.4*  Runnymede submerged, February 2014 (photograph by Matt White; Creative Commons: *https://creativecommons.org/licenses/by-nc/2.0/legalcode*).

the Digger community off the land they had occupied for three years, finding in favour of the development company Orchid Runnymede. The irony was not lost on the ecovillagers or their supporters. As the democracy campaigner Anthony Barnett observed, 'It is a grotesque scandal that on the day the high and mighty, queen and premier, gathered at Runnymede meadow to cover themselves in self-congratulation at giving the entire world the rule of law, the law should be used to destroy the woodlands of Runnymede for foreign registered property developers'.[41] Whilst the Diggers may have been forced to move on, the struggle for memory on this little, famous patch of land looks certain to continue.

Although monuments now populate the meadow, the prospects for more aggressive development of the riverside landscape are limited.[42] This site of memory is also the site of periodic erasure. It is the floodplain's very instability and impermanence, subject to regular inundations by the Thames, that most guarantees its survival. For a few decades in the latter half of the twentieth century, this liability

---

41  Ibid.
42  Recent initiatives to construct a substantial Visitors' Centre at Runnymede in time for the eight-hundredth anniversary of Magna Carta were quashed amid some acrimony; current plans for development of the site centre on non-intrusive ways of shaping the visitor experience through digital technologies. See Tanya Gupta, 'Magna Carta: Passions Still Running High in Runnymede' (BBC News website 14 June 2013) <http://www.bbc.co.uk/news/uk-england-surrey-22882941>.

seemed to be a thing of the past. As a history of Runnymede published in 1995 noted, flooding had been common 'Before river management became as sophisticated as it is today', but the A308 had not been submerged since 1959.[43] Yet in today's era of human-made climate change and catastrophic weather events, the aspiration to control the flow of Britain's rivers seems more and more unattainable. In the great floods of January and February 2014, the memorial piers designed by Edwin Lutyens loomed up out of what seemed a limitless expanse of water (Figure 10.4). Nature is less and less the teacher of moderation Denham hoped it would be. Perhaps no lines of his poem seem more prescient today than those concluding verses that picture the river breaking its banks and 'mak[ing] his power his shores'.

43 *Runnymede: A Pictorial History*, p. 12

# Bibliography

## Manuscript Sources

### Bodleian Library, Oxford

MS Ashmole 36, 37
MS Aubr. 6
MS Clarendon 43
MS Douce 357
MS Eng. poet. e. 4
MS Fairfax 40
MS Rawlinson A. xlvi
MS Rawlinson D. 398
MS Rawlinson Poet 26
MS Tanner 52
MS Tanner 306
MS Wood 398

### British Library, London

Add. MS 4180, fol. 104
Add. MS 29,577, fol. 44b
Add. MS 36,916, fol. 62
MS Egerton 2421, fol. 39r
MS Egerton 2550, fols 14–15
LC 5/137
MS Harley 6947

### The National Archive, Kew

LC 5/137
SP 20/10, no. 169
SP 29/8, no. 1

### National Library of Scotland

Adv. MSS 19.3.4

### Nottinghamshire Archives

MS DD/Hu1

### Princeton University Library

MS Taylor 34

### Sheffield University Library, Sheffield

Hartlib Papers

### Surrey History Centre

2118/2/5

### Worcester College Library, University of Oxford

MS 216

### Yale University Library

MS Osborn


## Printed and Electronic Primary Sources

*A most miraculous and happy victory obtained by James Chudleigh Serjeant Major General of the forces under the E. of Stamford, against Sir Ralph Hopton and his Forces …* (London, 29 April 1643).

*A most true Relation of divers notable passages of divine providence in the great deliverance and wonderfull victory obtained by the Parliament forces under the command of the Earle of Stamford* (London, 1643).

*A perfect diurnall*, 3 (10–17 July 1643).

———, 4 (17–24 July 1643).

———, 49 (15–22 May 1643).

———, 51 (22–29 May 1643).

Anderson, Robert, M.D. (ed.), *A Complete Edition of the Poets of Great Britain*, 13 vols (London: John and Arthur Arch, Bell and Bradfute and I. Mundell and Co., 1792–95).

Anglo, M.N. [Maurice Newport], … *Carmen Votivum* (London, 1665).

Aston, Thomas, *The Short Parliament Diary of Sir Thomas Aston*, ed. Judith Maltby (London: Offices of the Royal Historical Society, 1988).

Aubrey, John, *'Brief Lives', Chiefly of Contemporaries, Set Down by John Aubrey, between the Years 1669 & 1696*, ed. Andrew Clark, 2 vols (Oxford: Clarendon Press, 1898).

———, *Aubrey's Brief Lives*, ed. Oliver Lawson Dick (London: Peregrine Books, 1962).

Bampfield, Joseph, *Colonel Joseph Bampfield's Apology: 'Written by Himself and Printed at His Desire' 1685*, ed. John Loftis and Paul Hardacre (London: Associated University Presses, 1993).

Baron, Robert, *Mirza. A tragedie, really acted in Persia, in the last age. Illustrated with historicall annotations* (London: Humphrey Moseley, T. Dring, 1647).

Barton, William, *The Book of Psalms in Metre* (London, 1644).

Beaumont, Francis, and John Fletcher, *Comedies and Tragedies Never Printed Before And Now Published by the Authors Original Copies* (London, 1647).

Benlowes, Edward, *Theophila, Or Loves Sacrifice. A Divine Poem* (London, 1652).

Berkeley, John, *Memoirs of Sir John Berkley, containing an Account of his Negotiations with Lieutenant General Cromwell, Commissary General Ireton and Other Officers of the Army* (London, 1699).

'Biographical Sketches of Illustrious and Distinguished Characters: Lady Denham', in *La Belle Assemblée; or, Bell's Court and Fashionable Magazine* (London, England), Issue 141, 1 October 1820.

Birch, Thomas (ed.), 'State Papers, 1655: April (1 of 6)', *A collection of the State Papers of John Thurloe, volume 3: December 1654–August 1655* (1742), 332–48, British History Online <http://www.british- history.ac.uk/report.aspx?compid=55376&strquery=embroyle> [accessed 11 July 2011].

——— (ed.), 'State Papers, 1655: April (2 of 6)', *A collection of the State Papers of John Thurloe, volume 3: December 1654–August 1655* (1742), 349–63, British History Online <http://www.british- history.ac.uk/report.aspx?compid=55377&strquery=Denham> [accessed 11 July 2011].

——— (ed.), 'State Papers, 1655: June (4 of 7)', *A collection of the State Papers of John Thurloe, volume 3: December 1654–August 1655*, British History Online <http://www.britishhistory.ac.uk/report.aspx?compid=55390&strquery=davenant> [accessed 11 July 2011].

——— (ed.), 'State Papers, 1657: June (4 of 4)', *A collection of the State Papers of John Thurloe, volume 6: January 1657–March 1658* (1742): 362–375, British History Online <http://www.british- history.ac.uk/report.aspx?compid=55603&strquery=Denham> [accessed 11 July 2011].

Birkenhead, John, 'The four-legg'd Quaker', in *The Rump, or Collections of Songs and Ballads* (London, 1660), 358–62.

———, *The Four-Legg'd Elder* (London, 1647).

Bowels, Edward, *A letter from a minister in His Excellence his army, to a brother of his in London* (London, 1643).

Buchanan, George, *Paraphrasis psalmorum Dauidis poetica multo quam antehac castigatior auctore Georgio Buchanano; adnotata vbique diligenter carminum genera; eiusdem Buchanani tragoedia quae inscribitur Iephthes* (London, 1580).

Burgess, Daniel, *Psalms, Hymns and Spiritual Songs by the late Daniel Burges* (London: John Clarke, 1714).

*Calendar of the Clarendon State Papers*, ed. O. Ogle, W.H., Bliss, W.D. Macray, and F.J. Routledge, 5 vols (Oxford: Clarendon Press: 1869–1970).

*Calendar of State Papers, Domestic Series, 1640–1665*, ed. M.A.E. Green (London, 1875–86).

Camden, William, *Britain, or, a Chorographicall Description of the most flourishing Kingdomes, England, Scotland, and Ireland* … trans. Philemon Holland (London, 1610).

Carte, Thomas (ed.), *A Collection of Original Letters and Papers, Concerning the Affairs of England ... 1641–1660, Found among the Duke of Ormond's Papers*, 2 vols (London, 1739).

Cartwright, William, *Comedies, Tragi-comedies with other Poems* (London, 1651).

*Certaine informations*, 15 (24 April–1 May 1643) –17 (8–15 May 1643).

———, 17 (8–15 May 1643).

———, 19 (22–29 May 1643).

———, 26 (10–17 July 1643).

———, 27 (17–24 July 1643).

*Certain Verses Written by Severall of the Authors Friends.*

Chudleigh, James, *Serjeant Major Iames Chudleigh his declaration to his country-men* (1643).

Cook, John, *The New Theory of Generation, According to the Best and Latest Discoveries in Anatomy, Farther improved and fully displayed* (London, 1762).

Davenant, William, *The First Days Entertainment at Rutland House* (1656).

———, *Gondibert*, ed. David Gladish (Oxford, Oxford University Press, 1971).

———, *Luminalia* (1638).

———, *A Proposition for Advancement of Moralitie* (1653).

———, *A Proposition for Advancement of Moralitie* By a New Way of Entertainment of the People (London, 1654).

———, *Salmacida Spolia* (1640).

———, *The Siege of Rhodes: The First and Second Part* (London, 1663).

———, *The Tragedy of Albovine, first King of the Lombards* (London, 1629).

Denham, John, *On Mr. Abraham Cowley His Death and Burial Amongst the Ancient Poets* (London, 1667).

———, *The Anatomy of Play: Written by a worthy and Learned Gent.: Dedicated to his Father, to shew his detestation of it* (London: G.P. for Nicholas Bourne, 1651).

———, *Mr. Hampdens speech occasioned upon the Londoners petition for peace* (London, 1643).

———, *Poems and Translations with The Sophy. Written by the Honourable Sir John Denham Knight of the Bath* (London: Henry Herringman, 1668).

———, *A Prologue to his Majestie at the First Play Presented at the Cockpit in Whitehall* (London, 1660).

———, *A relation of a Quaker, that to the shame of his profession, attempted to bugger a mare near Colchester* (London, s.n., 1659).

———, *The Sophy* (London: Richard Hearne for Thomas Walkley, 1642).

———, 'The True Presbyterian without Disguise' (London, 1661).

———, *A Version of the Psalms of David, Fitted to the Tunes used in Churches, By the Honourable Sir John Denham, Knight of the Bath* (London: Jonah Bowyer, 1714).

Dennis, John, *The Causes of the Decay and Defects of Dramatick Poetry* (London, 1725).

———, *The Critical Works of John Dennis: Volume II, 1711–1729*, ed. Edward Niles Hooker (Baltimore: Johns Hopkins University Press, 1943).

Descartes, René, *Oeuvres de Descartes*, ed. Charles Adam and Paul Tannery, rev. edn, 12 vols (Paris: Vrin, 1964–76).

———, *The Philosophical Writings of Descartes*, trans. John Cottingham, Robert Stoothoff, Dugald Murdoch, and Anthony Kenny, 3 vols (Cambridge: Cambridge University Press, 1984–91).

Donne John, *John Donne: The Complete English Poems*, ed. A.J. Smith (London: Allen Lane, 1971).

Downes, John, *Roscius Anglicanus by John Downes*, ed. Montague Summers (London: Fortune, 1929).

Dryden, John, *Absalom and Achitophel* (London, 1681).

———, *Annus Mirabilis* (London, 1667).

Evans, John, *An Excursion to Windsor in July 1810* (London: Sherwood, Neely, and Jones, 1817).

Evelyn, John, *The Letterbooks of John Evelyn*, ed. Douglas Chambers and David Galbraith, 2 vols (Toronto: University of Toronto Press, 2014).

*Exploits discovered, in a declaration of some more proceedings of Serjeant Major Chudley, generall of the forces under the Earle of Stamford: against Sir Ralph Hopton* (London, 2 May 1643).

Felton, Henry, *A Dissertation on Reading the Classics, and Forming a Just Style* (London: Jonah Bowyer, 1718).

Gage, Thomas, *A New Survey of the West-Indias: Or, The English American his Travail by Sea and Land* (London, 1655; 2nd edn).

Godwin, William, *A Poetical Description of Bristol* (London, 1712).

*Good Newes from Plymouth* (London, 20 February 1643).

Gratius, Faliscus, *Cynegeticon. Or a Poem of Hunting by Gratius the Faliscian*, trans. Christopher Wase (London, 1654).

Hammond, Henry, *A paraphrase and annotations upon the books of the Psalms briefly explaining the difficulties thereof, by H. Hammond D.D.* (London: R. Norton, for Richard Davis, 1659).

*Happy news to England sent from Oxford* ([London,] 1643).

Herbert, Thomas, *A Relation of some Yeares Travaile, Begunne Anno 1626* (London: William Stansby and Jacob Bloome, 1634).

———, *Some Yeares Travels into Divers Parts of Asia and Afrique* (London: R. Bi. For Iacob Blome and Richard Bishop, 1638).

Hobbes, Thomas, *De Cive: The English Version*, ed. Howard Warrender (Oxford: Clarendon Press, 1983).

———, *The Elements of Law Natural and Political*, ed. J.C.A. Gaskin (Oxford: Oxford University Press, 1994).

———, *Leviathan*, ed. Noel Malcolm, 3 vols (Oxford: Clarendon Press, 2012).

Holland, John, *The Psalmists of Britain: Records of Upwards of One Hundred and Fifty Authors, Who Have Rendered the Whole or Parts of the Book of Psalms, into English Verse*, 2 vols (London: R. Groombridge, 1843).

Huckell, John, *Avon. A Poem* (London, 1758).

Hutchinson, Lucy, *Order and Disorder*, ed. David Norbrook (Oxford: Blackwell, 2001).

Hyde, Edward, *A Brief View and Survey of the dangerous and pernicious errors to Church and State, in Mr. Hobbes's book, entitled Leviathan* (Oxford, 1676).

———, *A Collection of Several Tracts of the Right Honourable Edward, Earl of Clarendon* (London: T. Woodward and J. Peele, 1727).

———, *The History of the Rebellion and Civil Wars in England*, ed. W.D. Macray, 6, vols (Oxford: Clarendon Press, 1888).

———, *The Life of Edward Earl of Clarendon*, 3 vols (Oxford: Clarendon Press, 1749).

Johnson, Samuel, *The Lives of the Most Eminent English Poets: With Critical Observations on Their Works*, 2 vols (London: P.C. and J. Rivington, 1821).

———, *The Lives of the Most Eminent English Poets: With Critical Observations on Their Works*, ed. Roger Lonsdale, 4 vols (Oxford: Clarendon Press, 2006).

——— (ed.), *The Works of the English Poets* (London, 1772).

Jonson, Ben, *Every Man in His Humour*, ed. Robert S. Miola (Manchester: Manchester University Press, 2000).

Killigrew, Thomas, *Comedies and Tragedies Written by Thomas Killigrew …* (London, 1664).

Kirkman, Francis, *A True, perfect and Exact Catalogue of all the Comedies, Tragedies and Tragicomedies, Pastorals, Masques and Interludes* (London, 1661).

Knowler, William (ed.), *The Earl of Strafford's Letters and Dispatches*, 2 vols (London: William Bowyer, 1739–40).

Lambarde, William, *Dictionarium Angliae Topographicum & Historicum: An Alphabetical Description of the Chief Places in England and Wales* (London, 1730).

Langbaine, Gerard, *An Account of the English Dramatick Poets* (London and Oxford, 1691).

Machiavelli, Niccolò, *Discourses on Livy*, trans. Ninian Hill Thomson (Mineola, NY: Dover, 2007).

Marshall, Stephen, *A plea for defensive arms, or, A copy of a letter written by Mr. Stephen Marshall …* (London, 1642, repr. 1643).

Martin, Benjamin, *Micrographia Nova: Or, A New Treatise on the Microscope, and Microscopic Objects* (Reading, 1742).

Martyn, John, *The Philosophical Transactions (From the Year 1732, to the Year 1744) Abridged, and Disposed under General Heads. In Two Volumes* (London, 1747).

Marvell, Andrew, *The Poems and Letters of Andrew Marvell*, ed. H.M. Margoliouth, 2 vols (Oxford: Clarendon Press, 3rd edn, 1971).

*Mercurius aulicus*, first week (8 January 1643).

*Mercurius aulicus*, sixteenth week (22 April 1643).

*Mercurius aulicus*, seventeenth week (29 April 1643).

*Mercurius aulicus*, twentieth week (20 May 1643).

*Mercurius aulicus*, twenty-eighth week (15 July 1643).

*Mercurius aulicus*, twenty-ninth week (22 July 1643).

*Mercurius Civicus*, 1 (4–11 May 1643).

*Mercurius Civicus*, 1 (4–11 May).

*Mercurius Civicus*, 7 (6–13 July 1643).

*Mercurius Civicus*, 8 (13–20 July 1643).

*Mercurius rusticus*, second week (27 May 1643).

Milton, John, *Animadversions upon The Remonstrants Defence Against Smectymnuus* (London, 1641).

———, *The Complete Prose Works of John Milton*, gen. ed. D.M. Wolfe, 8 vols (New Haven: Yale University Press, 1953–82).

*Musarum Oxoniensium* (Oxford, 1643).

Newcastle, William, Marquess of, *La Méthode Nouvelle et Invention Extraordinaire de Dresser les Chevaux* (Antwerp, 1658).

O'Neill, Daniel. 'A Brief Relation of the Affairs of England', ed. C.H. Firth, *English Historical Review*, viii (1893), 529–32.

Osborne, Dorothy, *Letters to Sir William Temple*, ed. Kenneth Parker (Harmondsworth: Penguin, 1987).

Ovid, *Metamorphoses*, trans. A.D. Elmville (Oxford: Oxford University Press, 2008).

Paris, Matthew, *Flores Historiarum*, ed. J.A. Giles (London, 1849).

Parker, Martin, *An Exact Description of the manner how His Majesty and his nobles went to Parliament* (London, 1640).

Pasquin, Anthony, [John Williams], *Poems* (London, 1789).

Peacock, Thomas Love, *The Genius of the Thames* (London: Hookham, 1810).

Pepys, Samuel, *The Diary of Samuel Pepys*, ed. Robert Latham and William Matthews, 11 vols (Berkeley: University of California Press, 1970–83).

Phillips, Edward, *Theatrum Poetarum* (London, 1675).

*Pompey the Great* (London, 1664).

Pope, Alexander, *Pastoral Poetry and an Essay on Criticism*, ed. E. Audra and Aubrey Williams (London: Methuen, 1961).

*Post and Daily Advertiser*, Monday, 20 October 1788 (London).

Priolo, Benjamin, *History of France under the Ministry of Cardinal Mazarine*, trans. Christopher Wase (London, 1671).

*Remarkable passages from Nottingham, Lichfield, Leicester, and Cambridge* (London, 1642).

Richardson, Jonathan, *Explanatory Notes and Remarks on Milton's Paradise Lost* (London, 1734).

Sandys, George, *A Paraphrase upon the divine poems* (London, 1638).

Shakespeare, William, *Henry V*, in Stephen Greenblatt et al. (eds), *The Norton Shakespeare* (New York: W.W. Norton, 1997).

———, *Pericles*, ed. Roger Warren (Oxford: Oxford University Press, 2003).

Sidney, Sir Philip, *Sir Philip Sidney's Defence of Poesy*, ed. Lewis Soens (Lincoln: Nebraska University Press, 1970).

*State Papers Collected by Edward, Earl of Clarendon*, ed. R. Scrope and T. Monkhouse, 3 vols (Oxford, 1767–86).

Steele, Richard, *The Tatler*, 4 vols (London: J. Parsons, 1794).

Stuart, Charles, *His Majesty's Declaration: to All His Loving Subjects, of the Causes Which Moved Him to Dissolve the Last Parliament* (1640).

———, *Eikon Basilike: The Pourtrature of His Sacred Majestie in His Solitudes and Sufferings* (1649).

———, *His Majesties Answer to the Nineteen Propositions of both Houses of Parliament* (Cambridge, 1642).

Suckling, John, *Fragmenta Aurea* (London, 1646).

Symmons, Edward, *A loyall subjects beliefe* (Oxford, 1643).

Taylor, John, *Mad Verse, Sad Verse, Glad Verse and Bad Verse* (London, n.d.).

*The Civil and the Ecclesiastical Systems of England Defended and Fortified* (London: T. Longman, 1791).

*The Court of Cupid. By the Author of the Meretriciad. In Two Volumes* (London, 1770).

*The Nicholas Papers: Correspondence of Sir Edward Nicholas, Secretary of State*, ed. G.F. Warner, 4 vols (London: Printed for the Camden Society, 1886–1920).

*The Poetical Works of the Earls of Rochester, Roscomon, and Dorset*, 2 vols (London, 1739)*The Quakers Shaken, or, A Warning Against Quaking* (London, 1655).

*The Round-head remembrancer* ([Oxford,] 1643).

*The Sucklington Faction, or (Svcklings) Roaring Boys* (London, 1641).

*The Whole Booke of Psalmes, collected into Englysh metre by T. Starnhold, J. Hopkins & others* … (London, 1562).

Thyer, R. (ed.), *The Genuine Remains in Verse and Prose of Mr. Samuel Butler, Author of Hudibras. In Two Volumes* (London, 1759).

Turberville, George, *The Noble Arte of Venerie or Hunting (1576)* (Oxford: Clarendon Press, 1908).

*Verses on the death of the right valiant Sr Bevill Grenvill* (Oxford, 1643).

Waller, Edmund, *Poems, etc. Written upon several Occasions, And to several Persons* (London, 1668; 3rd edn).

———, *The Poems of Edmund Waller*, ed. George Thorn Drury, 2 vols (London: Bullen; New York: Scribner's, 1901).

Ward, Edward, *A Riddle: Or, A Paradoxical Character of a Hairy Monster, often found under Holland* (London, 1725; repr. 1737).

Watts, Isaac, *The Psalms of David imitated in the language of the New Testament* (London, 1719).

Wood, Anthony, *Athenae Oxoniensis* 2 vols (London, 1721), ed. Philip Bliss, 4 vols (London, 1813–20; repr. New York: Johnson Reprint Society, 1967).

Woodford Samuel, *A Paraphrase upon the Canticles, and some select hymns of the New and Old Testament* (London, 1679).

———, *A Paraphrase upon the Psalms of David* (London, 1667).

## Printed and Electronic Secondary Sources

Achinstein, Sharon, *Milton and the Revolutionary Reader* (Princeton: Princeton University Press, 1994).

Adams, Joseph Quincy, *Shakespearean Playhouses: A History of English Theatres from the Beginning to the Restoration* (Boston: Houghton Mifflin, 1917).

Adamson, John, *The Noble Revolt: The Overthrow of Charles I* (London: Orion, 2007).

Allsopp, Niall, 'Sir Robert Howard, Thomas Hobbes, and the Fall of Clarendon', *Seventeenth Century*, 30 (2015), 75–93.

———, '"Let none our Lombard author rudely blame for's righteous paine": An Annotated Copy of Sir William Davenant's *Gondibert'*, *Library*, seventh series, 16 (2015), 24–50.

*Annales de Wifornia*, in *Annales Monastici*, vol. IV, ed. H.R. Luard (London: Longman, 1869).

Alter, Robert, *The Book of Psalms* (New York: Norton, 2007).

Aubin, Robert A., *Topographical Poetry in XVIII–Century England* (New York: Modern Language Association of America, 1936).

Aylmer, G.E., 'Collective Mentalities in Mid-Seventeenth-Century England, I: The Puritan Outlook', *Transactions of the Royal Historical Society*, fifth series, 36 (1986), 1–25.

———, 'Collective Mentalities in Mid-Seventeenth-Century England, 2: Royalist Attitudes', *Transactions of the Royal Historical Society*, fifth series, 37 (1987), 1–30.

Banks, T.H., Jr. (ed.), *The Poetical Works of Sir John Denham* (New Haven: Yale University Press, 1928, repr. 1969).

Barbour, Reid, and David Norbrook (eds), *The Works of Lucy Hutchinson*, 4 vols (Oxford: Clarendon Press, 2011–).

Barratt, John, *Cavalier Generals: King Charles I and His Commanders in the English Civil War, 1642–1646* (Barnsley: Leo Cooper, 2004).

Bawcutt, N.W., *The Control and Censorship of Caroline Drama: The Records of Sir Henry Herbert, Master of the Revels, 1623–73* (Oxford: Clarendon Press, 1996).

Beal, Peter, *Index of English Literary Manuscripts,* 2 vols (London: Mansell, 1980).

Bentley, G.E., *The Jacobean and Caroline Stage, Plays and Playwrights,* 7 vols (Oxford: Clarendon Press, 1941–68).

Beresford-Jones, R.D., 'The Oxford Mint and the Triple Unites of Charles I', *British Numismatic Journal,* 27 (1952), 334–44.

Berkowitz, David Sandler, *John Selden's Formative Years: Politics and Society in Seventeenth-Century England* (Cranbury, NJ: Associated University Presses, 1988).

Bernard Quaritch (Firm), *English Poetry before 1701* (1982).

Berry, Herbert, 'Sir John Denham at Law', *Modern Philology* 71.3 (February 1974) 266–76.

———, 'Sir John Suckling's poems and letters from manuscript', *Studies in the Humanities Departments of the University of Western Ontario,* no. 1 (1960).

Bevis, Richard, *English Drama: Restoration and Eighteenth Century, 1660–1789* (London and New York: Longman, 1988).

Birchwood, Matthew, *Staging Islam in England: Drama and Culture, 1640–1685* (Cambridge: Cambridge University Press, 2007).

Blackwell, Mark R., 'Bestial Metaphors: John Birkenhead and Satiric Royalist Propaganda of the 1640s and 50s', *Modern Language Studies,* 29.2 (Autumn 1999), 21–48.

Boeckel, Bruce, 'Landscaping the Field of Discourse: Political Slant and Poetic Slope in Sir John Denham's "Cooper's [*sic*] Hill"', *Papers on Language & Literature,* 34.1 (Winter 1998), 57–93.

Boswell, Eleanore, *The Restoration Court Stage, 1670–1702* (Cambridge, MA: Harvard University Press, 1932).

Braddick, Michael, *God's Fury, England's Fire* (London: Allen Lane, 2008).

Bradley, Jesse Franklin, 'Robert Baron's Tragedy of *Mirza*', *Modern Language Notes,* 34 (1919), 402–08.

Brayley, Edward Wedlake, *A Topographical History of Surrey, Volume II* (Dorking: Robert Best Ede, 1841).

Bronner, Edwin B., 'First Printing of Magna Charta in America, 1687', *American Journal of Legal History,* 7 (1963), 189–97.

Bruce, John (ed.), *Charles I in 1646. Letters of King Charles the First to Queen Henrietta Maria* (London: Printed for the Camden Society, 1856).

Budd, Adam, *John Armstrong's the Art of Preserving Health: Eighteenth-Century Sensibility in Practice* (Farnham: Ashgate, 2011).

Butler, Martin, *Theatre and Crisis, 1632–1642* (Cambridge: Cambridge University Press, 1984).

Butterfield, Herbert, *Magna Carta in the Historiography of the Sixteenth and Seventeenth Centuries* (Reading: University of Reading, 1969).

Caldwell, Tanya, 'John Dryden and John Denham', *Texas Studies in Literature and Language,* 46.1 (2004), 49–72.

Carte, Thomas, *The Life of James, Duke of Ormond ...,* 6 vols (Oxford: University Press, 1851).

Chalmers, Hero, *Royalist Women Writers 1650–1689* (Oxford: Clarendon Press, 2004).

Chamberlin, William J. (ed.), *Catalogue of English Bible Translations: A Classified Bibliography of Versions and Editions Including Books, Parts and Old and New Testament Apocrypha and Apocryphal Books* (Westport, CT: Greenwood, 1991).

Chapman, Hester, *The Tragedy of Charles II* (London: Jonathan Cape, 1964).

Clayton, Thomas (ed.), *The Works of Sir John Suckling, Volume II: The Non- dramatic Works* (Oxford: Clarendon Press, 1971).

Cogswell, Thomas, 'The Politics of Propaganda: Charles and the People in the 1620s', *Journal of British Studies,* 29 (1990), 187–215.

212   *Bibliography*

Coiro, Ann Baynes, 'The Personal Rule of Poets: Cavalier Poetry and the English Revolution', in Laura Lunger Knoppers (ed.), *The Oxford Handbook of Literature and the English Revolution* (Oxford: Oxford University Press, 2012), 206–37.

Collins, Jeffrey R., *The Allegiance of Thomas Hobbes* (Oxford: Oxford University Press, 2007).

Colvin, H.M. et al., *The History of the King's Works*, 6 vols, vol. V, 1660–1782 (London: HMSO, 1976).

Como, David, 'Predestination and Conflict in Laud's London', *Historical Journal*, 52.2 (June 2013), 263–94.

Cook, Judith, *Roaring Boys: Playwrights and Players in Jacobean England* (London: Sutton, 2004).

Cope, Esther (ed.), *Proceedings of the Short Parliament of 1640* (London: Offices of the Royal Historical Society, 1977).

———, 'The King's Declaration Concerning the Dissolution of the Short Parliament of 1640: An Unsuccessful Attempt at Public Relations', *Huntington Library Quarterly*, 40 (1977), 325–31.

Corns, Thomas N., *Uncloistered Virtue: English Political Literature, 1640–60* (Oxford: Clarendon Press, 1992).

———, 'Thomas Carew, Sir John Suckling and Richard Lovelace', in Thomas N. Corns (ed.), *The Cambridge Companion to English Poetry: Donne to Marvell* (Cambridge: Cambridge University Press, 1993), 200–20.

———, *A History of Seventeenth-Century Literature*, rev. edn (Oxford: Blackwell, 2014).

Cox, John D., *The Devil and the Sacred in English Drama, 1350–1642* (Cambridge: Cambridge University Press, 2000).

Croft-Murray, Edmund, *Decorative Painting in England, 1537–1837*, 2 vols (London: Country Life, 1962, 1970).

Crouch, David, *William Marshal: Knighthood, War, and Chivalry 1147–1219* (Harlow: Pearson, 1990).

Cust, Richard, *Charles I: A Political Life* (Harlow: Pearson, 2005).

———, 'News and Politics in Early Seventeenth-Century England', *Past and Present*, 112 (1986), 60–90.

———, and Ann Hughes (eds), *The English Civil War* (London: Arrowsmith, 1997).

D'Addario, Christopher, *Exile and Journey in Seventeenth-Century Literature* (Cambridge: Cambridge University Press, 2007).

Davis, Herbert (ed.), *The Complete Plays of William Congreve* (Chicago: University of Chicago Press, 1967).

De Groot, Jerome, 'John Denham and Lucy Hutchinson's Commonplace Book', *Studies in English Literature*, 48.1 (Winter 2008), 147–64.

———, *Royalist Identities* (Basingstoke: Palgrave Macmillan, 2004).

———, 'Space, Patronage, Procedure: The Court at Oxford, 1642–46', *English Historical Review*, 117.474 (November 2002), 1204–27.

Dobrée, Bonamy, *Sir John Denham: A Conversation between Bishop Henry King and Edmund Waller, at the Palace, Chichester, March, 1669* (Kensington: Cayme Press, 1927).

Dobson, Michael, *The Making of the National Poet: Shakespeare, Adaptation and Authorship, 1660–1769* (Oxford: Clarendon Press, 1992).

English Translation of Magna Carta, The British Library <http://www.bl.uk/magna- carta/articles/magna-carta-english-translation>.

Evelyn, John, *The Diary of John Evelyn*, ed. E.S. de Beer, 6 vols (Oxford: Clarendon Press, 1955).

Farmer, Brian R., *Understanding Radical Islam: Medieval Ideology in the Twenty-First Century* (New York: Peter Lang Publishing, 2006).

Feiling, Keith, *A History of the Tory Party, 1660–1714*, rev. edn (Oxford: Clarendon Press, 1965).

Firth, C.H., 'Sir William Davenant and the Revival of Drama during the Protectorate', *English Historical Review*, 18 (1903), 319–21.

Fischer, T.A., *The Scots in Sweden* (Edinburgh: Otto Schulz, 1907).

Fisk, Deborah Payne (ed.), *The Cambridge Companion to Restoration Theatre* (Cambridge: Cambridge University Press, 2000).

Fletcher, C.R.L., and Rudyard Kipling, *A History of England* (London: Doubleday, 1911).

Foster, William, *Thomas Herbert Travels in Persia, 1627–1629* (London: Routledge, 1928).

Fraser, Antonia, *The Weaker Vessel: Woman's Lot in Seventeenth-Century England*, (London: Phoenix Press, 1984).

Freehafer, John, 'The Formation of the London Patent Companies in 1660', *Theatre Notebook*, 20 (1965), 6–30.

Gardiner, S.R. (ed.), *The Hamilton Papers*, Camden Society, second series, 27 (London, 1880).

———, *History of the Great Civil War, 1642–1649*, 4 vols (London: Longmans, 1901).

Ghani, Cyrus, *Shakespeare, Persia, and the East* (Washington, DC: Mage, 2008).

Greg, W.W., *A Bibliography of the English Drama Printed to the Restoration*, 4 vols (London: Bibliographical Society, 1951–59).

Gronauer, Georg, *Sir William Davenants 'Gondibert'* (Erlangen: von Junge, 1911).

Gupta, Tanya, 'Magna Carta: Passions Still Running High in Runnymede', BBC News website 14 June 2013 <http://www.bbc.co.uk/news/uk-england-surrey-22882941>.

Habermas, Jürgen, *The Structural Transformation of the Public Sphere* (Cambridge: MIT Press, 1991).

*Ham House* (London: National Trust, 2005).

Hamlin, Hannibal, *Psalm Culture and Early Modern English Literature* (Cambridge: Cambridge University Press, 2004).

Hammond, Gerald, *Fleeting Things: English Poets and Poems, 1616–1660* (Cambridge: Harvard University Press, 1990).

Harbage, Alfred, *Sir William Davenant: Poet Venturer, 1606–1668* (Philadelphia: University of Pennsylvania Press; London: Oxford University Press, 1935).

———, *Thomas Killigrew: Cavalier Dramatist, 1612–83* (Philadelphia: University of Philadelphia Press, 1930).

Hardacre, Paul, *The Royalists during the Puritan Revolution* (The Hague: Nijhoff, 1956).

Hart, Clive, and Kay Gilliland Stevenson, 'John Armstrong's *The Oeconomy of Love*: A Critical Edition with Commentary', *Eighteenth-Century Life*, 19 (1995), 38–69.

Hazlitt, William Carew (ed.), *The Poetical Works of Sir John Suckling*, 2nd edn (London: Reeves and Turner, 1892).

Henning, B.D. (ed.), *The History of Parliament: House of Commons, 1660–1690* (London, 1983), online edition.

Holland, John, *Psalmists of Britain: Records of Upwards of One Hundred and Fifty Authors, Who Have Rendered the Whole or Parts of the Book of Psalms, into English Verse* (London: R. Groombridge, 1843).

Holt, J.C., *Magna Carta* (Cambridge: Cambridge University Press, 1965).

———, *The Northerners: A Study in the Reign of King John* (Oxford: Clarendon Press, 1992).

Hopper, Andrew, and Philip Major (eds), *England's Fortress: New Perspectives on Thomas, 3rd Lord Fairfax* (Farnham: Ashgate, 2014).

Hotson, Leslie, *The Commonwealth and Restoration Stage* (Cambridge, MA: Harvard University Press, 1928).

Howard, A.E. Dick, *The Road from Runnymede: Magna Carta and Constitutionalism in America* (Charlottesville: University of Virginia Press, 1968).

Hughes, Derek, *English Drama, 1660–1700* (Oxford: Clarendon Press, 1996).

Hume, Robert D. 'English Drama and Theatre: New Directions and Research', *Theatre Survey*, 23 (1982), 71–100.

———, 'Securing a Repertory: Plays on the London Stage, 1660–5', in *Poetry and Drama, 1570–1700: Essays in Honour of Harold F. Brooks*, ed. Antony Coleman, Antony Hammond, and Arthur Johnson (London: Methuen, 1981), 156–72.

———, *The Development of English Drama in the Late Seventeenth Century* (Oxford: Clarendon Press, 1976).

Huscroft, Richard, *Ruling England, 1042–1217* (London: Routledge, 2004).

Hutton, Ronald, *Charles the Second, King of England, Scotland and Ireland* (Oxford: Clarendon Press, 1989).

Jacob, James R. and Timothy Raylor, 'Opera and Obedience: Thomas Hobbes and *A Proposition for Advancement of Moralitie* by Sir William Davenant', *Seventeenth Century*, 6 (1991), 205–50.

Johnson, James W., *A Profane Wit: The Life of John Wilmot, Earl of Rochester* (Rochester, NY: University of Rochester Press, 2004).

*Journals of the House of Commons.*

*Journals of the House of Lords.*

Jung, Sandro, *The Fragmentary Poetic: Eighteenth-Century Uses of an Experimental Mode* (Bethlehem: Lehigh University Press, 2009).

Keblusek, Marika, 'Wine for Comfort: Drinking and the Royalist Exile Experience, 1642–1660', in Adam Smyth (ed.), *Pleasing Sinne* (Cambridge: D.S. Brewer, 2004), 55–68.

Kelliher, Hilton, 'John Denham: New Letters and Documents', *British Library Journal* (Spring 1986), 1–20.

———, review of Brendan O Hehir, *Harmony from Discords*, in *Review of English Studies*, n.s., 22.85 (February 1971), 79–81.

Kerrigan, John, *Archipelagic English: Literature, History and Politics, 1603–1707* (Oxford: Oxford University Press, 2008).

Kewes, Paulina, *Authorship and Appropriation: Writing for the Stage in England, 1660–1710* (Oxford: Clarendon Press, 1998).

Kinservik, Matthew J., 'Theatrical Regulation during the Restoration Period', in Susan J. Owen (ed.), *A Companion to Restoration Drama* (Oxford: Blackwell, 2001), 36–52.

Knapp, L.M., 'Dr. John Armstrong, Littérateur, and Associate of Smollett, Thomson, Wilkes, and Other Celebrities', *Publications of the Modern Language Association*, 59 (1944), 1019–58.

Kranidas, Thomas, *Milton and the Rhetoric of Zeal* (Pittsburgh, PA: Duquesne University Press, 2005).

Kroll, Richard, *Restoration Drama and 'The Circle of Commerce'* (Cambridge: Cambridge University Press, 2007).

Lacey, Andrew, *The Cult of King Charles the Martyr* (Woodbridge: Boydell, 2003).

Laing, David (ed.), *The Letters and Journals of Robert Baillie*, 3 vols (Edinburgh: Robert Ogle, 1841–42).

Lambert, Sheila, *Printing for Parliament, 1641–1700* (London: List and Index Society, 1984).

Lewalski, Barbara, *Protestant Poetics and the Seventeenth-Century Religious Lyric* (Princeton: Princeton University Press, 1979).

Lewcock, Dawn, *Sir William Davenant, the Court Masque and the English Seventeenth-Century Scenic Stage, c. 1605–1700* (Amherst, NY: Cambria Press, 2008).

Loftis, John (ed.), *The Memoirs of Anne, Lady Halkett and Ann, Lady Fanshawe* (Oxford: Clarendon Press, 1979).

Loloi, Parvin, *Two Seventeenth-Century Plays* (Salzburg; Oxford: University of Salzburg, 1998).

Loxley, James, 'Echoes as Evidence in the Poetry of Andrew Marvell', *Studies in English Literature*, 5.1 (2012), 165–85.

———, *Royalism and Poetry in the English Civil Wars: The Drawn Sword* (Basingstoke: Palgrave, 1997).

Maclean, Gerald, and Nabil Matar, *Britain and the Islamic World* (New York: Oxford University Press, 2011).

Maguire, Nancy Klein, *Regicide and Restoration: English Tragicomedy, 1660–1671* (Cambridge: Cambridge University Press, 1992).

Major, Philip (ed.), *Literatures of Exile in the English Revolution and Its Aftermath, 1640–1690* (Farnham: Ashgate, 2010).

———, *Writings of Exile in the English Revolution and Restoration* (Farnham: Ashgate, 2013).

——— (ed.), *Thomas Killigrew and the Seventeenth-Century English Stage* (Farnham: Ashgate, 2013).

Malden, Henry Elliot (ed.), *Magna Carta Commemoration Essays* (London: Royal Historical Society, 1917).

Mambretti, Catherine Cole, 'Orinda on the Restoration Stage', *Comparative Literature*, 37.3 (1985), 233–51.

Manning, Roger B., *Hunters and Poachers: A Social and Cultural History of Unlawful Hunting in England, 1485–1640* (Oxford: Clarendon Press, 1993).

Marotti, Arthur, *Manuscript, Print, and the English Renaissance Lyric* (Ithaca, NY: Cornell University Press, 1995).

McDowell, Nicholas, *Poetry and Allegiance in the English Civil War: Marvell and the Cause of Wit* (Oxford: Oxford University Press, 2008).

McElligott, Jason, *Royalism, Print and Censorship in Revolutionary England* (Woodbridge: Boydell Press, 2007).

———, and David L. Smith (eds), *Royalists and Royalism during the English Civil Wars* (Cambridge: Cambridge University Press, 2007).

———, and David L. Smith (eds), *Royalists and Royalism during the Interregnum* (Manchester: Manchester University Press, 2010).

McJannet, Linda, 'Bringing in a Persian', *Medieval and Renaissance Drama in England: An Annual Gathering of Research, Criticism and Reviews*, 12 (1999), 236–67.

McShane, Angela, 'Recruiting Citizens for Soldiers in Seventeenth-Century English Ballads', *Journal of Early Modern History*, 15 (2011), 105–37.

Meyer, Paul (ed.), *L'Histoire de Guillaume le Marechal, Comte de Striguil et de Pembroke, Règent d'Angleterre de 1216 a 1219* (Paris, 1891).

Milhous, Judith, *Thomas Betterton and the Management of Lincoln's Inn Fields, 1695–1708* (Carbondale: Southern Illinois University Press, 1979).

Miller, John, *James II: A Study in Kingship* (London: Wayland, 1978).

Miner, Earl, *The Metaphysical Mode from Donne to Cowley* (Princeton: Princeton University Press, 1969).

———, *The Restoration Mode from Milton to Dryden* (Princeton: Princeton University Press, 1974).

Morgan, David, 'After Abbas', *Times Literary Supplement*, 7 December 2012, 9.

Morrah, Patrick, *Prince Rupert of the Rhine* (London: Constable, 1976).

Morrill, John, *The Nature of the English Revolution* (Oxford: Routledge, 1993).

———, 'The Puritan Revolution', in John Coffey and Paul C.H. Lim (eds), *The Cambridge Companion to Puritanism* (Cambridge: Cambridge University Press, 2008), 67–88.

Mortimer, Sarah, 'Exile, Apostasy and Anglicanism in the English Revolution', in Major, Philip (ed.), *Writings of Exile in the English Revolution and Its Aftermath, 1640–1690* (Farnham: Ashgate, 2011), 91–104.

Nederman, Cary J., 'The Liberty of the Church and the Road to Runnymede: John of Salisbury and the Intellectual Foundations of the Magna Carta', *PS: Political Science & Politics*, 43 (2010), 457–61.

Nethercot, Arthur, *Sir William D'Avenant: Poet Laureate and Playwright Manager* (Chicago: University of Chicago Press, 1938).

Nevitt, Marcus, 'The Insults of Defeat: Royalist Responses to William Davenant's *Gondibert* (1651)', *Seventeenth Century*, 25 (2009), 287–304.

Newman, P.R., *Royalist Officers in England and Wales, 1642–1660* (New York: Garland Publishing, 1981).

Nicoll, Allardyce, *A History of English Drama, 1660–1900*, rev. edn, 6 vols (Cambridge: Cambridge University Press, 1952–59).

———, *A History of Restoration Drama* (Cambridge: Cambridge University Press, 1940).

Nora, Pierre, 'Between Memory and History: *Les Lieux de Mémoire*', *Representations*, 26 (Spring 1989).

Norbrook, David, *Writing the English Republic: Poetry, Rhetoric and Politics, 1627–1660* (Cambridge: Cambridge University Press, 1999).

Norton, David, *A History of the Bible as Literature*, 2 vols (Cambridge: Cambridge University Press, 1993).

O Hehir, Brendan 'The Early Acquaintance of Denham and Waller', *Notes & Queries*, n.s., 13 (1966), 19–23.

———, *Expans'd Hieroglyphicks: A Critical Edition of Sir John Denham's 'Coopers Hill'* (Berkeley and Los Angeles: University of California Press, 1969).

———, *Harmony from Discords: A Life of Sir John Denham* (Berkeley and Los Angeles: University of California Press, 1968).

Ollard, Richard (ed.), *Clarendon's Four Portraits: George Digby, John Berkeley, Henry Jermyn, Henry Bennett, From the Supplement to the Clarendon State Papers Vol. III (1786)* (London: Hamish Hamilton, 1989).

Orgel, Stephen, and Roy Strong, *Inigo Jones: The Theatre of the Stuart Court*, 2 vols (Berkeley: University of California Press, 1973).

Painter, Sidney, *William Marshal: Knight-Errant, Baron, and Regent of England* (Baltimore: Johns Hopkins Press, 1933).

Payne, Debora C., 'Patronage and the Dramatic Marketplace under Charles I and II', *Yearbook of English Studies*, 21 (1991), 137–52.

Peakman, Julie, *Mighty Lewd Books: The Development of Pornography in Eighteenth-Century England* (London: Palgrave, 2003; repr. 2012).

Pernal, Andrew B., and Rosanne P. Gasse, 'The 1651 Polish Subsidy to the Exile Charles II', *Oxford Slavonic Papers*, n.s., 32 (1999), 1–50.

Perringer, Alex, and T.V.F. Brogan, 'Ballad Meter', in *The New Princeton Encyclopaedia of Poetry and Poetics* (Princeton: Princeton University Press, 1993).

Pettegree, Andrew, *Reformation and the Culture of Persuasion* (Cambridge: Cambridge University Press, 2005).

Plomer, H.R., *A Dictionary of the Printers and Booksellers Who Were at Work in England, Scotland and Ireland from 1726 to 1775* (Oxford: Oxford University Press, 1932; repr. 1968).

Potter, Lois, *Secret Rites and Secret Writing: Royalist Literature, 1641–1660* (Cambridge: Cambridge University Press, 1989).

Quitslund, Beth, *The Reformation in Rhyme: Sternhold, Hopkins and the English Metrical Psalter, 1547–1603* (Aldershot: Ashgate, 2008).

Raylor, Timothy, *Cavaliers, Clubs and Literary Culture: Sir John Mennes, James Smith and the Order of the Fancy* (Newark: University of Delaware Press, 1994).

———, 'The "1653" Copy of Denham's *Coopers Hill*', *Yale University Library Gazette*, 71 (1997), 130–39.

———, 'Exiles, Expatriates, and Travellers: Towards a Cultural and Intellectual History of the English Abroad, 1640–1660', in *Literatures of Exile in the English Revolution and its Aftermath, 1640–1690*, ed. Philip Major (Farnham: Ashgate, 2010), 15–43.

———, 'Hobbes, Davenant, and Disciplinary Tensions in the Preface to *Gondibert*', in *Collaboration and Interdisciplinarity in the Republic of Letters: Essays in Honour of Richard G. Maber*, ed. Paul Scott (Manchester and New York: Manchester University Press, 2010), 59–72.

Raymond, Joad, *The Invention of the Newspaper: English Newsbooks, 1641–1649* (Oxford: Clarendon Press, 2005).

Reeve, L.J., *Charles I and the Road to Personal Rule* (Cambridge: Cambridge University Press, 2003).

Roebuck, Graham, 'Cavalier', in Claude J. Summers and Ted-Larry Pebworth (eds), *The English Civil Wars in the Literary Imagination* (Columbia: University of Missouri Press, 1999), 9–26.

Rosenfeld, Sybil Marion, 'Foreign Theatrical Companies in Great Britain in the Seventeenth and Eighteenth Centuries', *Society for Theatre Research Pamphlet*, series no. 4 (1955).

Rothstein, Eric, 'Discordia Non Concors: The Motif of Hunting in Eighteenth-Century Verse', *Journal of English and Germanic Philology*, 83 (1984), 330–54.

Rous, John, *Diary of John Rous*, ed. Mary Green (London: Camden Society, 1856).

Roy, Ian, 'The Royalist Council of War, 1642–6', *Bulletin of the Institute of Historical Research*, 35 (1962), 150–68.

Russell, Conrad, *The Fall of the British Monarchies, 1637–1642* (Oxford: Clarendon Press, 1991).

———, *Parliaments and English Politics, 1621–1629* (Oxford: Clarendon Press, 1979).

Sauer, Elizabeth, *'Paper-contestations' and Textual Communities in England, 1640–1675* (Toronto: University of Toronto Press, 2005).

Scott, David, 'Counsel and Cabal in the King's Party, 1642–1646', in Jason McElligott and David L. Smith (eds), *Royalists and Royalism during the English Civil Wars* (Cambridge: Cambridge University Press, 2007), 112–35.

Scott, Sir Walter (ed.), *Memoirs of the Court of Charles the Second by Count Grammont* (London: Henry G. Bohn, 1853).

Sharpe, Kevin, *Criticism and Compliment: The Politics of Literature in the England of Charles I* (Cambridge: Cambridge University Press, 1990).

———, *The Personal Rule of Charles I* (New Haven: Yale University Press, 1992).

———, *Image Wars: Promoting Kings and Commonwealths in England, 1603–1660* (New Haven: Yale University Press, 2010).

Smith, David, *Constitutional Royalism and the Search for Settlement, c. 1640–1649* (Cambridge: Cambridge University Press, 1994).

Smith, Geoffrey, *The Cavaliers in Exile, 1640–1660* (Basingstoke: Palgrave Macmillan, 2003).

———, 'Long, Dangerous and Expensive Journeys: The Grooms of the Bedchamber at Charles II's Court in Exile', *Early Modern Literary Studies*, Special Issue 15 (August 2007).

———, *Royalist Agents, Conspirators and Spies: Their Role in the British Civil Wars* (Farnham: Ashgate, 2011).

———, 'Royalists in Exile: The Experience of Daniel O'Neill', in Jason McElligott and David L. Smith (eds), *Royalists and Royalism during the Interregnum* (Manchester: Manchester University Press, 2010), 106–22.

Smith, Nigel, *Literature and Revolution in England, 1640–1660* (New Haven: Yale University Press, 1994).

Smuts, Malcolm, 'The Court and the Emergence of a Royalist Party', in Jason McElligott and David L. Smith (eds), *Royalists and Royalism during the English Civil Wars* (Cambridge: Cambridge University Press, 2007), 43–65.

Sommerville, Johann P., *Thomas Hobbes: Political Ideas in Historical Context* (Basingstoke: Macmillan, 1992).

Sorelius, Gunnar, 'The Rights of Restoration Theatre Companies in the Older Drama', *Studia Neophilologica*, 37 (1965), 174–89.

Sowerby, Robin Edward (ed.), *Early Augustan Virgil: Translations by Denham, Godolphin, and Waller* (Lewisburg, PA: Bucknell University Press, 2010).

Stern, Tiffany, *Rehearsal from Shakespeare to Sheridan* (Oxford: Clarendon Press, 2000).

Stevenson, David, *The Scottish Revolution, 1637–44*, 2nd edn (Edinburgh: John Donald, 2003).

Stoyle, Mark J., '"Pagans or Paragons?" Images of the Cornish during the English Civil War', *English Historical Review*, 111.441 (April 1996), 229–323.

Stubbs, John, *Reprobates: The Cavaliers of the English Civil Wars* (London: Viking, 2011; Penguin, 2012).

Summers, Montague, *The Restoration Theatre* (London: Kegan Paul, Trench, Trubner, 1934).

Tanner, Rory, 'An Appleton Psalter: The Shared Devotions of Thomas Fairfax and Andrew Marvell', in Andrew Hopper and Philip Major (eds), *England's Fortress: New Perspectives on Thomas, 3rd Lord Fairfax* (Farnham: Ashgate, 2014), 213–34.

Taylor, Gary, *Reinventing Shakespeare: A Cultural History from the Restoration to the Present* (New York, 1989).

Thomas, Keith, *Man and the Natural World: Changing Attitudes in England, 1500–1800* (London: Allen Lane, 1983).

Thrush, Andrew, and John P. Ferris (eds), *The History of Parliament: The House of Commons, 1604–1629* (Cambridge: Cambridge University Press, 2010).

Trease, Geoffrey, *Portrait of a Cavalier: William Cavendish, First Duke of Newcastle* (London: Macmillan, 1979).

Trevor-Roper, Hugh, *Religion, the Reformation and Social Change* (London and Basingstoke: Macmillan, 1972).

Turner, Ralph V., *Magna Carta: Through the Ages* (Harlow: Pearson, 2003).

Uhlig, Claus, '"The Sobbing Deer:" *As You Like It*, II.i.21–66, and the Historical Context', *Renaissance Drama*, n.s., III (1970), 79–109.

Underdown, David, *Royalist Conspiracy in England, 1649–1660* (New Haven: Yale University Press, 1960).

Van Lennep, William, Emmett L. Avery, and Arthur H. Scouten (eds), *The London Stage, 1660–1800: A Calendar of Plays*, 5 parts in 11 vols, Part I: 1660–1700 (Carbondale: Southern Illinois University Press, 1965).

Van Strien, 'Sir John Suckling in Holland', *English Studies*, 78 (1995), 443–54.

Wagner, Peter, 'The Discourse on Sex—Or Sex as Discourse: Eighteenth-Century Medical and Paramedical Erotica', in G.S. Rousseau and Roy Porter (eds), *Sexual Underworlds of the Enlightenment* (Manchester: Manchester University Press, 1987), 46–68.

Wallace, John M., ' "Examples Are Best Precepts": Readers and Meanings in Seventeenth-Century Poetry', *Critical Inquiry*, 1 (1974), 273–90.

Wasserman, Earl, *The Subtler Language* (Baltimore: Johns Hopkins University Press, 1959).

Weaver, Matthew, 'Cameron Condemned for "using Magna Carta day to push British bill of rights" ', *Guardian*, 15 June 2015 <http://www.theguardian.com/uk- news/2015/jun/15/david-cameron-magna-carta-push-british-bill-of-rights-claim>.

Weinbrot, Howard D., *Britannia's Issue: The Rise of British Literature from Dryden to Ossian* (Cambridge: Cambridge University Press, 1993; repr. 2006).

Wilcher, Robert, *The Discontented Cavalier: The Work of Sir John Suckling in Its Social, Religious, Political, and Literary Contexts* (Newark: University of Delaware Press, 2007).

———, *The Writing of Royalism, 1628–1660* (Cambridge: Cambridge University Press, 2001).

Williams, Richard, *Runnymede: A Pictorial History* (Addlestone, Surrey: Egham-by- Runnymede Historical Society, 1995).

Woodforde, Dorothy Heighes (ed.), *Woodforde Papers and Diaries* (London: Peter Davies, 1932).

Woolrych, Austin, *Britain in Revolution, 1625–1660* (Oxford: Oxford University Press, 2002).

Worden, Blair, *God's Instruments: Political Conduct in the England of Oliver Cromwell* (Oxford: Oxford University Press, 2012).

Wormald, Brian, *Clarendon: Politics, History and Religion* (Cambridge: Cambridge University Press, 1951).

Wright, Louis B., 'The Reading of Plays during the Puritan Revolution', *Huntington Library Bulletin*, 6 (1934), 73–108.

Zim, Rivkah, *English Metrical Psalms: Poetry as Praise and Prayer, 1535–1601* (Cambridge: Cambridge University Press, 1987).

# Index